To
Build
in a
New
Land

Creating
the
North
American
Landscape

Consulting Editors:
Gregory Conniff
Bonnie Loyd
Edward K. Muller
David Schuyler

Project Editor:
George F. Thompson

To Build in a New Land

Ethnic Landscapes in North America

edited by

Allen G. Noble

The
Johns Hopkins
University Press

Baltimore
and
London

The Johns Hopkins University Press
701 West 40th Street, Baltimore, Maryland 21211-2190
The Johns Hopkins Press Ltd., London

The paper used in this publication meets the minimum
requirements of American National Standard for
Information Sciences—Permanence of Paper
for Printed Library Materials, ANSI Z39.48-1984.

Library of Congress Cataloging-in-Publication Data

To build in a new land : ethnic landscapes in North
    America / edited by Allen G. Noble.
       p.   cm. — (Creating the North American landscape)
    Includes bibliographical references and index.
    ISBN 0-8018-4188-7. — ISBN 0-8018-4189-5 (pbk.)
    1. Ethnology—United States.   2. Ethnology—
Canada.   3. Material culture—United States.   4. Material
culture—Canada.   5. Human geography—United
States.   6. Human geography—Canada.   7. United
States—Geography.   8. Canada—Geography.
I. Noble, Allen George, 1930–   .   II. Series
E184.A1T6   1992
970′.004—dc20   91-20753

Contents

Contents

Preface and Acknowledgments

THE NINETEENTH CENTURY augmented the North American physical landscape with a rich and varied cultural tapestry produced by the diverse groups settling therein. Some of these ethnic communities had resided in North America for centuries, but in the nineteenth century their cultural landscapes achieved full flavor. Other ethnic groups were newcomers who broadened and diversified the North American scene.

Earlier books on the vernacular architecture of North America have focused mostly upon particular regions or small areas or, less often, upon particular structures. *To Build in a New Land* is the first book-length work to draw specific attention to the different cultural landscapes that a large number of ethnic groups created in North America. Many of these unique landscapes are in danger of being greatly diluted in their effect, or even of disappearing entirely.

For the most part, the chapter authors are specialists in dealing with a particular community. Often they are the descendants of pioneer settlers of the peoples they study. In a few cases, the authors have no familial connection to their group, but have been intrigued by its unique cultural landscape as a result of travel or residence therein.

Each chapter deals with a particular ethnic group and with the cultural landscape each group created. In some instances, that landscape is comprehensive and well-established; in others only a few relict features remain to document the presence of the group. In most locations the particular ethnic landscape is intermixed with features from the larger American cultural landscape.

In the introduction, I discuss the major components of migration to North America before, during, and after the nineteenth century. Thereafter the chapters are organized in a roughly geographical framework for the continent. Chapters 2, 3, 4, and 5, which constitute Part 2, discuss some of the early groups migrating to northeastern North America from the British Isles, Germany, and France. Part 3 contains chapters covering representative groups for southeastern North America. The different adjustments to settlement conditions of quite disparate peoples—ranging from American Indians in the mid-Atlantic area to Scots-Irish and English in Appalachia, Blacks and Creoles on the Atlantic and Gulf coastal plains, and Cajuns in the Mississippi River delta—are examined to discern the cultural landscape that resulted from each adjustment.

Part 4 treats a number of northern and eastern European communities who occupied different parts of central North America. The communities include Belgians, Danes, Norwegians, Finns, German-Russian Mennonites, and Czechs. Part 5 looks at five quite distinct ethnic groups that settled in western North America. They are from five different places of origin and their effective settlement peaked in five separate time periods. Nevertheless, each group has left its cultural impact, although that of the Basques, discussed in Chapter 21, is only faintly visible. Finally, the concluding chapter summarizes the immigrant experience in the nineteenth century and afterwards.

No one would pretend that one book could present every ethnic community in every part of Canada and the United States. For example, more than forty different ethnic groups settled in the state of Wisconsin alone! But the ethnic groups in this volume do represent a comprehensive cross-section of the immigrant groups who chose to make North America their home. Each of the groups discussed in this book displays a material culture and a landscape that are unique to the community, which, although clear and strongly expressed in the nineteenth century, are now rapidly disappearing at the close of the twentieth.

As editor of *To Build in a New Land,* I feel a deep sense of gratitude for the patience, unfailing good humor, and the quiet competence of the chapter authors. They have made a long and difficult task an enjoyable one and have helped me to understand better and appreciate more fully the cultural landscape of North America. I feel confident that the readers of this book will share these same feelings.

I would also like to thank the following individuals, who made this publication possible: Karl B. Raitz, professor and chair of geography at the University of Kentucky, who read an earlier version of the manuscript, made many helpful comments, and suggested the inclusion of a model which now appears in my concluding chapter.

I am grateful also to M. Margaret Geib, staff cartographer in the Department of Geography at the University of Akron, who executed most of the drawings and many of the maps that enhance the volume; Hilda Kendron, who oversaw the typing and production of the manuscript at the University of Akron; George Thompson, of the Johns Hopkins University Press, who recognized the worth of the endeavor and who provided valuable direction and guidance throughout; Anne M. Whitmore, of the Johns Hopkins University Press, who blended the disparate writing styles of chapter authors into a coherent and readable work; Edward King, the book's designer, who labored long and with great skill over our assembled artwork and created a clear and appealing design; and the mostly nameless members of various ethnic communities who offered to chapter authors information, insights, and perspective.

Part I

Introduction

1

Migration to North America: Before, during, and after the Nineteenth Century

Allen G. Noble

IT IS A RARE American who does not feel superior to a foreigner."[1] Yet North American society is a product of migration, with each succeeding group of immigrants adopting, to a greater or lesser degree, the culture of their new homeland and, in the process, also altering the North American culture by broadening and expanding it by the addition of new cultural elements.

The process reached its culmination during the nineteenth century, a time of great change in the North American countryside. Largely empty at the beginning of the century, the land was mostly settled by its close. As this settlement ran its course, the ethnic character of the continent was modified drastically.

In no other characteristic of the landscape was the ethnic quality more pronounced than in folk building practices. Each group of people migrating to North America had strongly formed ideas about what sort of buildings were suitable, and even proper. Thus, they introduced into the North American countryside a range of structures that had the stamp of their society upon them. After settlement, and sometimes even during the process of migration, their ideas often changed, as they came into contact with cultures with different building concepts, as they adjusted to a new environment offering construction materials different from their accustomed ones, and as they found their living standards and sometimes their newly acquired technology improving. This book is the story not only of the attempts of some nineteenth-century immigrant groups, both representative and disparate, to recreate their familiar built environments in the new land of North America, but also of the changes in the cultural landscapes wrought during the nineteenth century by earlier-arriving and native peoples.

In this book, the term *nineteenth century* should not be thought of as beginning precisely in the year 1800 and ending exactly in 1899. Rather, because evolutionary developments have often blurred beginnings and endings, so that they cannot be precisely defined, emphasis on the nineteenth-century must be viewed as a measure of convenience. For some groups, developments that reached full fruition in the nineteenth century had their origins in an earlier time, and chapter authors have not hesitated to explore those previous periods. Similarly, many evolutionary trends first evident in the nineteenth century are pursued in some chapters well into the twentieth century. Nevertheless, as much as possible, the chapters of this book deal with ethnic landscapes of the nineteenth century as they persist into present day. The discussion can also be taken as a plea to identify, understand, and preserve these distinctive, but minority, ethnic landscapes in North America before time erases them.

The Process of Migration and Settlement

Mention or discussion of several themes associated with the migration and adjustment process appears in subsequent chapters. These themes include preadaptation, cultural selectivity, cultural borrowing, cultural devolution or simplification, accessibility, conditioning by chronic poverty, and the influence of religion.

The concept of preadaptation, initially proposed by Newton, helps to explain why some groups adjusted more easily and effectively to New World environments than others did.[2] Some groups, because of their evolved culture, economic condition, or lifestyle were already alert to, and prepared for, the conditions they encountered upon their arrival in North America.[3] Their settlement was effective, and elements of their culture live on in the New World. The best examples among the groups included in this volume are the Scots-Irish, discussed in Chapter 6, and the Finns, in Chapter 14. The Basques, discussed by William Douglass in Chapter 21, were also preadapted, but their herding economy prevented the fashioning of an extensive cultural landscape.

Having arrived in North America, the immigrant faced the necessity of selecting and employing cultural elements that would prove advantageous in the new environment. The immigrant was forced to decide which American (or other, non-American) traits had to be borrowed and adopted for successful reconciliation with American existence. The Scots-Irish adoption of Fenno-Scandinavian log building techniques is one well-known instance of such cultural borrowing.

At the same time that cultural borrowing was going on, a process of cultural devolution or simplification was also under way. Simplification occurred for several reasons. Often the Old World culture contained traits whose usefulness or practicality was doubtful in the harsher environment of the New World. These superfluous traits were quickly dropped to ensure survival in changed conditions. Newly acquired skills often proved more beneficial than certain traditional skills. The new immigrant society was frequently more limited, or less elaborate, than its Old World version. Certain resources common in Europe did not occur with the same abundance in North America. For example, the general lack of reeds suitable for thatching and the abundance of North American timber resulted in wood shingle or plank roofs, and timber frame or log walls, replacing thatch roofs and half-timber walls. In some instances, the causes of cultural devolution were more complex, as noted by Peter Ennals in Chapter 2 in the case of the Acadians in the Canadian Maritime Provinces.

Finally, certain other conditions or factors were operating. Accessibility of settlements clearly had a great deal to do with how effectively different ethnic groups occupied an area. The question of this effect will be dealt with more fully in summation in the final chapter. The extent of an area's resources, the limitations imposed by landform character, soil quality, climatic elements, and absence of timber, and the balance between population and resources are all factors that must be given consideration in estimating the persistence of any ethnic community's occupation of an area and its rate of acculturation. In Chapter 19, Alvar Carlson raises the important question of how chronic poverty acts to preserve vernacular landscapes. Both Matti Kaups (Chapter 14) and John Rehder (Chapter 6) also imply that levels of poverty have acted to preserve early vernacular forms. Malcolm Comeaux, on the other hand, suggests in Chapter 10 that improved living standards have contributed to the decline of the vernacular.

Colonial Migration

Successful Atlantic migration had been a feature of North American settlement since 1607 in the United States and 1608 in Canada. The settlements of the seventeenth and eighteenth centuries essentially represented a colonial phenomenon. Long after the close of the American Revolution, the North American population still was derived basically from immigrant stock from England and Scotland and to a lesser extent from Ireland and Wales. The small and static numbers of Amerindians hardly counted statistically, and the major non-English groups in each country (the French in Canada and Blacks in the United States) were politically isolated and had only limited impact on national life, although their impact was significant within limited areas. Neither group was growing, because immigration of further members was officially banned. The position of the French has been well described by Harris and Warkentin:

> For most French Canadians, France was a totally inaccessible and,
> especially after the Revolution, an increasingly alien land. By 1800
> nearly all the important merchants were of British background,
> the relative importance of the fur trade was rapidly declining, and
> French Canadians were cut off from direct commercial ties with
> the external world. Equally isolated from power within Quebec,
> and feeling the threat of an expanding English-speaking, Protestant
> population, French-Canadian life folded inward around its own
> institutions and myth.[4]

The migration and settlement of the French in Quebec is well documented. Much less carefully recorded are Acadian influences in the Maritime Provinces of Canada. Peter Ennals pursues this subject in Chapter 2 by tracing the French (Acadian) cultural impact. At the same time, he notes the modifications produced in Acadian culture by contact with outside sources, such as New England.

Early Atlantic migration was unspectacular in volume, yet steady and inexorable. In addition to the Scots, English, French, and Blacks, the two immigrant groups with the largest impact were the Scots-Irish (Ulster Scots) and the Germans. The former became the ideal of the self-reliant frontiersman, pushing the edge of settlement ever westward. Accustomed to the conflict arising from their occupation of marginal agricultural lands in northern

Ireland, where they were often exposed to a hostile Irish population, they adapted readily to the rigors and dangers of the North American frontier, in the process producing colorful and sometimes famous backwoods characters and leaders. John Rehder in Chapter 6 identifies a range of folk structures associated with both the Scots-Irish and the English in Appalachia, where the largest remaining assemblage of such buildings in North America is found.

The Germans were perhaps less colorful but ultimately more numerous and probably more prosperous. They established more compact and cohesive settlements, many of which have persisted to the present day. They continued to emigrate from Europe in large numbers throughout the nineteenth century, eventually establishing Germans as the numerically largest immigrant group in North America.

Nineteenth-Century German Migration

In the colonial and immediately postcolonial periods, most of the German immigrants came from the Palatinate and Swabia. By the 1840s, the origin of the migration stream had shifted to the western German provinces of Hesse, Rhineland, Westphalia, and Thuringia. By the end of the nineteenth century, however, northern Germany had become the most important immigrant source region.[5]

The long continuity of German migration, its magnitude in the nineteenth century, and its wide geographical distribution explain why two chapters of this book are devoted to German settlement. The original German colonists came to Pennsylvania, but well before the nineteenth century. Hubert Wilhelm in Chapter 4 discusses the later impact of the Germans in Ohio but notes that only a limited number of relic features from original German settlement have survived to the present day. Gerlinde Leiding, in Chapter 20, examines the German immigrant group in Texas, another area where they were an important early settlement component. Drawn from opposite source regions in Germany, migrating at a different time, and settling in a contrasting environment, the Texas Germans created a landscape quite unlike that of the Ohio Germans. In Ohio the earliest settlers (1820s) were from southwestern Germany and were succeeded in the 1830s by those from Lower Saxony, who have left the most tangible reminders of German culture. In Texas a handful of Neidersachsen immigrants (1830s) were followed by much larger numbers from the southwestern sections of Germany, who followed economic pursuits and erected buildings quite unlike those in Ohio.

Perhaps because in the nineteenth century virtually all Americans and Canadians, with the exception of Amerindians, were products of Atlantic migration, little official attention was paid initially to the steady stream of immigrants coming from Europe. At the beginning of the nineteenth century few restrictions existed on European immigration, and the U.S. government did not even bother to keep track of the numbers of Atlantic migrants until 1820. The Canadian authorities made more deliberate attempts to encourage English and Scottish settlers, perhaps because of what might have been perceived as a threat from the large French minority in the St. Lawrence River basin. Accurate Canadian immigration data began to be gathered at an even later date than did those of the United States, so much of

Allen G. Noble

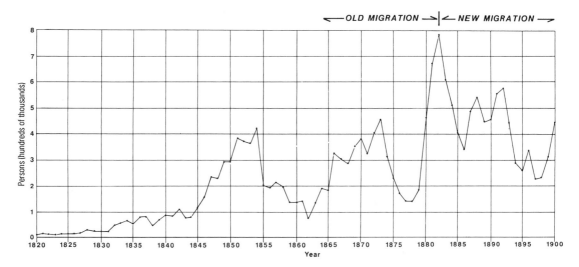

Fig. 1-1 Nineteenth-century immigration to the United States

the following discussion is based primarily upon U.S. information. In any event, early numbers were not large in either country, although proportional to the total population they were significant. Canadian immigration of the nineteenth and early twentieth centuries was less than one-fifth that of the United States, but Canada still ranks second as the country of destination for European emigrants.

The Ebb and Flow of Immigration in the Nineteenth Century and Beyond

Immigration to North America during the nineteenth century can be viewed as consisting essentially of three waves of varying intensity and magnitude (Fig. 1-1). The first great wave began about 1844 and increased in magnitude for ten years, after which there occurred a steady decline until the traumatic years of the Civil War. The second wave began during that conflict, extended to 1873, and was followed by a sharp decline over the next four to five years. The third and greatest wave of immigrants started in 1878 and persisted until 1898. Unlike the first two waves the third period was characterized by peaks, in 1882, 1888, and 1892. The areas of origin of European migrants also altered radically during this time.

The close of the nineteenth century saw the beginning of still another wave of immigration, which would not reach its peak until the second decade of the twentieth century. This major wave of migration was directed not primarily at rural areas, as the earliest ones had been, but to the rapidly growing urban centers, especially the larger cities oriented to manufacturing.

The First Wave of Migration

The first wave of migration had both political and economic origins and illustrates the importance of "push" factors impelling migrants to venture forth to new lands. A series of poor harvests over much of Europe, typified

Migration to North America

7

by the total failure of the potato crop in Ireland, drove thousands across the ocean in search of sustenance. At about the same time, political ferment rose to a dramatic peak in the revolutions of 1848 that swept across much of Europe. Most of these were abortive and thousands of political exiles sought refuge in the New World.

Although the famines and failed revolutions were the most conspicuous causes of the first wave of migration from Europe to North America, other less spectacular factors were also at work. In the German states, for example, the crop failures and widespread local famines coincided with the lifting of laws that restricted emigration.[6] The easing of other restrictions, such as tolls and levies on the Rhine, Main, and Nekar rivers, also contributed, along with the popularization of the river steamboat, which made seaports more accessible to greater numbers of residents of the interior.[7]

The Welsh, who came to North America largely as a part of the first wave of migration, may be taken as a typical example of a people who came in response to several factors. To escape the restrictions of the established church in the United Kingdom was certainly a consideration for some migrants.[8] In other instances, the custom of primogeniture induced younger (and thus effectively disinherited) sons to set off to the New World, where the carving out of an estate, denied at home, was an option for them. The discovery of slate deposits in North America, and later of abundant lead and zinc ores, held out the prospect of immediate and steady employment for Welsh miners, struggling with intermittent employment in dwindling deposits in Wales. Finally, the establishment of a discriminatory U.S. tariff on tinplating acted as a stimulus for the movement of a segment of that Welsh industry to the United States. The result of all these factors operating independently of each other was to sustain a steady Welsh migration, beginning in the eighteenth century, continuing throughout the nineteenth, and lasting well into the twentieth.

The Welsh did not scatter over the continent as did the English and, to a somewhat lesser degree, the Scots-Irish and Germans; rather they settled initially in small ethnic enclaves. Oneida County, New York became their largest settlement, although numerous smaller and earlier settlements in eastern Pennsylvania are well known. Southern Ohio also became an important destination for Welsh migrants. Michael Struble and Hubert Wilhelm, in Chapter 5, trace the vagaries of Welsh culture in Southern Ohio, where a New World Welsh vernacular building originated—the ty capel.

Basically, the impetus for migration was often simply the incompatibility of the rapidly growing rural and small town population of Europe and the inelastic land supply. Consequently, most migrants throughout the nineteenth century were peasant farmers, trades people, and craftsmen, mostly of middle-income status, neither very wealthy nor extremely poor. The very wealthy had little to gain through migration, except in the case of a few political exiles. The very poor rarely had the resources to migrate no matter how desperately they might wish to. The Irish were the notable exception to this generalization.

Allen G.
Noble

Irish Immigration

The Irish migration was born of desperation. The failure of the potato crop in 1845, 1846, and 1848 and the miserably small harvest of 1847, combined with severe winter weather, resulted in the starvation of millions. At the same time landlords, anxious to consolidate their holdings and to realize profits from tenant rents, drove destitute and starving laborers off the land, often by burning or knocking down their already miserable hovels, leaving them homeless and destitute. For many Irish rural folk, the only alternative to starvation and death was the hazardous journey across the Atlantic. But,

> very few of the poor Irish who fled from Ireland in the famine emigration were destined to achieve prosperity and success themselves; the condition to which the people had been reduced not only by the famine but by the centuries which preceded it was too severe a handicap, and it was the fate of the Irish emigrants to be regarded with aversion and contempt. It was not until the second or third generation that Irish intelligence, quickness of apprehension and wit asserted themselves, and the children and grandchildren of the poor famine emigrants became successful and powerful in the countries of their adoption.[9]

The scope of Irish emigration during the last half of the nineteenth century is unmatched elsewhere. In the short span of sixty years, from 1845 to 1905, half as many persons as lived in Ireland at the time of its greatest population migrated to the United States.[10] That they were able to make the journey is due largely to two factors. First, the landlords, and less often the government, frequently agreed to finance passage in order to rid themselves of this surplus and destitute population. Second, the nature of north Atlantic shipping was unbalanced. By 1845 hundreds of British ships annually brought stores of North American timber to a protected British market. The return trip, however, was unprofitable. The lack of development and the small population of North America offered only a limited market for British manufactured products. Thus, ships went partly empty or with low-value coal or salt as ballast. Carrying immigrants at extremely low fares enabled the shipowners to make the return Atlantic voyage economical.[11]

The emigrants left Ireland with virtually nothing of value and arrived in North America with even less in the way of possessions and resources. This helps explain many of the circumstances and characteristics of the early Irish experience in North America.

Once they had arrived in the New World, the Irish found their mobility largely restricted. Most of them had no resources to go farther. Hence in the United States, Irish families remained mostly in eastern coastal areas, at least for a generation. New England was especially densely settled by the Irish, but all major population centers in the northeast acquired huge Irish populations. The largest numbers settled in the vicinity of New York City and Philadelphia, although the proportion of Irish to total population was highest in Boston. Even in Philadelphia the Irish, by 1870, constituted over half the foreign-born population.[12]

While large numbers of Irish disembarked in Canada, at ports along the St. Lawrence River, most sought to cross the border and enter the United States. British Canada had little attraction for the Catholic Irish.[13] In their minds, freedom and economic opportunity lay on the other side of the international boundary. Nevertheless, some Irish did remain permanently in Canada, often joining small, already existing Irish settlements which dated from the early years of the nineteenth century.[14] In Chapter 3, Brian Coffey examines the housing construction materials employed by the Irish and by English and Scottish settlers in Ontario. The poorer Irish consistently used less costly and less prestigious materials than either of the other groups.

In fact, in most parts of North America distinctive architecture directly attributable to the Irish is difficult to find. In urban areas the Irish moved into existing housing and so left little architectural imprint. In rural areas their initial poverty and the fact that they had occupied hovels in Ireland and lacked any strong vernacular architectural heritage discouraged the development of an American-Irish architecture. Despite the fact that throughout the nineteenth century the Irish established a strong tradition as construction laborers, much of this work involved periodic migration, which may help explain the lack of community development.

Irish emigration reached a peak in the early 1850s, but it remained high throughout the balance of the nineteenth century. The Irish thus also contributed to the second great wave of immigrants to North America.

The Second Wave of Migration

The American Civil War was the culmination of a decade of increasingly strident sectional bitterness and strife, largely over economic questions in which slavery played a steadily enlarging role. In 1855 the territories of Kansas and Nebraska, then in the midst of active land settlement, became the initial battleground. The bloody riots and feuding and the specter of total civil war, could hardly fail to discourage immigration to this most active frontier. The number of immigrants fell almost steadily from 1854 to 1862 (see Fig. 1-1). Then, however, as the shortage of labor created by the call-up of volunteers and draftees for military service began to be felt and as the North asserted its dominance over the Confederacy so clearly that the end of the war was just a matter of time, the number of immigrants climbed. This second wave of migration was terminated by the economic panic of 1873 and the depression of the last half of the 1870s.

Whereas the first wave of migration illustrated the importance of the "push" factors that encouraged movement, the second wave demonstrated the even greater significance of "pull" factors. The critical importance of political stability, and above all of economic growth, is clearly seen. It must always be borne in mind that the abundance of good agricultural land in both Canada and the United States throughout the nineteenth century acted as a great magnet for Europeans. As Davie notes, "all forms of migration have in the last analysis the insatiable desire to get more land."[15]

One of the smaller but more interesting groups participating in the second wave of migration was the Belgians from Walloonia, who settled in the Door peninsula of Wisconsin beginning in 1846. William Laatsch and Charles Calkins review the distinctive buildings of this group in Chapter 11. Perhaps because of their relative isolation, the Belgians have been able to retain much of the traditional character of their settlements.

Another little-studied group who began their migration to South Dakota during this period was the Czechs. In Chapter 16, John Rau discusses their settlement, with an emphasis on the building technology that they employed.

Allen G. Noble

Scandinavian Immigration

Among the immigrant groups who made up the second wave of migration, were several from Scandinavia. Numerically, the Norwegians led, followed closely by the Swedes, then the Danes, and at a great distance, Icelanders.

Throughout the nineteenth century Scandinavian settlers generally avoided Canada in favor of the United States. The exception was the Icelanders, who created small settlements in Utah, on Washington Island in Wisconsin, and in the extreme northeastern corner of North Dakota, but who formed much larger permanent settlements in Canada. The largest of these were north of Winnipeg in Manitoba, on the west shore of Lake Winnipeg, and east of Saskatoon in Saskatchewan, although the latter was a product of the third wave of European migration.[16] In both Canadian areas, the Icelanders first built log, and then later wood frame structures. Only the Manitoba buildings have been studied carefully by architectural historians.[17]

Early log structures were rough and had little that reflected Icelandic vernacular building traditions. The Icelanders, coming from a treeless country, had no traditions of log construction and had to pick up rudimentary techniques from others. As they became more experienced, their log houses began to evidence stronger characteristics. The quality of workmanship improved, dovetail notching replaced saddle notching, and logs were more carefully shaped, fitted, and hewn.

A door on the gable or on the side near the gable, helped to differentiate the Icelander's one-and-a-half-story log houses from those built by other immigrant groups (Fig. 1-2). The position of the door recalled the internal plan

Fig. 1-2 A typical Icelandic log house from Manitoba. The one-room structure is covered with weatherboarding. Note the unusual position of the door. (Drawing by M. M. Geib.)

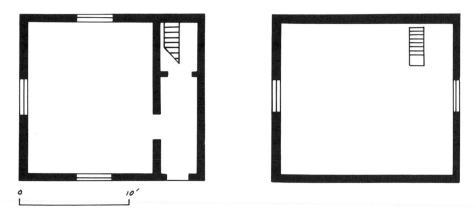

Fig. 1-3 Floor plan of an Icelandic house in Manitoba

of the Icelandic passage house, a distinctive structure which became the standard house type in Iceland from the thirteenth through the nineteenth centuries.[18] The early Canadian Icelandic structure was, however, smaller. In fact, it represented just one unit of the larger Icelandic passage house, which consisted of several rooms joined by a front-positioned cross passageway. The Canadian Icelandic house often had just two rooms, one on each floor. The ground floor room served as a live-in kitchen and the upper room as a sleeping area. Later on, a shed-roofed addition expanded the house, permitting the kitchen to be moved to the addition and leaving the main room as a living-working area.[19]

Structures built after the turn of the century, although they resembled the earlier dwellings, more often than not were quite different. For example, what formerly had been erected as shed-roofed, lean-to additions to log houses were now frequently built as enlarged, but free-standing, shanties. Log construction of gable-roofed houses was supplanted by wood frame construction, but the form and the size of the building did not change much. The floor plan of one such house (Fig. 1-3) from the Manitoba Icelandic settlement,[20] reveals an interesting similarity to Norwegian "sval" houses found in Wisconsin.[21]

Despite these modifications the basic gable-and-shed house became the standard house type within the Icelandic settlement in Manitoba. The main part of the house expanded to incorporate two rooms per floor, and a side hall and stairway provided an echo of the earlier "sval" plan arrangement. The shed-roofed part of the house contained the kitchen and was typically attached to the rear gable of the house. It was normally wider than the rest of the house to accommodate an outside door into the kitchen. This configuration was distinctively Icelandic (Fig. 1-4).

Other Scandinavian groups, numerically much larger than the Icelanders, have left a larger imprint on the North American landscape. In contrast to the Icelanders, the Norwegians settled overwhelmingly in the United States, particularly in the north central part of the country, where in some sections they became the dominant ethnic population.[22]

Despite their wide distribution and relatively large numbers, surprisingly little has been written about Norwegian vernacular architecture. (Even

Fig. 1-4 A typical Icelandic gable-and-shed house
(Drawing by M. M. Geib.)

less has been produced on the closely related Swedish immigrant architecture.) In an attempt to redress this imbalance, William Tishler, in Chapter 13, provides a detailed analysis of Norwegian vernacular architecture in Vernon County, Wisconsin, the center of one of the largest and most concentrated Norwegian settlements in North America.

The Danes, beginning in 1864, followed a migration pattern somewhat different from that of other Scandinavian groups. First, the numbers involved were not as large as those of Norway and Sweden and the migration came somewhat later. Second, the Danes were less inclined than the Norwegians and Swedes to settle in homogeneous ethnic communities. Thus, they too have largely escaped the attention of students of vernacular architecture. Furthermore, because of the later date of their settlement, many Danes occupied structures built by earlier immigrants, who had moved on. In a few midwestern communities, however, the Danish imprint persists. In Chapter 12, Signe Betsinger examines the Danish structures, and the people who built them, in several areas of Iowa and Minnesota. In the absence of distinctively designed exterior construction, it is often interior decoration that provides the clues to Danish origin.

The Third Wave of Migration

Beginning in 1878 the number of migrants began to climb until in 1882 it reached the highest single yearly total of the entire nineteenth century. Not only were numbers high in 1882, but that year also marked a significant shift in the ethnic composition of the immigrant population. The period before 1882 is usually spoken of as the "old" migration, while that after is called the "new" migration (Fig. 1-5). The old migration consisted of peoples originating primarily in northern and western Europe. Prominent among these peo-

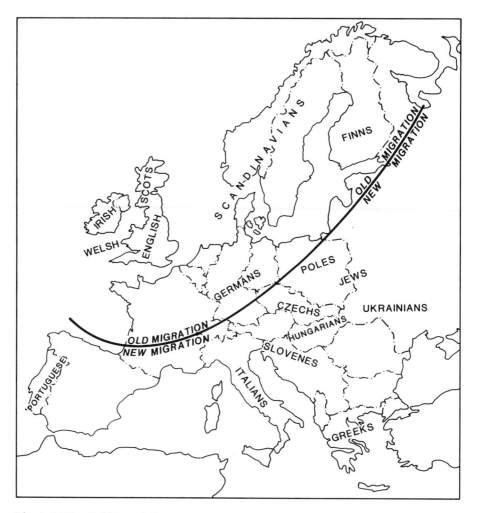

Fig. 1-5 The "old" and the "new" migration to North America and some of the more important migrating groups

ples were the British, the Irish, the Germans, and the Scandinavians. In the new migration peoples of southern and eastern Europe, especially Italians and Poles, predominated. The line of demarcation between the old and new groups was not sharply defined, however. For example, the peak of old migration may have occurred as late as 1882, but peoples from northern and western Europe continued to migrate to North America well into the twentieth century.[23] By the same token, the earliest Italians and Poles arrived in small numbers early in the nineteenth century. Nevertheless, a perceptible shift in migrant origins did occur, and after 1882 the balance lay with the Italians and Poles and other peoples of southern and eastern Europe.

The magnitude of the third wave of migration was larger than those of the first two waves, with much higher peaks and deeper intervening low periods. The great influx of settlers in the late 1870s and during the 1880s was

Allen G. Noble

14

related to the extension of railroads, especially the Great Northern, into the Great Plains and the resulting initially high prices and expanding markets for wheat. Technological innovations, such as the invention of barbed wire, the perfection of agricultural machinery, and the development of deep well drilling and the windmill, were also of significance in facilitating settlement on the western plains.

Beginning in 1893, however, the rate of migration entered a period of steep decline, which continued with one year's exception until 1897 (see Fig. 1-1). The decline in migration was the result of a combination of causes. The high grain prices of the early 1880s were replaced by steadily declining farm prices in the late 1880s and 1890s. Farmers mortgaged farmland to buy machinery in a desperate attempt to expand farming to an economical level. Hence, mortgage debt and subsequent foreclosures increased substantially. Finally, the weather became a problem as settlement was extended into drier and drier areas. A ten-year cycle of below-average rainfall beginning in 1887 broke the backs of many farmers.[24] Each of these conditions contributed to the collapse of the economy in the American West in the 1890s, culminating in the panic of 1893, the demand for free coinage of silver by impoverished western farmers, and the formation and growth of the Populist Party. After 1897 economic and physical conditions improved and migration began to climb once again as the nineteenth century ended.

As might be expected, the third wave of migration was extremely diverse. One group that more or less typifies the disparate heritage of the third wave is the German-Russian Mennonites of Manitoba. The group originated in the sixteenth century in the northern Netherlands, moved first to the Vistula delta in what is now northern Poland, then to the Ukraine–Black Sea area of Russia, and finally to Canada, and less commonly to the United States. Throughout these movements the community maintained its cohesive character. The nature of the German-Russian Mennonite community and its reaction to conflicting currents of tradition and innovation are considered in Chapter 15.

Another group that might be viewed as more or less transitional between the old and the new migration is the Finns, who formed an important part of the third wave of migration. Matti Kaups, in Chapter 14, discusses the vernacular building forms utilized by the Finns in the upper Great Lakes region. He also comments upon the difficulty of accurately measuring the number of Finnish migrants because of the double counting that occurred when young Finnish males returned to Finland and subsequently came back to the United States. In some cases this happened many times, and the individual was counted each time.

The situation was not unique to the Finns. Among later Italian immigrants it was considered to be a regular and common occurrence, and almost two million repatriates can be identified in the first third of the twentieth century.[25] In ethnic communities early migration was often primarily composed of young males. "The proportion of the sexes evened out after the first or second decade [of migration] when the men of the advance guard had saved enough money to send for sweethearts or families, or when demand for domestic servants provided jobs for girls."[26]

A final group whose migratory participation barely falls within the nineteenth century was the Ukrainians, who first migrated to Canada in 1891. The vernacular architecture of this group is discussed by John Lehr in Chapter 17.

Nineteenth-Century Changes in Earlier
Migrant or in Aboriginal Communities

The nineteenth century also saw great changes in ethnic communities whose migration had occurred largely at the very beginning of the century or even prior to that time. Some of these changes were produced by the westward spread of Anglo or "mainstream" American culture accompanying the fulfillment of "manifest destiny." The war with Mexico and the addition of thousands of square miles to the national territory of the United States brought both Indian and Spanish-Mexican groups into the American fold. In the eastern half of the continent, the continuing increase in numbers of settlers sometimes forced earlier arriving or original ethnic groups into more compact settlement, and in all cases it altered the material culture of these groups. Finally, the upheaval both before and during the Civil War left an imprint upon the former slave community.

The impact of Black material culture during the nineteenth century was felt most strongly in the southeastern United States, the region of its greatest concentration. Unlike all other migrant groups, Blacks arrived in the New World in captivity. Their ties with their own culture were either totally severed or severely damaged. Their only hope for survival rested in cultural adaptation.

> The old values, the sanctions, the standards, already unreal, could no longer furnish guides for conduct, for adjusting to the expectations of a completely new life. Where then was [the Black] to look for new standards, new cues—who would furnish them now? He could now look to none but his master, the one man to whom the system had committed his entire being: the man upon whose will depended his food, his shelter, his sexual connections, whatever moral instruction he might be offered, whatever "success" was possible within the system, his very security—in short, everything.[27]

Philippe Oszuscik analyzes, in Chapter 9, the cultural borrowing by Blacks in southeastern United States during the 19th century from both English and French Creole sources. At the same time that extensive cultural borrowing was occurring, Blacks were striving to preserve certain elements of their own African heritage and culture. The success of these efforts is also documented.

Not only Blacks were attempting to preserve their culture against the onslaught and pressure from "American" settlement, so also were the various Amerindian populations, but with limited and mixed success. Frank Porter discusses, in Chapter 7, the myriad problems that faced some of the eastern woodland Indian groups as they attempted to preserve their way of life and make those adaptations necessary for cultural survival.

In the less densely settled West, Indian communities were more successful in maintaining their distinctive ethnic orientation. In Chapter 18, Stephen Jett chronicles the evolution of Navajo material culture from its an-

Allen G.
Noble

16

cient beginnings in prehistory, through periods of conflict with the Spaniards and with other Indian groups, to the modern period of challenge from "American" settlers and culture. A combination of geographical remoteness and ethnic cohesiveness has served to permit the Navajo to maintain much of their traditional culture to the present day.

Spanish Mexicans not only impinged against the Navajo but also came into conflict with other groups. They were most successful in establishing themselves in the Rio Grande valley. Their initial settlement there occurred as early as the end of the sixteenth century. Alvar Carlson, in Chapter 19, traces the evolution of their settlement and their architecture through the nineteenth century and up to the present time. Paramount to his discussion is an examination of the connection between the continued impoverishment of the community and its tendency to fragment land resources. Both conditions help to explain the perpetuation of the vernacular material culture of the region.

Another group able to maintain its separate identity, although its material culture is now rapidly disappearing, is the Cajuns of southwestern Louisiana. In Chapter 10, Malcolm Comeaux points out that the Cajuns "developed a unique farmstead . . . that provided a distinctive look to the land," but it has now largely outlived its usefulness, so only remnants of the former cultural landscape continue to exist.

The situation is similar for the Creoles, who occupy a larger area of lower ethnic settlement density throughout much of southeastern United States. Philippe Oszuscik, in Chapter 8, looks at the evolution of this community from its origins in the seventeenth-century Caribbean world, through the nineteenth century and the impact of "American" culture, up to the present day, when a modest resurgence of Creole ethnic pride is identified.

Ethnic Groups and Urban Occupations and Settlement

The ethnic groups whose vernacular architecture is considered in this volume became, for the most part, residents of the small towns and the rural countryside in North America. By the end of the nineteenth century, the countryside was largely occupied, so immigrants increasingly sought their fortunes in nonrural communities and occupations. As immigration shifted from the old to the new after 1882, and from rural destinations to urban, some ethnic groups began to be associated with certain types or ranges of occupations. Slovenians sought and found employment in foundries and mills, Lithuanians in slaughter houses and meat-packing plants, Portuguese in fishing, Greeks in food service activities,[28] Italians in building trades, barbering, and specialized small crafts such as shoe repair,[29] and the Poles in steelmaking and coal mining. Russian and Polish Jews continued to be shopkeepers and traders as they had been in Europe and, additionally, found jobs in the garment industry. Other groups found urban employment, but they are not so easily stereotyped; and never was an ethnic group's occupational category exclusive or comprehensive—not all Greeks ran restaurants or owned fruit stalls or candy shops and not all of these facilities were ever exclusively Greek. Nevertheless, enough truth exists in these stereotypes to make the concept helpful in explaining the orientation of each of these later immigrant communities.

As immigrants poured into the United States in the closing years of the nineteenth century, their numbers were sufficiently high that cohesive ethnic neighborhoods of a distinct character were created in North American cities. The phenomenon occurred in urban centers of all sizes. In the smaller cities a particular ethnic group might eventually come to dominate and characterize the entire city, at least in the popular mind. Examples could include Portuguese in Fall River, Massachusetts, Greeks in Tarpon Springs, Florida, Armenians in Riverside, California, Spaniards in Tampa, Florida, Finns in Ashtabula, Ohio, and Italians in dozens of cities, including, appropriately, Rome, New York.

In some cities, the influx of later European migrants and their settlement in closely defined sections or neighborhoods sometimes had the effect of displacing earlier immigrants or their descendants, and in the process causing those earlier settlers to establish their own better-defined and usually more compact areas. The settlement sequence in Utica, New York, is a case in point.[30] The earliest settlers in Utica were basically of English or Irish origin. The former, together with settlers whose origin was non-French Canadian, constituted the bulk of the city's early population and consequently were well distributed throughout the city. The Irish, initially attracted by employment opportunities in transportation and construction (created by the building of the Erie and Chenango canals), also diffused throughout the small territory of the early nineteenth-century city. By the middle of the century, two other ethnic groups, reflecting the more rural settlers of the surrounding countryside, also had established themselves prominently in Utica. The central part of the city, on the flood plain and lower terraces of the Mohawk River, housed large numbers of Welsh (Fig. 1-6). In the countryside, the Welsh were already well established, especially on the Tug Hill Plateau several miles northwest of the city.

After the completion of the Chenango Canal in 1836, German workers, attracted by machine shops, textile factories, breweries, and other manufacturing plants, which grew up alongside and as a consequence of the canal, located on the expanding west side of the city.[31] Other Germans had long been established in the Mohawk Valley east of the city, where names such as German Flats and Palatine Bridge betrayed the ethnic origins of these settlers even before the revolutionary war. Both the Welsh and German immigrants to Utica were, in a sense, extensions of the older rural settlements of their countrymen.

The end of the nineteenth century saw a great influx of Polish and Italian immigrants, neither of whom had established rural communities nearby. The Poles occupied West Utica in the vicinity of the growing textile and other mills, following a pattern typical of immigrant settlement in the latter half of the nineteenth century in North American industrial cities.[32] As the Polish neighborhoods expanded, they began to replace the Germans, who gradually migrated southward and, less often, eastward as their family incomes and status increased. Eventually some Polish families also moved outward, especially westward toward New York Mills and Whitesboro, suburban communities that had originally attracted their own Polish millworker populations.

The much larger number of Italian immigrants to Utica settled in a

Allen G.
Noble

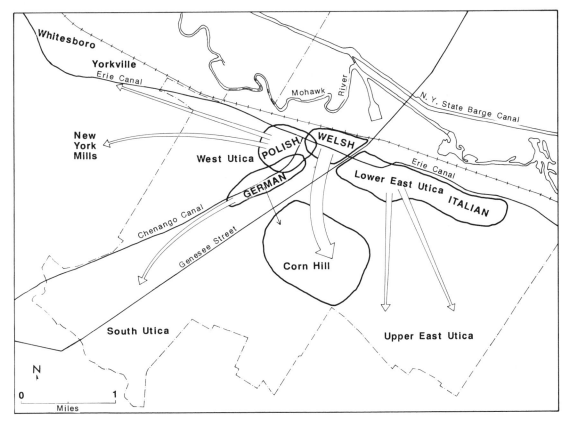

Fig. 1-6 Ethnic neighborhoods and migration patterns in Utica, New York

largely underdeveloped section of the city, East Utica. The possibility of cultivating large kitchen gardens on the fertile river terraces may have been an original attraction for these people, who had been mostly peasant farmers in Italy. Employment was secured in the brickyards, foundries, shoe factories, knitting mills, bakeries, and arms plants.[33] The Italian sections of East Utica, centered on Bleeker Street, became the most cohesive neighborhoods of the city in the early twentieth century. Eventually, their steadily growing numbers and economic success permitted some of them to move both south and southeast into more affluent and less crowded residential areas.

Throughout the nineteenth century the Welsh, impinged upon by both Poles and Italians and particularly by the commercial and industrial expansion of the growing city core, shifted southward to the Corn Hill section of the city (see Fig. 1-6). At the same time, a smaller number of Germans was moving to the same neighborhood. Over time, Corn Hill, located on the river valley's southern slope, developed a strong Celtic-Germanic character.

After World War II the distinctive ethnic character of German and Welsh settlements rapidly disappeared, but Polish neighborhoods are only now in the process of change and assimilation and East Utica remains strongly Italian.

Migration to North America

The Italian Migration

In the largest North American cities, the establishment of ethnic neighborhoods became a hallmark of their urban geography, emphasizing and reinforcing the cosmopolitan nature of these great centers of settlement. Toronto, Chicago, Cleveland (Fig. 1-7), and New York probably had the greatest diversity of ethnic neighborhoods. Frequently, in these large cities the numerically dominant groups established more than one settlement. Often these separate settlements were based upon place of origin in Europe. Thus, in New York City in 1928 at least twenty neighborhoods had populations that were between 50 and 90 percent Italian.[34] The largest and historically most important of these were New Italy (now called Little Italy), settled by migrants from throughout southern Italy; Italian Greenwich Village and Soho (Litte Italy or New Little Italy), a community largely of northern Italians; Italian Harlem (*originally* called Little Italy), populated by Calabrians; Italian Hell's Kitchen and the Italian Bronx (south of Fordham Road), both with a mixed Italian population; and Bensonhurst, settled largely by Sicilians.

Early Italian migrants came mostly from northern Italy, were from artisan, professional, and business classes, and came in modest numbers. Not until the late 1880s did the tide of Italian migration swell to large size and its composition shift largely to peasants from the south.

Although most were peasant farmers, they came at a time when little unoccupied agricultural land remained in the eastern half of the North American continent. Only a few immigrants had the funds or motivation to move on beyond the humid agricultural East. Some of the most characteristically Italian rural settlements grew up on deposits of glacial muck soils, by-passed by earlier migrants because they had been unusable until drained in the late nineteenth or early twentieth century. The Italian colony around Canastota, New York, based upon the raising of vegetables, may be taken as representative of a large number of such communities. Another typical Italian rural settlement was that associated with vineyards. Locations such as Napa Valley, California, and the Finger Lakes of central New York (Naples, for example) come easily to mind.

Still, most Italians of necessity settled in urban areas. The attraction of the extended family and agricultural village proved virtually irresistible:

> In New York, for example, Mott Street between East Houston and Prince held Neapolitans, as did Mulberry Street. On the opposite side of Mott Street were the Basilicati. Calabrians settled Mott Street between Broome and Grand, Sicilians lived on Prince Street, and the Genoese were on Baxter Street. Italians even settled along village lines. In Chicago western Sicilians congregated together, with the immigrants from Altavilla on Larrabee Street; the people from Alimena and Shiusa Sclafani on Cambridge Street; those from Bagheria on Townsend Street; and the people from Sambuca-Zabut on Milton Street. When neither family nor neighbors could be found, the new immigrant settled with other southern Italians.[35]

Gilbert has observed the same phenomenon of strong family and geographic village co-existence among Portuguese immigrants in New Bedford, Massachusetts.[36]

*Allen G.
Noble*

20

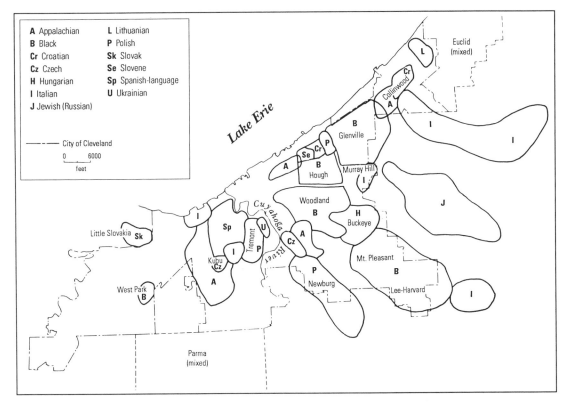

Fig. 1-7 Ethnic neighborhoods in Cleveland, 1960

The Poles in Urban America

The latest of the large nineteenth-century ethnic communities to evolve in the United States was the Poles. They may be taken as an example of what happened to the final group of European migrants who, although they began to arrive in North America in the nineteenth century, were most important in the opening three decades of the twentieth century. These peoples include not only the Poles, but Italians, Greeks, Portuguese, Slovenians, Croatians, Hungarians, Slovaks and Czechs, and Russian and Polish Jews.

Although records exist of Polish migration to North America during the seventeenth century, large-scale migration did not begin until after 1870. The truly vast numbers of Polish did not come until the first fifteen years of the twentieth century. At least three distinct major streams of migration from Poland can be identified, each associated with a different time period and a different part of Poland (Fig. 1-8).

Initially, Poles emigrated mostly from the Prussian- (German-) controlled areas of western and northern Poland.[37] German migration to North America from these same places had been going on for some time and may explain why Poles from this area migrated long before Russian Poles and Austrian Poles.[38] Communication in the German language from the earlier German emigrants to family and friends left behind in Prussian Poland were often shared with Polish acquaintances, and sometimes were even published

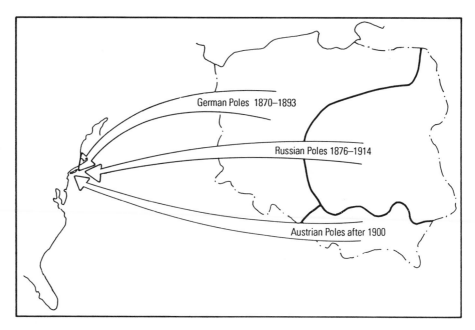

Fig. 1-8 The three streams of Polish migration to North America

in local newspapers. The German-speaking Poles were quick to recognize that their facility in the German language would enable them to adjust to North America much more readily than would their compatriots who spoke only Polish. The dissipation of Bismark's "Kulturkampf" to Germanize the Polish peasantry and the growing industrialization of Germany, providing manufacturing jobs, had the effect of greatly reducing Prussian Polish migration after 1893.

As German Polish emigration declined, its place was taken by outward movements from Russian Poland, which began as early as 1876.[39] The impetus for migration was essentially similar to that which had sparked the German Polish movements—restrictions of personal freedoms, a campaign of "Russification," the introduction of universal military training, and the lack of opportunity for the Polish peasant to gain or expand his own agricultural land resources.

In a sense, the Polish peasants were following the memorable observation of George Pierson that "flight can be an escape from the future as well as from the past." In their case, migration was a way, at least in part, of avoiding change.[40] The exodus from Russian Poland gained momentum by the turn of the century and continued up to the beginning of the first World War. The final Polish migration was from Austrian Poland, the southern fringes of the country. This mass movement did not really begin until the twentieth century.

Regardless of the part of Poland from which they originated, the Polish immigrants, as often as not, attempted to find suitable land for homesteading, but the good land was often already taken. Although a few distinctly Polish rural settlements did emerge, such as those on Long Island, in the Connecticut River valley, and in central Texas, the greatest numbers of Polish workers chose the coal mines, steel mills and other factories to gain their

Allen G. Noble

22

livelihood. In Pennsylvania, for example, the earliest Polish settlements of significant size were in the northeastern anthracite belt of the state.[41] Somewhat later, Poles settled in bituminous coal mining centers elsewhere in the state.

Throughout the eastern and midwestern parts of the United States, the Poles became essentially urban dwellers. As they occupied growing sections of cities such as New York, Chicago, Buffalo, Detroit, Cleveland, Milwaukee, and smaller places, the Poles first crowded into substandard housing. In some cities population densities reached almost unbelievable levels. For example, a Polish neighborhood in Chicago in 1901 "averaged 340 persons per acre, and a three block area housed 7,306 children."[42] Large peasant immigrant families customarily took in boarders and lodgers, but as time passed and the earlier arriving male workers married or sent for families in Europe, they established residences of their own and the crowding became less acute.

Like other immigrants in American cities, the Poles tend to cluster, forming distinct ethnic neighborhoods. These groupings resulted from both positive and negative factors. Positive elements encouraged settlement in some locations in a city, whereas negative factors worked to prohibit or discourage residence in certain other urban areas. Among the positive factors were (1) the presence of ethnic fellows speaking a common language and offering mutual support, (2) the low level of inner-city rents, (3) the location of appropriate churches and other ethnically oriented institutions, and (4) close proximity to places of employment or to public transportation routes. Negative elements included: (1) the residential segregation practiced in "better" neighborhoods, (2) higher rent levels in the outer city, (3) the necessity to use the English language in most parts of the city, (4) and the overt discrimination found in both public and private facilities.

Influenced by both sets of factors, Poles and other immigrant groups often established neighborhoods with strong ethnic characteristics. Kantowicz, for example, notes that in 1898 in eleven precincts of the "Division Avenue Polish Downtown" of Chicago, settlement by Poles reached over 86 percent of the total population. In one precinct of this neighborhood it was 99.9 percent Polish—one non-Pole out of 2,500 residents![43]

Because the Poles, and other urban-dwelling immigrant groups did not initially homestead or own their land, they accepted whatever housing already existed when they arrived. Consequently, Polish neighborhoods in large American cities are usually difficult to distinguish from those of other communities. For the most part, all of these neighborhoods consist of small, one-and-a-half or two-story frame houses of uninspired design, but of a construction sturdy enough to have survived for almost three-quarters of a century. Occasionally, some clues to ethnicity are provided. For example, in east Buffalo a distinctive add-on house type characterizes the Polish district (Fig. 1-9). As the family grew and prospered, its fortunes were reflected in additional rooms being added to the rear of the house. This type of house is so common in east Buffalo that it may be used as an index of Polish settlement.

A few other cultural indicators are also present. Front yard gardens on the small residential lots are often encountered, but these are also characteristic of other eastern Europe groups. More reliable are signs in neighborhood shopping areas, which helpfully and proudly proclaim "Polish Spoken Here." Polish language signs advertise dry cleaners, bakeries, lawyers, other

Fig. 1-9 Typical Polish house, Buffalo, New York, 1987.
(Drawing by M. M. Geib.)

commercial and service establishments, and even vacant properties. In the largest cities, entire market complexes and complete shopping centers serve the large Polish population (Fig. 1-10). That the signs usually are in both Polish and English attests to the fact that cultural assimilation is well under way.

Now, signs are often written in English only but still carry a strong ethnic message. Such elements further confirm the progress of cultural assimilation. Polish cultural centers and Polish-American facilities of all kinds preserved a part of Slavic culture, on the one hand, and helped the immigrant to adjust to American culture, on the other. Some of these facilities, such as the Goral restaurants in Chicago, attempt with distinctive architecture to recreate a part of Poland. Less pretentious, but perhaps more indicative, are the names of neighborhood bars, lounges, and social clubs, such as the Chopin Club, the Warsaw Inn, and the White Eagle (Fig. 1-11).

Another certain mark of the integration of Poles into American life is evidence of their military service in defense of their adopted country. The Polish League of American Veterans facility functions in many Polish neighborhoods as the local social center for males.

These facilities, along with community centers, social clubs and cultural organizations have functioned as support groups to assist the Polish immigrant in the move toward participation in the larger American community. Perhaps the most visible symbols of the final assimilation are the substantial European-style brick and stone churches, in whose front yards fly large American flags.

Allen G.
Noble

Fig. 1-10 Signs in Polish at the entrance to the Broadway Market, Buffalo, New York, 1987. (Photo by A. G. Noble.)

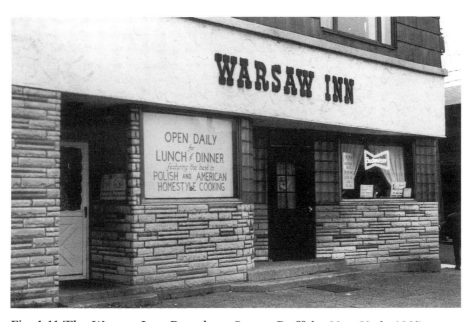

Fig. 1-11 The Warsaw Inn, Broadway Street, Buffalo, New York, 1987. (Photo by A. G. Noble.)

Part II

*Northeastern
North America*

2

Acadians in Maritime Canada

Peter Ennals

ACADIAN settlement along the Atlantic coast of Canada is arguably the oldest sustained European settlement north of the Spanish outposts that dotted the lower fringe of North America from the last quarter of the sixteenth century. Although the Acadians never constituted a large or imposing presence, Acadian history and Acadian life are remarkable, in the homeland of Maritime Canada or in the Cajun diaspora. The history is overwhelmingly a record of survival, as Acadians faced the full force of the emerging Anglo-American culture, which, with its imperious insistence on use of the English language, its militantly Protestant religion, and its liberal and utilitarian political and economic institutions, sought to obliterate and assimilate the tiny, weak, residual Maritime French population in ways never tried in Quebec. Tenacious and profoundly adaptive, Acadians have managed, in Maritime Canada at least, to preserve significant elements of an antecedent cultural identity and language, in spite of episodes of forced migration and, for the past century, the seductive call of North American popular culture.

An examination of Acadian housing forms and building practices provides a means of understanding the broader patterns of cultural change and adaptation that lie at the heart of Acadian survival. This chapter probes that experience in the context of the larger changes occurring within Anglo-American vernacular house building and settlement practices.

The Early Settlement History of Acadia

By 1800 Acadian French settlement had occupied the landscape of Maritime Canada for almost two centuries (Fig. 2-1). The first European settlement in the region began in 1603 with a small party of French commercial adventurers led by DeMonts, Poutrincourt, and Champlain, who overwintered on Dochet's Island near the mouth of the Ste. Croix River astride the modern-day border between Maine and New Brunswick.[1] After a disastrous winter, the intrepid leaders of this tiny and still tenuous commercial enterprise moved, in 1604, to establish a more commodious base at Port Royal, across the Bay of Fundy. All of this came after a century or more of European seasonal fishing and whaling contact with the lands around the Gulf of St. Lawrence, especially on the rich continental shelf of Newfoundland. The

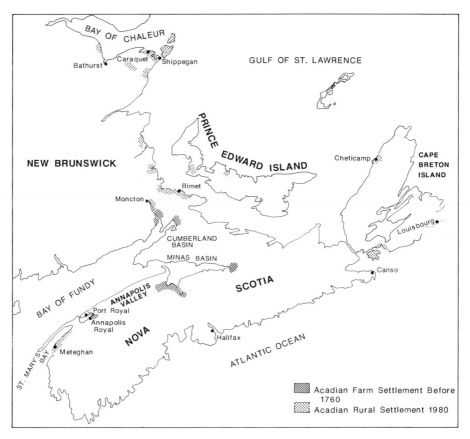

Fig. 2-1 Past and present settlement in Acadia

founding of Port Royal marked the establishment of a lasting European presence, though it progressed slowly and without evident commitment. Indeed, any historical reading of this region leaves one to marvel at the speed with which the main thrust of French colonial interest pushed past the Maritime region into the heart of the continent. While the French entrée to North America was through the geographically complex, but economically discouraging, Maritime coastal zone, the greater fascination and opportunity was soon seen to lie to the west, in the heart of the continent. Despite the shift in the frontier of colonial activity, a small coastal colony persisted.

Acadia, as this colony became known, corresponded roughly to the three modern provinces of Nova Scotia, New Brunswick, and Prince Edward Island and extended into the present-day U.S. state of Maine. The Acadian people sprang from a small population of settlers, probably no more than five hundred immigrants in all, most of whom had come as *engagés,* or indentured laborers, either to trade in furs or to fish, the two regional enterprises that had first tantalized French authorities. By 1632 those who chose to stay in the colony had begun, with official encouragement and their own familial land aspirations, to develop an agricultural orientation. Over the next generation small bands of settlers spread around the Bay of Fundy in tiny, and usually kin-related, clusters wherever good saltmarsh habitats could be exploited. Agriculture was largely subsistence farming, emphasizing cattle and bread grains wherever possible.

Largely by-passed and cut off from the pivot of French colonizing energy, which by 1650 had moved into the St. Lawrence valley, where fur trading opportunities were far superior, Acadia found itself curiously in the midst of, but effectively on the fringe of, a great geopolitical drama. It was a society caught in the seam between the more dynamic forces emanating from France and England, both of which were probing the continent with growing effectiveness and expanding populations. Illustrating this condition is the fact that the British took possession of mainland Nova Scotia under the Treaty of Utrecht in 1713, leaving Isle Royale (Cape Breton) and Isle St. Jean (Prince Edward Island) along with most of present-day New Brunswick and part of Maine, to France, guided by what proved to be an imprecise and ill-defined document. In reality the competing national sovereignty over both halves of Acadia was ambiguous at best. The main body of the Acadian population found itself nominally under British rule, yet life changed little; there were few signs of British authority, and almost no British population was inserted into the colony during the succeeding four decades. Here then, was a colony populated by French men and women but unsupported by the sustaining colonial impetus to supply new settlers from the homeland.

By the early decades of the eighteenth century the great marsh meadows of the Bay of Fundy allowed Acadian farmers to produce surpluses of livestock and other foodstuffs, which found a ready market in the fishing towns of the outer coast and, later, from the 1720s through the 1740s, in the garrison and population at Louisbourg. An equally important, if not more bouyant, trading outlet for livestock and other products was the New Englanders, who sailed north regularly to procure cattle and other products in considerable volumes. With the advent of British claims to Nova Scotia in 1713, Acadian farmers were left to survive by their wits. Most sought to effect a detached and neutral position in order to ensure the success of their trading activities, which were divided between the hostile nationalities.[2]

Evolution of Acadian Culture

Although the residents of this outpost achieved a modest prosperity compared to their peasant counterparts in France and soon worked out solutions for sustaining agriculture in an unfamiliar habitat, they found themselves unable to reap the great economic rewards of other more favorable locations to the south and west. They also may have been experiencing some cultural devolution or atrophy through official and institutional neglect and their own tendency to stay rooted in place rather than join the swirling tide of men and women probing the continent.[3] Through the eighteenth century, Acadian society seems to have been one that, if anything, simplified its social structure considerably by making seigneurial title largely irrelevant. No great fortunes were amassed and only tentative and fragmented intrusions came from institutions such as the church and the state. It was, in short, a setting in which a French folk cultural life, having been transplanted, was altered through experiment to reflect a new environmental and social reality. It thereafter existed with little outside interference, even to the point of taking on dimensions of a kind of post-European tribalism.

The nature of this way of life has hindered modern scholars from reconstructing patterns of cultural practice because little documentary record was evidently generated. Travelers' accounts, many of them written by British visitors after 1713, when mainland Nova Scotia fell under British control, disparage the Acadian practices, as will be noted later. Certainly, insofar as housing and settlement structure is concerned, these accounts portray a picture of extreme, even grim, rusticity. Later events, namely *"le grand dérangement"*—the Acadian term for the cruel and calculated British deportation and dispersal of the French-speaking population after the final British conquest in 1758—ensured that much of the written record and most of the housing stock were destroyed.

Henry Wadsworth Longfellow's romantic portrayal of Evangeline notwithstanding, not all Acadians were dispatched to southern American colonies. The dispersal was wide; some fled to France or England; others landed in such geographically disparate locations as St. Pierre and Miquelon in the Gulf of St. Lawrence, and Martinique in the Caribbean; many were absorbed into the populations of Boston, Savannah, and other seaboard cities. A sizeable colony did, of course, regroup in Louisiana. In all, it is estimated that 8,000 of the 10,000 Acadians were deported during 1755 and 1756.[4] The majority of those who remained took to the forests of what is now New Brunswick, and a significant new refugee colony emerged around the Bay of Chaleur (see Fig. 2-1). Within a few years, as ethnic and political pressures eased, many Acadians were able to drift back into the parts of the region from which they had been driven. However, in returning they were constrained by the presence of a new English-speaking population.

The new population was initially anything but homogeneous in its geographical origins. It consisted of New Englanders, many of whom had some experience in the region through longstanding trading connections with the Acadian farmers, or as irregular troops sent to garrison British forts in Nova Scotia or to carry out the conquest of the French at Louisbourg. Later, in the 1770s, colonies of British settlers, recruited in Yorkshire or driven from coastal and highland Scotland, arrived to plant themselves firmly along the northern coast of the region. Soon waves of Loyalists exiled from Massachusetts and other colonies flooded the region, and by the early nineteenth century large numbers of Irish, Scottish, and English settlers sought a home in the region. The chronology of their arrival and the localized settlement patterns of these newcomers tended to produce geographically separate and ethnically distinct cells of population, yielding a particularly heterogeneous cultural template in which the post-expulsion Acadian settlements were but another element in the complex matrix.

By the beginning of the nineteenth century, the geography of Acadian occupation of the region had shifted profoundly. In pre-expulsion times, Acadian agricultural settlement was concentrated in Nova Scotia, particularly in the upper and lower Annapolis valley, with outlying settlements on both the Minas and Cumberland basins at the head of the Bay of Fundy (see Fig. 2-1). Beyond this core was a handful of fishing settlements dotting the outer Atlantic coast, the most notable among them being Louisbourg on Cape Breton Island and a settlement at Canso on the mainland. In post-expulsion times, Acadian occupation of Nova Scotia was restricted to minor settlements on the western coast of Cape Breton Island, especially around

Cheticamp and on the outer Fundy shore around St. Mary's Bay. By 1800, the greatest weight of Acadian occupation had been planted in New Brunswick, with major settlements strung along the northeastern coast, especially around Caraquet and Shippegan and in the southeast near Moncton.

Evolution of the Acadian House to 1900

We have little tangible evidence with which to judge the form of the pre-expulsion Acadian house. British military authorities, and the Acadians themselves, razed most of the existing settlements, and any buildings that did survive apparently have not withstood the rigors of the two succeeding centuries. Moreover, the Acadians left little documentary record of their housing; and, given their somewhat cloudy antecedency in France[5] and an apparent simplification of European culture generally in Acadia, it is difficult to make assumptions about the nature and form of their early housing. Nor is it logical to assume that Acadian houses mirrored the house-building experience of New France. It is apparent from the vantage point of the twentieth century that Acadian and Quebecois culture evolved along distinct paths. Linguists have identified significant dialectical differences and patterns of usage; folklore and other elements of material culture show similar distinctions. Recent work on the early housing of Quebec suggests that there were no exact French prototypes for houses in Quebec. Rather, like all of the early emigrant populations on this continent, *les canadiens* adapted some of the regional housing practices of their native country to the newfound abundance of timber and the new climatic imperatives. Thus, in Quebec the European techniques of building in stone, in half-timber with stone filling (*colombage pierrotté*) (Fig. 2-2), and in half-timber with brick filling (*colombage bousillé*) gave way in the eighteenth century building entirely in wood, using a distinctive log building technique called *pièces-sur-pièces*, in which squared beams were laid horizontally one on top of another and were slotted into upright posts placed at approximately ten-foot intervals[6] (Fig. 2-3A).

Undoubtedly, early building in Acadia replicated the building technique of the homeland. The impressive research surrounding the reconstruction of representative elements of the great colonial French fortress at Louisbourg has found both archaeological and documentary evidence of some of these practices. Today visitors can see reproductions of buildings using many of the techniques noted above, in both pure French provincial transplants and in hybrid building techniques that reveal the transition toward a new technology utilizing the region's abundance of wood.

Louisbourg was the exception rather than the rule. The single largest urban settlement, the seat of the governor, and home to an administrative, military and mercantile elite, in Louisbourg, not surprisingly, some residents could attempt to reproduce familiar or pretentious housing following the conventions of provincial France. Colonial authorities brought large numbers of building tradesmen and artisans to Louisbourg, helping to ensure a building pattern different from that seen further afield in the colony.

Ordinary Acadian housing, both within the walls of Louisbourg and more particularly beyond in the rural villages and hamlets of the mainland, seems to have been cruder in form and construction. Contemporary accounts describe the colony's houses as "no more than badly built cottages

Fig. 2-2 *Colombage pierrotté,* half-timber with stone infilling, as executed at the Louisbourg reconstruction. (Drawing by P. Ennals.)

with chimneys of clay."[7] Many structures were built of tree trunks piled one on another without even having been squared; some were based on heavy piles driven into the ground.[8] Other accounts describe houses as low buildings roofed with thatch or "wretched dwellings of mud and wood," although some were apparently covered with shingles or boards.[9] Even on the eve of expulsion, after nearly a century and a half of settlement, Acadian houses could be described as "wretched wooden boxes without conveniences, and without ornaments, and scarcely containing the most necessary furniture."[10] Recognizing that such uncomplimentary accounts must always be judged in the social context of their authors—inevitably in this case members of an opposing military or administrative establishment—we are nevertheless left with a picture of buildings universally constructed of wood in the simplest of forms. The construction techniques probably consisted of a related pièces-sur-pièces method using dovetailed corners (*queue d'aronde*) and the *poteau en coulisse* method, in which unfinished logs were fitted horizontally into slotted upright posts. An even cruder method, *piquet* or *poteaux en terre* (Fig. 2-3B), with posts sunk into the ground to form a palisade-like wall, was no doubt very common; and some buildings were apparently built *en torchis*—that is, using a wattle and daub infilling between the timber frame.[11]

We can only conjecture that these houses reproduced the simplest of floor plans, the principal element of which was a large multipurpose room (*salle commune*), which served as kitchen and dining, living, and work space and which probably served as a sleeping area—perhaps being curtained off as the need arose (Fig. 2-4). The evidence at Louisbourg also suggests mar-

Fig. 2-3 Forms of log construction: A) *pièces-sur-pièces*, B) *piquet*.
(Drawing by P. Ennals.)

ginally larger houses consisting of two rooms, with the chimney stack in
some cases dividing the rooms. These houses appear to be the Acadian version of the so-called hall and parlor dwelling, in which the *cuisine* was equivalent to the hall, while the parlor space was invariably used as a separate bed
chamber (*chambre*). With the house set on a crude foundation of stones and
tamped clay, enclosing a pit cellar, and with perhaps the addition of a loft
area above the main floor, the dwelling was complete (Fig. 2-5).

The Reductive Character of Acadian Houses

Visually, the assemblage of buildings reconstituted at Louisbourg leaves
no doubt of a French origin. A transplanted French aesthetic is unmistakable
in the proportions defining roof lines and the detailing of facades, for example the preponderance of casement windows. In the same way, a distinctive
French stamp came to be imposed on the evolving building tradition in Quebec, and one can even detect elements of this same aesthetic in the surviving
buildings of Quebec's frontier outposts in the middle Mississippi Valley. Surprisingly, this same evocatively French imprint cannot be identified in the
surviving landscape of Acadia. The literary descriptions of early Acadian
dwellings provide no hint of a vivid exterior aesthetic; indeed, the suggestion is just the opposite. Combined with the surviving evidence of late-
eighteenth-century Acadian houses, we are left to conclude that the greater
body of this population—especially that residing on the mainland of Nova
Scotia—lost contact with these aesthetic principles. Without a local resident
elite, and cut off from a class of professional building tradesmen or the body
of published design ideals, Acadians seem to have executed housing that was

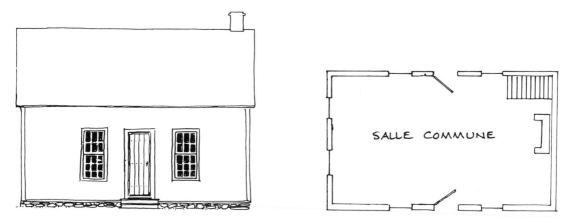

Fig. 2-4 Typical single-cell-plan house. (Drawing by P. Ennals.)

notable for its crudeness and utility rather than its expression of social or artistic sensitivity. In Quebec there were significant numbers of building tradesmen sent out to serve the larger colonial establishment. Many of these people came to reside in Quebec City and there is evidence that there emerged a kin-related community of these practitioners that existed through several generations.[12]

Houses with essentially these simple reductive features and plan, and dating to the post-expulsion period of the late eighteenth and early nineteenth centuries, have been documented in the Acadian-dominated areas of New Brunswick.[13] Several have been relocated and restored as part of the Village Historique Acadien outdoor museum near Caraquet, New Brunswick (Fig. 2-6). Many more can be found still in the towns and villages of Acadian New Brunswick, though they frequently are buried beneath the accretions of a century or more of additions and popular makeovers. The basic

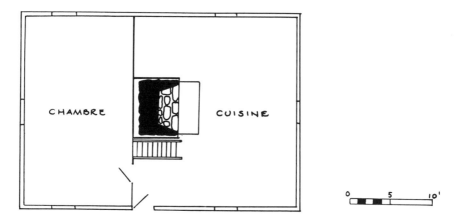

Peter Ennals

Fig. 2-5 An example of the Acadian hall-and-parlor plan, the Joseph H. Boudreau house, Bimet, New Brunswick, ca. 1795. (After Bernard LeBlanc, in Brun, LeBlanc, and Robichaud 1988.)

Fig. 2-6 Maison Leger, Village Historique Acadien, Caraquet, New Brunswick. (Drawing by P. Ennals.)

plan, which is, in effect, a single structural cell, was the simplest of European rural dwelling plans. The product of localized folk or peasant culture, it occurred widely in France and Britain, rendered in a variety of building materials and given a varied outward appearance by regional or localized differences in roof form and material, window and door placement, and so on.[14] Frequently, in western Europe and later in North America, house builders expanded the scale of houses and took the opportunity to alter the internal space by utilizing the location of the chimney and hearth as the dividing line between halves of the house. In other instances one might create a cross passage where doors on either side of the house opposed one another, thereby establishing a de facto hallway, even though the space may not have been set off by a wall or screen. Colonial examples of these simple folk houses illustrating both the single-cell plan and the hall and parlor plan were to be found from the time of first settlement up and down the eastern coast of North America where, in the hands of colonial settlers, this European dwelling was adapted to local materials and conditions.[15]

For the Acadian people, houses of this type suited their lifestyle admirably. They were comparatively inexpensive to build, especially when constructed using Acadian log techniques. Indeed, much of the work could be performed by the prospective owner using materials readily at hand, and as with other folk groups in isolated frontier settings, Acadians developed a strong tradition of self-sufficiency in building, as well as in other crafts.[16] Interior walls were typically covered in boards; plaster was rare before the 1850s. Boards could be produced at sawmills, when local sawmills became generally available after 1830; previously they were prepared by hand in saw pits. Perhaps more important is the way in which the house was suited to the informality of Acadian culture and life. Much has been written romanticiz-

Acadians in Maritime Canada

ing Acadian life since the deportation.[17] Let it simply be said that until as late as the mid-twentieth century, the Acadians in the Maritime Provinces remained preponderantly a peasant society. Isolated by ethnicity and geography from the main currents of North American society, they lived out a simple and spartan existence by seasonally harvesting in the waters, forests, and farms. Family, church, and community were the sustaining agencies that gave focus to their lives, and one still sees something of this written into the modern landscape in the form of the closely settled rural street villages that stretch almost continuously along the New Brunswick north shore, as well as along the Acadian coasts of Nova Scotia, that is, at Meteghan in Digby County and at Cheticamp in Cape Breton (see Fig. 2-1).

In such a world, the family was an economic unit as well as a social unit. There was little labor specialization, and families tended to be self-sufficient and independent. However, social custom and inclination produced a high degree of visiting between kin and neighbors. The house, and particularly the large, multipurposed salle commune, the focal point of which was the hearth, was a welcoming space in which much of the folk life, recreation as well as the daily toil and the instruction of the young, necessarily took place.[18] In a society whose customs, traditions, and way of life remained comparatively stable through the two socially tumultuous centuries after 1755, this dwelling form, in much of New Brunswick, passed into the 20th century without major alteration to the fundamental organization and use of space.

The Influence of English Building on Acadian Building

What is striking about this dwelling form among Acadians is that by the beginning of the nineteenth century, if not earlier, it was being constructed using a timber frame building technology very similar to that used by English-speaking settlers of the region. Indeed, the earlier solution of pièces-sur-pièces building, although continued into the nineteeth century, seems largely to have been replaced by a system of box framing, with paired rafter trusses as roofing members.

Typical of these houses is that built by Joseph H. Boudreau at Bimet.[19] Built in 1795, the Boudreau house (Figs. 2-5 and 2-7) was a one-and-a-half–story dwelling. Perhaps somewhat larger in dimension (32′ × 23′) than most Acadian houses, the ground floor still consisted of only two rooms—*cuisine* and *chambre*. A single large hearth and chimney stack occupied the center of the dwelling and opened onto the cuisine; behind the chimney pile was a board wall enclosing the chambre. It is believed that a steep stair set against the chimney provided access to the upper floor. Entry to the dwelling was through a door set near the middle of the long wall. It opened first into a small foyer formed by the side of the stair and the door leading to the chambre, then into the cuisine. The arrangement must have provided some protection from winter drafts and screened life within from visitors to the door. Double-hung windows on either side of the front door were matched in opposing positions on the rear wall and by similarly aligned, smaller half-windows in the knee wall of the upper story. Single windows in the end walls on the lower level completed the openings. The exterior was covered with rough board sheathing neatly set into a rabbet on the face of the structural

Fig. 2-7 The Joseph H. Boudreau house, Bimet, New Brunswick, ca. 1795. (After Bernard LeBlanc, in Brun, LeBlanc, and Robichaud 1988.)

members, so that the boards fit flush against the posts. Over this, clapboard siding could be nailed directly to the upright posts.

How and why this further change in building process was accomplished begs an answer, and here the longstanding interaction between New England and the Maritimes comes into play. Recent historical reconstruction efforts in the town of Annapolis Royal (formerly Port Royal), Nova Scotia have underscored the fact that a small but influential population of New Englanders was present in Acadia long before the explusion in 1758. Dwellings such as the Adams-Ritchie house, which may date to the 1740s, were the houses of a succession of New England merchants and derived from their origins. This type of house, in construction technique, floor plan, and exterior appearance, replicates a common New England form and, in fact, may have been erected by house framers brought in from Massachusetts. No doubt, the arrival of other merchants and administrators, and the travels of Acadians themselves back and forth from Boston to the Maritimes, before "*le grand dérangement*" would have permitted at least a passing familiarity with New England ways. Moreover, the arrival in 1749 of what proved to be the vanguard of a larger English-speaking population in Nova Scotia, increased the opportunities for cultural borrowing, the wholesale relocation of the residual Acadian population to other parts of the region notwithstanding. It seems likely that Acadians may have sought to conceal their ethnic identity, and thus reduce their social and political vulnerability, by constructing houses that looked like those of their colonial masters. Perhaps, too, a growing consciousness of social distinction expressed through housing induced the more prosperous Acadian farmers to copy the building practices of the Anglo-American newcomers. Whatever the reason, Acadians were led eventually to the acceptance of an alternative house-building approach, one that was easily adapted to the relative simplicity of the Acadian folk dwelling form.

Acadians in Maritime Canada

Having adopted and converted one dimension of a new building technology to their own folk culture, it was inevitable that Acadians would find other opportunities to absorb new ideas. Indeed, by the middle of the nineteenth century they apparently were responding to elements of the emerging vernacular architecture of the Maritimes.[20] Significantly, the elements adopted were utilitarian and selective. Thus, building techniques such as balloon framing became general, while log techniques all but disappeared by the end of the century. Shingles and clapboard and external decoration were also borrowed—particularly the simple vernacular forms of neoclassical trim and some of the common regional dormer designs. Thus, by the end of the nineteenth century many Acadian houses came to look little different in outward appearance from the ubiquitous rural vernacular cottages of the Maritimes. There were, however, significant differences in floor plan between the Acadian folk houses and those being built for the wider Maritime society. The majority of the latter used a center-hall plan with flanking formal parlors in the front of the house and kitchen and service rooms at the back of the dwelling (Fig. 2-8).

As was the case elsewhere on both sides of the North Atlantic, the execution of houses with more complex and functionally defined floor plans and the tendency of ordinary housing to mimic the design vocabulary or the established "high style" idioms gave rise to a series of popular of vernacular housing types. Because these new forms of housing were widely promoted

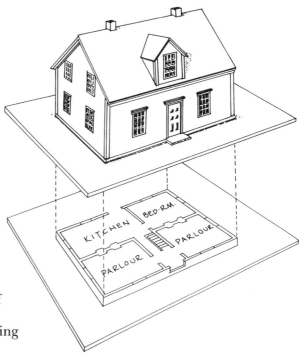

Fig. 2-8 The prototype of the Maritime vernacular dwelling, ca. 1860. (Drawing by P. Ennals.)

through carpenter's manuals, journals, and newspapers, they came to have a broad geographical currency by the middle decades of the nineteenth century. English-speaking Maritimers were well connected to the means by which these new fashions were promoted. Acadians were not, and any new innovations probably were absorbed by them more slowly and from direct contact and local observation rather than by the written word.

Nevertheless, during the second half of the century there were modifications in plan and design taking place which established an updated version of the Acadian house. A technological change—the arrival of cook stoves and small heating stoves, which became widely available after 1860—allowed a freer life within the house. No longer did activity need to revolve around the hearth, especially during the long winter months; now, rooms could be heated separately, functions could be carried on independently. Specifically, this innovation resulted in the creation of a small kitchen wing (Fig. 2-9), leaving the former cuisine as a more conventional parlor or living room. As a result of this change, the front door often ceased to be functional. The kitchen remained the center of life, and entry to the house came to be through the kitchen door. Indeed, in many surviving examples and many houses constructed in recent times, there is no stoop or stairway leading to the front door. In the case of some new houses, the front door gives access to a large porch on which the family can sit, but no stairs are provided to the ground. Improved heating also led to the transformation of the upper story from an unfinished and undifferentiated *grenier* or attic into two or more bedrooms. The addition of a central dormer or "cross gable" (after the Maritime vernacular fashion) aided this transition by providing more light and head room for an upstairs hall or landing.

More prosperous Acadians adopted one or the other of the house forms currently in fashion in the region at the time of construction. Thus, one sees examples of center-hall plan houses, the commonest Maritime vernacular house after 1840, of the "upright and wing" house of the 1860s and 1870s, and of the "four square house" popular in the period between about 1900

Fig. 2-9 Typical late-nineteenth-century Acadian dwelling with kitchen wing added. (Drawing by P. Ennals.)

and 1925. Also present are several local versions of the west coast "bungalow," which seems to have had a modest Maritime popularity during the period between the world wars. No doubt this cultural borrowing was aided by the increasing ethnic pluralism that was a characteristic of much of northern and eastern New Brunswick. Beginning in the 1860s Acadians began to move with greater frequency to the cities of the region, as well as to the factory towns of New England where these ideas could be assimilated.[21]

The Evolution of the Acadian House after 1900

During the twentieth century, Acadians continued to build houses that preserved the essentials of the longstanding folk plan. However, most houses were smaller, and they were owner-built at a time when house construction had generally become the preserve of contractors. The presence of these houses on the outskirts of cities such as Moncton and Bathurst, beyond the range of by-law restrictions and municipal building codes, suggests a low economic status of the owners. Yet, more recently, especially after the introduction of universal federal social welfare programs, such as unemployment insurance, a new level of prosperity has led to the transformation of these houses. Rather than building a new "modern" house or moving to a more fashionable neighborhood, many have opted to perform radical surgery on their earlier structures. Houses have been lifted onto new foundations, thereby providing a full basement into which family recreation rooms and other service rooms could be incorporated. Others have had the roof raised to create a full second story. In terms of plan, a movement developed to subdivide the old cuisine space into a front living room and a rear kitchen, no matter how tiny the resulting rooms. One bedroom and a bathroom typically occupy the remainder of the main floor. All of this produces a house not significantly different in arrangement from the common dwelling plans in mid-twentieth-century Canada.

The most recent alterations are typically to the exterior of the house. New siding and new sash and door combinations have become widespread and one quickly notices the Acadian habit of using bolder, more vivid colors on the exterior dwellings. Aquamarines, pastel blues and yellows are common, as are brighter hues of these colors. It is not uncommon to see upper and lower stories painted different colors, often with jarring results. House painting is probably more common now than in the past. Formerly, paints were relatively expensive and many people allowed their siding or shingles to weather naturally to a silver grey, painting only the more expensive sash and door, if anything. The common Maritime color for houses is white with black trim. The long Acadian tradition of self-reliant, owner-occupied building lives on, and Acadian house owners have become conspicuous consumers of all the latest handyman fads and "house beautiful" fashions. Many seem to have a particular attraction to stone facing, while others use a variety of siding materials without apparent regard to architectural convention and harmony. Indeed, in village after village, one notes that many of these Acadian houses are in an almost continual state of alteration. Sometimes this situation arises because the owner's finances prevent immediate completion, and the array of building materials bought at a bargain in odd lots is evident from the diverse coverings on different sides of the house. In other cases, the

Peter
Ennals

42

house serves rather as a palimpsest of changing fashion as the owner tests his creativity and responds to each new design concept.

Conclusion

It is evident, then, that while Acadians developed a house form of their own in the New World, they failed to produce a house that was outwardly distinctive. The Acadian house has none of the readily identifiable and evocatively French images of the Quebec house, for example, with its flared eaves, suspended gallery porches, or rich applique of the sash. While there are clear echoes of France in the plan of the house, there is no apparent continuity of style, and one is struck by the depths to which Acadian material culture as a whole seems to have lost its French roots. Perhaps the forced transience of the deportation era had a profoundly disconnecting effect on Acadian artistic traditions, with only the oral culture being able to survive, by virtue of its greater portability. It is more likely that there was a cultural devolution taking place before that time. By the nineteenth century, Acadians found it easier to become cultural borrowers of architectural elements and style, although they apparently were more reluctant to alter their internal use of space. In the present resurgence of Acadian cultural nationalism there is a visible yearning among many younger Acadians to connect with their heritage through a revival of earlier housing styles. Ironically, the absence of an overtly distinctive Acadian architectural tradition has led many to adopt the Quebec revival styles, none of which ever existed in Acadia. The rapidity with which older houses are being transmogrified or are being surrounded by new "builder styles" only highlights the difficulty and ambivalence that Acadians face in recognizing their heritage.

3

The Irish, English, and Scots in Ontario

Brian Coffey

THE QUESTION of cultural relationships in use of construction materials has received little attention from researchers concerned with early North American building practices. Nevertheless, assumptions and stereotypes regularly surface in both nineteenth- and twentieth-century writings, and they reinforce unsubstantiated notions regarding cultural bias in the selection of construction materials. Examples include references to a Scottish preference for stone construction, a German penchant for squared-log building, and widespread Irish acceptance of shanties or similar hovels.[1]

This chapter explores the question of cultural links to nineteenth-century building-material use through the example of Irish, English, and Scottish settlers in Ontario, Canada. For the year 1850 the settlement pattern and associated construction materials of each group are examined, on a county-by-county basis in order to evaluate the impacts of natural resource availability and levels of economic development. Further, to assess the importance of the groups' varied economic conditions and their length of settlement, a detailed study of a single township is presented.

The study is based on a sample taken from manuscript census data collected for the 1851–1852 *Census of the Canadas*.[2] The materials of houses (shanty, round log, squared log, frame, brick, and stone) owned by persons born in Ireland, England, and Scotland have been recorded.[3] The sample, drawn from counties containing a mix of housing stock, includes 3,146 Irish householders, 1,989 English settlers, and 1,776 Scottish residents.

In aggregate the data reflect a cultural bias in building material selection (Table 3-1). This is especially true for the Irish occupation of the shanty, the relative Scottish preference for stone construction, and a greater than expected English occupancy of frame dwellings. Further, all groups made extensive use of log construction techniques. By the mid-nineteenth century nearly 50 percent of all English settlers lived in log dwellings. For Scottish colonists this figure rose to nearly 65 percent, while approximately 70 percent of all Irish residents occupied log structures. The figures are interesting in that none of the groups had a log tradition before settling in Ontario. Presumably, they were quick to adopt this standard frontier dwelling, which, by the time significant numbers of Scots, English, and Irish arrived, was a

Table 3-1. Ethnic Occupancy of Houses, by Construction Category, 1851

	Shanty	Round Log	Squared Log	Frame	Brick	Stone	Other	Totals
English	7.3%	39.0%	1.1%	43.6%	4.1%	3.2%	1.7%	100.0%
	(146)*	(775)	(22)	(867)	(81)	(63)	(35)	(1,989)
Irish	24.0%	45.7%	2.0%	23.6%	1.3%	2.9%	0.5%	100.0%
	(755)	(1,438)	(62)	(743)	(40)	(92)	(16)	(3,146)
Scottish	8.7%	52.3%	3.0%	24.2%	4.7%	6.0%	1.2%	100.1%**
	(155)	(928)	(53)	(429)	(83)	(106)	(22)	(1,776)

Notes: Based on sample of manuscript census data for 1851–1852 *Census of the Canadas*.
*Values in parentheses indicate number of samples in each category.
**Total exceeds 100% due to rounding.

common feature of Ontario's landscape. However, distinct regional variations exist for all groups, suggesting that a variety of factors were at work in
the making of this landscape. The settlement patterns and associated use of
construction materials of each group are discussed below.

The Irish

Irish colonization of Upper Canada, as the area that is now Ontario was
then called, began after 1815, first with the immigration of Ulstermen and
later with large influxes of Irish Catholics. The total Irish immigration to the
province during the first half of the nineteenth century is difficult to determine, both because immigration records are sketchy and because large numbers of incoming Irish traveled on to the United States after their arrival in
Canada. However, some early concentrations of Irish can be noted. In 1818
approximately 120 Irish Protestants migrated to London Township in Ontario County[4] (Fig. 3-1). Five years later, more than 500 southern Irish took
advantage of government assistance and migrated to Upper Canada, ultimately settling in the Bathurst District.[5] A second large-scale assistance
program was undertaken in 1825 when an additional 2,000 Irish Catholics
sailed for locations in Peterborough County.[6] Finally, from 1817 to 1819
about 3,500 British subjects who landed at New York were persuaded to go
to Upper Canada.[7] Most of these were Ulstermen who ultimately settled in
the vicinity of Rice Lake, which is on the border between Peterborough and
Northumberland counties.

It was not until 1829, however, that extensive Irish immigration to Upper
Canada began. In that year, 9,614 Irish were reported to have arrived at Quebec.[8] Over the next twenty years more than 375,000 Irish landed at that
port.[9] Most of the Quebec arrivals who stayed in Canada settled in Ontario,
and by mid-century 176,267 Irish were counted in that province.[10] Found
throughout the province, the Irish accounted for about 19 percent of the
total population (Fig. 3-2). They exceeded the combined total of all other
European immigrants, and in only seven counties did they comprise less
than 10 percent of the population.

During the first half of the nineteenth century, the dominance of log

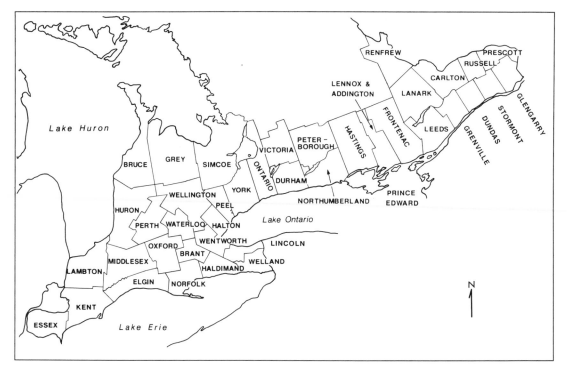

Fig. 3-1 Counties of the Province of Ontario, 1851

construction more than anything else characterized the Irish house in Upper Canada (Fig. 3-3). Throughout Ontario more than 70 percent of the Irish lived in some sort of log dwelling. Of these, about one-third occupied shanties and most of the remainder owned round-log houses (fewer than 3 percent had hewn-timber dwellings).

Shanties were crude, temporary dwellings which settlers occupied until a log house could be erected. Typically these were small, one room huts about six to seven feet high with a sloped roof (Fig. 3-4). Often a hole was cut in the roof to vent an open fire built in the middle of the floor, although more elaborate shanties had clay chimneys. However, it was not unusual to find shanties with only three sides, providing minimal shelter from the elements. In such cases a large fire was usually built on the open side for warmth and protection from wild animals.

While the Irish did occupy shanties to a greater extent than did the Scots or English, considerable regional variation is evident in their use of this dwelling type. In eastern Ontario's more isolated counties Irish occupancy of shanties was quite high. For example, in the interior county of Renfrew, 67 percent of all Irish settlers lived in shanties. In Carlton County, also inland from the St. Lawrence, the rate was 38 percent, and in neighboring Lanark the figure was 32 percent. In contrast, the St. Lawrence River counties, which were settled earlier, reflected much lower rates. In Glengarry, for example, only 10 percent of Irish settlers lived in shanties; in Stormont the rate was 12 percent; and in Grenville the figure was 20 percent. Despite the lower occupation rates along the St. Lawrence, Irish occupation of the shanty was

Brian Coffey

46

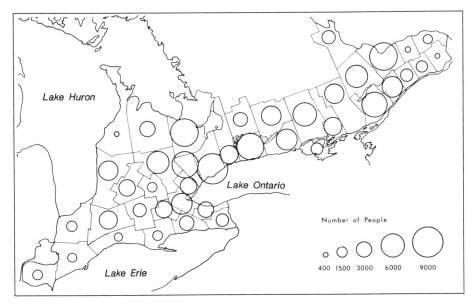

Fig. 3-2 Irish population of the Province of Ontario, 1851

generally somewhat higher in eastern Ontario than in the southwestern region (see Fig. 3-3).

The difference between Irish use of the shanty in the east and that in the southern and southwestern portions of the province can be related both to length of settlement and to the particular backgrounds of the Irish immigrants. Protestant settlement during the early nineteenth century was found in the counties fronting on Lake Ontario and to the south and west.[11] Most of these Ulstermen were farmers, a class able to adapt to Upper Canada's frontier environment. Ulster immigration predominated until 1840, after which the majority of Irish immigrants were Catholics.[12] Largely unskilled, the Irish Catholics worked as laborers, many initially settling in the Ottawa-Rideau area. Edward Mills notes that by the 1850s the "enduring settlement patterns by the two Irish groups were . . . formed. . . . Major concentrations of Ulstermen remained located in central and southwestern Ontario, while Catholics prevailed in eastern countries, outlying lumbering regions, the Peterborough-Lake Simcoe region and most towns and cities."[13]

Variation in shanty use, then, appears related both to length of settlement and to the economic and social background of the two Irish groups. Their large-scale use of the shanty at mid-century may also be due in part to the fact that the Irish Catholics appear to have maintained their shanties for longer periods of time than did other ethnic groups.[14] Precise reasons for this are unclear. In 1841, however, one-room cabins constituted over 40 percent of Ireland's houses. "Their major characteristics were a square floor plan with sides usually around fifteen feet, puddled mud floors, thatched roof, a chimneyless open hearth, small windows, walls of stone, sod or mud and no internal divisions."[15] Not only does the Irish house share some similarities with the shanty, the Irish occupant of a shanty in Upper Canada probably had as good a dwelling as the one left behind in the Old World.

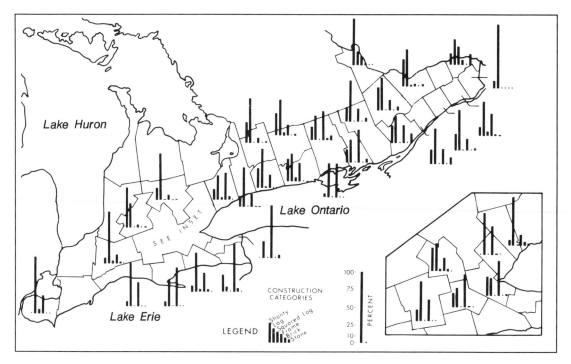

Fig. 3-3 Houses in Ontario owned by Irish settlers, by construction category, 1851

Further, the average Irish laborer lacked the expertise and wealth to construct an "elaborate" frame, brick, or stone dwelling. Non-log structures only gradually diffused into Upper Canada's Catholic Irish settlements from other immigrant groups.[16]

The use of hewn-log construction was not common among the immigrant Irish; provincewide only 2 percent of the population lived in hewn-timber dwellings. Further, in only two counties did the Irish use of squared timber exceed 5 percent—Renfrew (12 percent) and Prescott (25 percent). Both areas were associated with lumbering and the use of hewn-log construction in them was common among all cultural groups (Fig. 3-5).

When building non-log houses, the Irish settlers did show a slight bias for stone dwellings. Approximately 10 percent of all Irish settlers occupying non-log residences had stone houses. Given that stone houses accounted for approximately 6 percent of the province's frame, brick, and stone units, Irish occupancy is somewhat greater than expected. For the most part, these dwellings were found in eastern Ontario. In Grenville County, for example, nearly 9 percent of all Irish settlers lived in stone houses. In Lanark County the figure was 6 percent and in Leeds and Prescott counties the figures rose to 12 and 14 percent, respectively. Such values do not, however, reflect unusual concentrations. In most of these areas other groups occupied stone houses to a greater degree than the Irish. Thus, here, as elsewhere in the province, the Irish generally occupied the least substantial housing.

Brian
Coffey

48

Fig. 3-4 Log shanty, eastern Ontario. (Photo courtesy Ontario Archives, St. 1005.)

The English

The English constituted the second largest foreign-born group in Upper Canada at mid-century. Although settlement by them began gathering momentum in the 1820s, it was only after 1830 that large numbers of English-men began to arrive in the province. Cowan reports that in 1831 and 1832 nearly 28,000 arrived at the port of Quebec.[17] Other peak years included 1836 with 12,000 arrivals, 1842 with 12,000, and 1847, when more than 31,000 English disembarked.[18] In all, from 1830 to 1850 more than 180,000 people from England are reported to have landed.[19] Of these, many undoubtedly continued on to the United States; the census records indicate only 82,699 English-born residents in Ontario at mid-century. They were distributed throughout much of the province (although the easternmost counties experienced only scant English settlement), with major concentrations found at the western end of Lake Ontario (Fig. 3-6).

The English were the best housed of the three groups in question, with fewer than one-half of their number living in log houses (Fig. 3-7). Thirty-

Fig. 3-5 Hewn-log house typical of Ontario. (Photo courtesy of the Public Archives of Canada.)

nine percent lived in round-log units, one percent occupied hewn-log dwellings, and 7 percent dwelt in shanties. To have achieved such a high quality in housing by mid-century was somewhat unusual, for the English were not early arrivals but immigrated largely after 1830. However, government assistance for emigration from the British Isles was more commonly given to the poor of Scotland and Ireland than to the English, and general economic conditions were better in England than elsewhere in the British Isles for

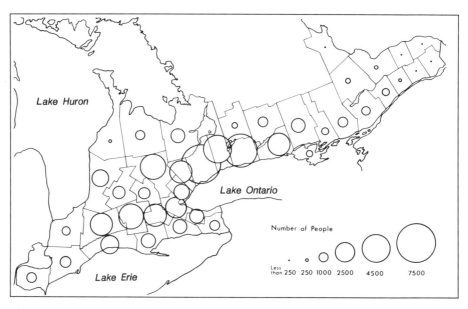

Fig. 3-6 English population of the Province of Ontario, 1851

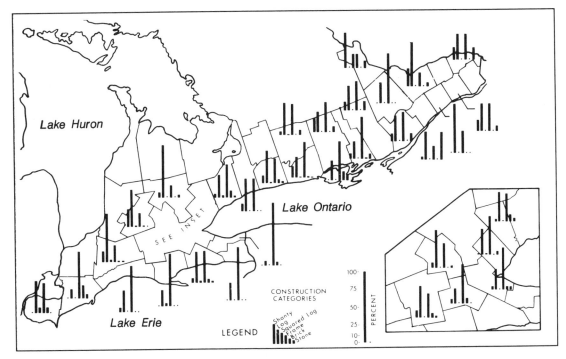

Fig. 3-7 Houses in Ontario owned by English settlers, by construction category, 1851

much of the nineteenth century. Thus, the average English immigrant was self-financed and probably in a better position to construct a substantial house than his Irish or Scottish counterpart.

For the most part, high rates of English occupancy of log housing were limited to the more remote portions of the province. For example, in Carlton County 85 percent of the English settlers lived in log structures. In adjacent Renfrew County this rate was 70 percent. High log-house occupancy rates can also be found for English settlers in the more isolated reaches of southwestern Ontario (see Fig. 3-7). However, such areas generally had similar rates for all groups, and, in general, the English in any given region had more substantial housing than their Irish and Scottish neighbors.

As a rule, then, the English in longer-settled areas showed widespread use of frame, brick, or stone, while in interior regions they commonly exhibited round-log construction (see Fig. 3-7). In only two areas did the English make use of hewn-log construction: in Essex County (7 percent) and in Renfrew County (20 percent). The former area was slow to develop and saw extensive hewn-log use by most groups. The latter county was a lumbering region and again an area where most immigrants made use of hewn timbers in building.

When considering only non-log housing, few unusual patterns emerge for the English. Approximately 6 percent of all non-log English houses were of stone, a rate lower than those of the Irish and Scots. However, given the total number of stone houses in the province, this rate is as expected. Similarly, their use of brick (8 percent) was as expected.

In 1851 nearly 76,000 native Scots lived in Upper Canada, accounting for about 8 percent of the total population. While they were found throughout the province, the greatest concentrations of Scots extended inland from Lake Ontario into the south-central region (Fig. 3-8).

Scottish settlement of Ontario began in the eighteenth century. In 1784 nearly 1,500 Highlanders left New York to settle in the easternmost townships along the St. Lawrence.[20] These were followed by other Scottish Loyalists fleeing the Revolution, who took up residence in the same vicinity. Additional Highlanders came to the area directly from Scotland after the Loyalist moves. In 1786, for example, 520 Highland Scots arrived, and in 1790 nearly 100 are reported to have immigrated.[21] Small numbers continued to arrive throughout the early nineteenth century.

Lowland Scots settled Upper Canada primarily after 1815. One of their first settlements was founded in Lanark County, where 1,400 migrated in 1816. The greatest Scottish settlement, however, was in the southern and western areas of the province, where large numbers of both Lowlanders and Highlanders arrived throughout the second quarter of the nineteenth century.

The reputation that the Scots have as builders of Upper Canada's stone houses is supported by the sample, but only to a certain extent. Overall, 6 percent of all Scots lived in stone dwellings in 1851, the greatest percentage among all the groups in question. One might suggest that this was a matter of circumstance, in that large numbers of Scots settled in the regions where building stone was readily available. In examining the eleven counties with more than one hundred stone houses at mid-century, the percentage of Scots

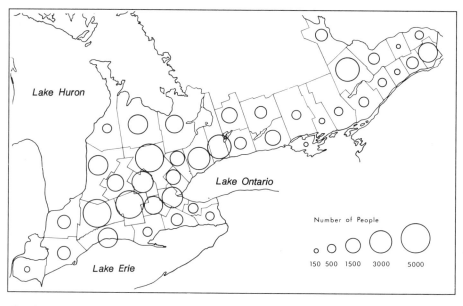

Brian Coffey

Fig. 3-8 Scottish population of the Province of Ontario, 1851

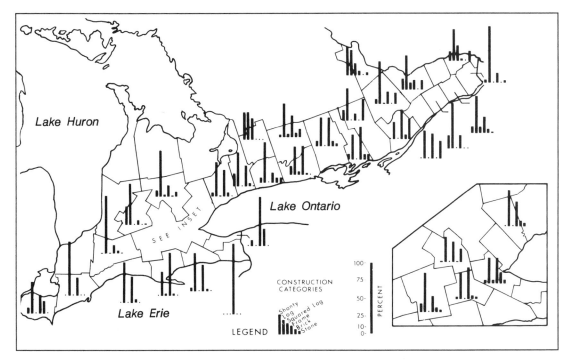

Fig. 3-9 Houses in Ontario owned by Scottish settlers, by construction category, 1851

utilizing stone was, relative to the other two ethnic groups, greatest in nine of the counties (Fig. 3-9). In those areas where building stone was to be had, some portion of each group constructed stone houses. However, given that the Scots led in stone construction more often than any other single group, it appears that there was a definite bias toward stone on the part of Upper Canada's Scots. Further, only 24 percent of the Scots sampled occupied frame dwellings. This is a low figure, considering their use of stone, and is another indication of their inclination toward the stone house.

A relatively large number of Scots (nearly 5 percent) occupied brick residences. Often these dwellings were associated with those immigrants who settled the southern and southwestern portions of the province. For example, in Lincoln and Wentworth counties, both at the head of Lake Ontario, 15 to 20 percent of the Scots owned brick houses. In areas where stone was not available, it seems that the Scots chose a similar building material.

Finally, a distinction can be made with respect to the construction materials of the Highland and Lowland Scots. The Highlanders who settled Upper Canada had a reputation for avoiding contact with other ethnic groups.[22] They were primarily tenant farmers possessing few nonagricultural skills. It is suggested that their self-imposed isolation, coupled with their occupational background, resulted in the slow development of the areas they settled. The Lowland Scots, on the other hand, had more varied backgrounds and interacted with other settlers to a greater degree.

In most of the Scottish-settled areas with high percentages of non-log

The Irish, English, and Scots in Ontario

53

houses, owners were of Lowland origin. In areas occupied by Highlanders, log structures were much more common, even in Highlander regions that had been settled for decades. The Highlanders' preference for log construction, along with the abject poverty of many Scots upon their arrival, accounts for the fact that nearly 65 percent of Upper Canada's Scots lived in log houses at mid-century.

Among types of log structures, the Scots displayed a similar preference for the most substantial. Of all Scots who lived in log houses at mid-century, only 14 percent occupied shanties, a figure lower than that for the Irish (34 percent) and the English (16 percent). At the other end of the log scale, the most durable and expensive type, 5 percent of Scottish log householders lived in squared-log structures, a rate exceeding that for the English (2 percent) and the Irish (3 percent). Thus, while the English may have been able to leave their log dwellings sooner than other groups, the Scots repeatedly demonstrated a relative bias for more expensive log and non-log houses.

Economic Status and Length of Settlement

Generally, land in Ontario was available for settlement only after surveys were completed. The survey system was based on townships, which were usually nine by twelve miles if bordering on a navigable waterway or, if inland, ten by ten miles. Each township was subdivided into concessions (bands running the width of the township), from which individual lots were created.

Examination of ethnic settlement patterns on a lot-by-lot basis permits greater understanding of the roles that economic status and length of settlement played in choice of construction materials. To consider the impact of these factors, the settlement patterns and levels of land development of the three national groups are examined for Augusta Township in eastern Ontario. Cross-tabulation of 1848 manuscript census records with manuscript assessment data for the same year reveals that 296 houses were owned by persons born in the British Isles. These include the residences of 211 Irish colonists, 50 English settlers, and 35 Scots. The locational patterns of the groups, considered in conjunction with the construction materials used, provide a general overview of their settlement chronology (Fig. 3-10, Table 3-2).

It appears that first in the settlement sequence are the Scots, who by 1848 were more likely to have occupied non-log houses than were English or Irish settlers. By 1848, 34 percent of all Scots had made the transition to frame or stone houses. This, coupled with the fact that a majority of Scots lived in the first two concessions, those nearest the coast, suggests a fairly early arrival date. Many were probably a part of the Scottish immigrations to the regions in 1815 and 1816.[23]

The English occupied slightly fewer non-log houses than did the Scots, with 28 percent of the English population owning frame or stone units. In addition, English-born immigrants were less likely than the Scots to have settled near the St. Lawrence; the first three concessions held 36 percent of the English but 70 percent of all Scots. However, 54 percent of all English settlers were in the half of the townships nearest the river (concessions I-V).

The Irish appear to have been the last of the groups to have arrived. Fifty-eight percent of the Irish immigrants occupied the remoter half of the township with approximately one-third living in concessions VIII, IX, and

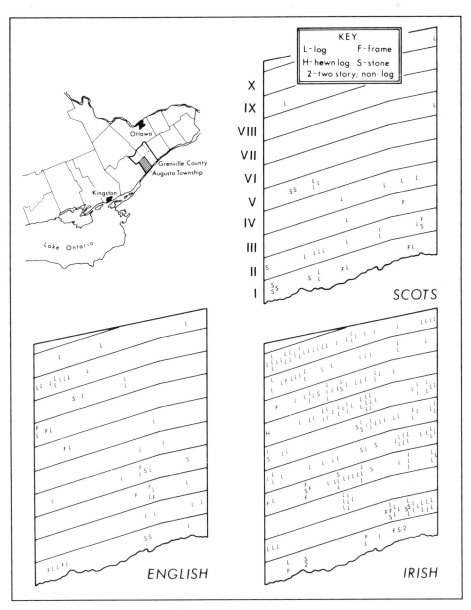

Fig. 3-10 Augusta Township: Construction materials used, by ethnic group, 1848

X. This area did not begin to receive extensive settlement until after 1830, and as might be expected, almost 90 percent of all Irish families lived in log dwellings.

The amount of land owned and developed by each group supports this chronology and lends credence to the contention that economic conditions played a role in the transition from log to non-log housing (Table 3-3). Scots, with the highest non-log occupancy rate, owned more land and had more acreage devoted to crops and pasture than did the English or Irish. On the

Table 3-2. Ethnic Housing Ownership, by House Type,
Augusta Township, 1848

	Log	Squared Log	Frame	Stone	Two-Story Non-Log
English					
Percent owning dwelling type	72	0	18	10	0
Number	36	0	9	5	0
Irish					
Percent owning dwelling type	87	0.5	5	7	0.5
Number	183	1	11	15	1
Scottish					
Percent owning dwelling type	66	0	11	23	0
Number	23	0	4	8	0

Source: Manuscript assessment rolls and manuscript census rolls, Augusta Township, Ontario, Canada, 1848.

other hand, the average Irish settler was the most likely to live in a log house and own the least amount of land. Further, the typical Irish householder cleared only about half as much land as did the average Scot and about 60 percent as much as did the typical English settler.

In looking past the log house, however, some variation in the selection of a frame or stone house is seen to have existed among the various groups (Table 3-4). First, a preference for stone among both the Scots and the Irish is apparent, with 67 percent of the Scots and 60 percent of the Irish choosing this material when building non-log houses. For English residents the figure drops to 36 percent.

In comparing the relative increases in stone and frame construction over time there appears to be some correlation in stone house construction rates and the rapid in-migration during the 1820s and 1830s. Between 1820 and

Table 3-3. Ethnic Land Ownership and Development,
Augusta Township, 1848

	Average Acreage Owned	Averaged Acreage in Crops or Pasture	Percentage of Population Occupying Non-Log Units
English	111	34	28
Irish	103	20	12
Scottish	116	41	32

Source: Manuscript assessment rolls and manuscript census rolls, Augusta Township, Ontario, Canada, 1848.

Table 3-4. Ethnic Occupancy of Non-Log Structures,
Augusta Township, 1848 (percentages)

	Frame Dwellings*	Stone Dwellings*
Anglo-Canadian	57	43
English	64	36
Irish	40	60
Scottish	33	67

*Based on occupancy of frame and stone units lower than two stories.
Source: Manuscript assessment rolls and manuscript census rolls, Augusta Township, Ontario, Canada, 1848.

1849 the number of frame houses owned by landed persons in Augusta approximately doubled, increasing from 50 to 110, but the number of stone houses grew more than tenfold, with 85 such units raised (Figs. 3-11 and 3-12). The increased activity in stone house building in the township also corresponds with the arrival of the Scots, after 1815, and other groups (especially the Irish) after 1830.

Nearly 70 percent of the stone houses were erected during the 1830s and 1840s, after the completion of the nearby Rideau Canal. Masons had been

Fig. 3-11 Frame house, Augusta Township. The owner of the house claims that it is one of the earliest houses in the township, ca. 1795. Although this is impossible to verify, a frame house is known to have been on this lot prior to 1820. (Photo by B. Coffey.)

Fig. 3-12 Nineteenth-century stone construction on a house in Augusta Township. (Drawing by M. M. Geib.)

imported to work on the canal and many stone houses in the Rideau region are attributed to their handiwork.[24] To test this, the birthplaces of masons living in Augusta Township in 1848 were determined from the census for that year. In all, ten masons were found. One was Scottish, four were Irish, three were English, and two were born in Upper Canada. Thus, if any ethnic associations are to be drawn between stone houses and their builders they would point to the Irish. However, it would seem that stone house construction was not so much related to any group as it was to the arrival of skilled foreign labor of diverse origins.

Further investigation suggests that a similar situation existed throughout much of the province. A study of the nativity of nearly eight hundred building tradesmen living in different townships along the St. Lawrence and Lake Ontario, revealed that nearly 75 percent of all masons and bricklayers had immigrated from the British Isles (Table 3-5). Of these, most were English and Irish (64 percent), while Scots constituted 10 percent of the total. Only 12 percent of all masons and bricklayers were born in Upper Canada.

With respect to carpenters the situation was nearly the reverse. Native Upper Canadians comprised 45 percent of the woodworking class, while Britons accounted for about 35 percent. Such figures suggest that labor availability was at least partially responsible for the locational and numerical disparities that existed between frame and brick and stone houses during this era.

Brian Coffey

58

Table 3-5. Ethnicity of Building Tradesmen, Upper Canada, 1851*

	Carpenters		Stone Masons and Bricklayers	
	Percent	Number	Percent	Number
American	13	84	13	19
Canadian	45	294	12	18
English	14	90	34	49
French Canadian	6	37	0.5	1
Irish	14	90	30	42
Scottish	8	54	10	15
Other	—	2	0.5	1

*Based on sample of 796 tradesmen from 1851 manuscript census.

Summary

The impact of cultural heritage on choice of construction material is apparent in a number of cases. This is especially true for the Scottish use of stone and, to a lesser extent, brick as construction materials, when building non-log structures. Further, the early references to Irish occupation of shanties are valid observations. However, lack of capital and the absence of skilled labor coupled with length of settlement appear to have been the major forces that shaped this relationship. On the other hand, the Irish shared some of the Scot's preferences, in that they too exhibited a tendency to use stone as a building material when they were able to build other than log dwellings.

Despite these associations, the regional variations evident at the middle of the nineteenth century indicate that several factors shaped this cultural landscape. Resource and labor availability, regional economic development, length of settlement, and the capital available to the members of each cultural group all must be taken into account. Cultural heritage, then, is but one of a number of elements whose interplay created the built environment still evident in Ontario today.

The Irish, English, and Scots in Ontario

4

Germans in Ohio

Hubert G. H. Wilhelm

THE UNCERTAINTY over whether the English or the Germans came in greater numbers from Old Europe to the new lands of America remains and may never be solved. There is, however, little question that Germans were the predominant immigrant group in Ohio. In fact, in only three census years, 1950, 1960, and 1970, did the Italian-born slightly outnumber the German-born in Ohio. By 1980, however, Germans were once again the prominent foreign-born group in the state, just as they had been throughout most of Ohio's settlement history.

Why is it that so many Germans made their new home in Ohio? That question is not difficult to answer. Ohio offered land and work at the time Germans began to leave the "Fatherland" in increasing numbers. The greatest German migration to America came during the nineteenth century, between 1830 and 1890. During those sixty years, 4.4 million Germans, representing nearly one-third of the total immigrant population, entered the United States.[1] They had left their home provinces for various reasons, but three stand out: rural landlessness, urban unemployment, and political discontent.

During the early 1800s, several of the German-speaking western states (Hessen and Baden-Wuerttemberg, for example) were in the throes of the "estate movement." Similar, at least in its effects, to the enclosure movement of the British Isles, the estate movement resulted in peasants losing their land to large estates. In the towns and cities unemployment was rampant, as the traditional craft industries lost their privileged state protection to a Prussian-inspired, nationwide trade union known as the Zollverein. The crafts were decimated by increased competition and, of course, by the rise of the industrial system. Finally, the ranks of potential emigrants were swelled by two unsuccessful popular uprisings, in 1830 and in 1848. The politically discontented would eventually carry their ideals to America, where they became specifically known as the "forty-eighters."

As Germany experienced dramatic changes in its economic, political, and social fabric, which inevitably produced heightened internal population pressure, Ohio had joined the growing union of states and was attracting both American migrants and foreign immigrants in large numbers. Ohio, which had been formed in 1803 from the Northwest Territory, became the first trans-Appalachian state to offer enormous acreages of excellent agricultural land and work opportunities in the rapidly expanding settlements. Thus, the combination of migration pull in Ohio and emigration push in Germany produced a predominantly Teutonic immigrant stock in the Buckeye State. Once this ethnic base was established, cultural affinity kept German immigrants coming to Ohio.

Because of this cumulative immigration effect, Ohio registered its largest German-born population, 235,668, in 1890, but the German ethnic strain was already well established by 1850 (Table 4-1), when Ohio's agricultural frontier had finally spread across the Black Swamp of northwestern Ohio and when the state's industrial and urban growth began in earnest.

Ohio's Germans are from every part of the old Reich; however, the earliest settlers (1820s) were primarily from the southwestern provinces, especially the Palatinate and adjacent areas of the Bavarian Rhineland and Baden-Wuerttemberg. Many of these were refugees of the Napoleonic Wars, which had devastated large parts of the Rhineland. They were also relatives or neighbors of earlier German immigrants to America who had settled principally in Pennsylvania and whose descendants are known to us today as the Pennsylvania Dutch. In fact, many of these early nineteenth-century German immigrants settled for a time in Pennsylvania before following the lure of cheap land to Ohio. They came with others of their kin and settled in and around Stark and Tuscarawas counties (Fig. 4-1). To this day this particular area of the state is strongly Pennsylvania-Dutch in its cultural expressions, including the largest concentration of Mennonite and Amish church congregations in the state.

The Palatinate Germans coming into Ohio were quickly joined by those from various other provinces, but especially Baden-Wuerttemberg, Hessen, Bayern, Hanover, and Niedersachsen, essentially the western and southern parts of the country. Of course, the true regional origins of German immigrants in Ohio, or for that matter anywhere in the United States, are difficult to know. The manuscript schedules of the population census are no help; the

Table 4-1. Origin of Immigrants in Ohio,* 1850

Country	Number	Percent
Germany	70,236	48.1
Ireland	32,779	22.4
England	19,509	13.4
France	6,326	4.3
Wales	5,045	3.5
Canada	4,606	3.2
Scotland	4,003	2.7
Switzerland	3,000	2.1
Others	488	0.3
Total	145,992	100.0

Source: Wilhelm 1982.
*Does not include city wards of Cincinnati, Cleveland, Columbus, Dayton, and Toledo.

Germans in Ohio

Fig. 4-1 Areas of concentrated German settlement in Ohio, 1850

Hubert G. H. Wilhelm

census taker would simply list persons as German if they spoke that language, although they had most likely indicated that their birthplace was in Bayern, Wuerttemberg, or Hanover. The same is true of naturalization documents, which do not distinguish between the old political subdivisions of Germany. Therefore, reliance has to be on other sources, especially genealogies and certain cultural criteria, for example, religion or family names that are traceable to particular German regions.

Distribution of German Settlers in Ohio

The distribution of German settlers in Ohio definitely is not random; it reflects a number of different influences, including the effect of clustering of kin. The Germans, particularly because of language contrast, became geographically much more localized in Ohio than was true of American migrants or of other foreign immigrants, who usually had an English language background. Figure 4-2 shows the percentage distribution of German settlers by 1850. Two principal generalizations can be made concerning their distribution in Ohio: they were primarily found in western Ohio, and they settled in the better farming areas of the state.[2]

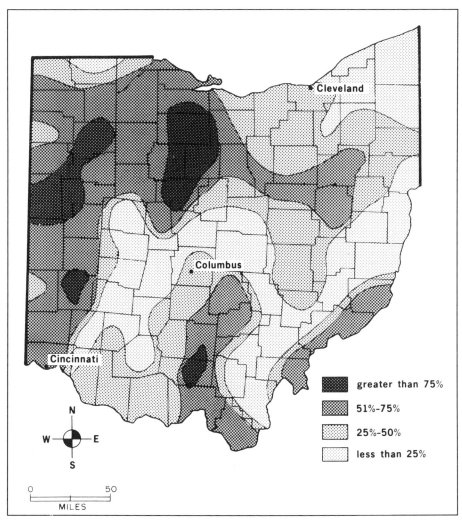

Fig. 4-2 Distribution of German population in Ohio, 1850 (percentages of total population). (Source: 1850 U.S. population census. Map used by permission of the editors, *Ohio Geographers*.)

Germans in Ohio

63

The Germans' strong presence in Ohio's rural and agriculturally important areas reflects the peasant background of many of the immigrants and their arrival in Ohio during the expansion of the state's agricultural frontier. The western lands of Ohio were not surveyed until the 1810s and 1820s and, therefore, land sales in this area began at a time coincident with the arrival of large numbers of German immigrants.[3] They entered this western area either through lake ports, especially Sandusky, or by way of Cincinnati. Most Americans would readily recognize the latter city, along with Milwaukee, as truly "German" towns. In Ohio, Cincinnati certainly carries this identifier, although Cleveland, Columbus, Dayton, and Toledo also have large contingents of Germans. The importance of Cincinnati to German immigrants dates from the late 1700s when descriptions comparing it to towns along the Rhine River reached Germany and potential immigrants. As early as 1795, a German businessman in Cincinnati by the name of Martin Baum actively recruited German craftsmen for his sugar refinery, foundry, and fleet of steamboats, thereby contributing to the initial impetus of Cincinnati toward becoming a German town.[4] German immigration to Cincinnati increased rapidly after 1830. By 1850, Germans were 27 percent of the population of the city, and grew to 41 percent, 133,000, in 1900.[5] For many of these Cincinnati Germans, the city became a jumping-off point for settlement in western Ohio. The wedge of German settlement northward from Cincinnati is especially well shown in Figure 4-2. Indeed, the area of heaviest settlement concentration, in west central Ohio, indicating more than 75 percent of German immigration, was settled by a group from Niedersachsen (Lower Saxony), who pushed northward from Cincinnati in 1833, close on the heels of the departing Shawnee, and who purchased land in Auglaize and Mercer counties.

Similarly, German immigrants came through Lake Erie ports into north central and northwestern Ohio. Here they converged with the Germans expanding from the eastern core area of Stark and Tuscarawas counties, forming by 1850 an area of especially heavy settlement concentration, including the counties of Marion, Crawford, Seneca, and Sandusky (see Fig. 4-2). The line of strong German settlement from the east to the west follows an Ohio vernacular region known as the "Backbone Country." It is the high land dividing Ohio River from Lake Erie drainage and is a region of glacial soils and ideal agricultural conditions.

Besides Ohio's Backbone and the western counties, another area of German settlement by 1850 follows what I have termed the riverine counties. Although less well known as an area of German settlement, the riverine region includes Pike County, which in 1850 had the highest concentration of German settlers of any county in the state (Table 4-2). The riverine settlement region follows the Ohio and Scioto rivers, beginning with Monroe County and continuing along the Ohio River to its confluence with the Scioto and north along the Scioto to Ross County (see Fig. 4-2). Here the Germans became primarily town dwellers, contributing their energies to the early shipping, salt manufacturing, iron making, coal mining, and canal building of the region. Descendants of German settlers who arrived in this area in the 1840s and 1850s remain conspicuous there through family and business names found in Marietta, Pomeroy, Portsmouth, Waverly, and Chillicothe.

The distribution of German immigrants in Ohio established during the

Hubert G. H. Wilhelm

Table 4-2. Highest Concentrations of Germans in Ohio Relative to
All Immigrants, by County, 1850

County	Germans	Percent All Immigrants
Pike	1,067	93
Auglaize	2,438	92
Mercer	988	92
Crawford	2,287	85
Seneca	2,940	83
Putnam	853	79
Montgomery	1,450	78
Marion	1,023	77
Holmes	1,362	74
Hocking	599	74

Source: Wilhelm 1982.

early years of their settlement did not change in subsequent decades. Rejuvenation of the German ethnic strain in the rural areas became negligible with the passage of time. In towns and cities there was a continuing addition of new immigrants, but hardly in the numbers to provide for a distinct German settlement effect. A recent study by Noble defining ethnic regions in Ohio confirms my generalization that the early areas of German settlement retained their attraction for later arrivals. Accordingly, in a thirty-seven–county area, Germans were the dominant foreign group both in 1850 and in 1950. By 1950, however, the actual number of German immigrants was smaller, and, according to Noble, "visual evidence of the group and any cultural impact resulting from their settlement might well be lacking"[6] because of rapid assimilation with the dominant American culture.

The Imprint of German Settlement

Indeed, although the Germans were the principal immigrant group in Ohio, they left relatively few settlement traits on the landscape. This is not to say that their settlement effect has been insignificant. In fact, one could argue that Ohio's general political conservatism, unusual for an industrial labor state, is representative of the traditional values of the state's most important immigrant group, who collectively espoused individual rights and the idea that the best government is one which governs least.

There are, of course, a number of reasons that explain the relative lack of German settlement traits in the landscape. Perhaps the most important relates to the time when Germans came into Ohio. By the middle of the last century, when German immigration in Ohio was at its peak, settlement in both town and countryside was beginning to be facilitated by inexpensive, standardized manufactured products. Traditional tools were being replaced by popular American material items such as the John Deere steel plow, wire fencing, balloon framing in construction and in standard building types.

The German immigrant readily adopted these American forms, thereby contributing to the creation of a midwestern American cultural hearth.

Another reason German settlers have left a fainter imprint is that they came after 1820, usually moving into areas already occupied by American migrants or other immigrants. As a result, they were rarely in a position to establish the first settlement of an area, which might have contributed to a lasting imprint of their occupancy. An exception to this generalization can be found in Auglaize and Mercer counties of western Ohio, where German settlement forms persist to this day. More will be said about this particular area later on.

Finally, the German immigrants, because they did not wish to stand out as being different, worked actively on assimilation. Once the language barrier was overcome, there was little else obstructing their integration with the rest of the population. The two world wars obviously accelerated this effort at assimilation. As a result, the survival of German settlement forms was ephemeral; they may reveal themselves today only in antiquarian features.

There remains, nevertheless, sufficient landscape evidence to study the effect of German settlement in Ohio. Much of that evidence is, perhaps, more indirect than direct, as for example, the influence of inheritance practices and the related stability or persistence of land ownership. The latter appears to be a characteristic of German rural settlement in Ohio, but it deserves much more investigation before definitive conclusions can be reached.

The direct German settlement imprints are especially related to the continuation of particular construction techniques and building types. In fact, one can say that wherever Germans settled in Ohio, they quickly introduced or expanded an existing practice of brick construction of houses and other structures, especially churches. Particularly West Germans, who were strongly represented among the immigrants to Ohio, came with a well-established tradition of masonry construction techniques.

Of course, quite often the masonry building technique was secondary to timber framing and the brick was used as a filler or nogging between the hand-hewn timbers. This half-timber or *Fachwerk* construction is representative of German and Pennsylvania-Dutch settlement in Ohio. I have located this type of construction in three separate areas: Monroe County in southeastern Ohio, Holmes and Tuscarawas counties in eastern Ohio, and Auglaize and Mercer counties in western Ohio. Each of these areas has a history of German and Pennsylvania-Dutch settlement. It is likely that half-timber construction survives as a relic building method in other German and Pennsylvania-Dutch settlement areas of the state.

The most substantial amount of half-timber construction with brick nogging is found in the German-settled areas of Auglaize and Mercer counties. Here the settlers had emigrated from Muensterland and Niedersachsen (Lower Saxony) in northwestern Germany, a region where brick masonry construction, with or without timber framing, was well established. On the till plain of western Ohio, the settlers continued the traditional building method of half-timbering. Their small frame houses were built of either hand-hewn or milled timbers, and the spaces between the uprights were lined with handmade and sun-dried bricks. Usually the bricks were made right on the farm from the plentiful supply of glacial clays that can be found in western Ohio. Through the efforts of historic preservation officials in the

Hubert G. H. Wilhelm

66

area, more than one hundred half-timber houses have been located. According to these officials, this type of construction was used until the early 1900s.[7]

Half-timber construction among the German and Pennsylvania-Dutch settlers of eastern Ohio relied on a different nogging technique. Brick nogging is hardly ever found. Instead, small wooden boards or slats were dropped between the uprights and then smeared over with a mixture of clay, grass, and straw. Sometimes, the daubed-in parts were plastered with a combination of sand and lime and then whitewashed (Fig. 4-3). The practice of whitewashing half-timber houses was traditional in central and southwestern Germany and was probably continued for that reason in Ohio. Originally, the plaster and whitewashing may have served an aesthetic purpose or been used to protect the clay nogging. In any case, houses of this kind, unless covered by siding, deteriorated rapidly in the humid and rainy conditions of eastern Ohio. No wonder, then, that the locals refer to them today in their Pennsylvania-Dutch dialect as *Dreckhaeuser* or mud houses.[8]

Perhaps nowhere else in Ohio is the German immigrant's preoccupation with brick construction better preserved and revealed than in Columbus's German Village. A restored part of the city covering several city blocks, German Village functions today as one of the principal tourist attractions of Columbus. It is located in the south end of the city and began forming in the early 1800s when German immigrants, primarily from Baden-Wuerttemberg settled this part of Columbus. The Germans worked at draining the swampy southern part of town, in the process obtaining the raw material for the houses and business structures that today characterize the area.

Fig. 4-3 German half-timber house, Holmes County, Ohio.
(Photo by H. Wilhelm.)

Among the variety of brick houses in German Village, including a large number built in high Victorian style, there are those which indicate traditional, vernacular origins. One type that particularly stands out is often referred to in Ohio as a "German house" or cottage. It is a small story-and-a-half house of frame or brick construction with central or gable-end chimneys. The entrance to the house is commonly on the long side. This is true even though the house was oriented with the gable side facing the street, as shown by the two examples from German Village in Figure 4-4. I have located this type of house in other German settlements in Ohio, including Auglaize and Mercer counties and in the Ohio Valley area. For example, in the town of Pomeroy in Meigs County in southeastern Ohio, a house very similar to those in Figure 4-4 was identified to me as "the German house." However, it is frame built, partially banked, and rests on a foundation of hand-cut sandstone blocks. It is one of the older surviving structures in a part of town that was settled predominantly by German immigrants.

Besides German Village in Columbus, the other area that offers the best possibilities to see and study this small German house is in Auglaize and Mercer counties. In many respects this is the area of Ohio where one must go to study the imprint of the German settlement. Settled in the 1830s by immigrants from the Muensterland and Lower Saxony, the area is characterized by an extraordinary degree of stability in land ownership and land use and by an overall orderliness and cleanliness in the landscape. It is also one of the few rural districts in the state that has been subjected to a detailed historic building survey.

To experience this part of Ohio is to be transported to a different world.

Hubert G. H. Wilhelm

Fig. 4-4 A pair of "German" houses in German Village, Columbus. (Photo by H. Wilhelm.)

Fig. 4-5 Chapel style house in the German settlement area of Marion Township, Mercer County, Ohio. (Photo by H. Wilhelm.)

The first obvious contrast with other rural parts of Ohio is the great number of tall, brick church spires jutting above the lush corn, soybean, wheat, oat and alfalfa fields. Under the leadership of an energetic Swiss priest, Father Brunner, the German Catholics organized into a number of parishes, which are identified by the large Gothic brick churches. The cloister Maria Stein became the religious and administrative center for the settlement district.

The farmsteads themselves are distinctive, for the house, the barn, and a variety of other outbuildings. The small German house appears frequently (Fig. 4-5). It was termed the "chapel style" house by the local surveyors because they felt that these small houses had been influenced by the slightly earlier construction of brick churches.[9] Of course, the chapel style house also occurs in frame or half-timber, the latter always sided. The form of the house, however, is the same—story-and-a-half with steeply pitched roof, gable-end chimneys, and entrance on the long side. On the first floor there are always four rooms, including the kitchen, placed toward the right rear. The upstairs is divided into two rooms. This type of house has one of three different floorplans (Fig. 4-6).[10]

Among the smaller outbuildings on these German farmsteads are summer kitchens, smoke houses, ice houses, and slop houses. The last were of particular importance in the past, when hog raising was more important to the region than it is today. While the area has been shifting increasingly to cash-crop production of corn and soybeans, many of the farmers continue with their traditional practices, including keeping dairy cows.

Because the descendants of the original German settlers in the Auglaize-Mercer area continue with the traditional mixed farming of fieldcrops and livestock, their need for a large barn persists. In fact, my first acquaintance with the settlement area came because of its barns. One day, I received a call

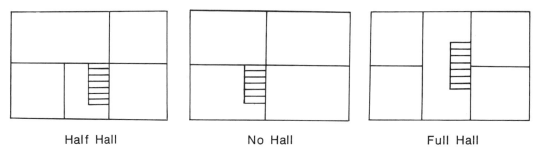

Half Hall   No Hall   Full Hall

Fig. 4-6 Typical floorplans of chapel-style German houses

from the state historic preservation officer in the area inquiring about the possible relationship of these barns to those common in the settlers' home area in Germany. Indeed, when first viewing these structures one is reminded of the large housebarns of northwestern Germany. The roof, especially, appears immense because of its steep pitch and makes the barn a distinctive feature in the landscape. However, in contrast to the Lower German housebarns, which are entered through the gable, those in western Ohio are at ground level with one or two driveways and are entered from the long side. The driveways are slightly elevated and are flanked by stalls and storage areas. Because some of these barns consist of five bays and, therefore, are quite long, the steeply pitched roof becomes a very prominent part of the superstructure.

Many of these large barns in Auglaize and Mercer counties were probably built during the latter part of the nineteenth century. Their main timbers are hand-hewn and fitted together in mortise and tenon fashion. A revealing detail of that construction was the "Dutch mortise."[11] Use of this construction detail is concentrated between Lower Saxony and Friesland, in northwestern Germany and parts of the Netherlands. It involves a mortise that is totally cut through the timber, allowing the tenon of the interlocking beam to protrude (Fig. 4-7). The survival of this specific construction detail in rural western Ohio is one more example of the diffusion of this and other traits and forms by a group of German immigrants there. Because of its outward similarity with the northwest German housebarns and because its appearance differs from that of the popular American barn of the area, the historic building surveyors named it the Saxon barn.[12]

I am not aware of any uniquely German method of land subdivision and settlement distribution in Ohio. However, in Marion Township of Mercer County, the distribution of surviving half-timber cottages and property frontages follows the main road west through the township (Fig. 4-8). This road (state Route 119) is located on the St. John's Moraine and joins the hamlets of Maria Stein, St. John's, St. Rose, and Cassela. The German settlers who entered the poorly drained parts of western Ohio in the 1830s and 1840s were fortunate to locate on the higher ground before they were able to fill in the remainder of the township toward the north and south. In the process, a greater density of properties and structures sprang up along the road, creating a distinctly linear settlement pattern. This kind of pattern was not unfamiliar to these settlers, who had come from similarly flat and poorly

Hubert G. H.
Wilhelm

Fig. 4-7 A Dutch mortise as a framing detail of a barn in Marion Township, Mercer County, Ohio. (Photo by H. Wilhelm.)

drained areas of northwestern Germany. In fact, linear dike villages (*Marschhufendoerfer*) occur regularly in that part of Germany. The Germans of Mercer County, in adapting to local advantages of terrain, also were continuing a traditional practice of settlement location.

The pointed steeples of brick-built Gothic churches remain a reminder of the German Catholics and Protestants who settled Ohio north of the Auglaize-Mercer region. Of course, settlement in these northwestern parts of the state, including the Lake Plain and the notorious Black Swamp, proceeded at a more deliberate pace than it did anywhere else in Ohio. Poor drainage, distance from established settlements, and remnant Amerindian populations (the Wyandot were the last group of Indians to leave Ohio for the western United States, in 1842)—these were the most serious impediments to occupancy of the area. However, the swarm of land-hungry German immigrants, following their established migration patterns northward from Cincinnati, westward across Ohio's Backbone Country, and through the lake ports of Sandusky and Toledo, were attracted by the flat and potentially fertile lands of northwestern Ohio. By 1850, there were 4,778 German-born residents in the region (Table 4-3), the entire foreign-born population of which was 8,270. The Germans in this area were in a 10 percent greater concentration than in the entire state in 1850. It should be added that an additional 796 residents were from Switzerland and France, the latter group primarily of Alsatian origin. These groups added to the strong Germanic influence in this area. By 1850, the core area of the German settlement extended from Allen and Van Wert counties northward through Putnam and Hancock to Defiance, Henry, and Wood counties (see Fig. 4-1). Because the majority of these counties remained rural and agricultural, their ethnic

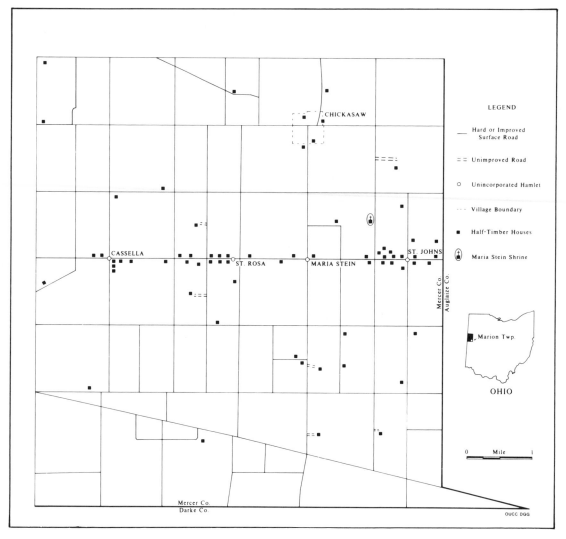

Fig. 4-8 Distribution of half-timber houses illustrates linear settlement pattern in Mercer County, Ohio. (Source: Ohio Historic Inventory, Marion Township, Mercer County, Ohio. Research and map by Mary Niekamp, 1979. Copyright *Pioneer America Society Transactions*.)

character did not undergo dramatic changes after the initial settlement period. In fact, Noble, in his attempt to identify ethnic regions in Ohio, shows that the northwestern counties of Ohio as late as 1950 remained predominantly German in their foreign-born population.[13] Only Wood and Allen counties were exceptions. Both, of course, have sizeable urban centers in Lima and Bowling Green, whose ethnic mix favors other than German nationals.

While the tall-spired, brick-built Gothic churches evince the German imprint, the houses and other buildings are American. Three reasons are suggested to explain this lack of traditional German material culture. For one,

Hubert G. H. Wilhelm

72

Table 4-3. German-born Population of Northwestern Ohio Relative to
All Foreign-born Residents, by County, 1850

County	German-born	All Foreign-born	Percent
Putnam	853	1074	79
Wood	706	1155	61
Lucas	640	1553	41
Hancock	529	833	64
Defiance	525	737	71
Allen	468	713	66
Van Wert	321	454	71
Henry	317	450	70
Williams	220	515	43
Fulton	150	664	23
Paulding	49	122	40
Total	4778	8270	59

Source: Wilhelm 1982.

the later settlement of the area coincided with a time of the nineteenth century when popular settlement forms such as houses and barns were accepted
in favor of traditional ones. Secondly, the Germans did not settle in northwestern Ohio in a very cohesive fashion. They came to this area as individuals or as family units, buying land and mingling with their native American
neighbors, who had been similarly attracted by those promising level lands.
Because residences were widely dispersed and because communal activities,
other than the weekly church visit, were not frequent, the Germans quickly
became part of that greater American rural farm population. Finally, the
built-up landscape of northwestern Ohio is essentially a later-nineteenth-
century expression of eclectic Victorian forms, houses and barns alike. As
soon as the area was drained and its real agricultural value became obvious,
the economic lot of its residents improved dramatically. The result was that
people were able to afford "modern" things, including more contemporary
styles of houses and other buildings. So, the old structures were replaced
with new ones and, in the process, the possible material legacy of specific
ethnic groups, including the Germans, was lost.

The German Relict Landscape of Northwestern Ohio

What then, if anything, does remain of the German settlement influence
in northwestern Ohio? Besides family names and infrequent place names, as
for example Glandorf and Leipsic in Putnam County, and New Bavaria and
Deshler in Henry County, there remains the stability in land ownership and
the general appearance of the rural landscape. The German farmer in
America has been stereotyped as stubborn and hard working, as one who
pays his bills on time and whose land and buildings reflect his preoccupation
with and pride in farming. The latter two indeed appear to be collective

traits of the population within the area of traditionally German settlement in northwestern Ohio. The agricultural landscape is one of orderliness and tidiness. The farmsteads are well kept, clean, and symbolic of the area's general prosperity. The outbuildings are painted, usually red, and include attractive decorations around doors and along the vertical and horizontal margins of buildings, especially barns.[14] These decorations are in the form of stylistic arches and columns. They are in white, which stands out dramatically on the dark red of barns and other structures (Fig. 4-9). Although this type of farm building decoration is not restricted to northwestern Ohio, it is in this area, especially in Putnam and Henry counties, that it occurs most frequently and is most elaborate. Its development appears to coincide with the area's strong involvement with popular Victorian architecture, requiring the use of a variety of colors and wall adornments. While the German presence in the area has nothing directly to do with the origin of this decoration, Germans are renowned as imitators, and if one farmer painted white pilasters on this barn another would surely follow, if only to do it better.

The German Influence in Southeastern Ohio

Stability in occupancy and care of the land is noticeable among the descendants of Swiss and German settlers in the coal mining country of Ohio's Appalachia. The riverine areas of Meigs and Monroe counties (see Fig. 4-1) serve as excellent examples. These counties are located in a region of strong settlement convergence by American migrants and European immigrants. Early river towns, such as Marietta and Pomeroy, served as settlement foci because of the availability of work in coal mining, salt making, tar burning (naval stores), and shipbuilding. Germans from other regions of the United

Hubert G. H. Wilhelm

74

Fig. 4-9 Barn decoration, Henry County, Ohio. (Photo by H. Wilhelm.)

States and also directly from Germany began arriving in large numbers during the 1830s and 1840s. Unlike in other parts of Ohio, many of these Germans came as common laborers and settled in the towns. These "town" Germans adapted quickly to American ways and left no discernable material traits other than a few German-type cottages or houses and the ubiquitous Gothic brick- or stone-built churches.

There are, however, nonmaterial and social elements of these communities that reflect the German settlement influence. For example, the entire riverine area is a staunchly Republican part of the state, representative of the conservative traditions of its population. Furthermore, I have heard it discussed by natives of the Pomeroy area that the anti-German fervor engendered by World War I never was an overt characteristic of the town and that certain German cultural practices, for example religious services held in German, persisted for a longer time in Pomeroy than in most places. The reasons cited were physical isolation and the large number of ethnic Germans who settled there.

Approximately one-half of the Germans who had settled in the riverine counties by 1850 acquired land and farmed. Although the land is marginally suitable for agriculture, most of these settlers survived, first as dairy farmers and in more recent years by raising beef cattle. Their houses and barns are vernacular American forms of the late 1800s, although in Monroe County a number of forebay barns, probably introduced from Pennsylvania, survive.

By the end of the nineteenth century, the entire region of eastern and southeastern Ohio became either actual or potential coal-mining territory. This resulted in dramatic changes in land tenure, from private to corporate ownership. Many among the hillside farmers followed the lure of quick money and sold out. One can hardly blame them, because farming in southeastern Ohio was, and still is, at best an onerous task.

The riverine counties of German settlement (Monroe, Washington, and Meigs), although less affected than their neighboring counties, nevertheless were not spared the economic, social, and environmental impact of coal mining. Land abandonment by farmers was less typical here, however, particularly in the traditionally German townships in Monroe and Meigs counties. I suggest that the combination of a concentrated German farm population and reduced pressure on their land for mining purposes, because the neighboring counties bore the brunt of it, explain the persistence of ownership and agricultural land use in these townships.

The contrast with the typical Appalachian landscape is especially apparent as one travels through the central and northern parts of Monroe County. Here one encounters a well-cared-for rural area of tidy farmsteads, fields of corn and oats, and fine looking pastures with better looking cattle. It is an island within an area of shaft and strip mining, mobile homes, and abandoned farms whose fields and pastures are covered with the brush and scrub of vegetational succession. An earlier observer of the Monroe County landscape wrote that the Germans had achieved "wonders with the land making it the best farmland in the State of Ohio. In 1880 almost every farm had a small vineyard of fruits. In contrast with the slovenly character of much of our native American farming there is an air of neatness and thrift."[15] These are harsh words, indeed, but they reflect the contrasting approaches to rural land use by very different settlement groups. The Germans followed a crop and livestock economy and practiced soil and land conservation.

The American settlers of the area, whose background was derived from the Appalachian hills of Pennsylvania and Virginia, paid little attention to intensive crop farming. Instead, they favored grazing and gardening, including a small patch of tobacco.[16] In contrast to the orderly lands of the German farmers, their settlements would appear more natural, even wild. Traditional Appalachian land use was less "rooted in the soil," because of the mobility of its practitioners. They would abandon the land more readily than their German counterparts. In fact, in Monroe County land initially occupied by German Palatines remains to a great extent in the same families who occupied this area 150 years ago.

Owl Holes

In both Monroe and Meigs counties a trait of building decoration survives which, in one way or another, relates to the German ethnic presence. This trait is the owl hole: small decorative cut-outs high up on one or both gables of barns. Owl holes, usually in the form of a heart, can be found throughout northern and central Germany. The hole, as its name indicates, provides access for barn owls, whose presence is greatly valued because they help keep the rodent population in check. Owl holes are also widely distributed in the eastern United States and Canada and may in some cases have been added to barns simply for decoration, rather than utility.[17] They can be found scattered throughout southeastern Ohio. There are, however, two areas where they have a clear concentration. One is in the eastern townships of Meigs County and the other coincides with the northern tier of townships in Monroe County. Both are traditional German settlement areas.

The owl hole shapes differ between these two areas. In Meigs County, diamond-shaped holes, usually occurring singly, are most common. In Monroe County, diamonds, stars, and half moons are typical (Fig. 4-10), and these are often found as multiples of one kind (usually three) or one of each shape. Toward the western part of the county, another shape—the cross—becomes quite characteristic. The reason for this contrast is not known, but it may reflect the larger number of Catholics in the western part of Monroe County. Oral historical evidence for Meigs County supports the often-made generalization that owl holes were cut by carpenters either to identify a specific crew of barn builders or to reveal their association, especially common in southeastern Ohio, with Freemasonry, indicated by the frequently used half moons and stars.[18]

Conclusion

In contrast to Pennsylvania, Wisconsin, and Missouri, Ohio is rarely recognized as a predominantly German immigrant state. Of course, everyone knows about Cincinnati and its Teutonic past, if for no other reason than the city's historic importance as a brewing center. That same recognition, however, does not apply for the state as a whole. The reasons lie with the distribution of German settlers in Ohio and the time of their arrival. Although there were some counties where German settlement concentrated, in general these settlers became widely distributed throughout the important agricultural

Hubert G. H.
Wilhelm

Fig. 4-10 Owl holes in the form of star and crescent cutouts, Monroe County, Ohio. (Drawing by M. M. Geib.)

parts of northern and western Ohio. Because the Germans entered the state two or more decades after the initial thrust of settlement into the Ohio Country, they rarely represented the first effective settlement group. Instead, they moved into areas which were already occupied by American settlers.

In the towns a similar situation prevailed. Besides Cincinnati, other cities, such as Dayton, Columbus, Cleveland, and Toledo, had large German populations. But, as in the rural areas, in these cities the German immigrants joined already existing populations, which outnumbered the newcomers. As a result, both in the rural areas and in the towns, the German population quickly adapted to the dominant culture. The two world wars greatly hastened that assimilation process.

The later entrance of the Germans into Ohio and their lack of group cohesion discouraged the establishment and survival of traditional elements of their material culture. In an article discussing the German contributions to the townscape of Cincinnati, Becker and Dailey make the point that the Germans built the kind of structures popular in America at the time and that "there was no articulate expression of a German architecture."[19] Traditional German settlement forms that might have existed did not survive for long, because the Germans, with very few exceptions, settled in those parts of Ohio that would experience rapid development. This certainly would apply to those living in towns of some size, and, I believe, was equally true of the German settlers residing in the countryside. As has been shown, the Germans occupied the prime agricultural lands, especially in western and northern Ohio. That ideal physical base and the German farmer's attention to traditional crop and livestock agriculture made him a very successful rural entrepreneur, one whose progress would be measured by having the "right" kind of house, barn, and other outbuildings. Thus, the traditional material trait influence, if at all present, was at best ephemeral.

Germans in Ohio

77

The German settlement legacy in Ohio is, then, not principally of a material nature; it must be sought in certain economic, political, and social practices. For example, the expanding number of German-type festivals in the state is evidence of the "cultural rebound" effect that Ohio's major foreign immigrant group is presently enjoying. In the final analysis, however, the German settlement legacy may be purely attitudinal, revealing itself in attachment and care of land and homestead—a landscape ethic, in other words, that is difficult to quantify and that probably defies objective analysis.

Hubert G. H.
Wilhelm

5

The Welsh in Ohio

Michael T. Struble and Hubert G. H. Wilhelm

THE UNITED STATES has often been referred to as the "melting pot" of the world. Such a notion assumes that the new immigrants were assimilated into mainstream American culture. But some Europeans went to great lengths to preserve their national identity. The Welsh, particularly, did not assimilate as readily as did many other groups. Their cultural traditions, especially their language, and their geographical isolation set them apart from other immigrant groups in the great American pioneer experience.

The Welsh people made their first appearance on the North American continent as Nonconformists seeking relief from religious intolerance in Wales. Welsh Baptists arrived in the Plymouth and Swansea areas of Massachusetts as early as the 1630s and in adjacent Rhode Island slightly later.[1] In 1682, Welsh Quakers came into the Pennsylvania wilderness, having entered into a colonization agreement with William Penn which involved settlement of some thirty thousand acres.[2] These settlements were located northwest of Philadelphia and included such places as Merion, Radnor, Haverford, Goshen, and Reading.[3] Additional Welsh settlements were founded in northwestern Delaware. From there several groups of Welsh Baptists migrated to the South.

The Welsh colonies in the South originated in early 1736 with a large settlement at Welsh Neck on the Pee Dee River in South Carolina. Some thirty-eight Welsh Baptist churches ultimately grew up in South Carolina. A smaller Welsh settlement existed in New Hanover County, North Carolina along the Burgaw Creek and the Black River.[4]

The great migrations of the nineteenth century brought Welsh farmers to Oneida County, New York, and Gallia, Jackson, Meigs, Delaware, and Licking counties in Ohio.[5] In Licking County the settlement was even called Welsh Hills.[6] The 1850 census, the first census to list residents on a township by township basis by place of birth, indicates the Welsh as a significant percentage of the total immigrant population. In Gallia County they represented 57 percent, in Jackson County 74 percent and in Meigs County 20 percent of the total immigrant population.[7] The Welsh land settlement continued westward to the newly opened farmlands of southern Wisconsin and Minnesota. The settlements in Wisconsin included Waukesha, Genesee, and Racine, while those in Minnesota were clustered in the area of Blue Earth, southwest of St. Paul.

In Meigs County, the Welsh, second only in numbers to the Germans, represented 20 percent of the total immigrant population. Settling along the Ohio River in a back-to-back line of communities that included Middleport, Coalport, Pomeroy, Kerr's Run, Minersville, Calloway, and Syracuse, they worked as coal miners or in the salt industries. The Welsh were especially numerous in Minersville, a town developed around two hills with obvious ethnic names, Welshtown Hill and Dutchtown (Deutscher) Hill. This chapter focuses upon the Welsh settlements in southern Ohio. The pertinent questions to ask at this point are, where did the Welsh in southern Ohio come from, why did they leave Wales, and why did they select a part of Appalachia as their home?

Welsh immigrants came primarily from two areas in Wales, the central farming region of Cardiganshire and the industrial and mining parts of southeastern Wales near Monmouth and Glamorgan (Fig. 5-1). In Cardiganshire, most of the land was owned by the gentry, while the majority of the people were renters and tenants. Among families fortunate enough to own land, the laws of primogeniture contributed directly to emigration. Welsh farm families were large, and with the oldest son inheriting the land, the remaining children had to be content with working as farm laborers or going off to work in the factories and mines of southeastern Wales. Landholding was viewed as giving not only social prestige but economic security; if the rest of the children wished to own land, they had to go to America, where land was plentiful and cheap.

Also, in Wales, both rural and urban populations were adversely affected by the Corn Laws, enacted after the disastrous and costly Napoleonic Wars. These laws increased the prices of food and commodities, which were scarce, and of rents, and added further pressure to emigrate. In addition,

Michael T. Struble and Hubert G. H. Wilhelm

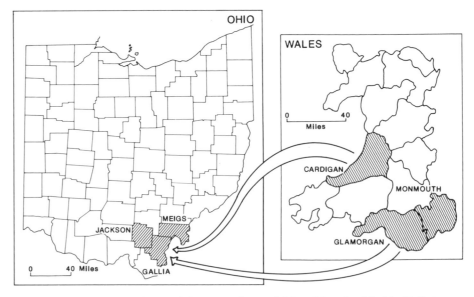

Fig. 5-1 Migration of the Welsh to southern Ohio. (Map by M. M. Geib.)

during the latter part of the nineteenth century, United States economic policies adversely affected certain Welsh industries. The Welsh tinplate industry was hit particularly hard, and many Welsh tin workers eventually migrated to the United States.[8]

Certain individuals encouraged the settlement of particular immigrant Welsh communities:

> The Gallia and Jackson settlements had attracted few settlers. Then the Rev. Edward Jones, a Calvinistic Minister arrived to preach to the settlers. Impressed with the area, Jones later returned to his native Cardiganshire and wrote a pamphlet extolling the virtues of the settlement. The Welsh, always impressed with the writings of the clergy, read the pamphlet and soon the Gallia-Jackson settlement became a household word in Cardiganshire. Beginning in 1835 and continuing for some twenty-five years, the Welsh of that shire emigrated to the settlement in such numbers that the area was soon dubbed the "Little Cardiganshire." They spread over the various townships of the two counties. The result of the propaganda of the Rev. Jones was the turning of this relatively insignificant settlement north of Gallipolis into the second strongest Welsh agricultural settlement in America. The Gallia-Jackson settlement, which would number some six thousand Welsh settlers at the end of the emigration, rivaled the great Welsh settlement at Oneida County, New York.[9]

These closely knit groups of Welsh immigrants brought with them a culture that was unique in language, family and place names, and religious customs, and the Welsh character, exemplified by their love for music, their habit of hard physical labor, and their deeply felt religious convictions. Throughout their pioneering experience, and later on, they left a significant mark upon the landscape of southern Ohio.

The Welsh Cultural Legacy in Southern Ohio

One of the unique cultural features the Welsh brought with them into the wilderness was their intense love for singing. In fact, part singing may have had its origins among the Welsh. The historian Giraldus, writing in 1188, speaks of their skill in vocal music, which they sang in parts rather than in unison.[10] This skill and custom developed and was nurtured through the ages, and the Welsh people's love of song became a characteristic of their everyday life. It would be an understatement to say the Welsh became famous for their congregational singing in four-part harmony. This form of singing became a means of expressing their deepest emotions and was expressed in their hymns at religious services and in other social activities:

> If one were to ask what were the inherent characteristics of Welsh congregational singing, one would be tempted to say, thought and emotions. The singing itself cannot be considered apart from the words of the hymns. We find in the hymns every kind of emotions expressed—fear, joy, despondency, hope, delight, anticipation, and love. The experiences, when they are thoughtfully sung, produce a

religious fervor. This fervor, which is characteristic of Welsh congregational singing, is undoubtedly born of the words of the hymns and not the music. When a congregation is moved by the fervor it develops a complete self-abandonment and from this abandonment are born the warmth and volume. From it also, we dare say, is born harmony which is so peculiarly characteristic of Welsh congregational singing. Thus a man is moved to sing the bass or tenor part of the tune, not the air, and a woman to sing soprano or the alto, whichever suits her best. Here we believe lies the reason for the predominancy of part singing in Welsh congregational singing. Good singing produces good atmosphere. It then arouses our deepest emotions.[11]

The Welsh incorporated their love for singing in three particular institutions, which they brought with them to the New World, the *eisteddfod, gymanfa ganu,* and the *gymanfa*. The oldest of these institutions is the eisteddfod. Its origins are ancient and are associated with the festivities related to the selection of the chief bard. The position of the chief bard, one who was honored in competition in the fields of literature, poetry, music, or speech, is known to have existed in Wales as early as the tenth century. The earliest recorded eisteddfods date from 1450, in Carmarthen, and from 1523 in Caewys, Flintshire.[12]

When the great cultural revival in literature and music occurred in the late 1700s, the literature and customs of the Welsh became important, including the revival of eisteddfods. This interest in the arts and languages contributed to renewed Welsh nationalism and became an integral part of the Welsh national character.

Eisteddfods are competitions, held over several days, involving speaking, poetry, literary readings, and musical presentations. Originally, the ultimate winner would be awarded the bard's chair, in elaborate ceremonies. A national eisteddfod was held at Jackson in 1930, and, although drastically changed from its original form, the eisteddfod is still held annually in the Jackson City schools in Jackson County (Fig. 5-2).[13]

The gymanfa ganu and the gymanfa are Welsh religious institutions. Church music was important both on the Sabbath and at social gatherings. While these two forms differed in purpose, they both included hours of congregational singing. *Gymanfa ganu* may be translated as *assembly for sacred song*. While its origins were in Wales, it became popular among the Welsh Americans. These gatherings helped perpetuate the Welsh language after it had ceased to be the common form of communication. In the tradition of the gymanfa ganu, churches within a defined geographic area would alternate from year to year in hosting the event. Such gatherings would last for two days with choir and congregational participation.

Gymanfas, sometimes called *Cwrdd Mawr* or great meetings, are great preaching festivals. In these gatherings, planned long in advance, the Welsh people come from miles around to take part in the preaching festival and the congregational singing. At Moriah Church, the mother church of the Welsh Calvinistic Methodists in the Oak Hill area of Jackson County, temporary outdoor seating and facilities were necessary to accommodate the crowds of three thousand to six thousand people. Today, the lilt of the Welsh tongue is

Michael T. Struble and Hubert G. H. Wilhelm

Fig. 5-2 Illustration
from the official
program of the
Jackson eisteddfod,
October 2, 1925

but a faint echo of the past, but the tradition of gymanfa ganu and gymanfa
(Fig. 5-3) is still carried on.

The Ty Capel

The deep religious convictions of the Welsh people have had a most lasting impact upon the cultural and material landscape of Welsh settlements.
In Meigs County, the Welsh built five small chapels. All now stand quietly
amid small cemeteries overlooking the Ohio River. Some of these cemeteries
reflect other aspects of early ethnic settlement. In the Minersville Hill cemetery for example, the residents of Welshtown Hill rest peacefully alongside
members of the area's other significant immigrant group, the Germans from
Dutchtown Hill, with the remnants of a fence line between them. Also in
Minersville are the ruins of the foundation of the Soar Church of the Welsh
Congregation and its small adjacent cemetery. The tombstones in the cemetery indicate birthplaces in Carmarthen, Glamorgan, and Monmouth, Wales.
   In the settlements in Gallia and Jackson counties, the Welsh impact on

Fig. 5-3 Flyer advertising an
annual gymanfa, 1988

the landscape persists in the form of several small chapels and the unique architectural structure of the ty capel (house chapel).[14] A small building was built near the rural church structure, where dinner was served to the itinerant minister after the Sunday services. The ty capel also served as a meeting place to conduct church business and became an integral part of the Welsh custom of the *Cadw y Mis* or *keeping of the month* (see below).

Most of the first group of Welsh settlers in southern Ohio were Calvinistic Methodists. These people trace their origins to a schism between early Methodism's most noted leaders, George Whitefield and John Wesley. Wesley adhered to Arminianism, a theological line of thought attributed to Jacobus Arminius, a sixteenth-century scholar and religious leader in the Dutch Reformed Church. Arminius split with John Calvin over the issue of predestination, believing that it was too harsh a position because it did not allow human choice in the issue of salvation. The followers of Arminianism placed greater emphasis on God's mercy. This idea was embraced by John Wesley, and the emphasis on free will and the grace of God influenced the development of Methodism in England, in Wales, and in the United States.[15]

George Whitefield, conversely, placed more emphasis on Calvinistic theology and split with Wesley over this issue. However, he kept the organizational structure of the Methodist Church, for which Wesley is noted. Whitefield's followers became known as Calvinistic Methodists. They had Methodist organization, bureaucracy, circuit riders, district superintendents, and conferences.

The church was the nucleus of these small Ohio settlements of the Welsh, who owed their allegiance, sustenance, and all their leisure time to it.

Michael T.
Struble
and
Hubert G. H.
Wilhelm

84

They practiced a strict observance of the Sabbath, requiring all food to be prepared the previous day, to avoid labor on the Sabbath. The church services had singing, preaching, then lunch, then more of the same later in the day. The Sunday school, a Welsh creation, promoted literacy as church members read and studied the Bible. On Tuesday evenings there were prayer services and singing. On the Thursday before a Communion Sunday, a *seit* was held, which involved individuals testifying to their faith, talking about their fears and temptations, and giving consolation to others who had similar problems and concerns.[16]

Because the churches were relatively widely spaced, the institution of the ty capel evolved. The two earliest Calvinistic Methodist churches at Moriah, Ohio, founded in 1835, and at Horeb, Ohio, founded in 1838, were at nearly opposite ends of Welsh-dominated Jefferson and Madison townships in Jackson County. The distance between them of some ten miles was considerable in the horse and buggy days. The circuit rider was required to leave Moriah before noon to arrive at Horeb, tired and hungry, by dinnertime. One early minister was the Reverend Robert Williams, who came to the Moriah settlement in 1836. He traveled back and forth between Moriah and Horeb. When he arrived at Horeb, he would hurriedly eat some dry bread that he usually carried with him, before beginning the service.

Church members became concerned about the minister's not getting adequate food, and Margaret Edwards, a parishioner, took it upon herself to provide Mr. Williams with some "johnny cake" and milk before each service. The practice became a tradition, and soon other women of the church were taking turns providing meals for Mr. Williams and those who followed him to the pulpits of Moriah and Horeb.[17] Eventually, the men of Horeb Church decided to build a suitable structure for the minister so that he could both be served food and rest. On March 18, 1859, they made plans to build the first ty capel.[18]

The ty capel appears to be restricted to Welsh settlements in Gallia and Jackson counties (Fig. 5-4). Conversations with the scholars of the Welsh in America, such as Edward Hartmann, professor emeritus of history at Suffolk University, Boston, Massachusetts;[19] Phillips G. Davies, professor of English at Iowa State University, Ames, Iowa;[20] and Ann Knowles, a researcher of the Welsh colonies in Wisconsin;[21] indicate that the ty capel is unique to the settlements of southern Ohio.

The ty capels varied somewhat in size, depending on the resources the local church could provide for its construction. Some very small Welsh churches did not have ty capels. The fully elaborated ty capels consisted of two or three rooms, including a kitchen, parlor, and sometimes a small bedroom with a cot. Meals could be prepared, elders and members could gather, and a place of rest could be provided for the visiting minister.

With the building of the ty capel there also began the practice of the *Cadw y Mis,* the keeping of the month. In this practice, different families would be assigned for a month the total responsibility of taking care of the ty capel and preparing dinner for the minister, as well as providing for his horse. Any failure of a family to comply with these tasks would result in a fine. So, what began as a simple meal of corn bread grew into a formal social custom and a new vernacular structure unique to the rural American landscape in Gallia and Jackson counties, Ohio.

The Welsh in Ohio

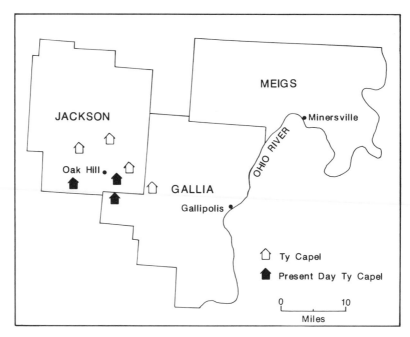

Fig. 5-4 Past and present locations of ty capel in southern Ohio. (Map by M. M. Geib.)

Only three house chapels remain today (see Fig. 5-4). Moriah Church (Fig. 5-5) was the first Calvinistic Methodist church founded in Madison township, Jackson County, in 1835. It lost its ty capel to a fire in August 1953. Horeb Church was founded in 1838, and its ty capel (the first one built) was torn down in the late 1970s because it had become so dilapidated its continued use was considered dangerous. Centerville Church, founded in 1841 in Gallia County, lost its ty capel in a fire in 1974. Soar Church in Jackson County, founded in 1841, was itself unique, in that it was made entirely out of brick, unlike the other churches in this area. The church and its ty capel were torn down by a local coal company in the mid-1960s. The only surviving ty capel are at Sardis, Bethel, and Peniel churches.

The church at Bethel was organized in 1841 and is currently an active Presbyterian church. Bethel, for the most part, enjoyed a larger membership than did most of its contemporary churches; it started with just sixteen members but peaked at one hundred fifty-one members in 1873.[22] This church was located near the charcoal furnace communities of Cambria and Washington. The neo-saltbox design was not duplicated in the other ty capel. The structure is now abandoned.

The church at Peniel in Gallia County was organized in 1870. Its ty capel is the smallest of the surviving ones. The structure serves as a kitchen for a nondenominational community church. Underneath the milled flooring of this ty capel, one can still see the original split log floor (Fig. 5-6).

Figure 5-7 shows the classical styling of the church at Sardis. This name was supposedly taken from a biblical passage that meant "place of few peo-

Michael T. Struble and Hubert G. H. Wilhelm

Fig. 5-5 The Welsh church at Moriah, Jackson County, Ohio.
(Photo by M. Struble.)

Fig. 5-6 The Welsh church and ty capel at Peniel, Gallia County, Ohio.
(Photo by M. Struble.)

Fig. 5-7 The Welsh church at Sardis, Ohio. (Photo by M. Struble.)

ple." Its original sixteen members, in 1843, grew to sixty-eight by 1879.[23] The building has the traditional two doors on the gabled front, typical of many rural churches in that time period. The women and children entered and sat together on one side during the services, while the men entered and sat on the other. This is now a Presbyterian church. Figure 5-8 shows the ty capel at Sardis. This ty capel has an unusual L-shaped floor plan and is by far the largest of the surviving house chapels. It consists of three rooms: kitchen, dining room, and parlor. The building is used on occasion today for various church related activities.[24] This structure has two fireplaces and the shutter decorations indicate a higher style than in other ty capel.

Over the years, use of the Welsh language in church diminished as the churches admitted people of non-Welsh background. The numbers of Welsh-born and ethnic Welsh in southern Ohio continued to decline as the regional economy changed and families moved on to other areas. In 1919, the Calvinistic Methodists formally joined the Presbyterian Church. Thus, this uniquely Welsh denomination, which dominated these settlements for more than eighty years, ceased to exist.

Welsh Barns

After helping to build the first road between Gallipolis and Jackson, early Welsh settlers in southeastern Ohio turned to farming. One can surmise that their early agricultural activity was subsistence farming. Both the hilly nature of the land in southern Ohio and its isolation would support this conclusion. No rural structures, such as barns, have been identified as distinctly Welsh in this part of Ohio. In some other areas of the United States, Welsh settlement has been associated with the occurrence of a two-level

Michael T. Struble and Hubert G. H. Wilhelm

88

Fig. 5-8 The ty capel at Sardis, Jackson County, Ohio.
(Photo by M. Struble.)

gable-entry barn. Although such barns were originally identified with the English Lake District,[25] they occur in some numbers in Oneida County, New York, and in central Pennsylvania, both areas of locally important Welsh settlement.[26] Even elsewhere in Ohio, a Welsh gable-entry barn has been documented.[27] But while the barns in Meigs, Gallia, and Jackson counties have some similarities with Welsh barns, their late construction (early 1900s) and apparent relationship to Appalachian loft barns suggest a different origin for these structures. No direct Welsh influence has been established.

Stone Dragons and a Welsh Contribution to the Industrial Age

Later Welsh immigrants moved into the mining and iron industries of southern Ohio. One of the greatest periods of prosperity there occurred at the outset of the Civil War. The price of iron rose to $90 a ton. Jefferson Furnace iron, used to make cannons, became famous throughout the world because of its high quality. The anchor trademark stamped on the Jefferson Furnace iron became the standard of excellence in those years. It was at this furnace that the iron was made for the famous Union ironclad, the Monitor.

The single greatest impact by the Welsh on the economic development of southern Ohio came through their involvement with the charcoal iron and related brick-making industries. The Welsh who came to this area were from the industrialized parts of southern Wales; they brought with them knowledge and experience in heavy industry. This type of background pre-adapted them to work in the isolated, self-sufficient, furnace communities of southeastern Ohio. Such isolation may have contributed to the clannish character of the early Welsh settlers. The ruins of the charcoal furnaces can

The Welsh in Ohio

89

still be seen today scattered on the landscape in the form of great stone stacks. Because during firing the stone chimneys belched smoke and flame, some picturesquely called them "stone dragons."

An address at the ninety-second anniversary of the founding of Jefferson Furnace gives us an idea about the beginnings of this remarkable enterprise: "On a beautiful Indian Summer day in the Autumn of 1854, the hills and the valleys of Jefferson Township were awakened by the sound of a whistle of a new industry that was to prove to be one of the most successful enterprises of its kind in the history of the charcoal iron industry."[28]

Two features distinguished the Jefferson Furnace. First, only Welsh-born males could be stockholders. The second was the long life of its operation, from 1854 to 1916. No other furnace produced for such a long period. The influence of the Welsh religion also had its effect on the operations of the furnace. In accordance with the very strong Welsh beliefs about work and the Sabbath, the original charter of the furnace stipulated that it was never to be operated on the Sabbath. At midnight Saturday, the fires were banked and all work stopped until the hour of midnight on Sunday. This pattern was faithfully observed for the entire sixty-two years of operation.

Another Welsh-owned furnace, the Cambria, was incorporated in the same year as Jefferson Furnace. However, lack of adequate capital and inexperienced management contributed to its demise in 1878.[29]

These furnaces were located in the Hanging Rock Iron District of Kentucky and Ohio. A description of this area is found in a report by Wilbur Stout:

> The Hanging Rock Iron District, as defined by the iron masters, embraced the furnace lands and also the adjacent properties over which iron ore, limestone, and charcoal were gathered. It included parts of Carter, Boyd, and Greenup counties in Kentucky and parts of Lawrence, Scioto, Gallia, Jackson, Vinton, and Hocking counties in Ohio. Within this field all the raw materials necessary for the smelting of charcoal iron were provided by nature in abundant quantities. The district in 1875 included 69 charcoal furnaces and 16 coke or coal furnaces.[30]

The Welsh settlement area of Jackson county included eleven charcoal furnaces. Of these, three furnaces—Monroe, Keystone, and Jefferson—stood out. Monroe was the largest furnace, producing as much as twenty tons of iron per day. Keystone, located on Raccoon Creek had its stack carved out of the sandstone hillside. It had a model community, with workers' houses, a two-story brick school, and a three-story brick company store with a horse-operated elevator.

The iron furnace was a tapering vertical shaft built of massive sandstone blocks positioned against a hillside. The sandstone was usually quarried nearby and brought to the site by ox-drawn wagons, to be pieced together by expert stonemasons. Special care was given to the construction of the interior of the stack to insure a lining with good refractory qualities. The lower part of the shaft had a hearthstone, and in its sides were openings through which air was blasted. Below the openings was the part of the furnace called the *crucible*, where the molten iron accumulated. Iron ore, charcoal, and limestone were stored at the top of the furnace and on the hilltop. At the base of the furnace was the *casting house,* a crude wooden structure where forms or molds were filled, and the *engine house* for the blowing devices.

During its operation, the stack was charged at the top with ore, charcoal, and limestone. These ingredients gradually descended inside the furnace during the smelting. The air introduced at the sides near the base and through the openings, called *tuyeres,* created the drafts necessary to create the intense heat that caused the ore to melt. The molten iron was trapped in the crucible and drawn off into molds of sand called pigs.

While the refining process was simple, the number of men required to operate each furnace was considerable. The direct result of the establishment of a furnace was the development of a furnace community. On average forty men were required to operate each furnace. Add to this figure the various colliers, timber cutters, ore diggers, and ox drivers and the total comes to about one hundred men.

Each furnace community of about five hundred people provided a cross section of Welsh society, with all its accompanying social, commercial, and religious activities. The residents developed local debating, speaking, and singing societies. They had spelling and mathematics contests. Musical festivals were common, and most communities had their own churches, which were the focal point of most Welsh activities.

It was common that the furnace companies provided homes for their workers. Almost uniformly these were log houses consisting of two rooms, a loft, and a lean-to in the rear. These were the style of structures familiar to the Welsh people, although they were built of different materials in Wales. At least one of these buildings survives from the Jefferson Furnace community. It was moved from its original site but still functions as a home.

Over the years, the iron demands of the American industrial revolution far outpaced the production capabilities of the charcoal iron industry, including the Hanging Rock district. Technology advanced to the point where other methods of iron production better met the quantity and quality demanded by the marketplace. The discovery of deposits of higher-grade ore in the Lake Superior region meant that the Hanging Rock district was no longer the center of iron production. The furnaces shut down, the equipment was sold, and the furnace communities were abandoned. Only the large stone stacks, erected on their hillsides, remained as silent memorials to an age of important industrial growth.

Legacies and Landscapes

What is left today of the Welsh pioneer experience? Once a year, on the last weekend of September, the faithful Welsh remnant gathers for the gymanfa, which alternates among the Oak Hill, Tyn Rhos, and Nebo churches. As has been done for over 150 years, the ancient Welsh tongue is raised in song and echoes among the windswept hills of Gallia and Jackson counties. Annually, the descendants of these early pioneers gather for the Welsh social event of the year, when they celebrate St. David's Day, in Oak Hill on the first of March. Surviving, in addition to the religious and social events, are the place names of the region. Tyn Rhos, Nebo, Bathania, and Bryn Hyfryd are in stark contrast to the usual names encountered in Appalachian Ohio.

Early conflicts in the Dutch Reformed Church and the Methodist Church gave birth to the Calvinistic Methodists. This group added to the cultural landscape of these hills with the construction of the ty capel. The distribution of these structures gave rise to the Welsh religious custom of the Cadw y Mis, the Keeping of the Month. Although the ty capel is a unique vernacular structure, houses and barns of the Welsh in this area do not appear to be distinctive or much different from similar structures used by other groups.

Also still surviving are the ruins of the charcoal iron furnaces. Welsh engineering and business talents and skilled labor helped to build these early industrial facilities. They have been quiet for some time now, but remain as a legacy of Welsh settlement in southern Ohio.

Perhaps the most personal and lasting presence of the Welsh settlers are their cemeteries (Fig. 5-9). To an outsider, the constant repetition of the names of Hughes, Williams, Morgan, Jones, Evans, Davis, and others may seem odd, but, they tell a story of a remarkable people—educated and deeply religious pioneers, who cleared the land, built their homes, raised families and worshipped in this wilderness. The pioneer settlers are now gone, but if one looks closely enough, one can still see their imprint among the hills and valleys of the land.

Michael T. Struble and Hubert G. H. Wilhelm

92

Fig. 5-9 The Welsh language tombstone of the Reverend David J. Jenkins, Horeb Cemetery, Jackson County, Ohio. (Photo by M. Struble.)

Part III

*Southeastern
North America*

6

The Scotch-Irish and English in Appalachia

John B. Rehder

A T THE beginning of the nineteenth century, the inhabitants of the southern Appalachian region comprised Scotch-Irish, English, Germans, and a few Welsh, Irish, and French Huguenot settlers, together with scattered Indian tribes. This chapter focuses particularly on the vernacular landscapes in Appalachia created by the Scotch-Irish and English ethnic groups, who together were numerically dominant.

Ethnic Origins

Most Scotch-Irish people originated as seventeenth century Presbyterian folk from Scotland, who emigrated to "plantations" established by King James I in northern Ireland's Ulster Province after 1609. Many Scottish emigrants to Ulster came from the Border country of present-day southern Scotland and northern England. Others arrived at various times from the western highlands of Scotland and the Hebrides Islands. Between 1717 and 1775 the folk collectively called Scotch-Irish, and their descendants, began major emigrations to the Americas, entering chiefly through the ports of Philadelphia and Charleston.[1]

Simple facts simply put cannot fully explain the complex events and the identity of the people who endured them. Less Scotch than most highland Scotsmen and far less Irish than Irishmen, the Scotch-Irish were still nearly as Celtic as other northern and western peoples of the British Isles. Should they be called Scotch or Scots, Ulster-Scots or Northern Irishmen? *Scotch*, the adjective, identifies whiskey or plaid cloth, but *Scot*, meaning Scotsman, begs for use of the term *Scots-Irish*. However, throughout the literature and especially in the American vernacular, *Scotch-Irish* is the accepted term and so it will be herein.

Just how many Scotch-Irish and English emigrants made their way to the Appalachian region is unclear. Dickson estimated 114,000 emigrants between 1718 and 1778.[2] Graham placed the number between 102,000 and 125,000 for the period 1707–1783.[3] An accurate enumeration of persons with Scotish-Irish ethnicity is impossible because the first U.S. census, in 1790, did not separately identify persons of Scotch-Irish ancestry. Using the

1790 census to proportion the population from 1775, Hanna estimated a total of 335,000 Scotch-Irish and Scots in the following numbers for the following states (in geographical order):[4]

Pennsylvania	100,000
Delaware	10,000
Maryland	30,000
Virginia	75,000
North Carolina	65,000
South Carolina	45,000
Georgia	10,000

Recent scholarly attempts to differentiate the groups from the British Isles have been met with disagreement. Some historians have attempted to separate the British Isles emigrants by surname.[5] Others argued against that methodology and deemed the estimates unacceptable.[6] Purvis estimated the 1790 population in percentages of total population per state in seventeen states for English, Welsh, Scotch-Irish, Scottish, Irish, German, Dutch, French, and Swedish.[7] If we convert his percentages into ratios between Scotch-Irish and English for the eight states in the Middle Atlantic and Appalachian regions, the results show a disproportionate number of English over Scotch-Irish (Table 6-1). The McDonalds' estimate based on Scotch, Irish, and Welsh surnames indicates smaller Scotch plus Irish to English ratios (Table 6-2).

The English contribution to the population dominates most estimates on a state-by-state basis, but nothing clearly answers these questions about the Scotch-Irish in Appalachia: Which Scots came from Ulster; which Scots were directly from Scotland and were they highland or lowland Scots; which Irish were from Ulster, and which immigrants were truly English, or should it matter? In spite of the discrepancies in numbers, the general pattern in each census after 1790 and until 1860 indicated that about half of the southern population was Scotch, Irish, and Welsh and about one-fourth of the

Table 6-1. Middle Atlantic and Appalachian Scotch-Irish and English Population, as Percentage of Total Population, 1790

State	Scotch-Irish	English	Ratio of Scotch-Irish to English
Delaware	9.2	63.3	1.0:6.8
Georgia	12.2	58.6	1.0:4.8
Kentucky	16.5	54.8	1.0:3.3
Maryland	10.4	52.5	1.0:5.0
North Carolina	15.8	53.2	1.0:3.3
Pennsylvania	15.1	25.8	1.0:1.7
South Carolina	18.9	47.6	1.0:2.5
Tennessee	17.8	50.6	1.0:2.8
Virginia	11.7	61.3	1.0:5.2

John B. Rehder

Source: Purvis 1984, p. 98.

Table 6-2. Middle Atlantic and Appalachian Scotch + Irish and English
Population, as Percentage of Total Population, 1790*

State	Scotch + Irish	English	Ratio of Scotch + Irish to English
Maryland	21.6	47.4	1.0:2.1
North Carolina	40.9	40.6	1.0:1.0
Pennsylvania	36.9	19.5	1.8:1.0
South Carolina	44.6	36.7	1.2:1.0
Virginia	32.2	49.6	1.0:1.5

Source: McDonald and McDonald 1980, p. 198.
*Data not available for Delaware, Georgia, Kentucky, and Tennessee.

population had come from western and northern England.[8] Perhaps the central issue here may not be how many persons were in the emigration, but how and where they settled in Appalachia and what was the personality of the vernacular landscape they created?

Migrations to the Appalachian Regions

Scotch-Irish migrations dominated the settlement history of the Appalachian region before the nineteenth century. Routes into the region were governed by location factors such as: ports of entry, land previously occupied by other European groups, the presence of Indian-held territory, established trails and wagon roads, and lands that were open to settlement.

Contrary to popular belief, the Scotch-Irish migration was *not* a case of uniform westward migration from the Atlantic shores of eastern North America. The migrations took the form of two widely separated streams entering through the ports of Philadelphia and Charleston and forming a pincer movement eventually creating an arc of Scotch-Irish settlement in colonial America (Fig. 6-1). The larger and clearly more important stream entered through Philadelphia, established an initial cultural hearth as a gathering place and staging area in the Susquehanna River valley west of Philadelphia in 1710–1730, and proceeded to take a major course southward following the Great Valley, to southwestern Virginia by 1735. From this part of Virginia, the route divided. One branch continued straight down the valley towards northeastern Tennessee, to linger there and later thread northwestward through Cumberland Gap, thrusting deep into Kentucky. A larger route went southeasterly passing through the Roanoak Gap and New River Gap to spill immigrants out onto the Piedmont region of North Carolina. Here a secondary hearth of Scotch-Irish settlement formed between the Yadkin and Catawba river valleys in the 1740s and 1750s.[9]

Another branch from the southeastern Pennsylvania hearth in the Susquehanna Valley area, pushed directly westward to form another Scotch-Irish secondary hearth in the Pittsburgh vicinity of southwestern Pennsylvania between 1768 and 1790.[10] Later, from this Pittsburgh hearth, continuing migrations would lead into the Ohio River Valley in the late eighteenth and well into the nineteenth centuries.

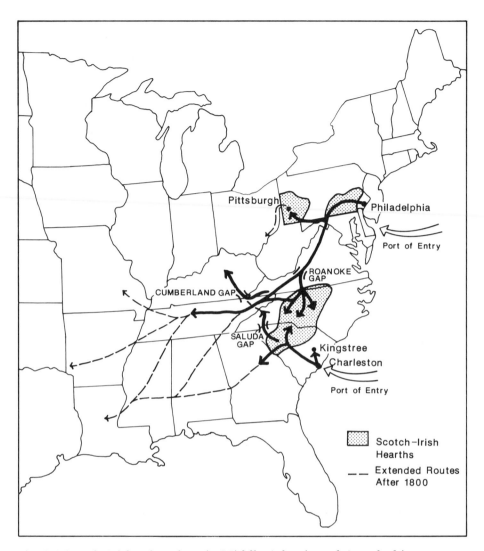

Fig. 6-1 Scotch-Irish migrations in Middle Atlantic and Appalachia, 1720–1790

The other arm of the pincers was the South Carolina stream of Scotch-Irish migration that began from the port of Charleston as early as 1732 and pushed seventy-five miles northward to Kingstree. As more people arrived, migration streams pushed inland to the upcountry of the South Carolina Piedmont to form another Scotch-Irish secondary hearth.[11] From this South Carolina Piedmont hearth, smaller streams pushed southwestward to Georgia and northeastward to North Carolina to eventually link up with the North Carolina Piedmont hearth mentioned above.

Throughout the region, secondary loops of migration and occupation continued. From the North Carolina Piedmont hearth, settlers led by Daniel Boone, James Robertson, and John Sevier in 1771–72 crossed the Blue Ridge Mountains of Southern Appalachia and followed the Watauga River

John B. Rehder

98

directly westward to settle northeastern Tennessee.[12] From these Watauga settlements, additional migration was carried overland and circuitously westward by way of the Tennessee River, to establish settlement in the Nashville Basin.[13] Meanwhile, many settlers coming down the Great Valley turned northwestward through Cumberland Gap and came to dominate the Blue Grass Basin in central Kentucky.[14] Others continued down the valley toward the areas that were to become Knoxville, Chattanooga, and Birmingham, as the threat of Indian attacks lessened and those lands were opened for permanent settlement.[15] From the South Carolina hearth, settlers moved northward through the Blue Ridge Mountains through Saluda Gap, to forge their way into the Asheville Basin and eventually westward to Tennessee.

Since the southern Appalachian region was the homeland of the Cherokee and other aboriginal groups, much of the land was closed to European settlement until after the 1790s.[16] Farther south, beyond Tennessee, Indian ownership of territory prevented major European incursions until after 1830.[17]

The English, meanwhile, were making progress moving inland, following river valleys from their Tidewater hearths along the Atlantic seaboard. Prior to 1760, from a well-established English-dominated hearth in the Chesapeake Bay area, additional peoples of various cultural and economic statuses began to move upcountry, following the James, the Potomac, and other rivers and eventually linking with the Shenandoah Valley and Great Valley settlements of the Scotch-Irish and Germans.[18] From the English-dominated, southern coastal towns of Wilmington, Charleston, and Savannah, additional English settlers moved westward to Appalachia. Ultimately by the opening of the nineteenth century, European settlement had expanded to embrace the core of the Appalachian region.

The Upland South and Appalachia

Appalachia represents a part of a much larger culture region known as the Upland South. For about twenty-five years, geographers have attempted to circumscribe the boundaries of culture regions in the United States.[19] Ideally, to determine the boundaries of a culture region one analyzes all diagnostic, material, and nonmaterial culture traits, then charts the geographic distribution of the keenest identifiers of the culture in order to draw conclusive boundary lines. Realistically, the task is done by relying on old-fashioned, yet scholarly, intuition based on field experience and reading knowledge, then drawing the boundary lines with an educated guess. Considering the late start for study and the many years over which cultural boundaries have become blurred, an area such as the Upland South presents, at best, confusing evidence upon which to base demarcation.[20]

The Upland South in the broadest sense is a culture region whose identity is based upon a Scotch-Irish heritage.[21] It is "upland" by virtue of the physical nature of its highland and cultural core—Appalachia. It is unquestionably "south," by virtue of its geographic location in eastern United States, but the region's controversial identity is blurred by its economic and social roots. Historically, the South could be subdivided into: Deep South or "lower south," which possessed a cotton plantation economy, slavery, and gently rolling to level landscapes; and Upland South, which had small-scale subsistence farming, few slaves or black population, and land with steeper slopes and higher elevation. Both souths are still "Anglo," by virtue of their Scotch-Irish and English heritages, and colloquially may be referred to by stereotypical appellations such as "Dixie, Bible Belt, red neck, white trash," or worse. Within the cultural and geographic milieu of Anglo America, Appalachia best serves as the heart and hearth of the Upland South.

The boundaries of the Appalachian region are debatable. Scholars and governmental agencies have chosen to delimit the region on the basis of elevation, geology, economy, poverty, political affiliation, cultural heritage, and less specific criteria.[22] Physically, the Appalachian region contains four major landform areas. The Piedmont, on the east, is an ancient eroded plateau with elevations up to 1,800 feet. The Blue Ridge Mountains and the Great Smoky Mountains form a mountain core with elevations ranging from 2,000 to 6,684 feet. The Ridge and Valley area, including the Great Valley, has parallel ridges and valleys aligned northeast to southwest with elevations of 1,000–2,000 feet. Finally, the Appalachian Plateau on the west may be divided into two parts, the Allegheny and Cumberland plateaus, with elevations of 1,500 to 4,000 feet.

The surface of Appalachia is forested, with numerous streams but few natural lakes. It was a land that offered the necessities of life—plentiful water, useful woodlands, selectively rich soils. But it also presented steep rocky slopes, areas with relatively poor soils, isolation and difficult transportation access caused by topography, and at times, harsh winters and scorching summers. The majority of early settlement focused upon the favorable soils and slopes adjacent to the Great Valley routeways that the settlers followed in the Ridge and Valley region. Only later did settlement expand to areas of lesser soil quality, steeper slopes, and greater isolation. The perception of the region's boundaries may not be as important as how we perceive the cultural vernacular landscape created by the Appalachian people.

The Vernacular Landscape

In any study of a people and their landscape, the initial occupancy or first effective settlement layer becomes paramount to the understanding of successive settlement layers.[23] That first permanent layer of European settlement created by Scotch-Irish, English, and German settlers in Appalachia established patterns that have endured through two centuries of land occupation.

The cadastral or survey system, by which property was measured, engraved a web of settlement evidence into the landscape. Land surveys relied on an English-based survey system called metes and bounds. Initial claimants were granted acreages in parcels allocated by the settler's choice of boundary lines to encompass selected soils, water, and woodland.[24] The cadastre followed a complex method of sightings to and from physical objects such as large rocks, trees, water features, and wooden or iron posts. Colorful boundary descriptions of points might have included: "the missing chestnut stump" or "the place where Will Smith's cow drowned in the river" or "two hollers into the swamp." In Appalachia today land is still sold with an imprecise disclaimer, such as: "fifty acres, more or less."

As land was claimed, surveyed, and settled, the result was a complex pat-

John B. Rehder

Fig. 6-2 Landscape evidence of the metes and bounds survey system on the Cumberland Plateau: Bledsoe County, Tennessee, 1964. (Source: U.S. Department of Agriculture.)

tern that appeared much like a crazy-quilt blanketing the surface (Fig. 6-2). The nineteenth-century landscape was characterized by property boundaries marked by fences and tree lines, irregular shapes of agricultural fields, and a network of trails and secondary roads that linked the holdings. Settlement became widely dispersed. Individual farms, though often in sight of each other, were clearly separate and apart. Unlike in the European homeland, the initial rural agricultural landscape here contained no villages, few hamlets, and few if any other rural agglomerations.

The Farmstead

The Appalachian farms reflected patterns in the arrangements of buildings that followed some from the Old World.[25] The house was situated near a water supply and near a means of transportation such as a path, creek, or road. The house site was on slightly higher ground to avoid local flooding. Deciduous trees, such as oak, hickory, or maple, shaded the house site. In the absence of lawn mowers, most yards were swept clear of grass and became clay- or sand-surfaced spaces. My friend and scholar of the cultural geography of the South, the late Milton Newton, once asked an elderly lady why she was sweeping her clay yard. He was searching for a rich folk explanation, but she answered, "Dangit, to keep it clean!"

Beyond the house, a variety of outbuildings were located as if they too had been swept out back or to the sides of the main house (Fig. 6-3). A barn, perhaps as big as the main house, was the focal point around which a myriad of much smaller outbuildings of cribs and coops clustered. Each building had its own function. The barn provided storage and protection for farm implements, hay, corn, and work animals such as oxen, horses, and mules. A complete farmstead maintained one or more corn cribs for storing corn; a smokehouse for curing, smoking, and storing meat; a spring house to protect the entrance to the main water supply at the spring or a "dairy" to cover the spring and to keep perishable milk products in cooling troughs under roof; an applehouse or roothouse for the storage of fruits and rootcrops; chicken coops, pig pens, and other animal enclosures; and an outhouse for obvious reasons. Beyond the house site and outbuildings stretched fields and pastures arranged in no particular size, shape, or alignment, bounded by fences of split wooden rails or later of wire and posts. Bottomlands, flat areas of rich soil along streams, were devoted to the most important crops—corn and tobacco. Tree lines followed fences and property lines, but woodlands, usually on steeper terrain and in somewhat larger units joined to fill in and partially obscure the landscape matrix.

John B. Rehder

Fig. 6-3 Outbuildings distributed around a house in Hancock County, Tennessee. (Drawing by M. M. Geib.)

Vernacular Construction Methods

Throughout nineteenth-century Appalachia, log construction was the primary building method; structures were built of horizontally placed, rounded or squared, hewn timbers, notched at the corners. The typology of corner notches used in Appalachia included saddle, saddle-V, V, half-dovetail, full-dovetail, square, half, diamond (Fig. 6-4), and half-log or semi-lunate crown notch.[26]

Corner notching has been suggested as a diagnostic tool for evidence of cultural identity. Which culture group or groups were responsible for the corner notching types found in Appalachia? Aboriginal Indian groups did *not* originate the technique, because their early wooden shelters were built with vertical posts and woven saplings. The use of horizontal logs with corner notches was a European introduction, used by Appalachian Indian groups only after contact with Europeans.

Despite the widespread use of log construction by the Scotch-Irish in Appalachia, the technique did not originate with them. Prior to coming to America, neither Scotch-Irish nor English culture groups had a history, or an apparent knowledge, of the use of wood in this way.[27] In Northern Ireland, Scottish settlers in 1611 built structures of stone and thatch just as they had in Scotland, while English immigrants at the same time were cutting and squaring timbers for structures built with half-timbering techniques.[28] Log construction did not exist in Britain at the time of emigration. Moreover, upon arrival in America, initial Scotch-Irish settlers from Ulster still lacked

Fig. 6-4 Log house with diamond corner notches, Grainger County, Tennessee. (Photo by J. Rehder.)

knowledge of log construction. In 1732 at Kingstree, South Carolina about seventy-five miles north of Charleston, the first homes of Scotch-Irish settlers were crude excavated earth pits roofed with pine saplings and sand.[29] The early English settlers in Virginia at first built cruck structures with walls of wattle and daub.[30] As early as 1610–1612, and for centuries thereafter, the English in the Tidewater region continued to build houses of framed, sawn timber.[31]

Not just one, but two, European cultural sources have been suggested for American log construction origins. The first championed by Jordan and Kaups and supported by the works of Wright, Mercer, and Weslager, proposes a Scandinavian origin for American log construction.[32] The second, as put forth by Kniffen and Glassie with support from Bucher, Wertenbaker, and others, argues for a German origin.[33] Supporting the Scandinavian origin is considerable field evidence collected by Jordan and Kaups. Notch types are more than coincidental, and cultural linkages between south central Sweden and the Delaware Valley are firm for the 1630s, albeit scarce in numbers for Swedish populations.[34] The German evidence, based on a larger population, suggests a connection between German immigrant builders of log structures in Pennsylvania and their homelands in Switzerland, southwestern Germany, and eastern German areas of Moravia, Bohemia, and Silesia.[35]

While the argument favoring a Germanic origin can be based on log building cultures with immigrant diffusions from German-speaking Europe to eighteenth-century southeastern Pennsylvania, the argument favoring the Scandinavian origin is based on physical evidence of log structures and notch types found in the Fenno-Scandian region and the historical evidence of Swedish immigration into the Delaware Valley adjacent to southeastern Pennsylvania in the 1630s.

For linkages to Appalachia, the pivotal introduction of log construction techniques was made by European immigrants who settled in southeastern Pennsylvania in the first half of the eighteenth century. Within this Pennsylvania hearth, cultural linkages were formed between German users of notching types and Scotch-Irish recipients. As both groups migrated throughout Appalachia, they exchanged culture traits through the process of acculturation, by which Scotch-Irish settlers and others learned the methods of log construction and notching that are now so closely identified with Appalachia.

House Types

For the geography of house types and the interpretation of their cultural significance we owe much to Professor Fred B. Kniffen. Through Kniffen's works, and those of his students and disciples, the study of vernacular or folk housing contributes much to the understanding of the American landscape. Folk houses reveal something about the personality of a culture region. They are representative of the folk who built them and as such are diagnostic culture traits that can be used to identify the culture or cultures involved in their construction. They allow us to trace the migrations and dispersals of folk cultures. Meanwhile, they stimulate us to seek answers to questions about source areas, points of origin, exact routes and times of diffusion, variations in types, styles, construction materials, and degrees of diagnostic reliability.

The house types of Appalachia largely follow the pattern of the English pen tradition in which a *pen* represents an individual room. In the typology, single-pen houses evolve into double-pen houses (two rooms), I-houses (two stories tall, two rooms wide, and one room deep), and larger houses (four rooms over four rooms). Construction techniques and materials for Appalachian folk houses may be of horizontal, rounded, or square hewn logs with corner notches, or of framed sawn lumber, brick, or stone.

Single-Pen Houses

The single-pen house is the basic form (Fig. 6-5). The typical one-room structure measures about 20' × 17' and has a single outside chimney at one gable. Usually the dwelling has a single story, but some may be a story and a half, with the sleeping loft supported by mortised loft joists in the ceiling above the main room. An interior ladder or a boxed stairway leads to the loft. A single front door, single back door, and optional windows provide access, air, and light. Appendages, additional structural attachments not considered in the typology of the single-pen, may include front and rear porches and a kitchen wing or shed.

Single-pen houses in the nineteenth century tended to remain much the same size despite variables of time, place, type of timber, and notch types. Investigating log single-pen houses in Alabama, Eugene Wilson measured thirty-eight examples to find that their outside dimensions averaged 20' ×

Fig. 6-5 Single-pen house with mortised loft joists and half-dovetail notching, Grainger County, Tennessee. (Photo by J. Rehder.)

17'1". Built between 1815 and 1895, these log single-pens represented three main types of corner notching: twenty were half-dovetailed, nine were square-notched, six were V-notched, and the remaider were either mixed or unknown.[36] Elsewhere in the South, Wilson examined seventeen other log single-pens, dating from 1726 to 1875 in Maryland, Virginia, Kentucky, and Tennessee, and found that they measured an average of 20'9" × 17'2".[37]

In Grainger County, Tennessee, John Morgan and Joy Medford, analyzed fifty-four log single-pens of a total inventory of 229 log structures.[38] The single-pens with average dimensions of 22' × 18', were built before 1860. Thirty-seven of the fifty-four houses were notched with half-dovetail notches; twelve houses were V-notched. The single-pens were built from three major timber types: twenty-one houses of pine logs, seventeen of yellow poplar, four of oak, and the remainder of mixtures of timber types.[39]

In adjacent Union County, Tennessee, Vincent Ambrosia compiled data on forty-nine log single-pens, including forty-two with half-dovetail notches, two with V-notches, three with saddle, one with saddle-V, and one with square notches. Thirty-five of the houses were built of yellow poplar timber, six of oak, six of pine, and the remainder mixed.[40]

In the Piedmont region of North Carolina, forty-four single-pen log houses were inventoried in the rural parts of Guilford County.[41] Their corner notching included eleven houses with V-notches, ten with half-dovetail, two with full-dovetail, one with square, and the remainder were unidentified. Measurements and timber types were not included in the study.

What can we conclude from these inventories and data analyses? First, single-pens are not perfectly square houses, rather they are small rectangles measuring approximately 20–22 feet by 16–18 feet. Such dimensions represent an unusual uniformity for dwellings constructed over a period of a century and a half and built by folk builders with no blueprints. One could surmise that the dimensions were governed by tree type and size or by the weight of the logs. Measurement might have been based on a certain number of axe handles, a paced-off distance, or some other folk means of measurement. Could the size have been based on traditional measurements carried from Europe? In early Britain, a standardized unit of measure, the rod (16 feet), was used for land measurement, for house bays, or room units, and was derived from the standard size of animal stalls (16' × 16'), originally the space needed to accommodate two pair of oxen.[42] This standard dimension came to the American colonies and was used for house bays in cruck structures in the earliest Virginia settlements.[43] In time, cruck structures gave way to timbered houses, but the 16' × 16' bay was retained and became the basis for the single-pen or square cabin of the English pen tradition.[44] Henry Glassie, studying the southern mountain cabin, interpreted the square cabin as English and the rectangular cabin (22' × 16') as a Scotch-Irish introduction. In dimensions, the rectangular cabin was a direct descendent of dwellings in western Britain and northern Ireland.[45]

To summarize, the dominant notches among surviving examples are half-dovetail, represented by 53.6 percent of samples in Alabama, 68.5 percent in Grainger County, Tennessee, 85.7 percent in Union County, Tennessee, and 42 percent for the single-pens with identified notch types in Guilford County, North Carolina. The V-notch is found in only 15.7 percent of the houses in the Alabama survey, 22.2 percent in Grainger County, and less than 1 percent in Union County, but it dominates the identified notch types with 45.8 percent in Guilford County. Temporally, the Alabama study revealed houses with half dovetail notches ranging in date of construction from 1820 to 1890.[46] In Grainger County, half-dovetail–notched houses were built from 1790 to 1915.[47]

Timber types indicate changing availability and choice of wood. In Union County, Tennessee, yellow poplar was used to construct 61.4 percent of log dwellings.[48] For Grainger County, three phases of log building emerge. Yellow poplar dominated in 53 percent of log single-pens in the first phase, dating from 1790 to 1850. In the middle phase, 1850–1880, oak and mixtures of oak, poplar, chestnut, and pine timbers were used. For the last phase from 1880 until the end of the log building period, about 1930, pine timbers dominated in eighty-one percent of the single-pen houses.[49] Of all timber types in Appalachia, yellow poplar (*Liriodendron tulipifera*) is unquestionably superior for the construction of log buildings, because the tree grows a tall, straight trunk with only a few limbs in the uppermost part of the mature tree. The tree is easy to cut down, lightweight and easily moved; the wood is soft, easily hewn, insect and rot resistant, and offers considerable durability. The change to the use of some hardwoods in the second settlement phase was likely governed by the availability of timber suitable for log house construction on specific sites. The change to pine was an imperfect choice because it is knotty, resinous, and rots relatively easily, but by the late 1880 until the 1930s it was probably the only sizeable and otherwise suitable timber remaining for log construction in this part of Appalachia.

Double-Pen Houses

Double-pen houses are represented by three subtypes: the basic double-pen, the saddlebag, and the dogtrot house. All double-pen houses are characterized by having two units or pens placed side to side so that the house is one room deep, two rooms wide, and a single story high. Chimney placement, the number of chimneys, and the spacing of pens are the traits that differentiate the subtypes.

The basic double-pen house, also called the Cumberland house, is characterized by having two adjacent pens, two gable chimneys, and usually, as in Figure 6-6, two front doors.[50] Optional windows, front and back porches, and an attached kitchen in back complete the structure. The house may be constructed of logs or of sawn planks, but like other small folk houses in southern Appalachia, it is rarely built of brick or stone.

In the surveys taken in Alabama, Tennessee, and North Carolina, the Cumberland house is poorly represented. Wilson's study in Alabama revealed only eight such houses; these represented various construction methods: three had half-dovetail notches, two were V-notched, one had square notches, and two were of frame construction.[51] No Cumberland houses were found in Union County, Tennessee. In adjacent Grainger County, our 1979 survey found six. However, the analysis covered only log single-pen houses.[52] The Guilford County, North Carolina surveys revealed ten houses of the basic double-pen type, with three log houses built with V-notches and seven houses of frame construction.[53] A major reason for the scarcity of this dwelling type in the areas of these surveys is that basic double-pens are more com-

Fig. 6-6 Basic double-pen or Cumberland house in framed, sawn lumber with a single exterior chimney, Grainger County, Tennessee. (Photo by J. Rehder.)

monly found on the western margins of Appalachia in the Cumberland and Allegheny Plateau regions. From there, the double-pen house type can be traced westward into the Nashville Basin, to Arkansas, and beyond. Another reason it was not found in the surveys is that the Alabama and Tennessee compilations were focused on log houses. The basic double-pen house in those areas appears more frequently in later time periods and in wood framing with sawn or milled boards, rather than log construction.

The saddlebag double-pen house is characterized by a single central chimney with a pen to each side. As with other multipen structures, the house could be built first as a single pen, with the second pen added at a later time (Fig. 6-7).[54] The saddlebag house gets its name from the imaginative conception of the chimney pile as a horse and the pens on each side as saddlebags. This house type, too, has a limited representation in the sampled surveys. In Alabama, the thirteen saddlebag houses comprised four of log (full-dovetail, half-dovetail, and V-notches) and nine of frame construction.[55] The Union County survey revealed six saddlebag houses, all built with half-dovetail notches.[56] In Guilford County, two saddlebag houses had V-notches and one had half-dovetail.[57] In eastern Kentucky, Carlisle's detailed study of the Paintsville Lake Dam area included three log saddlebag houses built between 1836 and 1865. Indicative of the evolutionary process in pen construction and of changing timber choices, one saddlebag had an older pen built in 1860 with half-dovetailed yellow poplar logs, while the second pen was built after 1865 with pine logs in a mixture of half-dovetail, V-, and square notches.[58] At a later time and in other places, framed saddlebag

John B. Rehder

Fig. 6-7 A saddlebag house with pens built at different times and using different construction techniques, Grainger County, Tennessee. (Photo by J. Rehder.)

houses were more frequent than log saddlebags, although the surveys in this case may be inadequate to support firm conclusions.

The dogtrot house is composed of two pens separated by an open-air passage, with a common roof covering all (Fig. 6-8). Outside end chimneys occupy the outer gables. Doors may be on the front, but more often the doors to each pen are in the open passage, called the dogtrot. Curiously, unlike other folk houses, whose names may be applied by scholars, the dogtrot is well known as such by folk in the regions where it is found.

In twenty-five years of examining southern mountain landscapes, I have found the dogtrot to be virtually nonexistent north of Virginia, and very scarce east of the Blue Ridge Mountains. The house has a spotty distribution in Kentucky, with some occurrence in central and southern, and especially western, Kentucky.[59] Although rare in east Tennessee, the dogtrot is well represented in the Nashville Basin and becomes increasingly frequent westward into Arkansas and the Missouri Ozarks, and southward across much of Alabama, Mississippi, northern and western (non-French) Louisiana and into central Texas.

The origin of the dogtrot house type is uncertain. Jordan and Kaups, Wright, and other investigators attribute it to Scandinavian origins.[60] Kniffen observed that the dogtrot house first appeared in southeastern Tennessee.[61] Wilson found a preponderance of dogtrot examples in northern Alabama.[62] Richard Hulan, looking at dogtrots in middle Tennessee, suggested that one should seek the origins for the house type in the Bluegrass Basin of Kentucky, settled by "old-fashioned Virginians."[63] In 1968, Glassie felt that the dogtrot was an Appalachian variation of the hall-and-parlor

Fig. 6-8 Dogtrot house with an open "dogtrot" breezeway between the two pens, Jackson County, Alabama. (Photo by J. Rehder.)

house from the English-settled tidewater region.[64] To date, no one has studied the dogtrot house in sufficient depth to reach an accepted conclusion about its origin. As these and other folk structures disappear from the landscape, the future work of the scholar who accepts this most important task will be made more difficult.

I-Houses

Closely related to the pen tradition is the I-house, a structure two full stories high, two rooms wide, and one room deep (Fig. 6-9). If any folk house in America can claim to be ubiquitous, it might be the I-house, whose distribution extends very widely across the United States. It may be found from Pennsylvania to northern Florida, to southwestern Louisiana and Texas, and all over the Midwest. The house appears occasionally in Utah, Washington, Oregon, and even in California.[65]

In Appalachia, I-houses have a special meaning on the landscape.[66] Kniffen suggested that the I-house represented a degree of rural opulence, a symbol of economic attainment in the Upland South, a region well known for its poverty.[67] His conclusions were supported by James O'Malley, whose study of I-houses in northeastern Tennessee indicated that they could be directly correlated to large landholdings, best soils, and gentle slopes.[68]

I-houses may be built of hewn logs, rounded logs, sawn lumber, brick, or stone. In a sample of 50 I-houses in portions of Grainger, Knox, and Sevier counties in eastern Tennessee, Karen Rehder found 41 I-houses constructed with framed sawn lumber, 8 of brick construction, and one stone I-house.[69] In Union County, 4 log I-houses, all with half-dovetail notches, appeared in

Fig. 6-9 An I-house that demonstrates past opulence, Grainger County, Tennessee. (Photo by J. Rehder.)

our 1979 comprehensive survey.[70] In Guilford County 116 I-houses were surveyed of which 8 were brick, 23 of logs weatherboarded, and 85 of frame construction.[71] Such surveys indicate the frequency of this house type, the general periods of construction between the 1790s and 1920, choice of building materials, and the survivability of I-houses in the Appalachian region.

Unlike the uncertain origins for other folk house types, that for the I-house points clearly to the British Isles.[72] Jordan found I-houses in the Fenno-Scandian source area but suggested a probable British origin for the I-house in America.[73] Outside gable chimneys are English traits, both in the tidewater region of North America and in England. The I-house in Appalachia, in terms of form, dimensions, gable-end chimney placements, and other diagnostic features, points conclusively to influence from the British Isles.

Four-Pen Houses

A final house type consists of four rooms on each of two floors (Fig. 6-10). Two versions exist, the simpler consists of just four rooms and the other has piles of rooms separated by a central hall. This house type has not been studied in Appalachia and its connection to the pen housing tradition is conjectural. As the largest house on the Appalachian vernacular landscape, the four-pen house signifies the highest degree of opulence in this otherwise poor part of America. Consequently, four-pen houses are scarce and are built of framed, sawn lumber or often of brick. They are relatively rare in stone and are never built of logs. While it is feasible to build I-houses and smaller structures with horizontal logs, it is quite a difficult undertaking to build a four-pen, two-story log house.[74]

Fig. 6-10 Four-pen house in Grainger County, Tennessee.
(Photo by J. Rehder.)

Barns and Outbuildings

The vernacular landscapes of Appalachia also display a distinct series of rustic barns and small outbuildings. Barns, much like houses, have an evolutionary pattern that proceeds from single cribs to double-crib, to four-crib, to transverse-crib barns.[75]

The single-crib barn is a one-unit structure built to store corn or other grain. Some single-cribs also provide shelter for farm implements with an overhanging gear shed (Fig. 6-11). Not all single-cribs have the gear shed, but the functions of storage and protection are constant.

The double-crib barn represents an expansion to two cribs or units separated by an open passage. Some double-crib barns have the superficial appearance of dogtrot houses, but the two structures do not share the same geographic distribution in the Upland South. However, Jordan notes a close correlation between double-pen houses and double-crib barns in Sweden.[76]

The four-crib barn represents a further expansion to a barn with a crib on each of four corners (Fig. 6-12). Open passageways crossing at the center separate the four cribs and a gabled roof covers the entire structure. Another method of expansion is the use of three or four joined cribs on each side of a central passage to create a transverse-crib barn. Both the four-crib and the transverse-crib barns are considered original American barn types, but with linkages through the single-crib barn to western Europe.[77]

Beyond the evolution of cribs lies the forebay barn. The diagnostic fea-

Fig. 6-11 Single-crib barn with gear shed, Grainger County, Tennessee. The roof was repaired and, unfortunately, remodeled after the photo was taken. (Photo by J. Rehder.)

Fig. 6-12 Four-crib barn, a restored structure rebuilt with original logs, Cherokee Orchard Road, Great Smoky Mountains National Park, Sevier County, Tennessee. (Photo by J. Rehder.)

ture is an overhanging loft or forebay that allows hay to be delivered from the loft to the barnyard. Forebay barns, also called cantilever barns, may have log cribs as support foundations. In a survey in east Tennessee, Moffett and Wodehouse discovered ninety-five log, two-crib, cantilever barns. Notch types were overwhelmingly half-dovetail, on sixty-nine of the structures.[78] One problem in barn type identification is that sawn lumber used as weatherboarding covers the expanded outer parts of many log barns. An enormous weatherboarded barn with a huge loft may be supported beneath by a pair of small cantilevered double-cribs for the foundation.

Appalachian forebay barns, smaller in the southern Appalachians than in the northern part of the region, trace to the German settled areas of rural Pennsylvania, where huge forebay barns dominate the landscape. They have been further traced to European source areas in central and eastern Switzerland, specifically to Canton Graubunden.[79]

The small outbuildings of the vernacular landscape have more variety in their function than in their form. They are characteristically used for smokehouses, root or apple houses, spring houses, dairy or milk houses, wash houses, and for other specialized storage or protection functions (Fig. 6-13). While most small outbuildings have one level, those built into steep slopes may have two levels with a stone root cellar and a wooden upper level. The form of a typical small outbuilding is that of a single square or rectangular crib, measuring about 12′ × 14′, with a front-facing gable, and a roof overhang at the gable entrance to provide shelter to the door.

John B. Rehder

114

Fig. 6-13 Spring house near Powder Springs, Grainger County, Tennessee. (Photo by J. Rehder.)

Fig. 6-14 Smokehouse showing characteristic white salt residue on the lower logs, Grainger County, Tennessee. This smokehouse was destroyed and used for firewood in the winter of 1978–79. (Photo by J. Rehder.)

In Grainger County, Tennessee, we analyzed twenty-six log smoke-houses as a part of a comprehensive historic buildings survey (Fig. 6-14). The smallest smokehouse measured 7'10" × 10'3"; the largest was square with 16'9" dimensions. Smokehouses with half-dovetail notches totaled 19, while six were V-notched and one was square-notched. Although many smoke-houses remain in the county, only one was still functioning as originally intended for the salt curing and smoking of pork.[80]

Other Landscape Traits

The Appalachian landscape contains other material folk features that carry cultural identities and values. On farmsteads, fields bounded by split rail fences give character to the landscape. The folk fences of Appalachia appeared in several forms: snake or worm (Fig. 6-15), stake and rider, post and rail, buck or reindeer (Fig. 6-16) fences, as well as stone walls. All but the stone fences were of wooden split rails; all enclosed agricultural fields. The snake fence was most widely used because it was light, portable, and effectively prevented livestock from entering cultivated fields. Rail fences met their demise after the introduction of barbed and smooth wire, and after the chestnut blight that destroyed American chestnut forests in the 1930s eliminated the building material for many of these fences.

Throughout Appalachia, water-powered mills, country stores, grave-yards, and bridges, fords, and ferries for crossing streams added to the landscape melange. Gristmills served as focal points for the exchange of goods, services, and gossip (Fig. 6-17). Later, country stores took up much the same

Fig. 6-15 Snake, worm, or zig-zag fence in Tazewell County, Virginia. (Photo by J. Rehder.)

John B. Rehder

functions, but with different forms and locations. The family graveyard, located on a farmstead knoll planted with evergreen trees to symbolize eternal life, also symbolized independence, as few church cemeteries and even fewer commercial cemeteries existed. Stream crossings offered yet another set of vernacular structures. Folk bridges took the forms of swinging cable bridges, foot logs, and others. Fords and ferries also continued in use until state and county governments accepted the responsibility of road and bridge building and maintenance in the 1930s and thereafter.[81]

In the late nineteenth century, coal mining created additional cultural landscapes in rural Appalachia.[82] Coal mine camps, coal loading tipples, railroad beds, mine shafts, and villagelike company towns with cheap board-and-batten frame houses wore everpresent coal dust coveralls and created a distinctive landscape expression of impersonal exploitation and poverty.

Fig. 6-16 This type of rail fence, variously called buck, reindeer, "Irish," Shanghai, and other names, is very rare in Appalachia. This one is in Floyd County, Virginia. (Photo by J. Rehder.)

Fig. 6-17 The Mabry gristmill on the Blue Ridge Parkway, Floyd County, Virginia, is one of the most photographed mills in America. (Photo by J. Rehder.)

The Ethnicity of the Landscape Contribution

Throughout this chapter, a search for origins of landscape traits has been paramount, as we have sought to analyze, synthesize, and explain the presence of certain vernacular landscape traits. Now we must connect these unraveling pieces of the landscape tapestry.

The English contribution is impressive, when one considers total influence. The metes and bounds survey system set the imprint of property into surface patterns of conspicuous complexity. House types evolved basically following the English pen tradition. The English influence is very strong for those houses with external chimneys. The I-house especially, traces to an English homeland. The controversial question of the origins of corner notching in log construction remains to be finally decided, but either German or Scandinavian sources, or both, are most likely. What were the landscape elements attributed to the majority of Appalachia's population? The dispersed settlement patterns and the sprawling arrangement of outbuildings on individual farms find identity with Northern Ireland and Scotland. Likewise, floor plan, size, rectangular shape, and off-set door opening have Scotch-Irish origins.

For some aspects of the vernacular landscape, the analysis is more open to question. Instead of seeking specific origins for individual vernacular landscape traits through cultural diffusion, we should also interpret the landscape for specific times and locations from the understanding and point of view of acculturation and, for some traits, from the perspective of independent invention. That is, we should recognize that many diagnostic traits attributed to Appalachia were indeed borrowed from other immigrant European cultures. Jordan and Kaups argue persuasively for a Karelian connection for many frontier cultural traits.[83] Furthermore, it is not too hard to believe that some folk settlers of Appalachia could have invented traits of their own, such as the dogtrot house type and the four-crib and transverse-crib barn types.

Geographers, folklorists, and other students of Appalachian folk culture may have been too quick to accept tradition as the full and complete explanation for all things folk. The Scotch-Irish were, and still are to an extent, a tradition-bound culture; but bound by what traditions and over what time period and place? We have already demonstrated that seventeenth-century Scotch-Irish immigrants were quick to adopt a completely foreign system of log construction techniques. They also adapted to a changing diet based on the marvelous variety of food and drink derivatives from corn. Throughout the settlement history of Appalachia, cultural traits were invented, introduced, borrowed, and kept. Common sense, as much as any cultural tradition, may explain many of the nagging questions that continue to be asked about the vernacular landscapes of Appalachia.

*John B.
Rehder*

7

American Indians in the Eastern United States

Frank W. Porter III

THE TRADITIONAL scenario of the process of acculturation of American Indians in the eastern United States, as well as the rest of North America, depicts two cultures—the aboriginal culture and the European culture—coming into direct, physical contact. This interaction resulted in major and permanent changes in the aboriginal culture. Such a highly ethnocentric perspective does not provide an accurate portrayal of what actually transpired. First, there never was a uniform or homogeneous aboriginal culture in the eastern United States. Major differences in language, settlement pattern, social organization, and material culture clearly distinguished the various tribal groups that occupied this vast and varied geographic landscape. Second, there never existed a transplanted "European culture" in the eastern United States. Instead, representatives from specific European countries—special interest groups, distinctive religious bodies, and potential settlers from varied backgrounds—emigrated to the New World, bringing with them their own unique motives, goals, and objectives, not to mention cultures. Furthermore, they arrived in the eastern United States at different times and places.[1] Such a complex situation is not easily explained by simply referring to it as the inevitable result of cultural contact and change.[2]

Acculturation of American Indians

There is a different perspective with regard to the process of acculturation. It clearly suggests that there was direct, and at times indirect, contact between two types of cultures, but this interaction occurred repeatedly among various specific cultures. The conditions surrounding their contact differed through time and from place to place. Admittedly, an almost immediate consequence of this contact among many of the smaller groups was the fragmentation of their tribal cultures. Communicable diseases, war, displacement, migration, confinement to reservations, and even passive resistance severely disrupted and altered the tribal cultures, because of a decline in population, a change in land tenure and settlement pattern and location of residences, a change in social and political organization, and an interruption of traditional subsistence activities. The final result produced a fragmented remnant of once complete cultures.

In time, most of these small isolated groups assimilated into White society to such a degree that they became virtually indistinguishable from their counterparts of Euro-American ancestry. The common pattern of acculturation among these groups was to borrow Euro-American traits and institutions and to blend them into a context of the older Indian way of life. Many anthropologists interpret such a situation as a survival of only fragments, of incomplete entities. D'Arcy McNickle strongly criticized such a myopic point of view and declared, "Any people at any time is a survival of fragments out of the past. The function of culture is always to reconstitute the fragments into a functioning whole. The Indians, for all that has been lost or rendered useless out of their ancient experience, remain a continuing ethnic cultural enclave, with a stake in the future."[3]

In their paper "The Integration of Americans of Indian Descent," Dozier, Simpson, and Yinger argued, "the place of Indians in American society may be seen as one aspect of the question of the integration of minority groups into the social system."[4] A significant key to understanding the process of integration of these surviving Indian communities into White society is to determine the changes that did occur in their aboriginal form of land tenure. Prolonged exposure to Euro-American culture assuredly altered the American Indians' concept of land tenure. Through time, those isolated, fragmented groups of Indians who chose to remain near their traditional habitats after their tribes were coerced from ancestral lands either borrowed or were taught or forced to accept specific facets of the Euro-American system of land tenure.[5]

Coincident with these changes in the aboriginal system of land tenure was the development of new Indian communities in the midst of a numerically superior White society. In addition, these surviving Indians gradually expressed a new attitude toward the physical environment and the technological means of exploiting its resources. In many respects the socio-economic activities in which these Indians participated and which were imprinted on the landscape during the nineteenth century are strikingly similar to those of the ethnic groups who emigrated from Europe, as they also struggled to become landholders. From a methodological point of view, any attempt to understand the changing pattern of land tenure, the formation and growth of new communities, and the process of the integration of Indians into White society during the nineteenth century and continuing to the present must utilize the same historical sources that are available for comparable studies of other ethnic groups in the eastern United States.

Myth of the Vanishing Indian

After more than a century of contact with European settlers, most of the tribes inhabiting the Atlantic seaboard had experienced a dramatic decline in population. In many instances these tribes were depicted as having become extinct. Henry Knox, the first federal official to have responsibility for Indian affairs, observed, "It is painful to consider that all the Indian tribes existing in those states now the best cultivated and most populous, have become extinct."[6] Behind this general acceptance of the eventual disappear-

Frank W.
Porter III

120

ance of the Indian firmly rested the belief that the Indian could not, or would not, adopt the White civilization. Sir Jeffrey Amherst echoed the sentiments of many Europeans and colonists when he declared, "I wish there was not an Indian settlement within a thousand Miles of this Country; for they are only fit to Live with the Inhabitants of the Woods, being more nearly Allied to the *Brute* than the *Human Creation*."[7] The Reverend Jedidiah Morse, commissioned by the president of the United States to report on Indian affairs in 1820, advised the Six Nations of Iroquois that they could not, "many years longer, live in any part of the United States, in the *hunter-state*."[8]

Several European travelers who visited the American colonies and fortuitously recorded their observations and experiences conveyed clearly the impression that the Indians were a vanishing people. Jaspar Danckearts, journeying through Maryland in 1679 and 1680, remarked: "There are few Indians in comparison with the extent of the country. When the English first discovered and settled Virginia and Maryland, they did great [wrong] to these poor people, and almost exterminated them."[9] François A. R. Chateaubriand similarly observed that "the Piscataways of Maryland; the tribes who obeyed Powhatan in Virginia; the Paroutis in the Carolinas—all these people have disappeared."[10]

The nineteenth century authorities were no less convinced that the American Indian in the eastern United States was on the verge of extinction. Scattered throughout magazines and periodicals published in the nineteenth century are articles about "the *last* surviving Indian" of the eastern United States. C. S. Rafinesque, for example, briefly discussed what he called "The Last Indians of New Jersey." Colonel D. Mead, in 1822, described "The Last Indians of Virginia" as a few individual Pamunkeys. Benson J. Lossing, in his testimonial "The Last of the Pequods," offered a slightly different twist. "Art, history, and romance have touchingly depicted that rare, melancholy person, the last of *his* race or nation, but have yet failed to portray that rare, melancholy being, the last of *her* race or nation," observed Lossing as he recounted his visit with Eunice Mahwee—"the last of the Pequods." Nathan Lewis, in a similar vein, described "The Last of the Narragansetts."[11]

Despite the rather grim tale penned by these early chroniclers, and the off-hand acceptance of the demise of the Indian by later generations, Indians in the eastern United States were by no means a vanishing race. The history of Indians in the eastern United States after contact with Whites must be viewed from the perspective of change and survival. After that contact, many tribes made adjustments (accommodations) to an ever-changing White culture. Some were successful; others were not.[12] The cultures of the American Indians have never been static. They have changed through time and at differing rates.

Origins of Surviving Indian Communities

During the greater part of the nineteenth century little attention was paid to the possible existence of small enclaves of Indians in the eastern United States. When, in the twentieth century, scholars finally did recognize and acknowledge the continued presence of Indians in this region, they did so with the assumption and belief that they were dealing with mixed-bloods, mestizos, or triracial isolates.[13] These Indian people, considered to be part

*American
Indians
in the
Eastern
United States*

121

White with varying proportions of Indian and Negro ancestry, were assigned a marginal social status. Who are these Indian people? How did they survive to the present?

In many instances the origin of surviving Indian communities in the eastern United States is unknown and unlikely ever to be determined. The most common opinion and widely accepted interpretation is that they formed through miscegenation between Indians, Caucasians, and Negroes. Many of these groups have to some degree been studied by scholars, but far too many others have been victimized in the publications of untrained laymen. Brewton Berry, in *Almost White: A Study of Certain Racial Hybrids in the Eastern United States*, accomplished the first serious and comprehensive survey of these isolated communities. It is not surprising that he confirmed the general confusion among the White and Black populations as to the origins of these people.[14] Recently, a small number of these communities have been investigated with rather interesting and, in some cases, startling conclusions.[15]

Although these Indian communities are scattered throughout the eastern United States, they frequently developed where environmental circumstances such as forbidding swamps or inaccessible and barren country favored their growth. It is difficult to locate one of these communities that is not associated with a swamp, a hollow, a remote mountain ridge, or the back country of a sandy flatwoods.[16] The remoteness and isolation of these settlements helped to maintain enforced and self-imposed social distance between White and Blacks and Indians. The habitat of these people, geographically and culturally isolated, was also typically rural. A majority of the people were involved in hunting, fishing, subsistence agriculture, lumbering, and collecting of herbs and roots.

The traditional habitats in which these small, isolated bands of Indians continued to reside during the eighteenth century became the focus of new communities, which grew and developed throughout the nineteenth century. Significantly, the events surrounding their earlier relationship with White society in the seventeenth and eighteenth centuries influenced, and in some cases determined, whether or not these new communities would be able to withstand the tremendous pressures exerted upon them by a hostile and racially biased White society during the nineteenth century.

Changes in Land Tenure

The antecedents of the idea of placing Indians in communities patterned after the Euro-American settlements are to be found in the colonial period. In several of the southern colonies, authorities repeatedly attempted to relocate entire tribes, to make them buffer zones between the tidewater settlements and the hostile tribes who resided in the back country.[17] In 1713, Governor Alexander Spotswood of Virginia recommended a plan for securing the frontiers with settlements of tributary Indians. Scattered tribes and bands would be consolidated in units at strategic points. In addition to being in a better position to resist attacks, the Indians would be more accessible to missionaries and teachers. Spotswood attempted to dispel any apprehension on the part of the Indians by explaining that they would have "a large tract of land to hunt in, a body of English to live among them and instruct their chil-

Frank W. Porter III

dren in literature and the principles of Christianity, to bring them to a more civilized and plentiful manner of living, and to establish a constant intercourse of trade between them and the inhabitants of this colony."[18] The Indians, in turn, would acknowledge their dependency on the king of England and were to hold their land by confirmed patents under the seal of the colony.[19]

In Maryland, the Piscataway Indians relinquished land to Governor Calvert and his settlers and agreed to move their villages northwest along the Potomac River. In this way, they would serve as a buffer between the Susquehannock Indians and the growing settlement at St. Mary's City. In return, they were to receive protection, provided by Governor Calvert.[20] In North Carolina, South Carolina, and Georgia, colonial authorities—forced to concentrate on large, powerful, and independent tribes—were not as successful in creating tributary tribes. They had the friendship of the larger tribes, vital to the security and welfare of these colonies, and that made establishing tributary tribes of Indians less important than it was in the Middle Atlantic region.

The practice of using tributary Indians for protection did not prove to be successful, and the ultimate result of being tributary Indians was, unfortunately, detrimental. Traditional settlement systems were altered, subsistence activities were severely disrupted, and economic and political relationships with neighboring tribes were rearranged.[21]

Using Indians as tributaries caused a major departure from aboriginal systems of land tenure. Beginning in the middle of the seventeenth century and continuing into the eighteenth century, several tribes throughout the colonies were placed on permanent reservations. These reservations—as administrative units—became a form of property which incorporated European adaptations of aspects of aboriginal land tenure and changes generated by colonial administrative practice and law. Significantly, permanent residence on reservations proved in many cases to be unsatisfactory for those tribes whose subsistence strategy reflected an economic adjustment to differing ecological zones. The success of their subsistence efforts depended entirely upon freedom of mobility and access to microenvironments within their habitat at critical seasons of the year.

Two mutually related problems developed from permanent residence on reservations. Reservations had been created with the explicit understanding that the Indians would reside within specific boundaries. After relatively brief periods of time, food resources (both flora and fauna) became sorely depleted. Forced to seek game outside the reservation, the Indians temporarily abandoned their dwellings. White settlers, interpreting this act as a violation of the reservation agreements, took possession of the land. Although some of these reservations have survived in the eastern United States, albeit reduced in size, many of the tribes lost or permanently abandoned their last vestige of land.

There were also attempts by missionaries to convert Indians and bring them together in small settlements where they would receive academic education and learn new skills. In New England the "praying towns" were artificially bounded communities within which heterogeneous groups of Indians were purposely isolated from encroachment by Whites. The purpose in establishing these towns was to facilitate control of the Indians by colonial authorities and to create an easily accessible population for the missionaries. Neal Salisbury has aptly observed that "the Algonquians who converted were those whose communal integrity had been compromised step-by-step—from the plague of 1616 to the treaties of political submission—and whose sources of collective identity and individual social stature had been destroyed."[22] Although the "praying towns" conformed outwardly to the dictums of the missionaries, they inwardly preserved much of their traditional belief system.[23]

One of the most notable examples of missionary activity in the Middle Atlantic region was the work of Reverend David Brainerd among the remnant groups of Indians in New Jersey. When Brainerd visited the Indians living at Crossweeksung in New Jersey, he found only a small number "and perceived the Indians in these Parts were very much scattered, there being not more than two or three Families in a Place, and these small Settlements six, ten, fifteen, twenty and thirty Miles and some more, from the Place I was then at." As a result of Brainerd's work among the Indians, they gathered "together from all Quarters to this place, and have built them little Cottages, so that more than Twenty Families live within a Quarter of a Mile of me." Within a short time, Brainerd excitedly exclaimed, "My people [went] out this Day upon the Design of clearing some of their Lands above fifteen Miles distant from this Settlement, *in Order to Their Settling there in a compact Form* [my italics], where they might be under Advantages of attending the public Worship of God, of having their Children Schooled, and at the same time a conveniency of Planting."[24] The Brotherton Indians, as residents of this community were called, remained "civilized" only as long as the Reverend David Brainerd and, upon his death, his brother John, were present.

Despite the efforts—in creating tributary tribes, reservations, and mission settlements—to bring the Indians together into compact settlements and to teach them new skills, by the close of the nineteenth century the general consensus was that the aboriginal population of the eastern United States could not, or would not, assimilate into White society.

Indian Removal

Between 1789 and 1820, the United States was neither strong enough militarily nor secure enough in its new role as a nation among nations to engage the Indians by force. The federal government pursued a policy virtually dictated by the military circumstances of the period: to make treaties with the Indian nations. Through the treaty process the United States acquired not only lands but also legal responsibilities to the Indians.

There was another important development during this period. The Louisiana Purchase in 1803 and the acquisition of Florida between 1812 and 1819 doubled the size of the United States. With the addition of new territory the problem of regulating trade with the Indians became even more difficult. Thomas Jefferson, ever aware of the deleterious effect on the Indians of contact between them and White society, proposed an amendment to the Constitution in 1803 to exchange Indian land east of the Mississippi River for land west of the river.[25] Although he was unsuccessful, the idea soon became a modus vivendi in government circles.

In 1830 Congress enacted the Removal Bill, which empowered the president of the United States to transfer any eastern tribe to areas west of the Mississippi River. Although the bill did not mention the use of coercion to remove the Indians, it was apparently understood that military force would be necessary. The tragic story of the "Trails of Tears" need not be recounted here. During the remaining years of the 1830s, most of the tribes in the eastern United States were removed. But what of those who chose to remain in their ancestral land? Those who soon were forgotten?

Behind the Frontier

The removal of the Indians east of the Mississippi was not complete. Groups of Indians, who for several reasons remained behind, were scattered throughout the eastern United States. Forgotten or neglected by Whites, they retained a sense of their Indian identity, gradually reconstituted a form of social organization and land tenure, and maintained a spatially defined presence on the landscape. I have identified three types of communities of Indians that survived and developed in the eastern United States during the eighteenth and nineteenth centuries: reservation communities, missionary communities, and folk communities.[26]

Reservation Communities

Reservation communities were able to survive as long as they retained possession of their land. Maintaining a land base was not an easy task. Of the several dozen reservations created in the eastern United States, only twenty-five are still in existence (Fig. 7-1). There are twenty state reservations and five federal. These reservations are in Connecticut, Florida, Maine, Massachusetts, New York, North Carolina, and Virginia.[27] Most of the general public is unaware of these Indian enclaves. It is only when land disputes erupt that public attention is drawn to them, as in the Passamaquoddy lawsuit in Maine in the 1970s.

Missionary Communities

The continued success of the Brotherton community was entirely dependent upon the energy and devotion of David and John Brainerd. After their deaths there was no one to take their place, and the community's reason for existence was gone. The Natick Indians, once a successful experiment in assimilation, were practically extinct by 1848. After 1810, they had a legal guardian, who supervised the sale of the last of their land in 1828. The Stockbridge Indians, who were greatly influenced by the missionary work of John Sargeant, had also attempted an experiment in Indian-White town living. By 1789, the Whites had forced the Indians out of the town of Stockbridge, Massachusetts. This group of Stockbridge Indians moved to Wisconsin in the early nineteenth century and created a new and viable community.[28]

Folk Communities

By the beginning of the nineteeth century, Indians throughout the eastern United States had been exposed to virtually every facet of Euro-American land tenure, economic activities, and religious practices. Increas-

American
Indians
in the
Eastern
United States

125

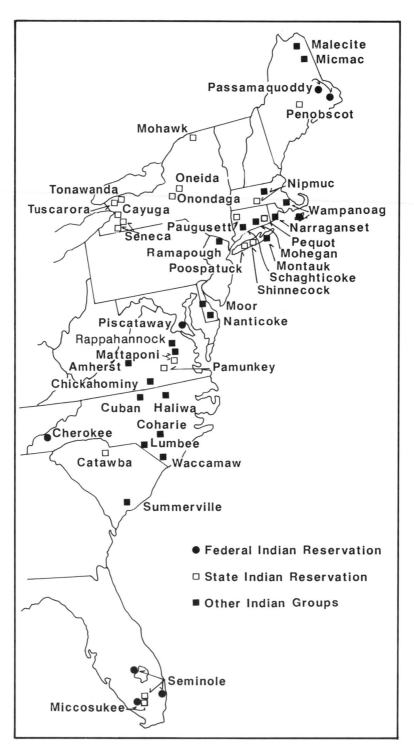

Fig. 7-1 Federal and state Indian reservations in the eastern United States in 1991

ingly, much of the Indian's material and nonmaterial culture was abandoned as it became more difficult for these remnant groups to survive in a White society. Because of the tremendous changes effected by Whites in the cultural landscape prior to 1800, the only economic system and viable form of land tenure in which the Indians could successfully participate was that practiced by Whites.

Folk communities developed as these surviving Indians began gradually to participate in the Euro-American form of land tenure. In many respects a folk community is quite similar to a folk society. Drawing upon the work of Redfield,[29] I have defined a folk community as a group (1) small and both socially and spatially isolated from other groups, (2) composed of people much alike in physical appearance, (3) similar in customary modes of behavior, (4) possessing a strong sense of belonging together, (5) with tightly knit social structures and clearly distinguished family relationships; and (6) economically self-sufficient with little class distinction.[30]

Initially, remnant Indian groups chose to reside in remote, isolated places—usually swamps, islands, or out-of-the-way necks of land. After years of exposure to harsh treatment by Euro-Americans, it made sense to these groups to choose sites that would afford them minimal contact with the outside world. These remote sites would have been perceived by contemporary European standards as marginal environments, unfit for large-scale commercial agriculture and lacking adequate transportation links with tidewater ports. In sum, these particular tracts of land served no strategic or economic purpose at the time and were not actively sought after by White settlers.

The maintenance of kinship ties played an extremely important role in the survival of these small, isolated groups. I have argued elsewhere that an analysis of the family hunting territory system offers a significant key to understanding the survival and persistence of these remnant groups.[31] Speck defined the family hunting group as a "kinship group composed of folks united by blood or marriage, having the right to hunt, trap, and fish in a certain inherited district bounded by some rivers, lakes, or other natural landmarks."[32] These family hunting groups had not only ties of kinship but a community of land and interest. The dispersal of small family hunting groups promoted "family isolation and a certain degree of permanency of residence in a particular territory."[33] It is my contention that many of the isolated and remote areas to which the remnant Indian groups dispersed were in fact traditional family hunting territories.

These years of residence in such isolated areas became a time of both self-imposed and externally enforced segregation. The isolation of these Indian groups permitted cultural change to proceed at a slow pace, allowing these groups to integrate selected material and nonmaterial culture of Euro-Americans into their own developing cultures. When they finally emerged from their remote habitats and began to establish folk communities, they usually retained only the knowledge that they were Indian and a social cohesion forged by shared hardship. Being neither White nor Black, by their neighbors they were commonly referred to as "the other people," or by a more disparaging epithet. These Indians had managed to preserve their

American Indians in the Eastern United States

127

identity during their years of isolation, and the racial prejudice directed towards them by unsympathetic Whites served only to strengthen the social bonds within the communities.

Separate and Marginal Racial Status

Almost without exception, the population of these folk communities was assigned a separate and marginal racial status, usually based on their distinct physiognomy. The non-Indian population did not distinguish any differences in the physiognomy of these people. Instead, they considered the Indians to be part of a larger racial classification: Blacks or people of color. However, social scientists who later visited these communities noted that phenotypic variation was present, with extremes of skin from light to dark and of hair from very curly to straight.

Because of the strong racial prejudice directed toward Indian folk communities, there has been a prevalent pattern of endogamous marriages. The Brandywine community (composed of Piscataway Indians) of southern Maryland is one of the few folk communities in which a detailed and thorough analysis of the kinship system has been performed. Among the Piscataway, the majority of marriage partners have been drawn from persons having one of fifteen surnames. Using baptismal and marriage records, Harte has identified seven family lines which constitute the *core* of the community. The other eight families, identified by Harte as *marginal* families, married into the groups some time later than 1870. There is no record prior to 1850 of an intermarriage between a core family and a marginal family, reflecting the significant degree of endogamy.[34]

It has been proposed that the Piscataway population had its early eighteenth-century origin in cross-racial unions, which were forbidden by colonial law. For the years 1702 through 1720, the Charles County court records mention nine convictions for producing illegitimate children with Piscataway surnames. All of these, with the exception of one marginal name, were females with core surnames. After 1720 there is an absence of additional indictments or convictions of persons with Piscataway names. Harte concludes that "these people (the original offenders and their offspring) had already isolated themselves from Whites and Negroes by segregating themselves into remote communities.[35] The evidence strongly suggests that all of them retired to isolated locations in southern Maryland. Today, they are collectively identified as the Piscataway Indians. However, they are also extremely factionalized, with at least three different communities claiming to be the descendants of the Piscataway Indians.[36] Endogamy is prevalent in almost every one of the folk communities of the eastern United States.

During these years of isolation, the Indians sought to exercise their traditional means of exploiting the land for foodstuffs. Their ability to subsist successfully diminished as more land was cleared for agricultural use by Whites. White population expansion during the nineteenth century engulfed the folk communities. Subsistence needs could no longer be satisfied by aboriginal strategies. Indian men, when so inclined, sought wage work on White-owned farms, at lumber mills, or in other light industries. Hunting and fishing remained the most important activities. The women sold produce from small gardens and sold or bartered various handcrafted items to

*Frank W.
Porter III*

128

Fig. 7-2 Cherokee pottery makers in North Carolina in 1888. (Courtesy Smithsonian Institution, National Anthropological Archives.)

local merchants and peddlers (Fig. 7-2). Through time, the Indians gained an intimate knowledge of the legal, social, economic, and political institutions of White society.

Participation in these institutions was not always achieved without conflict or hostility. During the nineteenth century and even into the twentieth century, the White population recognized only two classes of people: White or non-White. Unwilling, in many instances, to accept individuals claiming Indian ancestry, Whites subjected Indians to segregation in schooling, religious practices, residence, and social activities. The public school became the battleground for Indians in the eastern United States, for it was there that the question of their racial identity was explicitly challenged. In those states where Indians were most numerous, they were excluded from the White schools, and only under extreme duress would they attend schools for Blacks. In some communities, Indians constructed and maintained their own schools; elsewhere, missionaries provided education for them, or special schools were established by states, or they simply did not attend school at all. Despite this racial prejudice, Indian communities throughout the eastern United States fought for and won the right to have their own educational facilities. The North Carolina Lumbee's struggle to have schools of their own became the foundation for their pride, dignity, and recognition as an identifiable race.[37]

Racial prejudice among Whites also prevented many Indians from at-

American Indians in the Eastern United States

tending church. Many Indian communities established and maintained their own churches. In southern Maryland, the Piscataway attended the same Catholic church as Blacks and Whites, but they were relegated to a particular section of the church building. Unfortunately, the influence of the church in the development of eastern Indian communities has not been adequately studied. Although the schools are now integrated, some churches continue to reflect the division among Indian, White, and Black.

Material Culture of Eastern Indians

Racial prejudice has also had an adverse effect on the study of the material culture of American Indians in the eastern United States. As discussed earlier, it has been widely accepted that the majority of the Indian tribes in the eastern United States became extinct by the middle of the nineteenth century. Exceptions, of course, were noted. Anthropologists, however, viewed these particular tribes as "contaminated" because of their presumed extensive interaction with Blacks and Whites. As a result, they also believed that any material culture present in these communities would not be "Indian." Willoughby, for example, noted: "The Algonquians in the early historic days were expert basket makers. The excellence and variety of the old basket work of New England Indians . . . is represented today only by the degenerate splint basketry which is not worthy of a place upon the shelves of museums."[38]

Not everyone felt this way. Anthropologists such as Mooney, Harrington, and Speck made significant efforts to salvage as much as possible of the traditional Indian culture. Recording vestiges of the aboriginal language, collecting examples of traditional arts, crafts, medicinal cures, and folklore were of primary concern because these scholars firmly believed that such information would soon be lost or forgotten. Aside from these few early investigations, very little attention was directed at these communities until after 1930. By that time much of the surviving material culture had long since fallen into disuse and had been replaced by modern technology.

There continues to be an attitude among museum curators, collectors, and researchers that the material culture of eastern American Indians was vastly inferior to the crafts produced by tribes west of the Mississippi River. Most of the material culture of the eastern tribes that has found its way into museum collections remains in drawers or on shelves and is frequently uncataloged. These ethnographic collections are extremely important to our understanding of those eastern American Indian cultures which have vanished from the earth (Figs. 7-3 and 7-4). These artifacts are also significant to our understanding of the processes whereby certain of these tribes managed to withstand complete assimilation into White society. Researchers working in the field with the descendants of the original craftsmen can, in some instances, provide invaluable information about undocumented specimens in museum collections. They may also be able to offer examples of material culture that were not salvaged by the earlier generation of anthropologists.

One of the major problems with the material culture of American Indians in the eastern United States is inventorying it. What is there? How much of it? And where is it? Some collections are concentrated in large museums; and some are scattered widely in small repositories, many of them

Frank W.
Porter III

130

Fig. 7-3 Nanticoke yellow pine basket. Typical of the best workmanship of nineteenth-century eastern Indian groups. (Photo by F. Porter III.)

privately owned. Another obstacle is maintaining the integrity of these collections. They must not be allowed to deteriorate. They should be restored, kept for posterity, studied, and the information disseminated to the public. Furthermore, the philosophy of the collector can significantly influence the perception of the artifact. Collections of material culture can vary in purpose, content, and time frame. Why were certain objects collected? When were they collected? Who collected them? And how have they been studied?

Furthermore, the material culture of American Indians in the eastern United States should not be thought of simply as the preservation of artifacts from the time before Euro-American influence. From the outset, Indians came into possession of many of the material objects brought to the New World by Europeans (Fig. 7-5). The adjustment between the Indian and White cultures depended on the compatibility of cultural patterns. The general point seems to be that the economic relations of Whites and Indians were successful only when the two patterns readily integrated. The specific material culture borrowed by tribal groups can provide insights into how they adjusted to White society.

Fig. 7-4 Nanticoke eel pot. An excellent example of the material culture of a nineteenth-century eastern Indian group. (Photo by F. Porter III.)

Change in house types among the various communities of Indians in the eastern United States has not been thoroughly investigated. During the years of spatial and social isolation from non-Indians, surviving Indian families made a gradual transition from aboriginal to Euro-American types of housing (Figs. 7-6 and 7-7). Nineteenth-century historical records frequently mention Indians living in wigwams and lean-tos. Other families were observed occupying log cabins and simple frame houses. In time, the more successful Indian families purchased large two-story structures as their place of residence. Even then, however, traditional forms of housing remained in use. An unidentified Nanticoke woman from Maryland noted in the early 1950s that she had been born in a thatch-grass wigwam, which was located in back of her parents' "White" (i.e., typical American) house. Apparently there is a connection between this outbuilding structure and menstrual houses. Among the Oklahoma Kickapoo, birth took place near the family's house in a small hut that was also used for secluding menstruating women. Various other architectural structures were imprinted on the cultural landscape of these Indian communities, including log corncribs, longhouses, churches, and schools. Each of these buildings offers significant insight into the acculturation and the socioeconomic integration of Indians into White society during the nineteenth and twentieth centuries in the eastern United States.

Frank W. Porter III

132

Fig. 7-5 Log corn crib on the Isaac Harman farm. (Photo by F. Porter III.) This corn crib exemplifies the blending of American Indian and European cultures, the cultivation, harvesting, and storage of corn being native to the New World and log cabins and other similarly constructed buildings having been introduced into the New World by Scandinavians.

Patterns of sexual differentiation within the tribes may have been influential in determining which items of traditional material culture continued in use. For example, in many tribes the women owned the food, the shelter, and all household utensils. Men owned their hunting, war, and ceremonial equipment. After prolonged contact with White society, Indian warfare and many Indian ceremonies no longer retained as significant a place in tribal culture. Food, shelter, clothing, and household utensils, however, would continue to be essential to the survival of the families. It is not surprising that much of the traditional material culture still in use among the surviving Indian communities in the eastern United States during the nineteenth century and into the twentieth century were in these latter categories.

The periods of isolation that the folk communities achieved during the nineteenth century permitted the development of a communal order. There was a maximum of stability and a minimum of social change. It was during these periods of isolation that the traditional role and activities of the women preserved the integrity of the Indian families. The men continued to hunt and to fish, but they gradually made the transition from subsistence horticulture to commercial agriculture. These new economic activities resulted in the introduction of a vast array of Euro-American material culture into their

Fig. 7-6 An isolated Cherokee home in North Carolina in 1888. (Photo by J. Mooney. Courtesy Smithsonian Institution, National Anthropological Archives, photo no. 1000-B.)

Fig. 7-7 The nineteenth-century Isaac Harman farmhouse, in the Nanticoke community, Sussex County, Delaware, illustrates by its layout and form the adoption by eastern Indian groups of Euro-American cultural traits. (Photo by F. Porter III.)

way of life. The inventories of estates of these families attest to the growing importance of agriculture in their lives.

Summary

This chapter has hinted at some of the processes responsible for the presence of communities of American Indians in the eastern United States. Mission and reservation communities owed their existence to external factors. The development of a folk community was an involved process. Certainly the most important Euro-American institution adopted by the Indians was the notion of private property obtained by legal purchase. What prompted the decision to purchase land will perhaps never be fully ascertained. It would seem that after years of suffering the loss of their land to Whites, purchase of land would have been one of the few alternatives left from which Indians could choose. Whatever their motives, the Indians were able to amass a sufficient land base. Having secured real and personal property, and held together by the bonds of kinship, folk communities developed throughout the eastern United States. Simultaneous with their acquisition of land, the Indians were subjected to the same sort of racial prejudice, hostility, and segregation accorded to Blacks. This racial prejudice served the critical function of intensifying the self-imposed spatial isolation and cultural separation of the Indians in their relationship with the White and Black populations. In turn, the isolation of the Indians permitted cultural change to proceed at a slow pace, allowing the Indians to integrate selected material and nonmaterial Euro-American traits into their own evolving culture.

*American
Indians
in the
Eastern
United States*

135

8

French Creoles on the Gulf Coast

Philippe Oszuscik

FRENCH CREOLE is not always an easy identification to apply, in part because the term *creole* now has many meanings and connotations. Originally, the word was used by colonists of Spanish, French, or other nationality in the Caribbean and Mexican Gulf worlds to identify a person born in the New World rather than in the motherland, and it implied that the European individual had a better education and background. A Creole may have had a full European heritage, an African heritage (in the case of slaves), or a mixed heritage, such as the children of a European and an Amerindian or Black slave.[1] More recently, the term *creole* has been associated only with people having a mixed heritage, especially mixed racial backgrounds.[2] Even from the beginning, those of mixed heritage did constitute a large percentage of Creoles, because the first Europeans were adventurers and military personnel stationed in outposts that did not include European women as part of the initial settlement scheme. In 1702, a vessel arrived in Mobile with twenty-three marriageable young women.[3] This was the first ship with women on board sent to Louisiana, with the exception of a few officer's wives.

French Creole folk housing encompasses all of the housing of the French colonial periods on the Gulf Coast and in the Mississippi Valley plus that of the periods in which the French colonial heritage survived under the rule of the British, Spanish, and Americans into the early twentieth century. The nineteenth century, as will be seen, was a period of considerable ferment in French Creole house design. Today there is a revival of French Creole and Cajun house forms, at least superficially in exterior designs including *galeries*.

This chapter does not attempt to discuss every French Creole house variation. Plantation houses are discussed only when they represent basic plans or variations, and the existence of two-story vernacular urban house types is only briefly mentioned. Those who view folk and vernacular houses as monotonous and repetitive are particularly wrong in the case of the French Creole cottage. The French Creole cottage represents a number of compromises made by diverse groups that included Normans, Canadians, Amerindians, and Africans, although the form has always been dominated by the French influence. As a result of our melting pot culture, variety and surprise are what one can expect to encounter in the Creole landscape.

Historical Background

Unlike some ethnic groups, which migrated directly to the United States from their home countries, French emigrants dispersed in a more complex manner and over an extended period. Most authorities acknowledge that Normandy may have been the main European cultural hearth of the tradition. Adventurous French Normans explored the north Atlantic for fisheries and discovered and settled eastern Canada as early as 1534–1535.[4] Shortly afterwards, the French were contesting Spain's claims to the New World by seizing harbors and islands in the Caribbean. By 1624 the French claimed St. Christopher, and within forty years, Martinique, Grenada, St. Lucia, St. Croix, and the Lesser Antilles, as well as other islands of the Caribbean.[5] By 1629 French buccaneers settled Le Tortue (Turtle Island), off Haiti, and even on the western side of Haiti itself, called San Domingo or Ste. Domingue. Santo Domingo, long the capital of the Spanish Caribbean was on the eastern side of the island.[6] The French chose to live like the native islanders from whom the word *buccaneer* is derived. *Buccaneer* comes from the French, *boucanier,* which in turn comes from Arawak Indian, *boucan,* the Indian cooking spit or grate. Rodman describes buccaneers as a lawless lot of mainly French and English who were independent and acknowledged no sovereign. They hunted the wild cattle and boar left behind by the Spanish, who had deserted some of their western Hispaniola colonies. French and English buccaneers were followed by expatriate Spaniards, Dutch, Indians, and perhaps run-away Black slaves. The French Creole language, which includes words from English, Norman, Arawak, Dutch, Spanish and some African languages, originated in these buccaneer communities.[7]

These buccaneer communities were the cultural hearth not only of the French Creole language, food ways, and other cultural elements, but also of the folk tradition in housing. The French Creole cottage does not have a direct European model but was derived from a complex combination of ideas of the French experience from Normandy, Canada, and the Caribbean territory of the Arawak Indians, and to a lesser extent from African, English, and Spanish sources. The proof of the lesser strains may never be unraveled, as the important transitional cottages no longer exist; but, the major strains offer less debate.

In 1698, Iberville, Bienville Le Moyne, and other Canadian heroes were called to the court of Louis XIV in Paris to organize a secret expedition to colonize the Gulf Coast. However, the Spanish and English heard about it and formed their own expeditions. The Spanish beat the French to the Gulf Coast by two months, since they could outfit an expedition from Mexico. They selected Pensacola, with its deep natural harbor, to settle. Iberville and his men sailed first to Haiti, picked up supplies and crew replacements, who were Creoles, and made their way to the north Gulf Coast (Fig. 8-1). Discovering the Spanish at Pensacola, they sailed on to Dauphin Island and points farther west, finally choosing Ocean Springs, Mississippi for their outpost. Then in 1702 they shifted their colony to Mobile.[8] From these early beginnings numerous new colonies were established, including Kahokia and Kaskaskia, Illinois, ca. 1700; Natchez, Mississippi, ca. 1700; Mississippi Fort, Louisiana, ca. 1700; Natchitoches, Louisiana, ca. 1714; and New Orleans,

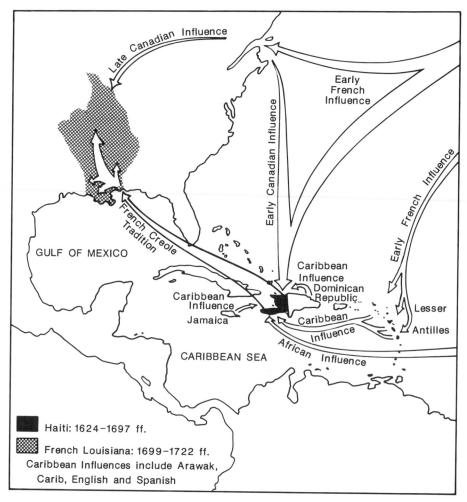

Fig. 8-1 French colonization of the New World

1718. Dauphin Island, Alabama, served as the French port of entry for goods and immigration until ca. 1722, when New Orleans became the capital.[9]

Before 1722, the main character of French culture and housing had already taken a firm hold. Many basic house plan variations existed, one- and two-story houses, with and without galeries. After 1722, newer developments, mainly refinements, spread from New Orleans. Mobile still influenced developments in housing during the 1720s, but slowly its importance declined in colonial Louisiana.

The basic French Creole cottage evolved in Haiti. It was brought to Ocean Springs and Mobile, and from these points it spread to the rest of colonial Louisiana (Fig. 8-2). New ideas absorbed by the French from the Indians will be discussed later. Furthermore, Canadian elements and modifications came primarily from the Le Moynes and their party in the colony rather than from Canadians coming down the Mississippi River.

Philippe Oszuscik

138

Fig. 8-2 French Creole cottage near Latham, Alabama, ca. 1910. (Photo by P. Oszuscik.)

French Settlement in the United States

The land claimed by the French was much more extensive than they could effectively occupy. To remedy this weakness, they purposely designed a scheme to lay claim to as much territory between the English and Spanish worlds as possible.[10] The French spread themselves thinly, but set up outposts at the limits of their claims. They began with Mobile in the east, to check the spread of the Spanish from Florida; then Natchitoches in the west, to check the Spanish from Mexico; Mississippi Fort, and later New Orleans, to hold the mouth of the Mississippi River; and then Natchez, Kaskaskia, Ste. Genevieve, and St. Louis up the Mississippi, and points farther north to Prairie du Chien, as well as outposts in the Ohio River valley to control northern access.

The French vaguely mapped their territory so that they could make claim to a peripheral site in the event that the English or Spanish tried to move to their lands. This chapter is concerned principally with the north Gulf Coast and the Mississippi Valley up to St. Louis, the area of most concentrated French settlement, even though other French sites existed in Iowa, Indiana, Ohio, and Michigan.

Experts on the settlement of Louisiana call attention to the "French triangle" when referring to all French areas of the state, with Alexandria as the apex, Lake Charles on the western corner, and New Orleans on the eastern, lower corner (Fig. 8-3). However, considering the vast territory settled by the French during the eighteenth century, this French triangle does not accurately represent the area in which French Creole cottages and other cultural evidence can be found. A truer picture can be obtained by imagining an expanded triangle formed by stretching each corner. Such stretching distorts the corners of the triangle until they hug the waterways of the Gulf Coast and the Mississippi River valley. The east corner should be stretched from New Orleans to Pensacola, the west corner to Galveston, Texas, and the apex at Alexandria extended to St. Louis. However, before reaching the Illinois-Missouri country, the extended shape would snap, leaving the existing upper part detached as an exclave. The French also moved up tributaries, such as the Red, Ouachita, Pascagoula, and Mobile/Tombigbee rivers, creating

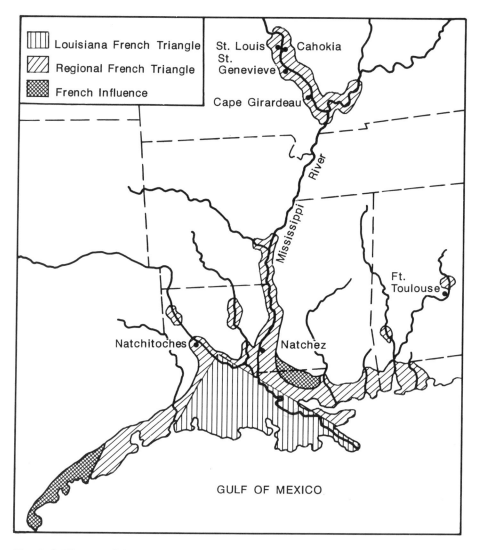

Philippe Oszuscik

Fig. 8-3 The Louisiana and regional triangles of French settlement

other exclaves. Occasionally, existing French Creole houses can be found outside the logical boundaries of even the former French territory. Such an example is a curious little French Creole cottage in Americus, Georgia.

Foreign Influence on French Culture

Until 1763, colonial Louisiana was almost exclusively French, although some Germans moved in during the eighteenth century. They provided food to the French, who initially tended to be poor farmers and who, furthermore, were concerned primarily with other economic pursuits. Some of the Germans were also brick masons or employed in the manufacturing of brick. Rather than trying to alter French culture, they accepted it.

More important than the minority groups in colonial Louisiana were the foreign powers, which interrupted the French rule and had a more lasting effect. Changes were evident in food ways, religion, and government. In architecture, however, most changes made by architects and engineers were limited to governmental or civic building. The French had already perfected a cottage type for the climate and weather, so the newcomers readily accepted the basic French ideas and modified them with their own.

From 1763 to 1801, the Spanish occupied New Orleans and the territory west of the Mississippi. Few changes were made to the basic cottage form during this period. The French regained the territory in 1801 and then sold Louisiana to the United States in 1803. The Acadians, who moved in during the Spanish period, adopted the small, basic French Creole cottage, making some innovations of their own.

The West Florida parishes experienced more complicated changes. First, the British controlled the area from 1763 to 1781, followed by the Spanish from 1781 to 1813 (1821 in Pensacola), when the area became United States territory. A few existing British Pensacola cottage drawings indicate that the general raised cottage form persisted, but larger structures were covered with clapboards. They also had single-hung doors, sash windows, and wall chimneys. Some also had a central hallway, reflecting current Georgian tastes. During the second Spanish period, the British ideas continued with no further changes to the house.

The British changes in materials and structural details, such as doors and windows, had a permanent effect on Gulf Coast houses. After 1813, Americans continued the practices introduced by the British, since most Americans came from the Carolinas. Although new cottage hybrids evolved during the American period, using the best attributes of the French Creole and the Georgian cottages, the basic French cottage lived on throughout the nineteenth century and into the early twentieth century. There are two reasons for this persistence. First, the cottage was better suited to the climate than a central hall house; second, a number of French Creole families remained in the area after American rule commenced.

Later, an area of Louisiana was settled by a group of French from former Acadia (Nova Scotia), Canada. Arriving destitute during the latter half of the eighteenth century, the Acadians settled on the least expensive and most available lands west of New Orleans. Rather than constructing a Canadian mode of housing, without galleries, they built small, simple cottages similar to the basic French Creole housing that had been erected in the area fifty years earlier. Thus, the Acadians patterned most of their cottages after the house type already proven to be suitable for the climate, with added touches of their own (see Chapter 10). An Acadian (Cajun) cottage or two will be presented in this chapter as an example of French Creole housing, when architectural elements are identical.

Pattern of Land Division

The French had a distinctive manner of dividing the land from the Gulf Coast to the Illinois country in colonial Louisiana, and these patterns survive today on farms and in some suburban lots. This landscape is easy to perceive, even where there are no French houses still in existence. Since the French settled along waterways, the colonial government had the insight to see that each farmer had river frontage, and they surveyed long, narrow land grants with the narrow side on the water. Today these rural layouts are known as *long lots* or *ribbon farms* (Fig. 8-4).

The long lot system reflects a medieval French influence of the *roture* or common fields. Modification of the system occurred in the United States, reflecting the changing cultural and political context of Louisiana. In every locale, shifts to new variations were made as changes of governments took place, from French to Spanish, then British, and back to the French.[11] The new variations still reflected the French folk system, perhaps because of the large number of French settlers remaining in Louisiana. However, under the British, an incoming British settler usually chose a British surveying tradition with broader rectilinear shapes. Eventually, the long lot survey system was abandoned, under American occupation during the early nineteenth century.

The earliest Creoles who settled along the Mississippi and other major rivers received the longest lots. Later-arriving Acadians and Creoles, who tended to settle on smaller streams and on bayous, received shorter ribbons, because these streams had smaller natural levees and narrower valleys.

Some French Creole and Cajun Elements

The main elements of French Creole culture that survive are found in house types, food ways, and religion, and in South Louisiana in language, folk arts, and crafts as well. Minor differences exist between Cajun and Creole food ways and cultural practices. In Cajun and Creole cookbooks most of the ingredients are the same, and titles of dishes are similar or exactly the same, although some Cajuns and Creoles challenge this notion of sameness.

Through an international synthesis of ingredients, the food known as Creole developed. A paradigm of a Creole dish, which is also Cajun in both its ingredients and dining ritual, is gumbo, a hearty soup. Many variations exist, including seafood, poultry, and vegetarian. In all of them, one begins with a roux, a base for gravies and sauces and a thickener—of French origin, it is made of butter (or oil) and flour. A soup must have either seafood or okra, a vegetable that originated in Africa, or both, to qualify as a true gumbo. The word *gumbo* may have been derived from the African word

Philippe Oszuscik

142

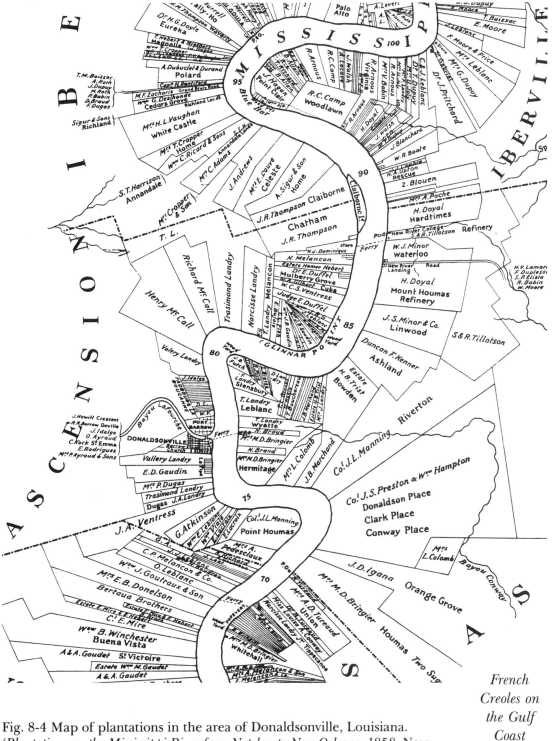

Fig. 8-4 Map of plantations in the area of Donaldsonville, Louisiana.
(*Plantations on the Mississippi River from Natchez to New Orleans, 1858.* New Orleans, La.: Pelican Book Shop, 1931.)

guingombo, meaning okra,[12] or from the Choctaw word *kombo,* meaning filé (ground sassafras leaves).[13] Okra was the African contribution, cayenne peppers were added to the recipe by the Spanish, and filé was contributed by the Gulf Coast Indians.

The ritual of cooking and eating gumbo is also a blend of traditions, a different culture influencing each cooking stage. The recipe is complete only after it is on the dinner table. It is during the eating ritual that the final, necessary, cultural mixing takes place: putting rice into a bowl, pouring the hearty soup over the rice, and adding filé as a final thickener according to each individual diner's taste.[14]

The Cajun and French Creole languages are similar but do differ in vocabulary and pronunciation. While Cajun can be compared to seventeenth-century Canadian French, French Creole also includes words from English, Dutch, Spanish, Arawak, and African languages. On the other hand, the Missouri Creole, Louisiana Creole, and Haitian Creole dialects differ from Cajun and from one another because of influences from other languages in each locale.

Wherever one finds the French Creole culture, one finds a concentration of Roman Catholic churches. While the larger churches, built before the mid-nineteenth century, were usually patterned after the twin-towered cathedrals of France, they were often built in a neoclassical rather than Gothic design. A simple vernacular church type also exists. It usually has a simple rectangular plan and is three to five window bays in length. The church often has a single square, bell tower placed over its entrance and on the central axis.

Formerly existing on a larger scale, but still surviving, is New World voodoo, which entered the culture by way of Africa. While voodoo priests and priestesses are not known to the general public, they can be found. At least one voodoo shop presently exists in New Orleans.

While music and folk arts and crafts are very much in existence in French Creole culture, the arts and crafts are not within the specialized knowledge of this writer. Cajun music is known to a much wider audience because of its association with folk and country song charts in the pop music industry. It is quite rhythmic and features a "fiddle" and an accordion as the primary instruments. A triangle is usually the only percussion included. While the folk singers still sing in Cajun French, a more modern country music version is usually in English. Some performers, such as Doug Kershaw, are known nationally. Delton Broussard and others have introduced a style, known as *zydeco,* that blends rock-and-roll sounds with traditional Cajun music.

Finally, some minor architectural features are typical of Creole areas. On existing Creole farms and plantations one can find *pigeonaries,* buildings for raising and keeping pigeons. Roof cisterns have also survived and represent a distinctive identifying feature. Two cisterns were often built symmetrically to the central axis of the main plantation house. While large cisterns were often of brick, those on smaller homes, including Cajun cottages, were wooden and looked like oversized barrels. The cistern provided a supply of potable water in regions where the ground water was permeated by salt and other pollutants to such a degree as to be only marginally usable.

Philippe
Oszuscik

Housing

A brief history of the migration of the people who founded Louisiana is also a record of the evolutionary development of the French Creole cottage. To summarize, the cottage's roots came from Normandy by way of Canada and the French Caribbean, especially Haiti, which was the main French stronghold in the Caribbean prior to, and at the time of, the colonization of the Gulf Coast and colonial Louisiana (see Fig. 8-1). It was in Le Tortue and Haiti that the semination of the French Creole cottage took place, probably by the mid-seventeenth century. The various folk strains that were initially involved were Norman, French Canadian, and Arawak Indian (or perhaps Carib Indian, whose culture was based upon that of the Arawak). The plans and form of the cottage came from French sources and ideas of an open tropical room, which came to be known as a galerie; later a porch came from the Amerindians. Thatching, and wattle and daub were traditions shared by all three sources. Whereas half-timber frames were common to Normandy and the Indians, the French Canadians had already begun making use of stone, brick, or horizontal hewn-log construction (*pièces-sur-pièces*) (see Fig. 2-3).

The French buccaneers lived on Le Tortue and western Haiti from at least the 1620s. Initially they lived like the Arawaks, in a hut called a *bohio* or *ajupa*, which was a one-room structure with its porched entrance on the narrow side. By 1650, however, France was intent on the serious settlement of Haiti, and governors were appointed by France to provide order. Wives were brought to Haiti from France, and soon (perhaps because of the wives) the buccaneers were giving up their bohios in favor of the Norman farmhouse or cottage. Houses in the towns were Norman as well. However, the buccaneers retained one important feature from the Indians, the galerie, and with that the Creole cottage was invented.

Some experts suggest that an African influence also can be seen in the cottage, since thatching and mud walls are commonplace in West African countries. About 1650, when Haiti was being transformed into a plantation culture, Africans were being imported into the country for labor. African inspired elements probably were woven subtly into the scheme, especially in Haiti. When the French settled on the north Gulf Coast, however, the Creole cottage was again modified through the syncretic process to include Gulf Coast Indian details and materials—Spanish moss in the half-timber, palmetto thatching and roof finials similar to those found on Indian structures. Figure 8-5 illustrates a plantation named Spanish Fort, at Pascagoula, as it appeared in 1726, with thatching and roof finials. A surviving structure of this plantation has Spanish moss in its walls.[15]

Theoretical Development

In theory, all folk housing stems from a one-room plan before developing into more complicated forms. The French Creole cottage is no exception. This does not mean that the first French Creole cottage consisted of a single room, because more elaborate basic folk plans were already in existence in Normandy and Canada. Any of the plans already established in Normandy could have been adopted.

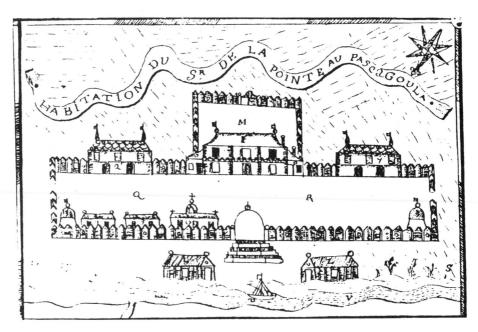

Fig. 8-5 Drawing of the plantation Spanish Fort, from *Carte de la Rivière des Pascagoula*. (Oszuscik 1983, 53.)

In Haiti, two sets of common plans were utilized for the French Creole cottage, and both were imported into the United States (Fig. 8-6). The question as to how and why two basic plans evolved and became acceptable remains, but an explanation is suggested below. Haiti was the most important French Caribbean stronghold in 1699, the year Iberville stopped in Haiti for a supply of food and men on the way to the north Gulf Coast. Early Louisiana maintained its contact with Haiti and continued to be influenced by this country.

First, both basic cottages may be traced to a two-room, medieval *salle-chambre* (hall-parlor), Norman plan (Fig. 8-7).[16] A number of cottages and small plantation houses still survive that have this plan or are variations of this plan, especially in Haiti. Examples in the United States include the Bequette-Ribault house, ca. 1787, in Ste. Geneviève; the commandant's house, Fort Jean Baptiste, 1732 (reconstructed 1979) and the Roque house, late eighteenth century, both in Natchitoches; and the Saragossa Plantation house, circa 1780, near Natchez. Just as rooms were added to the rear *galerie* of Saragossa around 1850, many houses in the landscape that are now three or four rooms were originally this basic two-room cottage, and further study is needed to uncover them.

When French Creoles searched for ways to convert the asymmetrical two-room medieval plan into a symmetical scheme, two possibilities were found and adopted. Unlike in the United States, where the distribution of the two common cottages seems to have no logical distribution pattern, a clearly defined geographic distribution exists in Haiti. The settlement pattern of Haiti stemmed from two main points, the north coast off of Le Tortue and the coast around the Gulf of Leogane in central Haiti. Dominated by

Philippe Oszuscik

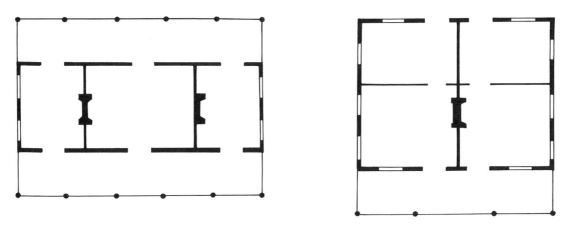

Fig. 8-6 Common French Creole floor plans in the United States

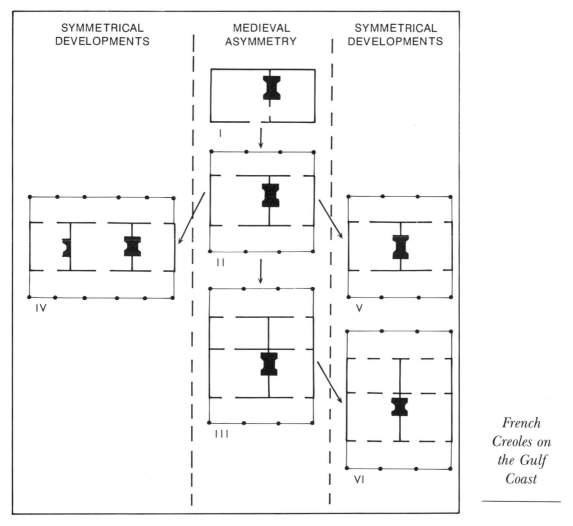

Fig. 8-7 Evolution of basic French Creole cottage plans

French Creoles on the Gulf Coast

147

French buccaneers, a large number of Spanish expatriates lived in the northern region and a large number of English expatriates resided in the southern communities. The influences of other nationalities living in the various French buccaneer communities, thus, may have been responsible for the two different sets of common folk plans that evolved and developed in Haiti: the three-room plan of the north and the two-room plan of the south.[17]

In Haiti and the United States the two-room plan expanded into that which is recognized as one of the two common French Creole cottages—the four-room plan. In French Louisiana the four-room plan became the preference during the nineteenth century, so more four-room than three-room cottages presently survive in the French Creole landscape. During the colonial period, however, the three-room cottage, which fell out of favor during the American period, was more popular. Perhaps the four-room cottage gained in popularity because it is boxy in shape, taking on a silhouette similar to that of the American Georgian cottage, which had arrived on the Gulf Coast by 1813.

Explanations of the popularity of the three-room cottage during the eighteenth century, when folk builders were looking for a symmetrical plan, include a tradition calling for a salle-chambre layout of two sizes; the thought of moving the internal partition to create two rooms of equal size was secondary to the idea of adding a third room. Moreover, precedents for a three-room plan already existed in Normandy. At Spanish Fort, a shop addition to the original plantation house was built about 1718. The shop was first changed to a medieval salle-chambre house and then expanded to a symmetrical three-room house later in the eighteenth century, after the main house was destroyed by a hurricane.

An evolution of the basic French Creole cottage plans might appear like those suggested in Figure 8-7. The diagrams represent a possible development from the medieval, asymmetrical two-room plan in the center to symmetrical folk plans. The left side illustrates the three-room plan, and the right side illustrates the two-room and four-room solutions.

Regardless of the variation among Creole cottages, all share some features. A preference exists for a centrally located chimney, which is placed within inner walls rather than outer. When the cottage evolved into the larger basic forms, the added rooms often did not have fireplaces; thus, the original salle-chambre rooms were the only ones to receive direct heat. Although the unheated rooms would get cold on the Gulf Coast for about eight weeks annually, the chimney was actually an added feature, since Creole houses in the Caribbean did not have fireplaces. The Gulf Coast French had to reach back to Canadian and Norman roots for its revival.

Another common feature of houses in the rural landscape, but not always in the urban context, is the galerie. The first cottages had only a front galerie, but in the subtropical Caribbean, the French soon realized that two or three galeries, or even galeries on all four sides, would keep the house ventilated with cool air, shutting out the direct sun. On the Gulf Coast, the galerie shuts out the sun in summer but permits the lower winter sun to shine in for solar heat.

The first cottages were undoubtedly constructed of *poteaux-en-terre* (posts-in-earth) with dirt floors, and in Haiti this type of construction is still used on the folk level (Fig. 8-8). The floors, however, are situated at a higher

*Philippe
Oszuscik*

Fig. 8-8 Two-room *maisonettes*, Gressier, Haiti. (Drawing by M. M. Geib.)

level than the surrounding earth, on podia called *banquettes*. Even the porch floor is elevated and one must step up to it from the ground. The Gulf Coast proved to be too swampy for earth floors during wet periods; consequently, wood floors were added to raise the floor above the dampness (Fig. 8-9). While poteaux-en-terre continued to be used, *poteaux-sur-solle* (posts-on-sill) became increasingly favored, until, by the second quarter of the nineteenth century, it had replaced the older medieval type of construction. Since some areas flooded excessively, cottages were often raised two, four, or six or more

Fig. 8-9 Bequette-Ribault house, Ste. Genevieve, Missouri, built ca. 1787–1800. (Drawing by M. M. Geib.)

feet off the ground, depending on the locale. The Bequette-Ribault house, built sometime between 1787 and 1800, in Ste. Geneviève, Missouri, is located at a site near the Mississippi River that is still flooded about every ten years, despite more effective and modern flood control mechanisms.

Several other features of the early cottages are worthy of mention. Steep roofs, of a forty-five to seventy-two degree pitch, were an element that can be traced to Canadian houses. French doors and windows also were used, and every room that fronted a galerie had external doors (see Fig. 8-7). Houses also had doors that were aligned from front to rear elevations. There was no communication between halves of the early four-room houses since the galerie fulfilled that function.

Other than the fireplace, the elements of the basic Gulf Coast cottage plan, including the steep roof, were common to houses in Haiti. The steep roof was not needed for throwing off snow, but was built out of a thatch roof tradition. It was retained for its efficiency in draining off the heavy subtropical rains.

The French were always open to experimentation with the ideas they encountered when setting up a colony. As soon as they landed on the Gulf Coast, the French not only scouted for mineral wealth, plants, herbs, and game but also searched for Indian villages so they could make arrangements for trade. They were also eager to learn from the natives those skills likely to ensure survival in the new environment, especially in reference to building techniques and materials.

In 1700, Father du Ru, a Jesuit priest, set up expeditions to learn the languages of friendly tribes, establish missions, and learn more about their building practices. He observed that the Indians planted posts in the earth with small stakes in-between on which to weave a wattle frame. He was intrigued that the Indians did all this without mortise and tenon, using only vines to tie parts together. In studying their daubing, he learned of a new material—"Spanish beard," as he called it, or Spanish moss—for the French to use in their *bousillage*.[18]

Father du Ru also noted and passed on to the French other devices, such as the use of finials in roof ridges and palmetto thatching. He observed that the village chief's house, which was larger than the rest, and the village temple were the only structures with galeries.

A primitive drawing of Fort Louis (1702) in Mobile, and descriptions of Bienville's residence reveal that the fort had a tile roof and finials that were similar to those used by the local Indians. Bienville's residence (the White chief's house) included a galerie. Soon many plantation owners were making use of building techniques such as roof finials, thatching, and galeries. Perhaps Indians were led to believe that plantation homes with galeries were those of chiefs. Before 1818, not every house had a galerie, especially in the middle of the community, as contemporary, primitive drawings illustrate. Some, no doubt, were built as tentative dwellings, but many had their own palisaded lots as on Dauphin Island. Many hastily built cottages had walls covered with bark rather than bousillage. When more permanent materials, such as shakes, became available, the French eagerly used them instead of thatching.

Philippe
Oszuscik

150

Variations to Basic Plans

Up to this point, basic house plans have been emphasized. The three-room cottage is represented by Spanish Fort, and the four-room cottage by the Levalle house and Cahokia Courthouse (Figs. 8-10 and 8-11). As mentioned earlier, the four-room basic plan evolved from the medieval two-room plan, which is still common in south Haiti (see Fig. 8-8). This medieval, asymmetrical layout exists in the United States, as in the Bequette-Ribault house (see Fig. 8-9). Many houses, including the Bequette-Ribault house, had additions made to them before their most recent restorations. By the time folk house studies began in the twentieth century, the four-room cottage dominated the landscape and any two-room cottage was viewed as a

Figs. 8-10 and 8-11 Lavalle house, Pensacola, Florida, second Spanish period, 1803; Cahokia Courthouse, Cahokia, Illinois, built in the 1730s. (Drawings by M. M. Geib.)

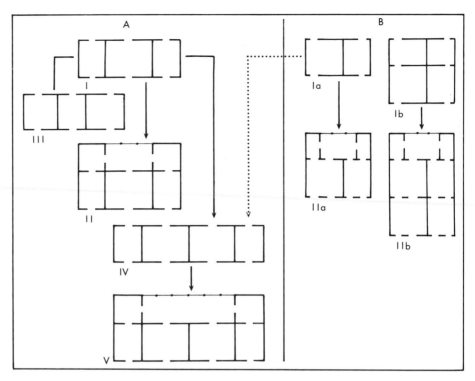

Fig. 8-12 Basic French Creole cottage plans and simple variations

half-cottage. In the reevaluation of basic plans, the two-room cottage has to be considered, because variations actually stem from this plan as well as from the four-room cottage.

Early variations of the basic cottage were made by creating a more complex core of rooms or by filling in galerie space (usually the rear galerie). When the three-room cottage was popular during the eighteenth century, there was much experimentation with this form (Fig. 8-12A). Often rooms were added, creating a longer, one-room-deep cottage, and spaces of the rear galerie were filled in, resulting in a range of half-rooms. To maintain symmetry, a pair of end *cabinets* separated by an open galerie was often built. Only the galeries that involve the partial filling in of spaces have been included in the diagrams. The two- and four-room cottages had only one main variation each (Fig. 8-12B). The variation involved the filling in of a rear galerie and a rear range of rooms of cabinets flanking a central galerie area. The Le Beau-Woody house (Fig. 8-13), built in 1840, is a good example of the two-room form expanded to include rear cabinets. It was possible for a common variation to have developed from the two- or three-room basic plan, reminding us that the three-room plan itself originally evolved from the two-room plan. Such an example, illustrating a four-room plan across the front with cabinets in the rear, is a plantation home near Pointe Coupe, Louisiana, built circa 1800. A fifth room was eventually added to the long range of this structure, on the end with the exterior chimney.

More complex variations occurred to houses with galeries on all sides

*Philippe
Oszuscik*

152

Fig. 8-13 Le Beau-Woody house, Rougon Chenille, Louisiana, built about 1840. (Photo by P. Oszuscik.)

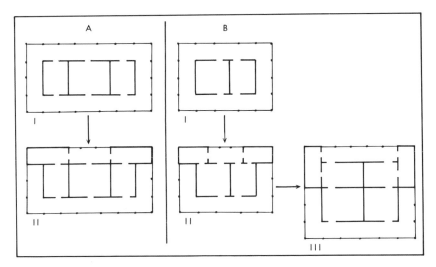

Fig. 8-14 Complex variations from basic French Creole plans: *A*) Three-room variations, *B*) Two- and four-room variations

(Fig. 8-14). Larger plantation houses are more likely to exhibit these or similar plans, but any basic cottage with complete verandas can be expanded into a complex form.

Half-Cottage Variations from the Nineteenth Century

While many of the foregoing variations developed during the eighteenth century, another group, which can be considered half-cottage forms, developed during the nineteenth century, mostly during the American period. These variations may have been influenced partially by American cottages. Some of the possibilities are illustrated in Figure 8-15. All variations in this figure stemmed from the four-room plan, now the dominant cottage in the landscape, and most can be found in the urban vernacular landscape.

The half-cottage plan was achieved by dividing the four-room plan longitudinally or laterally. The lateral type has a full two-room wide, four-bay facade and is always presented in a basic double-pen format (Fig. 8-15A, Fig. 8-16). It is useful to refer to this cottage as a four-bay, half-Creole cottage. It is possible that the Anglo-American double-pen had an influence upon nineteenth-century French Creole builders in their return to a two-room format, because the half-Creole cottage was then designed using a symmetrical room layout rather than the old medieval asymmetrical salle-chambre plan. The common variations that did occur involved the service wings, which tended to be long and often included more rooms than on the two-room front.

The half-Creole cottage that is divided longitudinally is one-and-one-half rooms deep (see Fig. 8-15B). A number of subcategories evolved from

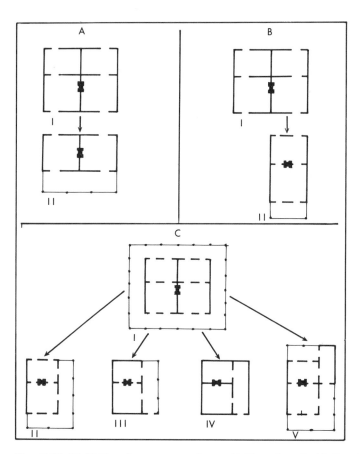

Fig. 8-15 Half-Creole cottage plans: *A*) Four-bay half-Creole plan, *B*) Two-bay half-Creole plan, *C*) Two- and three-bay cottage plans

Fig. 8-16 Four-bay half-Creole cottage, Bayou Le Batre, Alabama, mid-nineteenth century. (Drawing by M. M. Geib from a photo by P. Oszuscik.)

the basic two-bay front, such as one with a side galerie. Another has a three-bay front in which a door leads to the side galerie. A third variation that evolved from the three-bay front has a side hall. This last subcategory was probably influenced by the American townhouse, which had a three-bay front and was one-and-one-half rooms deep with a side hall. The American townhouse, however, is two stories high. More variations of the half-Creole cottage exist, such as the two-story Creole townhouse, that have identical plans to those discussed in this section (see Chapter 9).

One motivation for the changes may have been the influx of Americans. During the period when the Americans began to dominate the population, the French noted some of the new fashions and began experimenting with new devices so that their house forms would appear more American.

A question always present is, At what point do the new amalgamations cease to be French Creole and become American, or become French/American Creole? The latter term has never been formally used, but a large number of structures are actually Creole cottages that are equally French and American. By the late eighteenth century, Americans in the southeastern section of the country had already been introduced to the galerie, but it was by way of trade contact with the British West Indies. The British West Indies may have developed the galerie independently, or may have gotten it from the French. Carolinians moving into the Gulf Coast region shortly after 1763 and again after 1800 were already adding galeries to their cottages. Does the French cottage cease to be French when it uses American devices, such as a side hall or an external chimney, or when it uses American millwork, which became available in southern lumber yards, or when it uses a combination of these factors?

Americans moving into the Gulf Coast region also began to use devices that had proven successful for the Gulf Coast climate, such as steeper roofs and integral galeries instead of lean-to porches. A house developed that was a hybrid of the two cultures. It has a Georgian plan and external chimneys but includes the integral galeries and steeply pitched roof of the French. Throughout most of the Gulf Coast, this cottage is appropriately called the Gulf Coast cottage.[19] It also is referred to as a five-bay, central hall cottage, and by other names. Regardless of name, it represents a final American Creole amalgamation that was popular and that spread inland from the coast into the American sector. The French Creole cottage, however, remained coastal, except in Louisiana and a few exclaves up the Mississippi and other rivers.

Present Condition of French Creoles

These latest changes, as well as the evolution of the Gulf Coast cottage, occurred because the Americans entering British West Florida after 1763, Spanish West Florida after 1781, and Louisiana after 1803 exerted permanent influences upon the Gulf Coast culture. New lifestyles, foods, music, building materials, and ready-made sash windows and other architectural detail items, were available and preferred over the earlier folk traditions or handmade items.

Groups of French Creole and Cajun people still survive, speak French, and perpetuate old traditions, but modern American society has drastically changed their lifestyles. Yet, the groups persist, and French is not only still spoken but is being reintroduced in Louisiana schools, after having been forbidden in the state's classrooms for a number of years. Cajun and Creole foods have become popular from coast to coast, with the fame of their cooks growing and even the development of fast-food chains, such as "Popeye's." Creole and Cajun revivals are taking place in housing also. One Lafayette, Louisiana, firm will build a Cajun-style cabin almost anywhere, and the developers of many modern subdivisions are building modified "Creole style" exteriors, while including contemporary air-conditioned interiors. Nevertheless, the popularity of the external Creole design with a galerie reflects an ethnic pride that has resurfaced along the Gulf Coast.

Philippe
Oszuscik

9

African-Americans in the American South

Philippe Oszuscik

ONE GROUP often overlooked in its contributions to the southern land-scape is the Black American.[1] The main reason, perhaps, is that Afro-Americans were brought to the United States as slaves, and the White owners designed schemes to discourage the continuity of African traditions by providing American substitutes, by separating tribes and even families to discourage native languages and to encourage English, by outlawing voodoo and native traditional religions and by Christianizing the people, by supply-ing the necessary clothing and food stuffs, and by forcing them to become field workers, skilled laborers, and house servants for the White culture.

Needless to state, various traditions were not entirely eradicated; and many were ingeniously synthesized into the White southern culture—for example, even the southern accent to some extent, as "mammies" raised the plantation children. Since the Blacks did the cooking, okra and Afro-influenced preparations were added to the southern menus. Blacks may have been trained in blacksmithing and building trades by Whites, but their ethnic heritage is exhibited in the crafts of Europeans, such as wrought iron fences and other ornamental work. Certain innovations by Black carpenters and craftsmen, whether inspired from their homeland or not, led to new improvised details.[2] Such details are usually so subtle that it takes an expert to recognize them.

Unlike ethnic groups who migrated to the United States voluntarily, whether for adventure, economic advancement, or for religious or political freedom, Blacks were brought involuntarily and were deprived of their free-dom. In the United States, Black slaves were in all thirteen colonies and states until 1819, when slave importation was finally prohibited.

The slave culture persisted and expanded in the South until the time of the Civil War and the settlement of the slavery controversy. The area of pri-mary Black settlement includes the pre–Civil War slaveholding states and parts of border states, such as Kentucky and Missouri. After the Civil War, Blacks usually remained in the same areas, often near the plantations on which they had worked, in tenant houses on the plantations, in enclaves within a town where freedmen had already settled, or on the edges of such a town.

Some house types influenced by African-American tradition spread outside the Southeast as early as the late nineteenth century. This diffusion was not due to the migrations of Blacks but to railroad shipment of prefabricated house-building kits from centers such as New Orleans and Atlanta. The shotgun house, in particular, was prefabricated and shipped to factory, mining, and railroad communities to serve as company houses. By the late nineteenth century the origin of the shotgun house had become largely obscure, permitting them to be acceptable to Whites in the Southeast.

The products made by skilled slaves, such as wood carvings (walking sticks, spoons, boxes, chains, mortars and pestles), woven baskets (coiled grass baskets, which employ an African sewing technique), often bore decorative motifs that derived directly from Africa. Although modified by American techniques, materials, and ethnic traditions, these crafts still survive, largely in modified forms, with some African motifs.[3] There has been debate as to whether slaves learned of the coiled basket from the Southeast Indians or whether the Blacks taught the Indians this technique. Others have observed that both native Americans and Africans had coiled baskets, but sewing techniques and choice of materials were different.[4] Before the twentieth century, African-American baskets were mainly for agricultural purposes, and they lacked handles, since they were carried on the head; but modern baskets tend to be smaller and to be constructed with handles, so they will be more marketable to Whites.

Four cultural sources—Spanish, French, British, and, later, American— influenced the Black slave culture, including its housing. Nothing remains from the earliest Spanish and French beginnings in slave housing in North America. The prints and drawings that have survived are rare and not always reliable, as the slave housing was interpreted through European eyes. The earliest structures built for slaves usually exhibited a blend of details reflecting the slave owner's ethnic heritage. Thus, slave housing tended to be small, vernacular versions of the slave master's housing.

Knowledge of Black housing under the Spanish is sketchy at best. It is known that the Spanish permitted Blacks (South Carolinian fugitives) to enter Florida and set up Black communities. One colony of maroons (fugitive slaves) was established in St. Augustine. By 1746 there were 403 Blacks in the city, constituting 26 percent of the population. In 1739 a colony of thirty-eight families was established and Fort Mose was built on the frontier near Apalachicola.[5] Communities of Black maroons were rare in the Southeast, so some runaways may have joined Indian communities during the eighteenth century. While the French were still exploring the Gulf Coast, during their first years in the United States, Father du Ru, writing in Biloxi, recounted his exploration of the Red River on May 8, 1701: "We heard in all the villages [Indian] here that quite a large group of negroes and of mulattoes, men and women, have deserted [the Spanish] and are established in a separate district where they persist in their revolt."[6] These Spanish-speaking Blacks are the earliest known Maroons west of the Mississippi. They probably settled in northwest Louisiana or east Texas during the late seventeenth century, having migrated by way of Mexico.

Existing African-American housing in the Southeast bears influences primarily from American (British heritage) and French Creole sources. Consequently, the remainder of this chapter is divided into two major sections.

Philippe Oszuscik

The French tradition had the more profound and recognizable influence on existing house forms. In either case, the vernacular statements originated where settlers of these two European nationalities resided (Fig. 9-1). The French influence began on the Gulf Coast and penetrated inland from the south, up the Mississippi Valley. The British began on the Atlantic Coast and moved inland in a westward direction.

French-Influenced African-American Housing

African-American house-building practices bearing a French influence were imported into the United States, not during French colonial times, but during the American period (after 1801 in Louisiana). They are represented in the house form known by Americans as the shotgun, a term invented by the White population to visually describe the house, and its many variations. The basic and most common form is one room wide and three rooms deep (Fig. 9-2). Because the doors are traditionally aligned from front to back (Fig. 9-3), it is said that one could fire a gun into the front doorway and the bullet would come out the back. The structure was first built by Haitian refugees who arrived by the thousands in New Orleans between 1804 and 1809. Consequently, the form took hold quickly and strongly, spreading far beyond the French areas of the Gulf Coast. It became the most distinctly African-American house form, because it was developed by freedmen in Haiti rather than on White plantations.

Most shotgun houses exist in urban rather than rural landscapes. Neighborhoods that developed within city limits had to meet local planning codes, yet they retained an ethnic identity because of their house forms. In former Gulf Coast French communities, such as New Orleans, Biloxi, and Mobile, some mulattoes selected French Creole cottages rather than shotguns; therefore, it is common to see a mixture of French Creole cottages and shotguns in the same urban landscape. Neighborhoods and communities of Blacks that developed outside city limits and the jurisdiction of planning codes followed the general local custom of community planning, although in a more organic, looser manner. If a house existed in the path of a planned road, or if the terrain or a tree presented an obstacle, the road would detour around it and a strict grid pattern would not be maintained. Rather than having perfectly formed perpendicular intersections, corners would often be rounded according to the prevailing traffic flow. Improvisation rather than predetermined order is a desired Black aesthetic. An example of such practical planning can be observed in "Africatown" (Plateau), Alabama, a community that sprang from a boatload of Blacks, that was liberated by the United States Customs in 1859 in Mobile, during an attempt to smuggle them into Mobile as slaves.

The Shotgun House

A thorough history of the shotgun house appeared in a dissertation in 1975 by Vlach and in his subsequent writings in journals and books.[7] An abbreviated discussion, however, is appropriate here to ensure understanding and appreciation of this Afro-Creole house form. Vlach originally was interested in tracing the African legacy of this house form, and his research

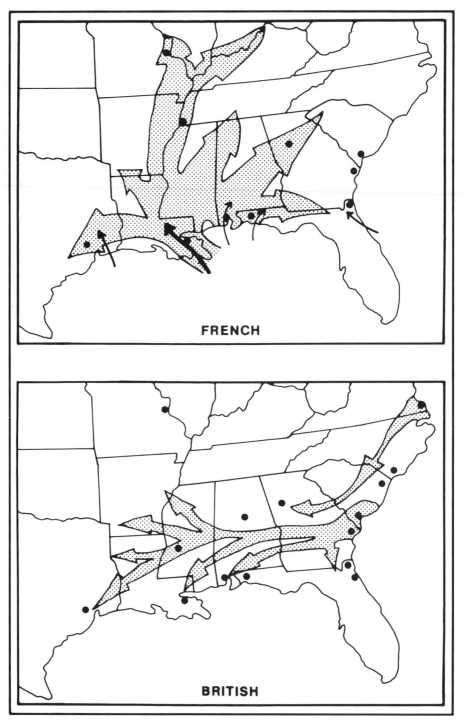

FRENCH

BRITISH

*Philippe
Oszuscik*

Fig. 9-1 Entry points and diffusion routes of French and British influence on
Afro-American housing in southeastern United States

Fig. 9-2 Exterior of a single shotgun house. (Drawing by M. M. Geib.)

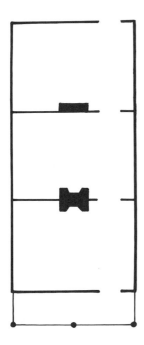

Fig. 9-3 Plan of a single shotgun house

led him to Yoruban houses in Africa. A second antecedent was the *bohio* (in Creole, *ajupa*) of the Arawak Indians in the Caribbean. The Arawaks had become extinct by the time slaves were imported into Haiti, but the bohio had been introduced and perpetuated there by French buccaneers (see Chapter 8). The bohio was a one-room dwelling with walls of mud daub and posts in the ground and possessed a thatched roof and a front porch. When the buccaneer became domesticated as a plantation owner, he moved out of the simple bohio and into a French Creole house, converting the bohio into slave quarters. Through the process of syncretism, each group saw something of the heritage of its own housing traditions in the slave quarters. Certain construction elements, such as posts in the earth (*poteaux-en-terre*), wattle and daub, and hipped thatched roofs, all of which could be viewed as

African-Americans in the American South

161

Creole features, had been commonly employed by Africans. As slaves were liberated over the years, the freedmen built on their small farms an expanded form of the bohio, so that it resembled the Yoruban two-room house. The result was the Haitian rural *caille*, the immediate antecedent to the shotgun. The Arawak format of an entrance on the narrow side with a porch was retained, whereas the Yoruban house had an entrance on the long side and was usually built without a porch.[8] Haiti, particularly the southern half, abounds with cailles today. Since these folk houses contain elements of African, Arawak, and French origins, they represent a Creole form of house tradition as much as the French Creole cottage does. In essence, they represent an Afro-Creole house form.

In Haitian villages houses are arranged in informal groupings or clusters. In dry areas, often, no grass is permitted to grow near the house, or in the entire compound of houses. The grounds are kept uncluttered and swept, such as at Saline Village and Odva Village, Haiti.

When freedman moved to the city, they built cailles in the more sophisticated materials, wood, brick, and half-timber, used by the French already resident in these urban areas. Today galvanized iron is a common roofing material and the gabled roof is commonly substituted for the hipped thatched roof. While all elevations of a house can take on a decorative emphasis, the facades are particularly decorative. Rooms began to be added to urban houses and the structures soon became three and more rooms deep.

Since it was freedmen who developed the shotgun, that house form was associated with their freedom. After the Haitian Revolution, this symbol was expanded into a nationalistic symbol of independence and a link with the African heritage. The French Creole cottage then became associated with the colonial French plantation culture.[9] Haiti became politically and culturally divided soon after the revolution. The southern half identified itself with its African heritage but the northern sector reinstigated a plantation culture.[10] As a result, more shotgun houses survive in the southern half of the country. French Creole cottages were not abandoned entirely; the light-skinned mulattoes often chose this house form, perhaps in an attempt to identify their French heritage.[11]

The Haitian Revolution disrupted not only the plantation culture but also many thousands of individuals—Whites, Blacks, and Mulattoes. Unrest persisted from 1791 until 1809, and thousands of Haitians left the country. In 1809 alone, 2,060 free Blacks came to New Orleans. The newly enlarged free Black community attained success. With a number of the Blacks in the building trades, they were able to establish and develop their own architectural environment and in this manner established the shotgun house in the United States.[12]

From New Orleans, the shotgun then spread inland. Haitians may have entered through other ports, such as Mobile, as well. Indeed, a large number of shotguns exist in other port cities, from Galveston and Port Arthur, Texas, to Pensacola, Florida. Even Jacksonville, Florida, on the East Coast, has a large concentration of shotguns, suggesting that Blacks may have entered through the port of St. Augustine in Spanish Florida. New Orleans, nevertheless, must have been the main port of entry because of its French culture and its early pre-eminence.

Vlach demonstrated that the Haitian and American shotguns share the

*Philippe
Oszuscik*

162

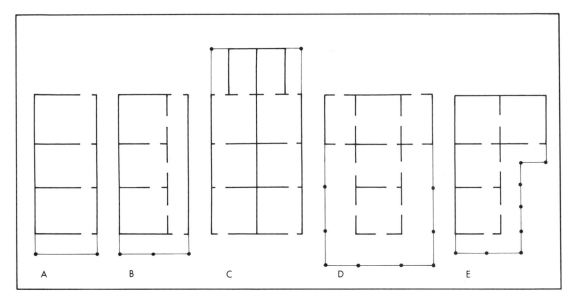

Fig. 9-4 Typical floor plans of the shotgun house and its sub-types:
A) single shotgun, B) three-bay shotgun with hall, C) double shotgun,
D) North Shore shotgun, E) lateral wing shotgun

same room sizes and ceiling heights, thus, proving that Haiti was the cultural hearth of this house type.[13] This was an important observation, since White Americans had assumed that they were responsible for its invention. Earlier writers thought it evolved from a temple-fronted Greek Revival cottage.

Subtypes of the Shotgun House

Haitians do not recognize the term *shotgun.* The urban caille is often referred to by the French term *maison basse,* or "low house." White Americans coined the term *shotgun,* and the label will persist in this country, even though *low house* is an appropriate descriptive term coined at the house tradition's cultural hearth.

In 1976 Vlach discussed three subtypes of the basic shotgun—the double shotgun, the camelback and the North Shore house. Since that time another variation, the lateral wing shotgun, has been recognized. Field work in Haiti suggests still more variations of the shotgun house (Fig. 9-4).

Even though it dates from circa 1900, the Smith shotgun house in Pritchard, Alabama, with its Caribbean hipped roof, board and batten siding, and board and batten windows, represents an early folk level of the basic shotgun. All of its occupants resided in it without electricity or water, and a wood burning stove was in the kitchen, which was at the back of the house. Originally, a chimney served fireplaces for the two forward rooms. In the Mobile area, doors often are aligned from the front porch to kitchen, but the back door of the Smith house is on a side elevation to serve a side rear porch rather than on the rear wall. Others have an integral side rear porch as an alternative.

The earliest surviving shotguns of New Orleans also have hipped roofs

African-Americans in the American South

163

and, like some urban Haitian shotguns, were often built without porches. The earliest shotgun I have examined dates from about 1840, and this second generation structure exhibits details of Greek Revival styling. The basic single shotgun can be found with one-bay, two-bay, and three-bay facades. Later in the nineteenth century the gabled facade became popular. Some examples on the folk level survive in the historic district called Africatown of Plateau, Alabama, although they date from the turn of the twentieth century. Such vernacular examples in urban areas are now more rare than the Victorian-styled examples.

A double shotgun is a duplex, or two single shotguns attached side-by-side under one roof. All examples I have encountered are urban rather than rural and may have been created in response to the rising cost of lots.

The camelback is a subtype that has a second story over the rear room, or sometimes over the back two rooms. Although more common in New Orleans, the camelback can be found in other cities along the Gulf Coast, such as Mobile. Another, but less common, variation is the double shotgun with camelback.

Vlach defined the North Shore type as having porches on three sides and rooms projecting from the rear room.[14] It received its name because people thought it originated in the small towns on the North Shore of Lake Pontchartrain. However, it exists far up into northwest Louisiana and along the Gulf Coast into Florida. Moreover, as with all shotgun subtypes, its antecedent is in Haiti. One I examined at Gressier, Haiti, for example, clearly has *galeries* on three sides. This subtype combines many elements of the French Creole cottage, such as verandas and doors on each elevation that open onto a galerie. Excellent examples in Louisiana exist at Abita. Most North Shore houses date from the late nineteenth century, judging from their Victorian trim. While all North Shore houses have galeries on three sides, not all form a T at the rear, which was once definitive of the style. Some form an L and others have no room off the sides, so many variations exist within the subtype.

A subtype that is similar to the North Shore shotgun was first identified in Biloxi, Mississippi, as the lateral wing shotgun.[15] This house occurs from Louisiana to Pensacola in sufficient numbers to be a major subtype. It always has a room projecting off the rear room, so the plan forms an L (Fig. 9-5). It can be found at the folk level in Haiti and on a higher vernacular level in Haitian cities. Many variations exist. It may be built with or without galeries or have from one to three galeries—one on the facade, one on the lateral wing, and/or one as a side galerie, which always occurs on the side of the lateral wing. Wherever a galerie does exist, there are doors to the corresponding rooms. Next, the lateral wing may be a prominent wing, projecting beyond the roof line of the main mass, as illustrated in Figure 9-5, or it may be a smaller room that projects out only to the edge of the main roof as in the Haitian caille. This type is nearly as common on the Gulf Coast as is the type with the larger wing with its own supporting roof. Perhaps the subtype evolved by enclosing the rear part of a side galerie to create more interior space. The next logical step was to create a larger wing. While most wings consist of one room, some long two-room wings exist on suburban lots.

The North Shore house can now be evaluated from a new perspective. Most are actually bilateral wing shotguns. Some are lateral wing structures,

Philippe Oszuscik

164

Fig. 9-5 Lateral wing shotgun house, ca. 1900, at 750 Reynoir, Biloxi, Mississippi. (Drawing by M. M. Geib.)

Fig. 9-6 The John Cox house, ca. 1900, Mobile, Alabama, an Afro–Anglo-American cottage type. (Photo by P. Oszuscik.)

but still retain the characteristic galeries on both of the main section's long sides. Romantic labels, such as *North Shore house* and *shotgun*, will remain; but descriptive terms such as *low house* and *lateral wing house*, and classification of subtypes by number of rooms and number and location of galeries, are more useful in making field notes.

Beyond the subtypes listed above exist more amalgamations. Some are Afro–French Creole and others represent Afro–Anglo-American cottage types. One example of the latter is the Cox house in Mobile, dating from about 1900 (Fig. 9-6). It is a lateral wing cottage with the wing projecting from the middle room rather than from the rear. A side hall replaced the side galerie element and a later owner added the small side addition next to the front door. The Victorian trim camouflaged the African-American shotgun heritage, elevating the cottage beyond being a recognizable shotgun in its White neighborhood.

High Houses

Field work in Haiti, reveals that all one-story shotgun variations exist in two-story versions. Furthermore, even more variations exist, because galeries are used only on the ground floor in some, on two floors in others, and in combinations of one and two floors in yet others. Some front galeries are cantilevered to produce another subtype. One variant combines commercial functions on the ground floor with housing on the second. Haitians refer to a two-story house that follows the shotgun plan as a *maison haute* or "high house" to differentiate it from the maison basse. When speaking Creole, the Haitian refers to the one-story maison basse as a *ticaille* (little house), to the two-story maison haute as a *caille enchanmotte* (charming house), or to both generally as caille (house).

Once one knows all of the shotgun subtypes and further variations, it is easy to correlate two-story equivalents. Moreover, it becomes easy not only to plot on paper the variations but also to visualize subclassifications that could hypothetically exist.

While the Gulf Coast has all, or most, of the possible variations of the one-story shotguns found in Haiti, the Southeast has adopted only a few of the basic high house plans. Some of the factors that may have been responsible for this are the landscape site, the economic class of the owner and the distance from the cultural hearth. With regard to the site, much of the inner city landscape in Haiti was high houses in which the ground floor has been converted from residential to commercial space and the upstairs remains living quarters. Cities on the Gulf Coast were already built in an Anglo-American tradition, and immigrants moved to the suburbs where there was less congestion. Thus, no pressing need for high houses existed. In larger cities, such as New Orleans and Jacksonville, Florida, where the Black population became dense, high houses developed, including the combined house over commercial store subtype.

Economic resources were a factor, because some of the variations are extremely complex, sophisticated, and filled with late Victorian as well as French half-timber details. Such houses exist in the exclusive, Creole neighborhoods of Port-au-Prince. Although some rich Creoles immigrated to New Orleans between 1804 and 1809, the majority that arrived in the city were of more modest means and selected the one-story shotgun form in which to reside.

Lastly, Haiti is indeed the source of one- and two-story Afro-Creole house types. I suspect that many of the more complex, two-story types evolved in that country during the nineteenth century after the main Creole exodus to New Orleans. Because there are fewer high houses and high house subtypes in the United States, they have largely been overlooked by housing experts in this country.

Philippe Oszuscik

The basic high house, with two-tier front galeries, can be seen in all southern cities of Haiti. The first story is usually brick and often stuccoed; this vernacular tradition has not died out, although both stories and the galerie piers of recent structures are now often built of concrete block, and even ferroconcrete. Usually, the second story is wood or half-timber. Balconies may have hand rails of a traditional design, although it is commonplace to see an X pattern on vernacular house types. The galerie friezes are treated similarly.

A variation of the basic house is the high house that has a cantilevered galerie (Fig. 9-7). This house differs from the basic example in that the space above the ground floor porch, which is usually a second story porch, is an enclosed room. The second story galerie is cantilevered over the street. It is easy to see how this subtype evolved. The ground floor was converted into commercial space, as in other early high houses because of urban expansion. Later structures were designed with commercial space from their beginning. Another vernacular subtype is a basic high house with a one-story side galerie. Another variation has a second story balcony continuing around the side of the structure.

Further discussion of Haitian high houses is unnecessary, since it is extremely rare to find a high house on the Gulf Coast that varies from the basic plan. However, to illustrate how complicated the analysis of high houses can be, I refer to one mansion encountered in the Bois Verna area of Port-au-Prince. While the ground floor was built in a bilateral plan of stuccoed brick,

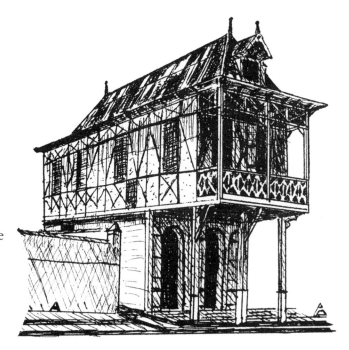

Fig. 9-7 High house with cantilevered porch, Port-au-Prince, Haiti, late nineteenth century. (Drawing by P. Oszuscik.)

the second floor was limited to the basic plan with a cantilevered front gallery in wood.

High Houses in Southeastern United States

The basic high house with two-tier front galeries can be found from Jacksonville to the Texas Gulf Coast, especially in Port Arthur, Texas. While use of the style moved up the Atlantic coast into Georgia and South Carolina, the number of such structures is smaller there. The American cultural hearth of this house type is clearly in New Orleans and the Gulf Coast. Furthermore, Jacksonville used to have block after block of high houses into the 1950s and 1960s, before expressways, but urban renewal officials and commercial developers called for them to be razed by entire blocks. The two examples pictured in Figure 9-8 narrowly escaped being part of an expressway. Just as in Haiti, high houses in the United States often have handrails with X-bracing and other patterns of the Caribbean and often have one-story shotguns as neighboring structures.

Many examples in New Orleans are built with balconies rather than with two-tier porches. Some also have a partial integral side porch, a feature also found in Port-au-Prince. Some towns in Louisiana, with their mixture of shotguns, high houses, and French Creole houses on the same street, closely resemble the Haitian urban landscape. Such a view can be seen in St. Martinsville. Its high houses have stores on the ground floor. One example exhibits a two-tier side galerie in addition to the front galerie and Caribbean patterns in the handrails.

Sometimes, a high house can be confused with a two-story French Creole townhouse (Fig. 9-9). The example in Mobile shown in Figure 9-9 could at first sight be mistaken for a high house, before one realizes that its plan is only two rooms deep. These homes also have antecedents in Haiti, and they are squarer than the high house.

More variations of the high house probably exist along the Gulf Coast, but they are scarce. Generally, more study and education of the general pub-

*Philippe
Oszuscik*

Fig. 9-8 High houses, ca. 1900, Beaver and Georgia streets, Jacksonville, Florida. (Drawing by M. M. Geib.)

Fig. 9-9 French Creole townhouse, nineteenth century, Mobile, Alabama. (Photo by P. Oszuscik.)

lic is needed in this area of vernacular architecture, as most people have little knowledge of the heritage of high houses. Some of the rare varieties could be saved before they are razed in the name of urban renewal if increased public awareness existed. To my knowledge, this chapter represents the first published analysis of high houses. A few scholars who recognize that these types of two-story houses do not relate to American or French Creole townhouse traditions tend to use the inappropriate term *two-story shotgun.*

British-Influenced African-American Housing

Unlike Afro-Creole housing, which bears more African and Arawak influences than French, African-American housing in the Southeast stems from an Anglo-American heritage and so exhibits a British influence. In fact, floor plans are identical to Anglo-American pen houses and the hall-and-parlor cottage (see Chapter 6, under "House Types").

While the shotgun house is primarily an urban vernacular entity that is found along the Gulf Coast and spread from formerly French areas, the Black Anglo-American cottages are found in the rural landscape and in small towns and villages. These cottages are on the East Coast and Atlantic islands, the areas in which the British colonies began. They spread inland with the westward expansion, when migrating White masters took slaves with them. The Southeast retained an agricultural economy into the twentieth century, just as some rural parts still do. The tidewater source of the Anglo-Americans is the cultural hearth for these African-American cottages.

The Slave House

The first British colonists in the Virginia and Carolina colonies built hall-and-parlor cottages as residences. While no wood examples have survived from the seventeenth century, due to a combination of weather and termites, a number of brick ones, such as the Thoroughgood house in Virginia Beach, are still in existence. By the end of the seventeenth century, large plantations were already developing. When landowners became prosperous, they gave up their modest hall-and-parlor cottages for more pretentious, larger homes. The hall-and-parlor cottages were adapted for slave quarters, servant houses, and kitchens. The use of hall-and-parlor houses for slave quarters on the eastern seaboard persisted into the 1860s.

While most slave and kitchen buildings were constructed of wood, a surprising number on islands and along the Atlantic coast were constructed of brick, tabby, or *coquina,* a soft shell rock found on the coast and first used as a building material by the Spanish in St. Augustine, Florida.[16] Excellent examples of surviving ruins and a partially reconstructed cottage, constructed in the early nineteenth century of coquina, are on Kingsley plantation on St. George Island, off the northeast coast of Florida near Mayport (Fig. 9-10).

Boone Hall plantation at Mount Pleasant, South Carolina, has a row of brick slave quarters with tile roofs near the main house that date from the early nineteenth century. The exterior of each of these small structures resembles that of a hall-and-parlor cottage, but the interior has been modified with the removal of a wall partition to create one large living area. The fireplace is located on the rear wall opposite the front door. The interior view reveals an exposed truss roof, which is typical for slave houses. Similar coastal brick slave cabins survive at the Hermitage plantation near Savannah, Georgia. These, however, have hipped roofs, suggesting influences from the

Philippe Oszuscik

Fig. 9-10 Slave quarters built of coquina, early nineteenth century, Kingsley Plantation, St. George Island, Florida. (Photo by P. Oszuscik.)

British Caribbean, although some writers have suggested that this trait shows an African influence.

Inland slave houses of the nineteenth century were usually single- or double-pen or saddlebag structures, which were derived from the Anglo-American folk culture, as defined by Glassie.[17] Log construction was used for early slave houses, but clapboards on a timber frame became a common method as well. Unlike most pen houses on the coastal plain built for use by Whites, which usually had a front and even a rear porch, slave cabins, more often than not, did not have porches. Sizes of slave houses were comparable to those of the period built for rural Whites. Some slave homes had flooring while others had dirt floors; but that, too, is a similarity shared in the folk houses of Whites.[18]

Two clapboard-sided, single-pen houses from Graves plantation, built circa 1830, have been restored and moved to the open air museum at Stone Mountain, Georgia. Each was built for a single family. The interiors have ceilings with exposed rafters, recalling a seventeenth-century Tidewater practice. On the rear wall, each house has its only window.

When Americans moved into Louisiana, they brought the single- and double-pen house forms with them. These were especially used for slave housing. Some saddlebag houses and a single-pen, dating from about the 1830s, on Wilham plantation, have been moved to the Louisiana State University open air museum. These have clapboard siding. In addition to wood doors, their entrances also are curtained against the hot climate. While the saddlebag house clearly is a double-pen, with its dual-pitched roof, extended without columns, to shade the facade. This type of roof, however, can be seen on folk houses in the Carolinas and Vlach documented a Kentucky slave saddlebag house with the same columnless overhang. He suggested the possibility of a subtle African influence.[19]

Rural Housing after 1865

After the Civil War, Blacks usually remained on, or lived nearby, their former plantations, working as tenant farmers. What had been slave cabins became tenant houses. When the houses were replaced about the turn of the century, the newer tenant houses still followed Anglo-American folk patterns and retained a severe appearance. In Georgia, Merritt observed that slave cabins of log or of vertical boarding were sometimes resurfaced with clapboards.[20] Merritt states that this was to disguise some of the structures' original features, perhaps because of the negative connotation associated with possessing former slave structures. Although this may be true, cracks and gaps in old folk structures can be insulated well with a covering of clapboards, especially log structures; and during the latter decades of the nineteenth century, White owners of folk houses were following the same procedure, which suggests that another reason for using such a covering was to hide the humble origins of a folk house form in general.

Board-and-batten saddlebags, such as the tenant houses in Marengo County, Alabama, are similar in appearance to their pre–Civil War relative, despite the fact that they may date as late as the 1930s. They were constructed with board windows and doors in the same severe aesthetic as a slave cabin. The porches of these structures are typical of Black tenant houses in

Fig. 9-11 Tenant saddlebag house, ca. 1870, West Baton Rouge Parish, Louisiana. (Photo by P. Oszuscik.)

Fig. 9-12 Single-pen house, late nineteenth century, Smithville, Georgia. (Photo by P. Oszuscik.)

Philippe Oszuscik

the Anglo-American plantation belt in that they are small, perhaps just large enough to shade the doors from sun and rain, suggesting that individuals of a tenant status had no time for just sitting. Such dwellings may have originally housed two families. A saddlebag tenant house in Louisiana, circa 1870 or later (Fig. 9-11), appears just as severe, but, perhaps because of its location in West Baton Rouge Parish, it features a French Creole type integral porch. The only features that distinguish it from a French half-Creole cottage are its severity of design, its two-bay facade, and its small scale. As with French Creole structures, it includes the use of different board widths on the galerie wall. Many saddlebag tenant houses in the area also have un-painted exterior walls, except for the front elevation. This treatment represents a tradition going back to the whitewashed or plastered, half-timber facades of the earliest Creole houses.

In looking at houses of rural land owners, pen houses again dominate. On the outskirts of Smithville, Georgia, a late-nineteenth-century single-pen house (Fig. 9-12) still features the typical simplicity of design, small compact interior space, and lean-to porch. Its neatly swept dirt yard exhibits a Black tradition with African origins also encountered in Haiti. Carefully groomed areas of grass grow at the gate and one corner of the front yard that adjoins the vegetable garden.

Some Black landowners had adopted the dogtrot house by the late nineteenth century, in areas where it was the favorite folk house of lower-income White farmers. An example near Sunny South, Alabama, even has detached upper chimneys, in the Carolina and Virginia Tidewater tradition. This structure is indistinguishable from dogtrots built by Whites.

Housing in Towns and Cities

In small towns, some Black landowners built the old, traditional, hall-and-parlor house. A typical one would date from the late nineteenth century. It is larger than many rural houses, severe in design, and quite compact and possesses a gallery smaller than the porches of counterparts owned by Whites. A fairly steep, gabled roof is reminiscent of the earlier hall-and-parlor houses.

Some Black-occupied vernacular duplex housing in Savannah, Georgia (Fig. 9-13) still resembles a tenant or slave row of saddlebags. Ironically, they

Fig. 9-13 Black-owned duplexes, late nineteenth century, Savannah, Georgia. (Photo by P. Oszuscik.)

are urban equivalents of such, built, perhaps, for factory workers. An aesthetic severity dominates their Classical revival details. Small porches, approached from the side rather than directly from the street, shelter the doors. Such porches may represent a British Caribbean influence.

In Charleston, White homeowners in the 18th and 19th centuries lived in two-story "single houses." Two-tier porches facing the side yard rather than the street became a typical part of these houses beginning in the 1780s. The idea of orienting the facade as well as the porches to the yard probably came from the British Caribbean, and may in turn be traced to the Spanish tradition. Most of the surviving examples of these urban houses in Kingston, Jamaica, are one story. Whether evolving from the Jamaican one-story source or from the two-story Charleston single house, one-story "single cottages" are often the form of housing now inhabited by Blacks in Charleston. Like the single house, these hall-and-parlor and central hall cottages have a door from the street leading to a porch, which in turn has a door to the interior. Most porches abut a service wing. Additions to many of these dwellings make them reminiscent of the shotgun, or possibly one of its subtypes.

Haitians came to Charleston after 1791, the same time they came to New Orleans, and shotgun houses still exist in Charleston today. The Jamaican urban house (Fig. 9-14) cannot be overlooked as a major influence to the single house. The raised Charleston cottage, in particular, must be compared to the typical Kingston, Jamaica, house that dates to the eighteenth century. The Kingston house traditionally has a double stairway leading to an entrance, usually onto a porch, which commonly is louvered. Some have side porches as well. A Jamaican or British Caribbean treatment of the porch

Philippe
Oszuscik

Fig. 9-14 Urban house, early nineteenth century, Kingston, Jamaica. (Photo by P. Oszuscik.)

is to alternate sash windows with louvered sections that can be adjusted to open or close. Nevertheless, the single cottage is a curious form that is just as much a Creole house form as the French Creole and Afro-Creole houses, although its origins are in the British Caribbean rather than the French Caribbean.

African-Influenced Houses

On rare occasions, a plantation owner would be liberal with Blacks who were constructing their own quarters and would allow them to include obvious elements indicative of their African heritage. Freedman and ex-slaves with memories of Africa are documented to have built "African" houses in the Southeast from the Carolinas to Louisiana.[21] Surviving examples are extremely rare, as it was illegal to bring slaves into the United States after 1819; thus, most ex-slaves had no living memory of African housing to duplicate.

One example to cite is the famous "African House" on Melrose plantation, dating circa 1800. The master was a Black French Creole, with the surname *Metoyer*. Oral history relates that Metoyer, a Louisiana native, asked a newly arrived African slave to build an African house. The resulting structure was a two-story, double-pen with extremely deep projecting eaves and a hipped roof (Fig. 9-15). Many experts do not challenge the account of the history of the structure, since it appears African to Americans. Other scholars are more skeptical, pointing out that the cantilevered support system for the eaves is not African. In fact, this structure does resemble quite closely the traditional buildings of Bresse, France which have identical deep

Fig. 9-15 "African house," ca. 1800, Melrose plantation, Melrose, Louisiana. (Photo by P. Oszuscik.)

eaves, steep-hipped roofs, and the same cantilevered support system.[22] Brick and wood shingles were substituted for typically African materials. However, its design still embodies an African spirit, and its material and structural substitutions underwent the same syncretic process characteristic of all Creole structures.

Conclusion

The Afro-Creole shotgun and high house have obvious syncretic origins in Arawak, African, and French sources. Freedmen developed these house forms in Haiti and included more French devices when building in the French colonial urban areas. The thousands of free Black Creoles who entered Louisiana were large enough in number to establish this Afro-Creole house in the United States.

The Black housing derived from Anglo-American traditions is more difficult to explain. Yet, differences from its White counterparts are apparent to the acute eye. One notes severity of design, small rooms, and few windows in tenements and slave quarters. Vlach observed that since these structures were built by Blacks, these elements represent African preferences and aesthetics. The Yoruba house has only a door for interior light, small rooms, and plain mud walls.[23] Thus, these house designs were derived through the same syncretic process as the shotgun and French Creole cottage. Africans and the English share certain house-building traditions, such as the two-room house, wattle-and-daub walls, hipped roofs, and thatching that permitted syncretism to occur. The "Creolization" process is merely more subtle in the development of Black houses in the Anglo-American landscape.

This chapter illustrates that most rural houses of freedmen, ex-slaves, and subsequent generations of these continued to be smaller, plainer, and to have fewer windows than the rural houses of Whites, and some later structures even had dirt floors (an African tradition). While porches were added to most post-slavery houses, they tended to be smaller than those on houses of Whites of the same vernacular tradition. Double-pens or two-room houses dominated the rural inland landscape into the twentieth century.

Black folk and vernacular house traditions are beginning to disappear from the southeastern landscape just as are many earlier White folk traditions. Like rural Whites, Blacks are moving into trailer houses and ranch style homes.

Philippe Oszuscik

10

Cajuns in Louisiana

Malcolm L. Comeaux

IT IS DIFFICULT to define the Cajuns of Louisiana as a cultural group. There is much controversy as to just who is a Cajun.[1] In the strictest sense, they are Gulf Coast residents who are the descendants of French speakers who once lived in Nova Scotia. There are, however, few pure Cajuns. It has been well over 230 years since the French migration from Nova Scotia. Many other ethnic groups have married into Cajun society, including Englishmen, Spaniards, Germans, and other Frenchmen. Some people in south Louisiana have no Cajun ancestors but consider themselves Cajuns because they have lived among Cajuns for a long period. It is best, therefore, to characterize a Cajun as a person who identifies himself or herself as such and is also perceived by others to be so. This individual is typically Roman Catholic, has strong family ties, speaks some French or has family members who do, and comes from a rural background.

The Acadian Movement to Louisiana

The Cajuns have had a turbulent history. In the early 1600s their ancestors began migrating from western France, particularly the Loire River valley,[2] to Nova Scotia, an area at that time called Acadia. By the middle of the 1700s they had grown in number, were prosperous, and were known as Acadians (see Chapter 2). Most were agriculturalists who farmed drained coastal land, but others were fishermen, herders, and hunters. In 1755 there occurred *le grand derangement*—about 10,000 Acadians were forcibly removed and their lands given to others. Several authors have written of this deportation, some quite emotionally.[3] The uprooted Acadians were either imprisoned or scattered. Most were shipped to the British colonies along the eastern seaboard of North America, but another large group was taken as prisoners to England and later exiled to France. Others were imprisoned until 1763 in Halifax, Nova Scotia. With no possibility of returning to their homeland, many of the Acadians began drifting to other parts of eastern Canada, but large numbers chose Louisiana as their final destination.

Most of the Acadian migrants to Louisiana arrived between 1765 and 1785. About 1,200 Acadians arrived from Nova Scotia and the eastern seaboard between 1765 and 1768, but small groups continued to arrive from those areas throughout the late eighteenth century. The only large organized migration consisted of about 1,600 individuals who had been interned in England and then exiled to France. The Spanish government transported these Acadians from France to Louisiana in 1785 in an effort to bolster the population of the colony they had acquired from France in 1762.[4] About 4,000 Acadians eventually reached Louisiana.

The Acadians settled in south Louisiana (Fig. 10-1) and slowly expanded outward, particularly westward and southward. The Acadians were among the first to settle many areas of south Louisiana. Other peoples were also attracted to south Louisiana. Large numbers of Germans settled upstream from New Orleans a generation before the Acadians arrived, and Spaniards occupied several other areas. Also, at about the time of the first Acadian settlements, English-speaking Americans began drifting into Louisiana as a part of their westward expansion. The Acadians, however, became the dominant group in rural south Louisiana, and many individuals from other groups were absorbed into the Acadian culture.

Almost everywhere the French settled in the New World they subdivided the land into long narrow strips, in what is called the long-lot system (see Figure 8-4). The French in Louisiana used this technique long before the first Acadians arrived, and the Spanish continued the system in many of their land grants. For a time, even the U.S. government continued the tradition of granting land in long lots in Louisiana, in the only instance in which

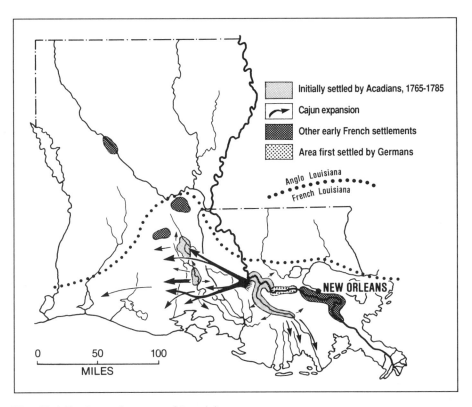

Malcolm L. Comeaux

178   Fig. 10-1 Early settlement of Louisiana

the U.S. government deviated from the rectangular survey system, once it had been established.[5] The long-lot method of surveying land, therefore, cannot be used to identify areas of Cajun settlement, for many other peoples, such as Germans, Spaniards, and Americans, were among the initial settlers of land thus subdivided.

The environment of south Louisiana was very different from that found in eastern Canada, and Acadian culture had to change in order for the Acadians to survive.[6] Such change occurred quickly—new crops were grown and new foods eaten, clothing styles were modified, new house and barn types were adopted, new words to describe local subjects were developed or adopted, and the like. By the 1870s these people were known as Cajuns, and their culture was quite different from that of their cousins who had remained in Canada, who are known to this day as Acadians. Some aspects of Acadian culture remained intact over the years, such as their adherence to the Roman Catholicism and their strong feeling for family ties. But, on the whole, the Cajuns of Louisiana, by the middle of the nineteenth century, had become a new people and developed a distinctive culture.

Throughout the nineteenth century the Cajuns were a rural people, and to understand Cajun buildings and construction techniques one must understand the Cajun farmstead. The Cajuns developed a unique farmstead that varied little from one region to the next, and it provided a distinctive look to the land. An understanding of the form and function of farmsteads can also provide clues to understanding landscapes and economy.[7] Knowledge of the Cajun farmstead is therefore important for an understanding of Cajun culture in general.

The Cajun Farmstead

Various elements typify the Cajun farmstead: the characteristic farmer's residence and the barns and outbuildings that shelter animals, store feed, and protect equipment; particular kinds of fences; and the use of certain types of vegetation. No two Cajun farmsteads were exactly alike, but certain basic traits were found in all.

The typical Louisiana Cajun farmstead of the nineteenth century was very different from the farmsteads of western France, the original homeland of the Acadians. In western France, farmsteads were usually in villages, abutted a road, and had buildings opening onto a central courtyard. Louisiana provided a new and challenging environment for early French settlers, and they apparently never tried to replicate the farmsteads of France.

The typical farmstead of the Cajuns was an aggregation of many small buildings set far back from the road (Fig. 10-2). Between the farmstead and the road was a pasture that was usually used to graze milk cows and horses. A road crossed the pasture and led to a carriage house, or *remise*, which was to the side and slightly to the rear of the home. The placement of the farmstead far back from the road and surrounded by a pasture seems to be an old cultural trait, for such farmstead layouts are found throughout French Louisiana. The building closest to the road was the house. It always faced the road and usually was the largest building on the farmstead, though sometimes a barn was larger.

The only building material readily available in nineteenth-century

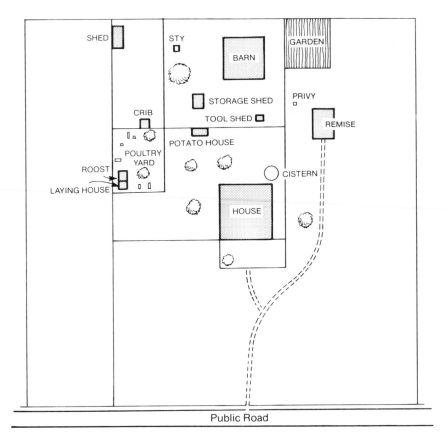

Fig. 10-2 Plan of a typical Cajun farmstead

southern Louisiana was cypress, and this wood was used in almost all construction. It was particularly important because it was (1) very durable, (2) less flammable than other woods, (3) easily worked, (4) readily split into shingles and boards, and (5) resistant to rot, a desirable feature in humid southern Louisiana. To acquire this wood, farmers entered swamps and girdled cypress trees in the fall, and then during the next flood felled the trees and floated them to the swamp's edge. To produce boards, the logs first were sawed into blocks about seven to nine feet long and six to nine inches wide. From these blocks boards known as *pieux* were rived with a large froe (*coteau pieu*) and maul. Except for their roughness, the resulting pieux greatly resembled milled lumber. There was always a demand for pieux,[8] and their production and sale had become a big business by the 1870s, particularly in areas not near cypress swamps.[9] All buildings were roofed with long shingles known as *merrain*, produced in a fashion similar to that of pieux. By the 1880s modern industrial techniques were being used in the cypress lumbering industry,[10] and at this time Cajuns began purchasing milled cypress lumber from the sawmills that lined most local swamps.

Most Cajun settlements in Louisiana were in open prairie environments; and a farmstead, surrounded by tall trees, resembled an island in a sea of grass. The cypress wood, unpainted except for the front of the house,

Malcolm L. Comeaux

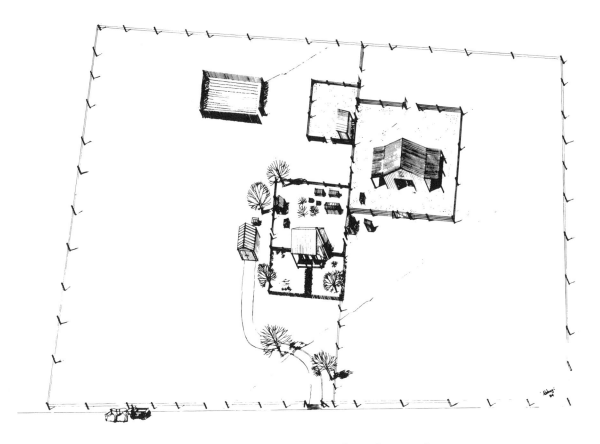

Fig. 10-3 A sketch of a typical Cajun farmstead in the late nineteenth century. (Courtesy D. Abbey, Louisiana State University.)

weathered with time into a dull grey color. From nearby, the dull grey color of the buildings and fences dominated the appearances of farmsteads. From a distance, however, they resembled areas of high vegetation that were a deep green color in summertime; in winter, when vegetation was dormant, entire farmsteads had a dull and dreary appearance.

There was always a particular order to Cajun farmsteads (Fig. 10-3). All buildings were built either facing the same direction as the house or at right angles to it. Doors to outbuildings usually opened toward the house, but if the buildings were off to the rear and side of the home, the doors usually opened as if to an imaginary courtyard to the center of the rear yard. Many fences were found on each farmstead. Fence lines always ran parallel to the sides of the house.

A study of American farmsteads in general, conducted in 1948, reveals that the Cajun farmstead was quite different from all others.[11] Another very detailed examination of the farmsteads immediately north of the French area, in the hill country of southeast Louisiana, revealed farmsteads there to be very different when compared to those of the French-speakers to the south and west.[12] Differences noted in the hill country included such things as farmsteads built near the road, different building materials and tech-

Cajuns in Louisiana

181

niques, fences meeting at odd angles, and so forth. The traditional Cajun farmstead of south Louisiana is truly unique.

The Cajun House

The house was by far the most important building on the farm. It was the only structure built with great care, and the only one to receive extensive maintenance. The house used by the Acadians in Canada was not suitable in the humid subtropical Louisiana environment, and the Acadians quickly adopted a house type that had been widely used in Louisiana before their arrival (see Chapter 8).[13] It was a house type that first evolved in the West Indies and had become the main house type of the Germans who lived near the Acadians' earliest settlement on the Mississippi (see Fig. 10-1). The basic house type was accepted by Cajuns, who then took it with them wherever they settled. Its use was so widespread that it became a true folk house, and local people always recognized it as the traditional "Cajun" house.

The Cajun house had several distinctive features (Figs. 10-4 and 10-5). The typical Cajun house was two rooms wide, had two front doors, and had no central hall. A chimney could be in the center or on the inside of the walls on one or both gables. The house had a steep, gabled roof, with the gable parallel to the bayou or road onto which the house fronted. The roof usually had no dormers and extended to cover a gallery that stretched across the front of the home. A stairway from the front porch gave access to the attic, which was used for storage and as a young men's bedroom (*garconniere*). It was very common to have two rooms, covered with a shed roof, added to the rear; and some time after construction almost all homes had a kitchen and dining area added, usually also to the rear, thus giving the house a T or L shape. The house was always built 2 to 3 feet above the ground, resting on cypress or brick piers. It was made of heavy frame construction, never of logs. The area between the heavy beams was filled with a nogging of mud

Malcolm L. Comeaux

Fig. 10-4 The Cajun house. (Drawing by M. M. Geib.)

Fig. 10-5 View of a typical Cajun home (the chimney on the inside wall has been removed). A wooden cistern, in very poor repair, is situated at the right rear corner of the dwelling. (Photo by M. Comeaux.)

and moss (*bousillage*). The sides and rear of the home were covered by clapboards (another use of pieux) to protect the nogging from the weather, but the nogging at the front was somewhat protected by the porch roof and was always painted or whitewashed, in contrast to that on the rest of the structure.

The Cajun Barn

The Acadians adopted a new type of barn upon their arrival in Louisiana.[14] The barns of Acadia had been quite large, and their main features included a side entrance and a threshing floor.[15] The barns of French Louisiana were very small structures. One probable reason for the small barns was environmental, as the mild Louisiana winters did not require extended stabling of animals, and relatively little animal feed had to be stored. The barns of southeastern Louisiana were particularly small, with structures as small as 12′ × 15′ being called barns.[16]

The Cajun barn is distinctive. Its origin undoubtedly lies with the Germans who lived nearby on the Mississippi. This type of barn first developed along the Mississippi River, but it reached its fullest development and greatest use in the Cajun settlements to the west of the river (Fig. 10-6). The typical Cajun barn had a recessed central crib, a gable-end front, and a squarish floor plan (usually 30 feet on a side) (Fig. 10-7). Corn was sorted in the central crib (*magasin à maïs*) and hay in the loft (*grenier*), while horses or mules were fed on one side and cattle on the other (both sides were called *écurie*).

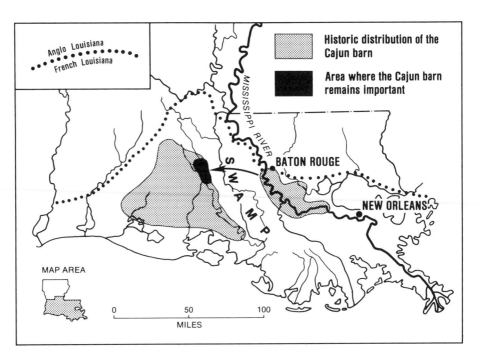

Fig. 10-6 Distribution of the Cajun barn

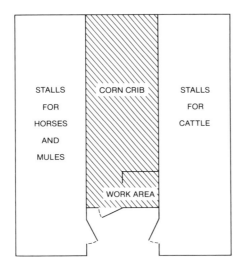

Fig. 10-7 The floor plan of the typical Cajun barn

*Malcolm L.
Comeaux*

Most Cajun barns had a shed appendage, resembling an open lean-to, added to one or both sides (Fig. 10-8). This addition (*appentis*), usually added long after the barn was built, was used for storage or for animal shelter. Most additions were built of heavy frame construction, though occasionally an old log crib had a barn built around it. The only lower part of the barn to have a floor was the crib. The sides usually were vertical boards nailed to the heavy

Fig. 10-8 A typical late-nineteenth century Cajun barn. (Photo by
M. Comeaux.)

frame, and battens were never used. The roofs were covered with handsplit
shakes (*merrains*).

Chicken Coops

Chickens were important on all farms and were raised primarily for
home consumption. The chickens were under the exclusive control of the
farmer's wife; she would raise and feed them, and if any hens and eggs were
sold she would keep the money for her own discretionary use.[17] On most
farms there were from five to seven small structures devoted to the raising of
chickens, usually located in a cluster near the rear of the house. Two of these
structures were of some size, the roost and the laying house, but the rest were
little more than cages.

The roost was one of the larger structures devoted to the raising of
chickens. The roost was called the *juchoir*, though some farmers called it *fort*.
Doors were locked at night, and the building was made safe from nocturnal
predators such as mink, skunk, opossum, or raccoon. Since chickens suffered
in the heat (it was not unusual for several to die during summer months) and
seemingly were unaffected by the cold, the sides of the roost were usually
made of slats, though one or more walls could be solid, particularly a north-
facing wall. A few farmers did not provide a roost, but allowed the chickens
to roost in small trees.

There were two types of roosts. The most common was a small building
(usually about 7 feet high, 10 feet wide, and 8 feet deep) built on the ground
with no floor (Fig. 10-9). On the inside were a series of horizontal slats, nearer

Fig. 10-9 A typical Cajun farm chicken coop. (Photo by M. Comeaux.)

Fig. 10-10 An elevated Cajun chicken coop, of the type commonly found in areas that tend to flood. (Photo by M. Comeaux.)

the ground at the front and rising stairlike to the back, where the chickens would roost. The second type was usually smaller and had a floor made of small slats placed close together. In south central Louisiana, in areas that tended to flood, this type was often raised on posts 4 to 8 feet off the ground (Fig. 10-10).

Another structure associated with chickens was the laying house (*poulailler*). It was oblong, had a dirt floor, and was about the same size as the larger type of roost. A series of nests (*nichées pour les poule pond*) lined the inside walls, and sometimes nests with a shed roof over them were attached to the outside of the laying house, or occasionally were free-standing.

There were also small cages (*cage à poulets*) built of cypress slats. Some were used to fatten chickens, others were used to stop hens from setting while others were used to hold hens with young chicks. One type resembled a small gabled roof sitting directly on the ground, but others were small square structures built a foot or so above the ground.

Other Outbuildings

There were many small outbuildings on the typical Louisiana French farmstead. Most were built of cypress planks placed vertically, and battens were not used. The better-built structures had gabled roofs, with the entrance usually on the gable end, though some rather mean buildings had shed roofs and an entrance on the side where the roof was highest. These buildings were also roofed with hand-rived cypress shakes.

Certain outbuildings were found on most farmsteads. By the beginning of the twentieth century all had a privy (*cabinet* or *comode*), usually a small square building. Almost all homes had a potato house (*patatrie*). A few were quite fancy (brick-lined to help keep it cool), but the vast majority were small, oblong, simply built buildings. A few farmers kept their sweet potatoes not in a potato house but in an earth-covered mound (*butte*).[18] Cows traditionally were milked out-of-doors, tied to a fence, and in inclement weather in the rear part of the barn. By the end of the nineteenth century, however, it was common for a farmer to have a small milking shed (*laiterie*). Small low sheds for pigs were common, as well as a sty to fatten pigs for a month or two prior to slaughter. The sty was a small, square, simply built structure made of widely spaced horizontal boards, with a floor about a foot off the ground. Most farmsteads also had several other small outbuildings, such as a storage shed or two, a smoke house, and a tool shed. To the side of the dwelling was a carriage house (*remise*) that in the twentieth century was invariably converted into a garage.

Fences

Fences were an important part of all Cajun farmsteads. Since domestic animals and plants had to coexist on farms, fencing was critical to the success of subsistence farming. Hedges were suggested as a solution to the fencing problem as early as 1807, and many Cherokee rose hedges still survive; but hedges did not solve the problems.[19] The only fencing material readily available were the pieux of cypress, and throughout the nineteenth century two types of pieux fences were used on Cajun farmsteads.

The oldest fence type employed closely spaced vertical pieux that were driven into the ground. This type of fence resembled the palisade walls of Indians and may have evolved from them. The vertical pieux fence was traditionally used around the home and farmstead, but never around fields. The earliest proven use of this fence along the Gulf Coast was in 1717, and it was found around houses wherever the French settled in the Mississippi Valley.[20] In 1811 a similar type of fence, around a home in St. Genevieve, Missouri, was described in the following way: "The yard was enclosed with cedar pickets, eight or ten inches in diameter, and six feet high, placed upright, sharpened at the top in the manner of a stockade fort. The substantial and permanent character of these enclosures is in singular contrast with the slight and temporary fences and palings of the Americans."[21] Such a description would have fit a Cajun fence of that era, except that the Cajuns would have used cypress pieux rather than round posts.

The original vertical pieux fence was about 6 feet tall. The pieux were driven into the ground, and as the bottoms rotted off the pieux were driven ever farther into the ground.[22] By the end of the nineteenth century runners had been added, nailed to the top and bottom of the fence to give it greater stability. By this time many of the pieux fences had become relatively short and had come to resemble picket fences.

The second type of fence commonly found on Cajun farmsteads was known simply as the pieux fence (or *pieux à travers*), and it had the pieux placed horizontally. In building this fence, slots were cut in relatively short pieux with a *peircer pieu*, a tool that resembled an adz with a narrow trough-shaped blade. These pieux were then placed vertically into the ground about 8 feet apart, and usually five pieux were placed horizontally through these slots. This fence type was unique to French Louisiana. A similar type of fence, known as the post and rail, was used in the North; but as the name implies, it was made of substantial posts, and rails were used rather than boards as in the pieux fence.[23] Throughout the deep South, including northern Louisiana, the principal pioneer fence was the snake fence (also known as zig-zag or worm fence), but these were never used by the Cajuns.

The pieux à travers fence was a good one; and with the pieux placed horizontally, considerably fewer were required than when they were placed vertically. This fence was used extensively, particularly around fields, large pastures, and smaller enclosures near the rear of the home. The one weak feature of this fence was the vertical pieux; they would rot in the ground and if driven in farther would no longer hold five pieux, for at least one slot would be underground (Fig. 10-11). By the end of the nineteenth century, the common way to repair this was to replace the vertical pieux with a post (usually of catalpa because of its resistance to rot) onto which the horizontal pieux were nailed. Many examples of very old pieux nailed to posts can still be seen. The old pieux were kept rather than replaced because by the late nineteenth century cypress had to be purchased and thus was expensive. It was difficult to cut holes for the pieux in the catalpa, and nails were relatively cheap by this time, thus the switch to posts and nails.

Gates in fences varied. The literature tells us little about early gates. One writer mentions that sometimes in a vertical pieux fence one of the pieux,

Malcolm L. Comeaux

188

Fig. 10-11 An old pieux fence. This fence now has only three horizontal pieux, but the holes in the vertical pieux at ground level suggest that the fence had five or six when new. As the vertical pieux rotted at the bottom they were driven farther into the ground. (Photo by M. Comeaux.)

known as the *passe pieu*, was unnailed so that it would be removed to allow passage.[24] The passe pieu was held in place by slats nailed to the tops and bottoms of its neighboring pieux. This "gate" was unique to French Louisiana. Older informants mentioned that locally made hinges were sometimes used in gates. They identified two gate types that required no hinges, although neither was unique to French Louisiana. One (Fig. 10-12), still commonly used, has two vertical posts placed close together with small horizontal boards running between them and supporting half the weight of the gate. The other end of the gate rests on the ground, and the farmer has only to lift it and swing the gate open. The other type had the gate built on a large post, the lower end of which fit into the hub of a wagon wheel while the upper end was supported by an iron loop attached to the fence. This arrangement supported the weight of the gate and allowed it to pivot.

As late as 1890 all fences were of pieux, but about that time wire fences (barbed wire and woven wire) were introduced, and they quickly began to replace pieux fences.[25] Fences of horizontal boards remain an important fence type at the rear of farmsteads, and a few houses still have picket fences around them, but by the middle of the twentieth century most fences were of wire. The wooden fences were never painted, and they added to the dull grey character of the typical Cajun farmstead.

Cajuns in Louisiana

Fig. 10-12 A hingeless gate. The left side of the gate is off the ground, resting on cross pieces between the two vertical posts. The farmer, to open or close the gate, raises the other end of the gate and swings it aside. (Photo by M. Comeaux.)

Farmstead Vegetation

Most Cajun farmsteads were located in open flat grasslands, and surrounding pastures, fields, and fencerows were usually devoid of trees. The farmsteads, meanwhile, had many trees and shrubs so they stood out as islands on the flat landscape.

A large variety of trees were planted on farmsteads. Some of these were simply shade trees, but many had other useful purposes. There were many fruit trees, such as fig, pear, persimmon, and citrus usually kept to the rear of the house. Also several pecan trees usually provided shade and nuts. In many prairie areas some trees, particularly the chinaberry, were grown for firewood. They were planted to the rear of the home and pollarded every other year, developing a grotesque appearance with huge trunks and tiny limbs. By the late nineteenth century some trees were grown for use as fence posts, especially catalpa trees, which were particularly resistant to rot.

Usually a small vegetable garden lay to the rear of the house. It was worked by the farmer in his spare time, and every farmer took great pride in his garden. All male visitors were expected to visit and comment favorably on it. A vertical pieux fence, high enough (about 6 feet) to keep out chickens, surrounded the garden (Fig. 10-13). There were problems with a pieux fence around a garden; it produced too much shade, it created a hot working space inside the enclosure, and it was expensive to replace. Consequently, high woven wire fences were adopted when they became available in the late nineteenth century.

The front yard was best described as "an enclosure within an enclo-

Malcolm L. Comeaux

190

Fig. 10-13 Enclosing gardens within high pieux fences was common in the nineteenth century. This farmer stands at the gate of one of the few surviving examples of this practice. (Photo by M. Comeaux.)

sure."[26] One researcher contends that the concept of this "double front yard" may extend back to Normandy.[27] If it does, it is about the only bit of the European farmstead that survived in the New World. The yard was usually surrounded by a high vertical pieux fence. Vegetation was dominated by flowers, and most front yards had jasmine bushes, which gave the yard a distinctive sweet odor. Maintenance of the front yard was the responsibility of the homemaker. She, along with any other person she could press into service, such as a young son, would usually use a hoe to scrape the ground, not allowing a weed or blade of grass to grow. This latter tradition was common in the American South, and it may have been an idea accepted by the Acadians when introduced to them.[28]

The traditional Cajun farmstead was set far back from the road and resembled an island in a sea of grass. Buildings were almost entirely unpainted, except for the front of the house; and so, with the extensive unpainted cypress pieux fences, the predominant visual characteristic was bleached, grey, rain-washed cypress. In summer the farmstead had a very pleasing appearance, but on a cold and overcast winter day, all of this grey, along with the grey of the dormant vegetation, produced a rather dreary look.

Summary and Conclusions

Many aspects of the farmstead were unique to southern Louisiana, or to the Cajuns themselves. The house used by the Cajuns was limited to southern Louisiana. It was well suited to the environment and the available technology, and it was found wherever the Cajuns settled. The Cajun barn, meanwhile, was unique to the Cajuns. It was a barn type that they developed, and it diffused with Cajun expansion westward, but not southward. It was well adapted to the environment and it fit the needs of these subsistence agriculturalists. The fences were also a bit unusual, but they too were functional. Some of the other buildings on the farmstead were distinctive, such as the elevated chicken roost, but the rest would resemble buildings on farmsteads elsewhere in the American South, except in the building material—very few in Cajun Louisiana were ever built of logs. There was also a characteristic shape and orderliness to the Cajun farmstead.

The traditional Cajun farmstead is rapidly becoming a thing of the past. Many elderly Cajuns try to maintain this old look of the land, but they are fewer each year. Few farmers keep animals, as they find it cheaper and easier to purchase milk, cheese, butter, eggs, meat, and the like. The grey and weathered cypress wood now brings high prices for decorative purposes in urban areas. As a result, barns and outbuildings are fast disappearing from the landscape, being dismantled and their wood sold. The typical farmstead of the 1990s consists of a brick home on a concrete slab located near the road, having few outbuildings except for a large "pole barn" to store farm implements. The traditional farmstead of the nineteenth century fit the time and place, and served the Cajuns well, but its usefulness has passed, and today only remnants of old farmsteads are left.

Malcolm L.
Comeaux

Part IV

*Central
North America*

11

Belgians in Wisconsin

William G. Laatsch and Charles F. Calkins

THE TITLE of the book *Old World Wisconsin: Around Europe in the Badger State*, published about forty years ago, suggests the importance of ethnic islands in the settlement fabric of Wisconsin.[1] Evidence of ethnic islands and their associated cultural landscapes remains throughout much of the state. One such island, settled by Walloon-speaking Belgians, can be found in northeastern Wisconsin's Door Peninsula, which is composed of parts of Door, Kewaunee, and Brown counties.

The Belgian Migration

Belgian immigrants were attracted to this area between 1853 and 1857 from their homes, primarily in the south central provinces of Brabant, Hanaut, and Namur. The push from the homeland was stimulated by crop failure in the 1840s and early 1850s, the decline of local and regional industries as industrialization and transportation became more centralized, and the pressures of continued population growth.[2] The primary magnet drawing the Belgians to northeastern Wisconsin was land at the government price of $1.25 an acre. Moving was vigorously encouraged by Antwerpen shipowners, whose agents actively sought passengers among the rural folk, and recruiters who, armed with guides and handbooks, advocated Wisconsin as a place to settle. However, the major exodus was relatively short lived. Restrictions by the Belgian government, because of falling Belgian land values, increased wage demands, the actions of corrupt and careless shipowners, and discouraging letters from previous emigrants, abruptly curtailed the mass migration in 1857.

The Belgian pioneers did not come directly to the Door Peninsula. Arriving in New York City they took the Albany-Buffalo road, sailed to Detroit, and took the train to St. Joseph, on the eastern shore of Lake Michigan. After crossing the lake to Milwaukee they chose a place some fifty miles north, near the city of Sheboygan. However, this area, occupied by Dutch and Germans, was unattractive to these Walloon-speakers, because of the language differences. Resident French-speaking immigrants informed them of the French Canadian population that lived in the lower Fox River Valley in the vicinity of Green Bay. It was here that the Belgians accidently encountered Father Edouard Daems, who was in charge of the Bay Settlement parish on the Door Peninsula, a few miles northeast of the city of Green Bay. It was, thus, through the presence and assistance of a Walloon-speaking Belgian priest that the Belgians began to acquire land and establish a Belgian settlement region.

The Belgian Settlement

By 1860, there were 3,812 foreign-born Belgians in the three-county area; this figure represented 33.7 percent of the total foreign-born population residing in Door, Kewaunee, and Brown counties at this time. Of these 3,812 Belgians, approximately 2,900, or 70 percent, had settled in the area that was to evolve into the rural Belgian ethnic island. The remainder had more of an urban orientation and were to be found in or very close to the city of Green Bay, which had a population of 2,275 in 1860.

Census data from as early as 1860 and current field research reveal a well-defined and persistent Belgian cultural area (Fig. 11-1). Within the area delineated on the map 80 percent of the farmland is in the hands of Belgians. This amounts to approximately 150 square miles with a population estimated at 10,000 persons.

The Belgian cultural region is bounded by other ethnic groups.[3] The sharpest line is to the southeast in Kewaunee County, where a well-defined Bohemian community is located. To the east and north the ethnicity is more varied, but Germans predominate. A Norwegian and a more distinct German community form a northeastern boundary. In terms of language, especially, these Teutonic and Slavic groups provide sharp contrast with the Romanic French Walloons.

A variety of material and nonmaterial elements can be identified that belong to the Belgians. Even to the untrained ear the English spoken by the locals can be recognized as being different from most "Midwesterneze." If one were to visit a Belgian home or join in a picnic at the local Roman Catholic parish, some of the food such as jutt, trippe, kaset, booyah, and Belgian pie would be unfamiliar. Some of the place names—Brussels, Namur, Thiry Daems—and common surnames such as LeMense, Baudhuin, Massart, and Jeanquart evoke European roots.

State Highway 57 cuts through the region, linking the city of Green Bay, and points south or west, to the Door Peninsula. At times during summer the highway carries bumper-to-bumper vacation traffic as city people are attracted to the physical and cultural features of Door County.[4] The vast majority of these people, intent on arriving at their destination swiftly and safely, pay little regard to the unique region through which they pass, giving the settlements of Namur and Brussels only passing recognition. Off the highway are a dozen or so villages having common components arranged linearly along a section line road. The village ensemble includes a Roman Catholic church, adjacent cemetery and rectory, a tavern or two, a two-room public school, a general store, cheese factory, mill, and a handful of residences, often situated above the commercial structures.

Around these small service centers are the dairy farms, which are relatively small by today's standards—80, 120, 160 acres. The pattern their fields exhibit is a checkerboard of rectangular plots, reflecting the U.S. public land survey system. The area has been surveyed some twenty years before the

William G.
Laatsch
and
Charles F.
Calkins

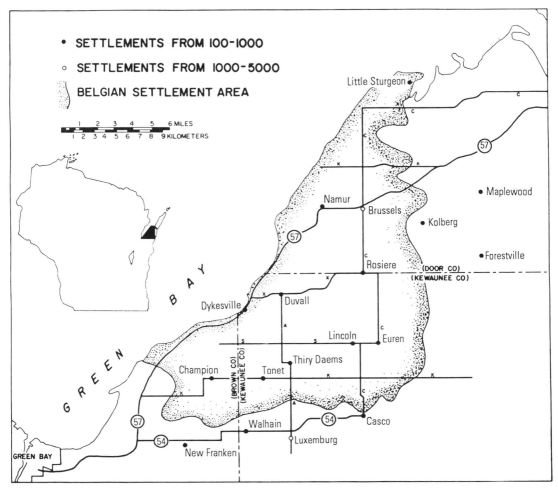

Fig. 11-1 Belgian settlement in northeastern Wisconsin. Eighty percent of the farmland within the stippled area is owned by ethnic Belgians. (Map by W. Laatsch, 1977–78.)

arrival of the Belgians. The resulting landscape, while not dramatic, is attractive, with the land surface form dominated by resistant Niagara dolomite, sculpted by glacial erosion, and later covered with a thin layer of till deposited as the glacial ice wasted away. The rolling land slopes gently to the east, following the Niagara cuesta as it dips under Lake Michigan. Interrupting the regular geometry of the countryside are low densely treed swamps and rough areas where the bedrock appears at the surface.

Extensive mixed forests provided logs for the first structures erected by the Belgians. Few of these buildings exist today. Most were leveled in early October 1871 by extensive and intense fires (exactly contemporaneous with, but unrelated to, the great Chicago Fire!), which destroyed buildings, crops, livestock, timber, and took more than 200 lives. The disaster was not without some benefits. The fire partially cleared thousands of acres, and land was thus more readily available for farming. A building boom also resulted from

Belgians in Wisconsin

the fire. Many of the trees, especially the conifers, though stripped of their foliage and badly charred, were left standing. If harvested and trimmed, often with a broadaxe, before the wood could rot or become insect infested, the salvaged logs could be used for building.

The Vernacular Belgian House

Thus the winter of 1871–72 was a period of timber harvest in anticipation of spring and summer construction. The resulting vernacular houses date from the late 1870s into the early 1880s. Modest in size and well proportioned, these houses are similar to one another in form, material, scale, and detail. Clearly the Belgian house type lends character and a distinctiveness to the area. The Belgians did not share a history of log construction that we associate with Northern or Eastern Europeans. Thus, much of the log work is not of the quality produced by ethnic groups who came from a log building tradition. Despite this lack of tradition, many buildings do exhibit tight joinery and refinements that reflect good craftsmanship. After the laying up of logs, most of the houses were eventually covered with a red brick veneer or with clapboards (Fig. 11-2). As recently as 1949, an old log home near Dyckesville was covered with red brick. Among the locals this process is more than cosmetic. Their explanations indicate that the veneer made the houses more weather resistant and that the brick, being fire resistant, alleviated fears associated with the 1871 conflagration. Of broader importance may have been the desire of the Belgians to adopt the building material common to their homeland, where brick and stone structures prevail. This cultural re-

William G. Laatsch and Charles F. Calkins

Fig. 11-2 A typical log and red brick veneer Belgian house, in the process of being restored. A summer kitchen with attached oven is to the rear. (Photo by W. Laatsch.)

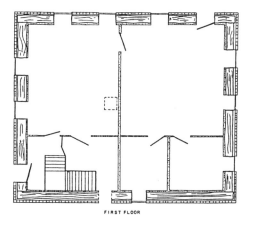
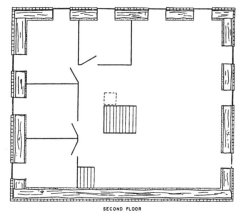

FIRST FLOOR   SECOND FLOOR

Fig. 11-3 The "four-and-two" floor plan is evident in this plan of the
Massart house, now restored at Heritage Hill State Park, Green
Bay, Wisconsin.

bound would have occurred at a time when the pioneer phase of settlement
had been completed and some wealth had been accumulated. (See Chapter
14 for a similar situation with the Finns.) In addition, brickyards developed
locally and in the Green Bay area in the early 1880s; and masons, many with
Milwaukee ties, were available to build the structures.

Fewer in number, but similar to the brick houses in proportion and scale,
are stone houses constructed from locally quarried dolomite. The appearance of this buff-colored irregular stone, coupled with the modest scale and
appropriate proportions of these houses, give them an especially European
look. While these houses are relatively few—a couple of dozen—when compared to the red brick structures, they are an almost dramatic addition to the
harmonious architecture found in the region.

Whether these houses are constructed of stone or brick, their floor plans
are similar; the plan of the Massart house may be considered typical (Fig.
11-3). Tishler has identified this floor plan as a "four-and-two, with four
small rooms along one axial wall and two large rooms along the other, with
one of the latter used as a living room and the other as a dining/kitchen
area."[5] The kitchen/dining area was, and is, the focus of activity within the
house.

As simple farmhouses, these structures reflect their utilitarian design
but are not without decorative elements. A "bulls-eye" window just under
the roof peak on the gable facing the road is a common feature (Fig. 11-4).
Known locally as builders' trademarks, these windows may be circular or
semicircular, plain or ornate. A cream-colored brick, contrasting with the
more normal red brick, is used as a decorative element around windows and
doors and on the quoins. Finally some houses have areas of elaborate decoration, where the mason has created designs in brick that contrast sharply with
the monotonous courses of stretchers.

*Belgians in
Wisconsin*

Fig. 11-4 An example of a builder's trademark "bulls-eye" window. (Photo by W. Laatsch.)

The Vernacular Belgian Barn

Belgian barns strongly reflect economic progress rather than perpetuating unique ethnic traditions, as the Belgian house does. The largest Belgian barn is the early-twentieth-century dairy barn; livestock are housed on the ground floor and the upper level is used for hay storage. The structure is framed with squared timbers and covered with vertical boards (Fig. 11-5). North of the village of Brussels are found raised or basement barns, which have dolomite foundations and a ramp or bank providing access to the loft. Roof shapes vary, with older gable roofs having been replaced by gambrel roofs in the early decades of the twentieth century. Three-bay barns are also common, their central threshing floor reflecting the dominance of the wheat era. These barns have now been adapted for other uses (Fig. 11-6). A barn of this type, consists of two log cribs linked by a frame roof covering a drive through. Single-crib cattle barns, granaries, pig sties, and poultry sheds of log, usually cedar, can be found in the farmyard. The proportion of log structures when compared to other buildings is truly remarkable, and it would be difficult to find a greater variety, frequency, or density of log structures anywhere in North America. Brick farm buildings are rare, but brick barns, sheds, smokehouses, pig sties—and even brick privies!—do exist; they cannot, however, be said to characterize the region. Connecting architecture is common, as barns and sheds have been joined forming ells or enclosing a yard, or linked end to end. The number, form, and size of these Belgian farm structures is probably not unique, but there is a decorative element that does stand out. This is a white five- or six-pointed star, 2 ½ to 3 feet

William G. Laatsch and Charles F. Calkins

Fig. 11-5 A dairy barn with a log granary is a common sight near Green Bay, Wisconsin. (Photo by W. Laatsch.)

Fig. 11-6 A log three-bay threshing barn adapted to shelter cattle. (Photo by W. Laatsch.)

across, attached to the gable end and immediately below the roof of the large dairy barn. The significance of the star is not yet clear, but the strongest indication is that it is a builder's trademark.

Research is continuing to explore whether these types of barns and ancillary structures are unique to the Belgian community. For example, a sharp difference can be observed between the Belgian barns and those in the Bohemian area, where three-gable barns predominate. Given the plethora of structures and the time demands of field research, the answers will be slow in coming.

There are, however, two structures in addition to the house that can be used as an index to Belgian settlement. They are modest in size and can be easily overlooked in a cursory view of a farmstead. These structures are the outdoor bakeoven[6] and the roadside chapel.[7]

The Belgian Bakeoven

The oven is a separate structure, although it does share a common gable end with the familiar summer kitchen. The kitchen, also a relic structure, is generally located a few steps from the back door of the house. Access to the oven's fire/baking chamber was gained through the summer kitchen. The oven rested on a platform which was constructed of local dolomite and stood 4 feet high, measured 7 ½ feet wide, and extended 6 ½ feet beyond the gable end of the summer kitchen. On top of this platform the oven was constructed. The oven was oval, resembling the shape of an egg that has been halved lengthwise and laid flat side down (Fig. 11-7). The interior of the oval-domed fire/baking chamber was 2 feet tall at the highest part, 4 ⅓ feet wide, and 5 ¾ feet deep. A small door (approximately 20 inches high) located 28 inches above the kitchen floor provided access from the kitchen to the oven.

Bricks made from local clays were used in constructing the fire/baking chamber and the chimney, which was built into the gable end of the summer kitchen. After the base was laid, wet sand was heaped onto the platform, packed, and molded until the required dome shape was attained. Using the sand core as a form, bricks were laid to produce the required shape. The same lime mortar used for bonding the brick was applied to the entire surface, thus sealing it. After the mortar hardened, the sand core was removed, and the interior of the fire/baking chamber was given the same treatment. Since baking was accomplished by radiated heat, the dimensions of the oven were critical. If the oven was too small, the bread burned, if too large, baking would be slow and uneven. To protect the oven from damage, a roof was constructed over the entire structure. The roof was framed and extended down to the platform. A square door, 22 inches on a side, in the gable gave access to the oven's domed exterior for periodic repair to the mortar.

Baking was done weekly, usually on Saturday, and more often at harvest time, the days preceding holidays, and the *kirmess*[8]—the kirmess (literally church mass) is an autumn festival celebrating the harvest season. A fire was started in the fire/baking chamber and allowed to burn until the desired baking temperature was attained. Smoke from the fire was drawn up a chimney situated in the wall common to the oven and kitchen. Two measurements were used to determine the actual baking temperature. Most commonly, the baker, usually the experienced farm wife, would watch the oven's interior. When a white powder coated the chamber walls it was felt that the oven was ready for baking. The second method for determining readiness was probably used less frequently. This required extending one's arm into the oven. If the arm hair was singed, the oven was ready. When the proper temperature

William G.
Laatsch
and
Charles F.
Calkins

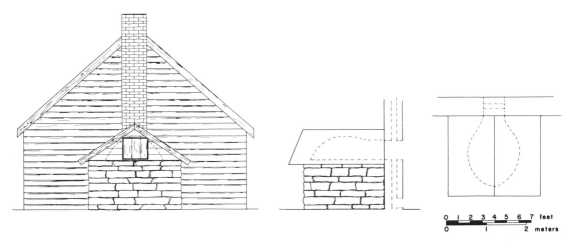

Fig. 11-7 Sketch and plan of a Belgian oven illustrate the dimensions, which were kept uniform to facilitate the baking process. (Drawing by W. Laatsch.)

was reached, unburned wood, coals, and ashes were raked into a cavity immediately below the chimney. Rectangular baking pans of bread dough were placed into the oven with a large paddle. As many as twenty-four loaves could be baked at one time. After the pans were inserted, a heavy iron door, mounted on hinges or designed to fit brackets, was put in place; the oven was sealed and baking commenced. The exact baking time remains a mystery. A typical respondent replied that the "bread was baked until done."[9] After the bread was baked and removed from the oven, the residual heat was used to bake pies. The typical Belgian pie, unlike the familiar fruit pie, was small (7 inches in diameter), thin, and lacked a top crust. Using a biscuit-like covering, the common fillings were prune, raisin, rice, or dried apple. The pie was covered with a thin layer of cottage cheese. As many as thirty pies were baked at one time.

Eighteen ovens still exist in the region, and of these, three or four could be placed in working condition with only modest repairs. Belgians interviewed in the field indicated that at one time nearly every farm in the area had an outdoor oven. Most of them were attached to the summer kitchen as described above. In addition, informants suggested that the free-standing oven was built and utilized by some area farmers. Unfortunately none of this type has been found through field research or identified through old photographs.

It is clear that the Wisconsin oven had its origin in Belgium. In a comprehensive monograph, Weyns details the Old World Belgian antecedent.[10] Photographs and sketches provided by Weyns reveal a great deal of similarity in the form, building materials, and function of the ovens on both sides of the Atlantic. However, some exceptions to these generalizations are apparent. In Belgium, the free-standing oven was not a rarity as it was in the United States. The presence of the free-standing oven there may be attributed to the moderate marine west coast climate, the fear of fire, and the fact that some of the ovens in Belgium were communal. Several families utilized

Belgians in Wisconsin

203

one oven, which was, as a result, in almost constant use. Dispersed rural settlement and the harsher winter climate in Wisconsin made the communal use of ovens impractical.

Another difference is the construction materials. In the old country, brick was used consistently for the fire/baking chamber and for the platform upon which it rested. Among Wisconsin Belgians local limestone was used since it was more readily available and less expensive than large quantities of brick.

A more limited use of ovens, that is, exclusively for baking, was characteristic in Wisconsin. Weyns reported a greater variety of uses in Belgium, including drying small fruits and seeds, roasting large quantities of meat, baking herring, and disinfecting feather beds and the clothes of the dead.

The Belgian Farmstead Chapel

While the oven provided food for the body, the small roadside chapel provided nourishment for the soul. At first glance, it could be mistaken for a tidy tool shed, or a commodious privy! A typical chapel is of frame construction and rectangular plan, measuring 9 feet in length and 7 ½ feet in width (Fig. 11-8). The gable roof stands 9 feet at the peak and slopes to 6 ½ feet at the eaves. Of the twenty-four chapels surviving, the largest is 12′ × 10′ and 10 feet high, whereas the smallest is 6′6″ × 5′6″ × 8′. The chapel sits a few inches off the ground and is supported simply by fieldstones at the corners or, more commonly, rests on a foundation of locally quarried dolomite.

Chapels generally have no windows; if present, one small window may be found in the door. Neither the window nor the door contains religious symbols, but a wooden or metal cross may be attached immediately above the door or to the roof peak (Fig. 11-9). Three stone chapels have crosses incorporated in the dolomite walls by the deliberate arrangement of the building stone or glacial erratics, which provide contrast in color, size, and shape. An inscription above the door may attest further to the building's religious function and clearly sets it apart from a tool shed or privy. These inscriptions are always in French and may be lettered on a board or stamped out of metal. Examples include: "Notre Dame des Aflices, Priez pour Nous," and "Saint Ghislane, Priez pour Nous."

Whether they are frame or stone, the Belgian chapels exhibit interior uniformity. The interiors are finished with lath and plaster, plastered wallboard, or, more recently, sheets of paneling. If plastered, the walls and ceilings are painted a pale color: white, blue, green, or yellow. Floors are commonly made of varnished hard or soft woods and occasionally are covered with linoleum, indoor-outdoor carpeting, or composition tiles.

William G. Laatsch and Charles F. Calkins

The focus of this one-room structure is the altar, located directly opposite the door. Wooden, two or three tiered, and usually without any cloth or lace cover, the altar provides a simple but adequate place for religious artifacts (Fig. 11-10). The center of the highest tier is reserved for an element of special significance; a cross, a crucifix, a statue either of the Blessed Virgin or of an appropriate saint. The lowest tier holds a variety of other symbolic items, including smaller statues, crosses, vases (with either artificial or fresh flowers), a container holding holy water, and a small receptacle for donations. Altars may display as many as two dozen items, all arranged system-

Fig. 11-8 The simple design and layout of the Belgian roadside chapel with prie-dieu and altar indicated. (Drawing by W. Laatsch.)

Fig. 11-9 Belgian roadside chapel viewed from the road. The distinctiveness of the chapel is clear and the inscription, "NOTRE DAME DES AFLICES PRIEZ POUR NOUS," is evident. (Photo by W. Laatsch.)

atically to achieve symmetry, in order to emphasize the dominant cross or statue. Furnishings are limited to a simply built kneeling bench (prie-dieu) and, in the larger structures, a wooden chair or two.

Just as the altar is crowded but orderly, the walls are similarly adorned with pictures and a variety of certificates. The pictures, often relatively large, usually depict a special saint. In many cases it is clear that they have a European origin and have been purchased at a notable shrine. Once, while I was interviewing an elderly Belgian gentleman at his chapel, he gazed at the pictures, turned and said, "I got arts wert tousans," indicating the value he

Belgians in Wisconsin

Fig. 11-10 The decorated altar and interior walls of a roadside chapel. (Photo by W. Laatsch.)

placed on his art collection.[11] In his heavily accented English, Mr. Vandertie was attempting to convey the belief that his chapel art works were worth thousands of dollars. The discrepancy between the perceived and real value is an indicator of the very high sentimental value placed on the chapel and its contents by most owners. (At the same time, he revealed a relic ethnic speech pattern, with the troublesome plurals and *th* sounds. This speech pattern persists in the rural areas inhabited by Belgians and among Belgians residing in Green Bay.) The certificates, on the other hand, are of local origin and acknowledge a baptism, first communion, marriage, or death. Those dated before 1920 are inscribed in French. Chapel walls, then, are like pages of the family Bible, where significant family events are recorded.

In most cases, a chapel stands on the farm of the family whose ancestors built the structure. If this is the case, the family continues to care for the building and its contents. Where the farm has changed hands, the new owner may assume responsibility for the chapel or, if no interest is expressed, a nearby relative or friend of the former owner may maintain the building. Whatever the case, the chapels are seen as important structures in the Belgian communities of the Door Peninsula.

There is no doubt that the general form of the chapels is secondary to their function. These are votive chapels that were built by devout Catholics and dedicated to, and in honor of, a saint or the Blessed Virgin in gratitude for favors sought or received through prayer. Although they may be used

William G. Laatsch and Charles F. Calkins

now for general purposes, such as family devotions, or as sites where people will gather on special occasions to say the Rosary, their primary function is a place of prayer for those who seek relief from types of distress similar to those that caused the chapels to be built initially. Several examples will illustrate this point.

One chapel still actively used was originally built in the late nineteenth century by the Constantine Flemel family near Rosiere. The Flemels had several children die in infancy as a result of convulsions. They subsequently built a chapel in honor of St. Ghislane (St. Ghislain), the patron saint of small children, so that the family would have a place to pray for the intercession of the saint. Their devotion and sacrifice in building the chapel at this time are significant because there were two Catholic churches within a two-mile radius of the farmstead. Following its construction and early use, the Flemels had three very healthy children born to them, each ultimately reaching adulthood. This chapel's miraculous reputation had continued and is attested to in the following letter:

Nov. 30, 1962
De Pere, Wisconsin

Dear Friends

I suppose you's [sic] will be surprised to hear from me, but I have a girl who falls in convulsions and I know ma took me over to that chapel where you are now for it, and they say it helped. Mabel mentioned its still up. I'd like to take Coleen there. We'll go this Sunday, Dec. 2 or next if we can't make it then. It will probably be around noon or after twelve so were [sic] home before dark. If you plan on going away leave it open and I'll leave a note that we were there. If we don't make it this Sunday, write and let me know if the chapel is still there. I put a card in the envelope. The one next door has a married sister that might come along too.

Thanks — Irene[12]

In another case, Joseph Derenne, who was born in Bousoux, Belgium, and came to Duvall, Kewaunee County, in 1887 at age 14, was diagnosed in 1902 as having incurable cancer. At the urging of his brother, the family decided to build a chapel in honor of Our Lady of Lourdes. The finalization of the building plans reportedly had a positive effect on Derenne's deteriorating health. While the chapel was being constructed, Derenne's brother returned to Belgium. He brought back a large piece of religious statuary, which was placed on the altar. Family members believed that the construction of the chapel was responsible for the miracle that further restored Derenne's health.[13]

Joseph Destree, a Belgian stone mason who had a reputation in the Door Peninsula for building with the local Niagara dolomite, got hot lime in his eyes in about 1870 while practicing his trade. Fearing for his eyesight, he built a chapel in honor of St. Adele, believed locally to be the patron saint of eyes, who herself had been born blind but had her sight restored upon baptism. Destree maintained his eyesight throughout his life.[14] The chapel remains in its original location and is maintained by his descendants. People with eye afflictions still come to the chapel with the hope of having their prayers answered.

Although the chapels are privately owned, they commonly are available or open to all, Belgians or non-Belgians, who care to use them. It appears that ten chapels are used on a rather regular basis, especially during late spring, summer, and fall. Deep snow accumulation during winter curtails access, and the cold weather discourages even the most faithful. Information about their usage was obtained through interviews, registrations in guest books, and observation. Three of the chapels had frequent visitations, six to eight per week, by family members, neighbors, and people from outside the immediate rural Belgian community. Of these, one was used consistently by the elderly owners, and it was well known that they encouraged and welcomed use by others. Its guest register for the summer months of 1981–1986 showed that visitors had come from Algoma, Green Bay, Luxemburg, Milwaukee, and Sheboygan, Wisconsin, as well as from St. Paul, Minnesota, and Hollywood, Florida. Presumably, many locals also used the chapel but did not bother to sign the register. Votive candles were provided for those visitors who had neglected to bring their own. Another of these three chapels was used frequently, but primarily by family members. The young farmer who owned it indicated that he and his wife used the chapel for prayers "at least a couple of times a week" and that his parents, who had formerly lived on the property, came from their home to maintain the chapel and pray in it "more often than we do, almost every day."[15]

The other seven chapels were visited an estimated six to ten times a month. This pattern of visits is characteristic of chapels owned by someone other than descendants of family members originally responsible for their construction. Although new owners, many of whom are not Belgian, will maintain the chapels, they do not use them with the same frequency that chapels identified with particular Belgian families are used.

The remaining fourteen chapels are used rarely, if at all. Five of these no longer function as chapels. The religious artifacts have been removed from them, but no new function has been assigned to the vacant buildings and they stand idle. The farmsteads on which these chapels are located are ones that have been purchased by people who are neither Belgian nor Catholic, who have moved into and have somewhat diluted the Belgian stronghold. They are rural nonfarm people who commute to nearby Green Bay to work. Their tie is not to the Belgian community and its customs.

Clearly, the chapel is part of the ensemble of buildings constituting the Belgian farmstead; yet, its distinctive function and, in turn, unique location on the farmstead tend to set it apart from the other buildings. At the time of construction, the chapel was placed adjacent to the road so that the faithful could have free and immediate access without having to enter the farmstead proper via a lane or driveway. To this day, chapel owners do not exercise the same kind of proprietary rights over the chapel as they do over the remainder of the farm in general. They view the chapel as community property, in part, and freedom of access is encouraged. Visitors park their cars along the road's shoulder and walk a few short steps to enter a chapel. The same certainly does not apply to the rest of the farm property, which is considered private; trespassing is overtly discouraged. The distinctiveness of the

William G.
Laatsch
and
Charles F.
Calkins

chapel's location is further enhanced by its being separated from the house, barns, and driveways by a low hedge, flower garden, or fence. Thus, the chapel becomes more of a sanctuary and less a farm structure.

Whereas proximity to a road is an advantage for both user and owner, it has been a disadvantage for the longevity of some chapels. Road widening, errant vehicles, and overzealous snowplow drivers have on occasion reduced a chapel to a pile of kindling wood. At least four owners have anticipated these possibilities and have moved their chapels a greater distance from the right-of-way.

Field work over the last decade has identified twenty-four chapels on the Door Peninsula. Of these, twenty-one are located in the Belgian settlement area. Most of the chapels are found in the vicinity of Rosiere, a hamlet on the Door-Kewaunee county line that continues to be the stronghold of Belgians.

Belgium's Walloon region was the source area for the Door Peninsula chapels. While such chapels in Belgium are similar in size and function there are notable differences. The Walloons built them almost exclusively of brick and stone. Instead of a rectangular door, the Belgian chapels feature an arched, often Gothic, entrance, and the door is often only a metal grill. Open to the weather, the interiors are rather plain with only a few plants flanking a statue or a crucifix. The locations of Walloon chapels in Belgium are less predictable than those of chapels in Wisconsin. They are found in urban centers, along rural roads, within forests, or incorporated into farmyard walls.

The Changing Cultural Landscape

Of the components of material culture, the red brick farmhouses, the oven attached to the summer kitchen, and the chapel are particularly distinctive elements in the Belgian landscape, while food, customs, and language persist as elements of the nonmaterial culture. The persistence of these constituent factors has been remarkable, as an analysis of plat maps and census data over the last twelve decades will show. Farms have remained in the founding families for generations. As families in the area grew, the farms could not possibly have supported the additional population. Fortunately, the industries of the nearby cities of Green Bay, Sturgeon Bay, and to a lesser extent Algoma and Kewaunee were expanding and were able to absorb the excess regional population. Thus, the young people were not required to live far from the home farm or village and could easily maintain contact with family, friends, and institutions. Through these frequent contacts, especially with the extended family, Roman Catholic parish church, sports league, or deer hunting camp, the culture was continually reinforced.

This is not to suggest that there has not been change. Buildings are destroyed, modified, or moved as age deteriorates them and their functions change. The hamlets, with their ensemble of church, cheese factory, general store, mill, tavern, school, and town hall are changing. A close examination will show that priests now serve several area parishes rather than just one, and there is encouragement from the Diocese of Green Bay to consolidate congregations. The small cheese factories have been unable to meet competition from larger, more modern and adaptable factories and have closed. The general store and mill also have closed as transportation has improved and they have faced competition from larger operations in nearby communities that could offer greater variety, lower prices, and access to a bank and post office. School consolidation occurred in this region in 1962, turning the rural school into a relic feature or adapting it as a dwelling or storage facility. So the functions of the hamlets have changed, and they are now primarily areas of residences only.

Other changes are occurring. Former urbanites have moved into the area, seeking the tranquility of the countryside. Frequently these individuals have little relation to the Belgian community. College-age Belgians are increasingly obtaining degrees and are often unable to find appropriate employment in the region, forcing them to move to Milwaukee, Chicago, or even the Sun Belt! Thus, the opportunity to transmit the culture to future generations will be curtailed.

Currently the culture flourishes, and it must be remembered that northeastern Wisconsin still has the greatest concentration of rural Belgians in North America. Individuals of Belgian descent are well known, respected, and hold leadership roles in the professions, public service, industry, the arts, and business, especially banking. The Peninsula Belgian-American Club is an exceptionally active organization, which sponsors and participates in ethnic events, hosts and exchanges visits with friends and relatives abroad, supports scholarships, promotes research and genealogical investigation, and acquires valuable archival material. Much of the archival material is deposited in the Area Research Center, University of Wisconsin at Green Bay, which houses an important research collection documenting the Belgian community. A major annual event is Belgian Days, held in Brussels each July. This celebration of Belgian culture attracts thousands and is often attended by the Belgian ambassador to the United States, as well as many European Belgians. Green Bay's Heritage Hill State Park continues to develop a Belgian farmstead, circa 1890. The ensemble includes a log-brick house, a number of barns, a summer kitchen with attached oven, and a chapel, all accurately restored and interpreted. The farmstead is enthusiastically supported by the devoted Belgian community and has appeal to Belgians and non-Belgians alike.

This Heritage Hill restoration has been a successful effort. Interest in and respect for ethnic groups has increased in Wisconsin, especially toward the Belgians. Among the Belgian community there is additional pride in themselves and their artifacts, especially houses, bake ovens, chapels, and barns. This is good news indeed for those who appreciate rural vernacular landscapes.

William G.
Laatsch
and
Charles F.
Calkins

12

Danes in Iowa and Minnesota

Signe T. Nielsen Betsinger

THE DANES' pattern of settlement has been unlike that of other Scandinavians. Kristian Hvidt, the librarian at the Danish Parliamentary Library and an authority on Danish immigration to America, says in *Danes Go West* that nine-tenths of the approximately 300,000 Danes emigrating from Denmark between 1864 and 1914 chose the United States and distributed themselves thinly.[1] Frederick Hale, in discussing some of Hvidt's earlier writing, notes that, after landing in the United States, many of the Danish immigrants found work in New York and New Jersey, and many more established themselves in a scattering of small towns in the Midwest. That the Danes did not cluster in the way other Scandinavians did may be due in part to their intermarriage with Germans, Swedes, and Norwegians. Because of the imbalance of the sexes among Danish immigrants, Danish males often married non-Danes, which encouraged assimilation into other ethnic groups. By 1914, Iowa had 10.4 percent of all Danish Americans, followed by Wisconsin with 9.6 percent and Minnesota with 9.4 percent.[2]

Experiences of the early Danish immigrants, as told in their stories and in letters to their homeland, are filled with accounts of stress, disappointments, determination, and courage. The midwestern Danes coped cleverly with the hardships that befell them as they broke ground and built homes in the wide open midwestern prairie. Tenaciously, they wrested a living out of a harsh environment, which challenged them with bitter cold winters and blisteringly hot summers. They risked planting crops, knowing full well that drought, hail, and insects could wipe out all their efforts, and they built homes despite the ever present threat of prairie fires and tornadoes. Nevertheless, they not only survived but succeeded in establishing strong communities. By the early 1900s, there were significant numbers of Danes in Cedar Falls, Elk Horn, Hampton, Kimballton, Newell, and Ringsted in Iowa, and Albert Lea, Askov, Clarks Grove, and Tyler in Minnesota (Fig. 12-1). This chapter focuses on the homes of Danish immigrants in two locations, the Elk Horn–Kimballton area in southwestern Iowa, and Tyler in southwestern Minnesota. Some background on what precipitated and facilitated the arrival of Danes in these areas follows.

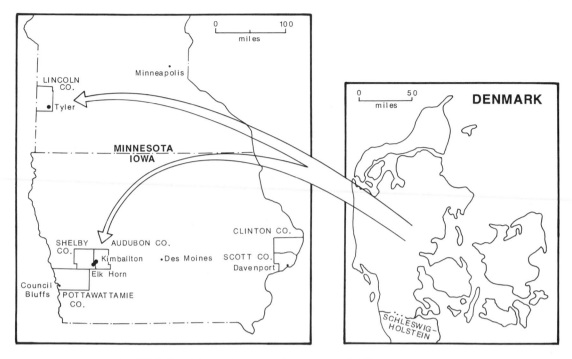

Fig. 12-1 Danish settlements in Iowa and Minnesota

Danish Migration to Iowa

Numerous early immigrants found their way to the prairies by steamboat and ox-drawn wagons. In the introduction to the reprint of the 1839 collection of John Plumbe, Jr.'s *Sketches of Iowa and Wisconsin* is a description of the tempo of the times in the Iowa area. About 1840, the population was increasing at a rapid rate. Although the growth in Illinois and Missouri was noteworthy, the rate in the Black Hawk Purchase exceeded them; between 1836 and 1840, the "Iowa District" increased fourfold. Not only were people pouring in from the eastern states, but they also came from across the Atlantic.[3] Although the number of Danes among these pioneers is unknown, they certainly must have played an important role in easing the way for the large influx of Danes that was to come forty years later.

Plumbe, a promoter of the railroad to the Pacific, in describing what in 1839 was known as the Territory of Iowa, depicted it as a grand prairie having rivers, creeks, and lakes bordered by woods giving shelter to animals and providing materials for building houses and fences. Plumbe estimated that three-fourths of the territory was without trees; however, isolated groves made the gathering of timber convenient.[4] Canadians, too, were interested in the possibility of emigrating. Plumbe wrote of the substantially large association called the Mississippi Emigration Company, which sent out delegates to explore western country, particularly the Territory of Iowa. Single Canadians were encouraged to come only with a single team and wagon. Those not choosing to come by team were offered the possibility of going first to Buffalo, from there by steamboat to Chicago, and then hiring a team for the

*Signe T.
Nielsen
Betsinger*

last stretch to Davenport or "any other place to which they wish to proceed." Large families with considerable furniture to be transported by team could go to Cleveland, then to the Ohio Canal to the Ohio River and "from there take a steamboat to Davenport or any other place they may wish." They were advised that those coming by the latter route could buy household furnishings more cheaply in Cincinnati than in Canada; if they were intending to build, they were urged to get doors and window sashes, glass, putty, and nails there also.[5]

The first railroad connecting the Mississippi River and the Great Lakes was completed to Rock Island, Illinois, in 1854; at about the same time, the Mississippi and Missouri line was built from Chicago and continued from Davenport to Council Bluffs, Iowa, over a bridge built in 1856.[6] The coming of the railroad was exciting, and because of it, dramatic changes occurred. It was a faster, more direct, and more sure means of transportation. Considering the possibilities that the railroad opened up, it is little wonder that those connected with steamboats were concerned and fought the railroad's progress.

The book *Iowa As It Is in 1855; A Gazeteer for Citizens and a Handbook for Emmigrants* [sic] reflects the determination of those encouraging western settlement. The objection to the building of the bridge at Davenport was forcefully opposed by the following statement: "The people of Iowa, Western Minnesota, and those who are to cultivate the fertile soils of Nebraska, will never consent to be shut out from the Atlantic and the great Western lakes by any pretended obstructions which a bridge built on the plan proposed may offer."[7]

The Mormons were some of the first White people who ventured into the area that is now Audubon and Shelby counties in southwestern Iowa. They were under the leadership of Brigham Young. After being driven out of Nauvoo, Illinois, in 1846, the Mormons went across Iowa on their way west. Just north of Omaha, Nebraska, they established what is referred to as Winter Quarters.[8] One of the important Mormon trails entered Audubon County in the southeastern part; this later became a stage road and part of the overland route to California.[9] According to Thomas Peter Christensen, it was upon the suggestion of a Danish Mormon, who crossed the continent to the Territory of Utah, that missionaries were sent to Denmark. Efforts to proselytize there began in 1850, and as early as 1852, converts were on their way to Salt Lake City. When the hand cart caravans came across Iowa, a considerable number of Danes were among the travelers. Many reached Utah, but some settled in western Iowa.[10] Some Mormons went to Utah but returned to Shelby County and vicinity because they did not agree with the practice of polygamy being followed by Mormons in Utah.[11] An 1889 history of Shelby and Audubon counties stated that the greater portion of the first settlement of Shelby County was from those who had broken off from the Mormons when Brigham Young took up the leadership.[12] The scattering of the settlers in western Iowa, near the Missouri, was due mainly to the need for water and natural game.[13] Christensen reported it would be difficult to know how many Danes the Mormons had brought to western Iowa by 1869. In 1870 there were approximately six hundred in Pottawattamie and Shelby counties; however, many of them had come in as railroad workers.[14]

Another significant reason for the influx of Danes was the unrest in

Schleswig-Holstein in northern Europe. A number of German Schleswigers and Holsteiners began arriving in Iowa in 1838; and ten years later, thousands of them had settled in Scott and Clinton counties. Those coming before 1864 were Danish subjects. They left because of economic and political dissatisfaction with the Danish government; and after 1864, when Prussia took over Schleswig-Holstein, the people continued to come, because of German oppression. Gradually more Danish Schleswigers settled along the Mississippi and then moved inland.[15] Some of these immigrants were to find their way eventually to Audubon and Shelby counties.

At the same time the Schleswigers were migrating to Iowa, so too were the Wisconsin Danes, who felt dissatisfied with the agricultural yields there. Some came to Monroe Township in Shelby County in 1865. Together with others coming directly from Denmark, they organized in 1874 a Baptist congregation, the first Danish-speaking denomination to establish itself in North America. Danish Lutherans were also moving in, arriving in Clay and Jackson townships. These two religious groups, the Baptists at Cuppy's Grove and the Lutherans in Jackson Township, were the core of the largest rural settlement of Danes in the United States; the area was eventually to be referred to as the Elk Horn–Kimballton settlement.[16]

Danish Migration to Minnesota

In Minnesota, the railroad played an important role in the settlement of Danes in Lincoln County. However, it was probably more as a facilitator of Danish settlement than as a direct cause, as it had been in Iowa, where the railroad had provided opportunities for the immigrants to work their way across the state. It was after 1880 that the Danes began to arrive in significant numbers in Lincoln County. This influx was the result of a concerted effort of the Danish Evangelical Lutheran Church of America.

Enok Mortensen has written a detailed history of the beginning of the Danish settlements in Lake Benton and Tyler. In *Seventy-Five Years at Danebod,* he notes that in 1884 the Danish Evangelical Lutheran Church of America purchased land from the Winona and St. Peter Railroad Company. The church appointed a body called the Land Selection Committee to locate an appropriate setting for a new settlement. A Danish minister, Pastor F. L. Grundtvig, headed the committee, which negotiated the land transaction. The agreement with the railroad carried with it the provision that for three years land that lay in Diamond Lake, Hope, and Marshfield townships would be sold only to Danes.[17] By 1886, approximately 270 Danes had purchased land in Lincoln County, and of these about 50 had settled on farms and the others had chosen the towns of Tyler or Lake Benton.[18] It was the combination of the westward construction of railroads and the sale of farmland that provided much of the incentive for Danes to settle in the nation's heartland. The symbiotic relationship between rails and land was critical for the survival of the rural communities.

Signe T.
Nielsen
Betsinger

Resources for Building

Although the Tyler, Minnesota, colony was organized approximately a decade after the Kimballton–Elk Horn settlement in Iowa began, the growth and development of the two settlements were much alike and the homes of the immigrants bore striking similarities. The immigrants in both settlements made good use of two important resources—natural and human. In the Kimballton–Elk Horn area particularly, there was an abundance of timber and water, whereas in Tyler the land was open and windswept. In both places a dread existed of the prairie fires that could destroy homes and timber. Survival depended on the settlers' ability to control prairie grass fires; the slightest spark could turn a prairie into a raging inferno. In addition to timber and water, the earth itself was a resource for home building. At first the immigrants created dugouts. Later they formed clay into bricks, fired them, and used them in building walls and chimneys. Other significant resources, the human kind, included—carpenters, cabinetmakers, painters, and bricklayers. They had learned their trades in Denmark, and their workmanship was superb. They were true craftspersons.

It is impractical to present a comprehensive listing of the immigrants' homes in these areas. However, a few examples will provide an insight into the Danish design characteristics that were transferred to the United States in the early years of settlement and into those that persisted up to and beyond World War I.

Late-Nineteenth-Century Houses in Iowa

One of the earliest Danish immigrant houses in Shelby County, Iowa, was a windowless dugout carved into the side of a hill. It had a single stove pipe and a few boards across the front, into which a door was placed. There was no covering on the dirt floor, and the walls were brushed with a mixture of lime and water. This dugout was built by Hans Nissen in 1873 and measured about 16′ × 16′ × 8′. About 1874 he built a second house. This 12-by-24-foot structure, shown in Figure 12-2, was a considerable step up from

Fig. 12-2 Exterior view of the Hans Nissen house, Shelby County, Iowa, built ca. 1874. (Photo, ca. 1879, courtesy Mrs. Alfred Nissen.)

the previous cave home.[19] Attached to the house by a shed-roofed passageway was an extension with what appears to be a peaked roof. The chimney suggests that it might have been a summer kitchen.

Nissen, who came from Schleswig, was a talented man. During the time he lived in the second house, he designed and built the sewing cabinet shown in Figure 12-3. A rare find, this sewing cabinet is unmistakably similar to the Danish *stolpeskab* (post cabinet), which may have originated in Copenhagen or near Øresund and was commonly found in Danish homes in the 1700s.[20] In Denmark it was placed in the corner of the main room on a bench, where it provided storage for valuable papers and money.

Another early house was built in 1874, for Hans J. Jorgensen, who came from the Island of Ærø, Denmark. Located in the town of Kimballton, this house originally had three rooms—a kitchen-dining room downstairs and two bedrooms upstairs. Figure 12-4 shows the way the house appeared in 1895 after additions had been made. Careful study of the first section reveals a resemblance to provincial houses found all over Denmark, where the long side of the house is the front.

The entire first floor of the original house measured 13′3″ × 21′5″. Jorgensen was one of the first settlers in the community; his house was open to friend and stranger, and many newcomers were invited in for a meal.[21] The east wing of the house was added as the family grew. Jorgensen was

Fig. 12-3 Sewing cabinet of *stolpeskab* design, built by Hans Nissen. (Photo by S. Betsinger.)

Fig. 12-4 Sketch of the Jorgensen house, Kimballton, Iowa, built ca. 1874. (Drawing by M.M. Geib from a photograph, ca. 1895, provided through the courtesy of Mrs. Thomas Thomsen.)

married in 1878 and had had ten children by the time his wife died. He re-married in 1894 and in this marriage had three children. With a large family and two hired men, obviously there was a need to expand the house and increase the number of bedrooms. This was done, but even with five bed-rooms there had to be three beds in a room downstairs to accommodate everyone![22]

Worthy of special mention is the interior decoration of the Jorgensen house. During the twentieth century, wallpaper was added to the house. Be-cause of a fire in 1969, the wallpaper, which had been damaged, was re-moved, revealing a stenciled ceiling in the living room. It had a stylized floral motif in reds, yellows, and browns, accenting the four corners, and a blue border along the perimeter of the ceiling and down the side of a doorframe. In the hallway there were imitation marble panels. A beautiful walnut stair railing was still intact. In the book *Dagligliv i Danmark,* discussions of rural farmhouses in Denmark include mention of painted wooden panels in Zealand in the late 1700s; they were also common in Southern Jutland. Along the west coast and on the islands, roccoco designs were favored, and from Rømø there is a record of undulating designs being used from floor to ceiling, spreading out on the ceiling boards unless they had been painted as framed marble. Apparently, traveling painters were common.[23] In America, stenciling was used in other parts of the country. Although the painter of the Jorgensen house is not known, because of the particular nature of the mar-belized panels, it seems likely that it was a Danish craftsperson who did the work.

Rasmus Hansen, a wheelwright, also from the island of Ærø, built the house shown in Figure 12-5, about 1879 for the Simonsen family. The front view shows Danish characteristics similar to those of the Jorgensen house. The long side of the house featured a centered front doorway under a dor-mer and was flanked by formally balanced windows, two on each side. The Simonsen house, too, was expanded as the family's needs grew. The ceilings

Danes in Iowa and Minnesota

Fig. 12-5 Simonsen house, Audubon County, Iowa, built ca. 1879. (Photo by S. Betsinger.)

were low downstairs, 6'10", built that way to conserve heat; the whole house was sited in a low area, to have protection from the winds.[24] There was a room which the family called the water room; where, as the name implies, water was kept.[25] It was reminiscent of a room in rural houses in Denmark called *bryggerset* (the brewery), which had a stone floor and where the home-maker washed clothes, butchered, and boiled sausages. In the Simonsen house, the water room had a loose brick floor. Later it became a *pulterkammer* (general storeroom), but it was used for cooking as late as 1916. The wood-work in the Simonsen living room, which was probably pine, was finished in grained enamel, probably painted by Peter Claude Hansen, a fine craftsman, well known for his expertise. Using combs and feathers, Peter Claude, as he was called, could transform a piece of plain ordinary pine into a beautiful oak grain.[26]

In 1894 the Jorgen Hartvigsens replaced their old farmhouse with one that was large for its time (Fig. 12-6). It had a 15' × 16' dining room, a 16' × 16' parlor, and a 14' × 14' bedroom on the first floor. The Hartvigsens had several children, they boarded a school teacher, and they had two hired men. The space was well filled.

An interview with Palma Sornsen, the Hartvigsens' daughter, revealed some interesting features in the house.[27] The deep cellar was unusual. Dug a couple of feet deeper than was commonly done, it was flooded with water and became a large cooling tank where milk could be lowered in kettles to be kept sweet. There was no bathroom in this house. The family used an out-house and managed baths ingeniously. The school teacher used a pitcher and basin in her room, children were bathed in a washtub in the house, and

Fig. 12-6 Hartvigsen house, Audubon County, Iowa, built in 1894. (Photo, date unknown, courtesy of Mrs. Charles Sornsen.)

for others, there was a washroom where a shower had been arranged by using a cream separator bowl which had a faucet. In the summertime, they drew water from the stock tank, which always had a clean supply, the bather hoping that the water had stood long enough to be warmed by the sun. If the cows happened to have drunk just before bath time, the refill could be cold!

In this house, too, there were painted designs on the ceiling. Mrs. Sornsen remembered that the dining room had a geometric design of lines and beautiful squares probably done by stenciling; the living room ceiling, done freehand, had angels painted in the center, and in each corner was a spray of flowers; in one bedroom there was a landscape on the wall; and in another bedroom there was a blue sky with floating clouds and stars including the Big Dipper and the Eastern Star. This interior painting was done by H. Hansen and Jens Kjar, Danish painters from Atlantic, Iowa.

Heat in the house was provided by a hard coal stove. Originally, lamps in the house were gas fueled, but an explosion occurred elsewhere in the community and the Hartvigsens decided that beacon lamps would be safer. Refrigeration, beyond the cellar cooling tank, was accomplished by an ice box filled with blocks of ice cut from a pond and stored in sawdust during the summer.[28]

Niels and Amanda Boelth lived in a house in Kimballton that was probably built in 1895.[29] Originally a Lutheran parsonage, additions had apparently been made as various ministers came and space needs changed. Niels Boelth came from Denmark and his wife was a second generation Dane. While there were no Danish design features on the exterior of the house, it is of interest that the Boelths chose interior furnishings that clearly bore Danish characteristics. Among them was a *pyramidehylde* (pyramid shelf), in the dining room, placed between two windows in a formally balanced arrangement.[30] The origin of this particular shelf is unknown, other than that it was purchased at a local auction. The pyramid shelf in general has a long history and is one of the few typically Danish furnishings found in late-nineteenth- and early-twentieth-century Danish American homes. Pyramid shelves were ordinary household items in Denmark in the 1700s.

Late-Nineteenth-Century Houses in Minnesota

Because the settlement at Tyler came a little later than those in Kimballton and Elkhorn, some of the earliest Danish houses in Minnesota date back to the very late nineteenth century. One such house, built in 1885 by Soren B. Skow, had three rooms—kitchen, living-dining room, and bedroom (Fig. 12-7) when originally built.[31] Its floor plan and overall proportions reveal this house to belong to a type called Baltic three-room houses, common to a large area surrounding the Baltic Sea and including Denmark.[32] The present study may be the first documentation of a Baltic three-room house built by Danes in North America, although many others are likely to have been constructed.

Another house, built in 1892 by Thomas Hansen, from Vejle, Jutland, originally consisted of a single room and was subsequently partitioned to separate the sleeping area from the kitchen. Figure 12-8 shows the house as it appears today. The lumber came from Chicago, Illinois, and Neenah, Wisconsin, and was sent to Tyler by rail.[33] Thomas Hansen's son, Carl T. Hansen, in recording his memories, said of the original house: "It remains part of the present house. I wonder how, with no modern tools, the house was built to stand the blistering heat of summer and the dreadful frigid winds and blizzards of winter all these years. There were no trees to cut for fuel. Twisted straw and dried cow pads were burned in the stove. It must have taken constant firing."[34]

Another early settler in Tyler was Mads Hansen. Born in Langeland,

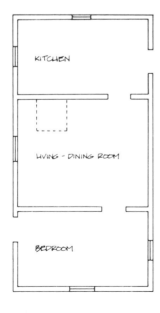

Fig. 12-7 Floor plan of the Skow (Holm) house, Tyler, Minnesota, built in 1885. (Drawing by I. Minciel-Waligora.)

Fig. 12-8 View of the east side of the Hansen house, Lincoln County, Minnesota. The south section was built in 1892. (Photo by S. Betsinger.)

Denmark, he and his wife Karoline, who was from Hedensted, Zealand, settled first in Neenah, Wisconsin, before coming to Tyler. Rather than building their house, they bought one that had been built in 1892.[35] The Hansen's daughter Clara Sorensen, now in her nineties, recorded some memories several years ago. In "Glimpses from My Eighty Years" she said:

> Our house was not very big—there were 3 rooms upstairs and a big kitchen, front room and my dad and mother's bed room and a clothes closet. We had a heater in the front room and a cook stove in the kitchen. There was a pantry connected to the kitchen and there of course we kept our dishes and food, but most of the food was kept in the basement. The basement was dark and to get there, you opened a door in the kitchen floor and from there, there were steps going down. The basement could be real interesting in the winter, because there, together with a lot of potatoes, was stored a lot of good things. Every year in the fall we bought a big barrel of good apples, a wooden pail full of jelly, one of salted herring. There was a big clay crock of salted pork, smaller crocks of fried meat covered with lard and hams that my dad himself had smoked with good old hickory wood. . . . Our drinking water was brought in from a well generally in the middle of the yard where you would pump the water by hand. A big pail with a dipper in it would serve the same purpose as the faucets over the sink does now. Water for washing dishes and clothes was caught outside in a big barrel in the summer time when it rained, and in the winter we melted snow. Then we graduated to a cistern.[36]

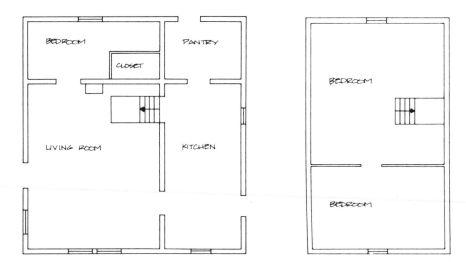

Fig. 12-9 Floor plan of the Simonsen house, near Lake Benton, Minnesota, built in 1895. (Drawing by I. Minciel-Waligora.)

Hans Simonsen and his wife, Marie Pedersen Simonsen, emigrated from Stubbum, Schleswig, to Clinton, Iowa, and then moved to a farm north of Lake Benton, Minnesota, where in 1895 they built the house whose floor plan is shown in Figure 12-9.

The original house had two rooms downstairs—a living room and a small bedroom. Hans Simonsen's grandson, Harold Simonsen, described the interior as he remembered it from his childhood. When the kitchen and pantry were added, the family had a cookstove in that section and used it only in the summer. During the rest of the year, they cooked on a kerosene stove in the living room. There was a round table, a cupboard that had glass doors, and an Aladdin lamp that always smoked. In the bedroom there was a wooden bed and an oak dresser that had an adjustable mirror with handkerchief drawers on either side.[37]

Post-Nineteenth-Century Houses in Iowa and Minnesota

Niels Bennedsen, who was a mason from Vejle, Jutland, constructed his own brick house. Although it did not have the symmetry typical of so many Danish brick houses, it was similar to them in the total feeling of the house, particularly in the interior. The arrangement of furniture and the furnishings themselves clearly harked back to Denmark. Flowers and doilies decorated the dining room. Photographs covered almost an entire wall in the study—in Denmark in the late nineteenth century it was common to hang many pictures in this way. A desk in the corner of the living room made by a Danish immigrant cabinetmaker, featured fine marquetry, squares of wood meticulously laid out diagonally giving a two dimensional effect. This desk might easily have been inspired by earlier Danish peasant furniture dating back to the sixteenth century.

One of the most spectacular houses in the Tyler area was named Kronborg (crown castle). Although no longer standing, it is still remembered by

Signe T. Nielsen Betsinger

222

many local citizens. Laurits and Anna Petersen, for whom the house was built, came from the island of Funen. They lived on a farm near Tyler and moved to town when Kronborg was completed in 1898.[38] An analysis of the house by Peter Grina suggests it to have been a development of the traditional Scandinavian manor house. The house was essentially a cube with symmetrical facades. The main level was above grade on a restricted base and was in the classical tradition, as was the string course marking the main floor line.[39] Used as a boarding house for several years, there was room for the Petersens, their daughter, their five sons, and the boarders.[40]

In light of the fact that Tyler was a new pioneer settlement, Kronborg was extraordinarily furnished. A chest of drawers that undoubtedly came from Kronborg was used in Askov, Minnesota, for many years by the Petersen's son, Hjalmar, while he was governor of Minnesota. The chest of drawers is reminiscent of Danish eighteenth- and nineteenth-century *dragkister* (chests of drawers).

The Mads Hansens, whose house was discussed in the previous section, built another house in 1910. The exterior had no Danish characteristics, but the interior bears a strong resemblance to interiors in Denmark during the same period, such as the one in Figure 12-10. There was use of much pattern, doilies, and plants, as well as many pictures on the wall.

Dr. Frode Nordskov Thomsen, was born in Ristinge, Langeland, and his wife, Astrid Hendricksen, in Copenhagen.[41] They were married in Chicago in 1907 and established their home in Tyler immediately after the wedding. In 1918 they built an elegant structure (Figure 12-11), which was designed by

Fig. 12-10 Interior of a Danish house on Ebeltoft, Jutland. Photograph taken before 1912.

Fig. 12-11 Thomsen house, Tyler, Minnesota, built in 1918. (Photo, date unknown, courtesy Mr. and Mrs. Helge Thomsen.)

an architect from Mankato, Minnesota. According to their son, Helge Thomsen, there was a large open foyer with a stairwell. Dark English woodwork and beamed ceilings were used throughout the living room and dining room. In writing about the house, Thomsen said:

> It was a gathering place for young people. It was a place of "refuge" when there were lengthy events at Danebod—a place for out of town people to find a quiet spot away from the hustle and bustle of activities up there. During the summertime the "rock garden" developed by F.N.T. in the 1930s (on site of his old tennis court) was an attraction unto itself with water lily ponds, gold fish, flowers of every variety and a "lyst hus" [gazebo].
>
> Music was a major activity in the house. The Danebod choir, The Tyler Male Chorus, The Tyler String Ensemble and make up groups all played and practiced there. . . . Winter afternoons were commonly dedicated to listening to music, listening on the old Atwater Kent radio. . . . It was a home for lonely souls. Mother and Dad would regularly invite lone persons who had no family in Tyler to share "nyt aars gaas" [New Year's goose] or a Sunday nite supper. . . . Celebration of events occurred on a regular basis. Christmas was perhaps the biggest celebration in the house. With many days of preparation by Mother, the event climaxed with Christmas eve dinner following the twilight church service. The dinner was the traditional Danish Christmas dinner—goose, red cabbage, rum pudding and citron fromage [lemon snow] followed by dancing and singing around the Christmas tree, closing with

"Nu har vi jul igen" [Now It Is Christmas Again] and present opening.[42]

Conclusion

In the eighteenth century in Denmark the rectangular, low, one-story house was common. Sometimes it was separate, standing alone, perhaps parallel to the barn, but often it was connected to three barns forming a square courtyard. In the two Iowa and Minnesota communities under discussion here, only one example is known where the house and the barn were under one roof. Although there have been no examples incorporating a courtyard in the two geographic areas covered in this chapter, Danish design influence did manifest itself in the houses, particularly in the use of the rectangular form and the symmetrical arrangements of architectural features on the exterior, which included a central dormer. The very earliest house designs tended to emphasize the horizontal rather than the vertical. The interior of these houses did not reflect the symmetry of the exterior, probably because building was relatively costly and space was limited.

Outstanding characteristics of the later houses in both Iowa and Minnesota were the departure from formal balance of architectural features, and an increase in the number and sizes of the rooms. During the period 1874 to 1930, there was a clear shift from small houses that had a minimum of decorative features to large houses where much attention was given to wall treatments, furnishings, and the physical comfort of the inhabitants. Although Danish influences quickly disappeared on the exterior of early houses, interiors continued to bear Danish characteristics up to and well beyond World War I. They were evident, to a certain extent, in the furnishings; some things were brought by the settlers from Denmark. Most exciting has been the discovery of some pieces of furniture handmade by Danish immigrants in the United States that definitely have their roots in the seventeenth and eighteenth centuries.

The manner in which furnishings were arranged also showed Danish influences. These included the use of much pattern, particularly small and controlled motifs, use of plants, heavy decoration of wall areas with pictures and bric-a-brac, placement of furniture at angles to the wall and of doilies and tablecloths in opposition to the underlying surface furniture lines, and the presence of much texture, such as in lace curtains and wicker furniture.

Part of the reason that interior arrangement of Danish houses remained more purely Danish than exterior construction is, no doubt, gender related. Outside influences came to the attention of men before they did to women. Men traveled greater distances from home than women, so their exposure to different construction ideas was greater. Cultural traditions could be kept alive in a home with portable objects. Furniture, pictures, wall hangings, and other decorative objects could be arranged with relative ease from house to house so that the familiar atmosphere was maintained. It was more difficult to maintain the familiar form and exterior of a house in different environments.[43]

13

Norwegians in Wisconsin

William H. Tishler

WITH SEAFARING long a part of their culture, Norse explorers visited
North America perhaps as early as the year 1000, and during the seventeenth century modern Norwegian migration to the New World began. Overpopulation in Norway, combined with economic disruption and
the limited amount of cultivable land, resulted in a mass exodus of the rural
bonder, or peasant class. Their numbers swelled the ranks of foreign-born
settlers in the United States, and in the nineteenth century only Ireland (see
Chapter 1) contributed a larger proportion of its population to North American settlement.[1] Americans of Norwegian descent eventually spread throughout most of the United States and Canada. However, their heaviest regional
concentrations are in the upper Midwest, where the best surviving examples
of their folk building tradition can be found.

The first group of Norwegian immigrants coming to the Midwest settled
in the Fox River valley region of Illinois. In 1837, a malaria epidemic devastated these colonies, and many of the survivors pushed northward, seeking
better farming land in Wisconsin. Here they established agricultural settlements on the prairies of Rock County at the southern edge of the state (Fig.
13-1). During the summer of 1839, a boatload of immigrants from Upper
Telemarken and Stavanger settled to the northeast near Lake Muskego in
Waukesha County. The following year Koshkonong, another Norwegian
settlement, was established on the fertile lands of neighboring Jefferson
County and southeastern Dane County. As new frontier lands opened for
development, these early colonies became an important primary destination
for other immigrants from Norway. By 1860, Wisconsin's 44,000 Norwegians
constituted nearly half of America's Norwegian population.[2] The state became a center for Norwegian-American life and served as a springboard for
the diffusion of Norwegian-Americans into Iowa, Minnesota, the Dakotas,
and other regions of the West. Here, and in other states with significant numbers of Norwegian-Americans, their ethnic pride and identity flourished,
and survives to this day.

Initial Shelter on the Wisconsin Frontier

Early Norwegian immigrant settlers often hastily erected crude shelters,
to provide some means of protection, before a better house—usually of log

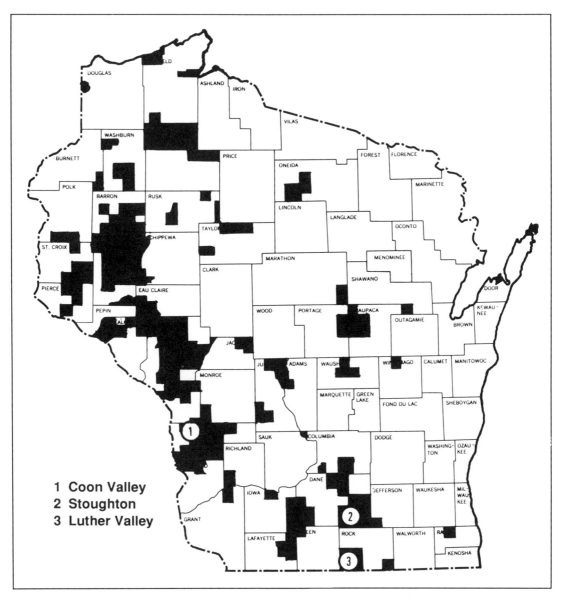

Fig. 13-1 Areas of Norwegian settlement in Wisconsin. (Source: 1905 and
1938 Wisconsin county maps of dominant nationalities; prepared by the
University of Wisconsin-Madison, Department of Rural Sociology, 1938.)

construction—was built. These primitive dwellings were fashioned from a
variety of readily available materials and sometimes even consisted of mere
dugouts carved into the ground. Information regarding these temporary
structures was sometimes chronicled in diaries, letters, and settlement accounts and is included in the extensive body of Norwegian-American literature. Construction plans for such abodes do not exist and photographs documenting this earliest phase of habitation are rare; few other available
records describe these impermanent shelters.

Several primitive initial dwellings are noted in the following accounts, the first of which refers to conditions in the Rock Prairie settlement, an area that encompassed portions of four townships in Rock County, Wisconsin, plus a small adjacent area in Illinois. Here, a later observer mused:

> The makeshift dwellings . . . must have been amusing sights. A . . . Norwegian family lived in a hay stack for three months, and surely their completed cabin must have had a feeling of real permanence, if not elegance, about it. At times a mother's duties were carried on in and around the wagon in which they bumped to their "home," or it may have been in a crude brush shelter hastily put together.[3]

The following statement refers to conditions encountered by another group, which also arrived in covered wagons:

> Once an immigrant family arrived upon the land of its choice, the immediate problem was to cultivate some ground and plant a crop as soon as possible. . . . Some kind of shelter was, of course, necessary, but a house was secondary in importance to the business of planting. In the days of covered wagons, weeks might pass with the family residing in the wagon boxes before cabins were made ready; sometimes tents were used. Frequently the first building was hastily improvised from any materials that happened to be handy—a mere shed or perhaps an underground habitation with dirt walls on three sides.[4]

Gullik Springsen, an early Rock Prairie settler, described his primitive shelter, built in 1841:

> My family and I lived near my spring through the autumn and far into the winter in a cabin woven of branches and thatched with straw. The flat cover of a chest brought from Norway served as a table, and all working was done outdoors. Only toward Christmas was I able to build a simple log house.[5]

Such primitive initial shelters were commonplace elsewhere in southern Wisconsin, for immigrants in the first wave of Norwegian settlement, including a group at the Lake Muskego colony:

> We had decided to make use of a mound out on a fine plot of ground with good drainage in all directions. . . . The mound was so large that by excavating down to the level of the surrounding ground we got a room twenty-four feet long, eighteen feet wide, and seven feet high. This first story was entirely underground. Over it we built a loft five logs high which rested on six pillars about seven feet in height. The walls of our dugout were so firm that there was no danger of a cave-in, and we merely needed to provide it with a wainscot in order to get a good, warm dwelling.[6]

In the Koshkonong settlement, Knud Hilliksen Roe, from Tiren in Telemarken, gave a description of his first habitation, built in 1843. The following year, he built a log house at the same location:

Our first dwelling was so near completion that my wife and I with our one child could find protection under its roof against wind and rain. The hut was made of leafy branches and each of its four corners was supported by an oak tree. There were no other settlers in the township at the time, so I was the first white man to light his hearth in Pleasant Spring.[7]

As Norwegian immigrants moved northward into newly opened areas of the state, at each new site the pattern reappeared; the first houses were makeshift, crude, and temporary. The following account describes four early non-log dwellings in the Waupaca County Norwegian settlement:

The first settlers in Farmington spent 3 winter months in a tent. Bears and wolves came sniffing around the tent and there was such a howling that they rarely got rest at night. . . .

Van Horn and his family settled in the Town of Dayton. He knocked some poles into the ground. Floor mats were used for walls and roof. As did others, Mrs. Van Horn had to cook food out in the open field. . . .

Gregar Gregarson Halla, from Hiterdal in Telemarken settled in the Town of Iola. He cut down and split the big aspen (poplar) logs which he raised up around a big oak tree. In this aspen tent, he stayed with his family until he managed to make himself a log hut. . . . Some of them took the fox as an example and dug a big hole in the hill. There they could have it good and warm.[8]

Another account describes sod houses—an unusual type of early dwelling in Wisconsin—in the Bruce Valley area of Trempealeau County. The year was 1868:

Sod houses were built on each homestead, and the families moved to their new homes. Barns were also built of sod. The dwellings were two-story structures, but contained no stairways. The second story was the children's bedroom, and when bedtime came they were hoisted into their quarters through a trapdoor in the so-called ceiling. . . . Bruce Valley, like all the other valleys in Trempealeau County at that time, contained no timber—mostly brush, and the valley bottoms were wet and marshy. . . . Yearly fires had stripped the terrain of trees.[9]

Early Log Construction

Where feasible, log construction was preferred for early built dwellings throughout areas of Norwegian settlement in Wisconsin (Fig. 13-2). Unfortunately, since most of these houses no longer exist, written sources of information must again be used to gain insights regarding their design, construction, and utilization. In addition to accounts published in the Norwegian-American literature, important architectural data have been obtained from homestead documents filed by Norwegian settlers claiming land under the Federal Homestead Act. The following accounts provide impor-

Fig. 13-2 Norwegian-American dwelling unusual because it utilizes vertical log construction, and is partially covered with brick. Located south of Valders, Manitowoc County, Wisconsin. (Photo by W. Tishler.)

tant information about these buildings and the often harsh living conditions of their inhabitants. In Waupaca County, for example,

> a settlement house was often built in great haste, and was therefore not either very tight or solidly built. . . . When the strong cold of the winter came, they would have to fire the stove all night, and when there was an end to the wood, the husband would have to go out and cut more. . . . If they had only a board shanty, this was also exposed and could be swept away by strong storms. A log cabin always "kept" better. . . . The first settlement houses were of different sizes. Some were only 12′ × 12′. Some of them 12′ × 14′, and some 14′ × 20′, and the height could be 8′, 10′, 12′, or 14′. If a house was 24′ × 16′, and 14′ high, it was called a fine house, or a great house. Houses of 12′ or 14′ were not divided up. But a building 24′ × 16′ × 14′ was most often divided into 3 rooms; a sitting room, bedroom, and a pantry. The steps up to the loft were on one side of the pantry with the entrance to the cellar underneath. The loft was divided into 2 or 3 rooms. The biggest houses were built in such a way that a side house could be added later.[10]

Further details regarding early log construction are vividly portrayed in the following account:

> An ordinary living house is built here in one day—at least up to the roof. Its walls are so open that in many places there are three or four inches between each log, and in the winter these openings

William H. Tishler

must be filled in with wood splinters and clay to make the house reasonably tight. Some of this chinking falls out and leaves holes so large that a cat could almost pass freely in and out. People seldom have more than one room, which must serve as a kitchen, dining room, and bedroom. There is a loft overhead which is far from being as tight as an ordinary hayloft in Norway and this must serve as a bedroom when there are more people in the house than there is room for downstairs. . . . Such accommodations . . . are so exposed to draft and drifting snow that sometimes the beds are almost covered in the morning with a foot of heavy snow.[11]

In February 1857, Olaus Fredrick Duus, a Norwegian pastor, wrote about the housing conditions of members of his frontier congregation in the same area:

I should like also to take you with me into the house of my friend, Torjer Mortensen, from Guldbrandsdalen, who lets me use his house when I preach in the district. . . . The house is like all the others here, with neither siding on the outside nor paneling on the inside. You walk directly into the living room, which is tremen- dously large compared to the average room here—it is eighteen feet each way. Along the wall on one side are some planks placed on log stumps, which serve as benches, while on the other side the bed, chests, and trunk all serve the same purpose. Right between the windows is a table . . . and behind the table is a stool made from the end of a board and four sticks. Chairs are not to be found and are still a luxury in at least half the houses in this settlement, since the farmers have come here too recently to be able to buy things that they can do without or that they can provide in a cheaper way.[12]

Other informative accounts of Norwegian log construction were made of farmhouses in Pierce County. One immigrant wrote the following to his fam- ily in Norway on January 13, 1861:

We built our house last spring, and were kept busy a long time, as it is large compared with such dwelling houses here in America. It is 16 ells [32 feet] long and 10 ells [20 feet] wide, inside measure, and two full stories high. The timbers are hewed of oak and also bev- eled, so it was a lot of work and it took a long time to erect. We have divided it in two, as the whole room would be too large for so few people to live in.[13]

A year later, in January 1862, he told of building another house for one of his countrymen:

After harvest last fall we contracted to build a house. . . . We were to build it of hewed timbers for $60, and we made fairly well by it as we averaged a dollar a day each. The house was 14 ells [28 feet] long and 10 ells [20 feet] wide and two full stories. We hewed the logs, which were of oak, on the ground before we hauled them up in place, but we did not bevel them as he did not wish to have the logs lie so close together. There has been a lot of building done here lately, as the houses have been poor, and there were very few who could do such work before we came.[14]

The Homestead Act of 1862 was used by many Norwegian immigrants to obtain land in Wisconsin. It provided up to 160 acres of free land to any citizen or intended citizen, 21 years of age, who would settle on and cultivate the land. After five years of occupancy, homesteaders could secure title and finalize ownership by completing a series of documents. These included sworn affidavits or "proof forms," which required a description of the dwelling plus other improvements made on their land claim. This could include information pertaining to accessory structures, the number of acres of land cleared, the amount of fencing erected, the principal crops grown, plus accounts of family and social relationships and other data that have also been useful in understanding ethnic origins.

A recent investigation of Norwegian homestead documents in Wisconsin provides important insights into early structures and other aspects of pioneer settlement. Coon Valley, located in western Wisconsin's Vernon County (see Fig. 13-1), purportedly "the most densely settled Norwegian area in the state,"[15] was selected for this study. Here, nearly all of the 334 homestead claims were made by Norwegian settlers. Coon Township, where 70 homestead applications were registered, was selected for detailed analysis. Within this township, 34 percent of the applicants claimed 40-acre parcels of land, 30 percent registered parcels ranging from 41 to 80 acres in size, and the others occupied land claims of 81 to 160 acres. The typical Norwegian homestead in the township was inhabited by a family averaging 5.2 members. After five years of occupancy, they had an average of 5 acres under cultivation and 16.3 acres enclosed with fencing.

While homesteaders' house dimensions varied, the most common measured 14' × 16'. The size of these dwellings varied from less than 100 square feet to more than 350 square feet, 200 to 249 square feet being typical. Houses were usually one-and-one-half stories in height and had a wood shingle roof, although sod, board, and birch bark roofs were sometimes noted. Board floors, one exterior door, and two windows constituted other frequently mentioned details. A stable was the outbuilding most commonly present, but many accounts also mention a granary, and blacksmith shops were noted to have been on two of the homesteads.

Fourteen of the proof documents indicated that fruit trees had been planted, but specific varieties were seldom mentioned. In some cases the types of cultivated crops were recorded, with wheat, corn, oats, and potatoes most frequently mentioned.

Surveys of Norwegian Folk Architecture

Several important surveys and studies of Norwegian folk architecture in Wisconsin have contributed important information regarding this ethnic group's building tradition in the state. The first, completed in 1973, was an analysis of Norwegian structures and their furnishings in the early Luther Valley settlement in Rock County (see Fig. 13-1).[16] Another important investigation was undertaken during the early research and construction phases of Old World Wisconsin, the state's highly acclaimed outdoor museum.[17] A

William H. Tishler

third source of data on Norwegian-American architecture was derived from surveys and research of the Coon Valley region for Norskedalen, an outdoor museum established to conserve the area's rich Norwegian heritage.[18]

The Luther Valley Study

Three forms of shelter were constructed by Norwegian immigrants in Luther Valley during the early (1839–1860) settlement period: timber structures, combination timber and stone structures, and stone structures. Timber structures were fabricated as a transient approach to the problem of shelter. Based upon information from seven documented timber buildings in Luther Valley, several timber house types were constructed in the area. These varied in size, ranging from 144 to 320 square feet and from one to two stories in height. Both dovetail and saddle corner-notching methods were used, and only one building was built of close-fitting unchinked logs, the traditional northern European method of log construction.

Eventually, when economy, time, and other factors permitted, a more commodious and permanent stone or frame house was built. The original log dwelling was then adapted to other uses, typically that of a granary or storage shed. In some cases, however, the original log structure was enlarged with an addition built of stone. Four structures built of a combination of timber and stone were documented in the Luther Valley area. In three examples the log portions had been sided over with sawn boards, and in one case the structure had been covered with a veneer of limestone. Two of the stone additions resembled the more formal, all-stone structures of the area. In the other two cases the stone additions were "smaller and unique in construction; clear-cut outgrowths of the needs of the owner-builders."[19]

The loose ledges of yellowish limestone that existed in much of Luther Valley provided the most readily available building material for the area. Norwegian settlers utilized stone for their larger and more refined dwellings, and several examples, built between 1845 and the late 1850s, have been documented. Most adhere to a rectangular, gable-roofed "classic Luther Valley form."[20] This generally consists of a central hall plan and symmetrical fenestrations—three bays on the front and back walls and two on the gable end walls. Many incorporate some Greek Revival stylistic features, including roofs with heavy neoclassical moldings and returning gable end cornices. Other common features include a central stone wall—frequently containing a chimney flue—and chimneys in the gable end walls. The masonry construction generally consists of loosely coursed limestone ashlar with irregular corner quoins and mortar raked with lines to suggest vertical and horizontal joints. Over time, some changes were made to these dwellings, including the addition of porches or summer kitchens and, in a few cases, alterations to the partitioning of interior spaces.

Coon Valley Folk Houses

Norwegian pioneer builders in the Coon Valley area continued their Old World log building tradition, but with several important modifications. Here, because coniferous wood was scarce, most immigrants built with available hardwoods, usually red and white oak, leaving spaces between the logs. These interstices were then filled with a chinking of wood strips and clay or lime mortar.[21] As Lars K. Brye, an early settler in Coon Valley, later noted, even suitable hardwood could be difficult to find:

> When the first immigrants came, the hills and ridges were not as beautiful as now. Then there were only small, thin woods—oak openings, everywhere. The forests must have burned several years before, for when the first settlers arrived, there were only a few small scattered bushes in the valley. These were not large enough for building timber, so men had to go well up into Skogdalen [Timber Coulee], where the timber was larger, to find lumber for building houses.[22]

Fifty-four surviving log houses were documented in a recent survey of the Coon Valley area.[23] These were categorized into three types: one room and one story with loft; two bays, one room deep with one story plus attic or two stories; and the *sval,* enclosed side stairway and passage with loft.

Eighteen of the dwellings can be classified as simple one-room cabins, with exterior dimensions ranging from $10' \times 12'$ to $17'8'' \times 20'6''$. No standard pattern of dimensions emerges for these structures, but many range from 16 to 18 feet square in size. Furthermore, sixteen of the one-room structures incorporate a length of approximately 16 feet for one of their walls, apparently a common module for Norwegian-American dwellings in the area.[24] These cabins were usually crude structures that lacked the carefully shaped and fitted logs and decorative carved details found in traditional Scandinavian buildings.

Living space in the simple one-room houses was at a premium. Typically, the main room (*stue*) served as parlor, bedroom, dining room, and kitchen, while the upper area or loft (*bod*) served as storage and additional sleeping space for the children. "People lived in small log cabins which usually consisted of only one room with a loft above," one observer noted. He added, "In one corner of the room was a bed made of some boards and laths nailed to the wall. In the other corner was a stove. There were, in addition, a homemade table and some benches, plus a cupboard where food was kept."[25]

Several common features occur among one-room log houses in the Coon Valley area. All were built with oak logs joined with full dovetail corner notches and were chinked with wood strips, clay, or a combination of both. With one exception, all have horizontal logs laid up to the eaves with board-and-batten or clapboard siding running to the ridge on the gable ends. Only one, a very early dwelling, exhibits the traditional Scandinavian full log gable end construction feature. Other characteristics of this building include steps to the loft consisting of three large wooden pins protruding from holes drilled in the wall, and unhewn purlins (*aas*) and a ridgepole linking the gable ends to support the roof. One other house also had a ridgepole and purlins in its roof construction.

After a few years in the small, one-room cabin, the immigrant family frequently built a more expansive dwelling. In some cases, the original log structure was retained and incorporated into the larger building—its identity concealed beneath vertical board-and-batten or horizontal clapboard siding.

The second type of log house found in the Coon Valley area had two pens, one large and nearly square (the stue) and the second a smaller space.

William H. Tishler

234

These rectangular houses are easily distinguished by a slightly off-center chimney constructed adjacent to the interior partition wall. They are symmetrical in outward appearance—the main entrance is usually centrally located in the axial wall, flanked by one or two windows, with the same window arrangement frequently repeated on the opposite side of the house. As in the one-room cabin, the staircase was usually placed against the wall and near the front entrance. This two-pen dwelling is a traditional Norwegian log house form.

When one-room log cabins were expanded into larger structures, the additions were built of logs, or were of frame construction, when cheap sawn lumber became available. In many, "a much favored arrangement was to adjoin two rooms on the first floor as *kjokken* (kitchen) and *stue* (parlor) and repeat the plan on the second floor as *soverum* (bedroom) and *bod* (loft)."[26] As in Norway, the bod was often used as a sleeping area for children during the winter or as a dry-storage facility.[27] Both one-story-with-loft and two-story versions were found in the area. Exterior dimensions of the two-bay houses range from 16'4" to 24'6" in width and 18'4" to 39'1" in length. Consistent with one-room cabins, the stue in two-bay houses frequently measured from 16 to 17 feet in length, reflecting the common size module found in Coon Valley folk houses.

In some dwellings access to the bod was by a staircase located within an enclosed passageway, or *sval* (Fig. 13-3). This form represented the third Coon Valley area house type. Rarely found in America, the sval is usually enclosed by logs extending from the upper portion of the building and sup-

Fig. 13-3 House with a *sval* passage on the lateral wall. One end of the sval, where stairs lead to the upper level, has been enclosed with a tight-fitting weatherboarding. Portage County, Wisconsin. (Photo by W. Tishler.)

ported by upright timbers. One end of this projection was then sheathed with sawn boards to serve as an unheated storage chamber. Two extant sval houses were identified in the survey and two more houses, to which access could not be obtained, strongly resembled sval houses. One specimen had interior walls of skilfully hewn and fitted hardwood logs and great care had been taken in shaping other details of the house.

A traditional feature in many areas of Norway, the sval is well documented in Norwegian folk architecture literature.[28] It was widely known in the Gudbrandsdal region of Norway, where many Coon Valley settlers had lived and where examples of svals in the mid-seventeenth century have been documented. In the European versions, the sval "might appear at one or both levels of the house and sometimes extend . . . along three sides, ending in a privy."[29] Its early use, particularly when it was on the second floor level, was assumed to be fortification, but it also served as a storeroom and weather buffer between interior heated areas and the outdoors. Some scholars suggest that the sval represented a transitional phase in the evolution of the single-room shelter into the larger, double-pen, or bipartite plan, in which the stairwell was contained within the core of the building.[30]

Twenty-five early outbuildings also were documented in the survey of Coon Valley. These log structures consist of granaries, corn cribs, sheds, chicken coops, and assorted barns. Few working farms retained more than two of the early structures, including the house. The low number of surviving relic buildings per farmstead is unexpected, since there are usually many specialized-function structures on traditional farms in Norway, where the number might be thirty or more.[31] Obviously, many agrarian buildings were lost over time from the forces of change so typical of American agriculture; however, fewer outbuildings were utilized on Norwegian-American farms in Wisconsin than on farms in Norway, because of the different agricultural, economic, and social conditions. Noting this contrast after observing the new farms of his countrymen, one immigrant wrote, "What we call a 'gaard' in Norway is a farm here, and a large farm here consists of dwelling house, a cellar and a stable."[32]

While as many as five types of early farmstead arrangements have been distinguished in Norway,[33] variations of only two traditional layouts were utilized with some frequency in Wisconsin. These are the courtyard plan, common to the scattered farmsteads in the broad valleys of eastern Norway, and the linear or double-linear forms found in the more precipitous areas of western Norway. In the latter, a lane or street that followed the contour of the land divided the dwellings located on higher ground from the down-slope barns and outbuildings. In Wisconsin, terrain characteristics had a similar influence on farmstead form. Arrangements suggesting loose courtyards can be found on prairies and other gently rolling areas, while versions of linear plans are more evident on Norwegian-American farms in the steep valleys of western Wisconsin.

To date, of all the surveys of Norwegian-American folk architecture undertaken in Wisconsin, the Coon Valley study has examined the largest number of surviving structures. Thus, the extensive body of information derived from it has been extremely useful in analyzing this ethnic group's patterns of building activity. Wood was the predominant building material used by Norwegian immigrant builders in the area. However, as in other portions of

Fig. 13-4 The deteriorated condition of this two-story log house reveals several details of the construction used in early Norwegian-American buildings in southern Wisconsin. These include interior and exterior wall surfaces hewn with a broad axe, extensive chinking, wood pegs placed at window and door openings for lateral stability, and interior wall logs mortised through the lateral walls. (Photo by W. Tishler.)

southern Wisconsin, where most of the state's Norwegians settled, only a few surviving buildings retain the tight joinery of the northern European method of log construction. Here obvious modifications were made through the widespread use of chinking and less-sophisticated (typically dovetail) methods of corner notching. One widely used feature of traditional Norwegian wood building that was retained, however, was the use of stabilizing pegs driven into vertical holes bored into the logs near door and window openings (Fig. 13-4).

Roof systems of Coon Valley houses reflected American influences, and traditional Norwegian characteristics were retained in only four houses. Here the use of horizontal logs to the peak of the gable end walls and massive purlins—common features in Norway—were noted in only four houses (Fig. 13-5). Most of the dwellings utilized hewn log rafters, and three incorporated an extended plate log protruding over the gable end to support a principle rafter. While a few sod roofs were used for a short time, roofing materials also represented important changes with the advent of cheap sawn shingles.

Norwegians in Wisconsin

Fig. 13-5 Detail of the gable wall of a one-room cabin built by a Norwegian immigrant at Coon Valley, Wisconsin in 1853. Note the log purlins extending below the roof overhang and the logs in the wall that extend to the roof peak. (Photo by W. Tishler.)

With two exceptions, all entrances were located near the center of the axial wall. Access to the loft was usually by a steep staircase (*traap*) located in one corner near the door. Typically, after one or two risers, the stair made a ninety degree turn continuing up to the loft. All staircases lacked handrails and were enclosed, and they frequently had a door at the bottom. During the months or years following initial construction, a root cellar (*kjeller*) in which to store perishable food was often dug beneath the house. Many remain and are frequently accessible through a trap door in the floor.

The Old World Wisconsin Outdoor Museum

Meticulous field investigations of Wisconsin's Norwegian-American architecture have been undertaken for Old World Wisconsin, the state's huge outdoor museum of ethnic immigrant culture. This research documented building types, characteristics, and availability, as well as siting patterns, furnishings, related settlement history and other information necessary for accurate restoration and interpretation. Buildings for two Norwegian farmsteads and a schoolhouse were acquired and restored and became part of the museum's elaborate recreated rural ethnic enclaves.

The Fossebrekke farm includes one of the oldest houses at the museum,

William H. Tishler

built in the Luther Valley settlement in 1841. A Fossebrekke descendent later noted that it had housed "as many as 17 persons in the first winters."[34] Originally located near a spring, in a small clearing in the surrounding forest, it provided shelter during a subsistence-level existence that depended on wheat-growing and trapping. Built of square-hewn, chinked oak logs, it has three windows on the ground floor and a single door in the lateral wall. Measuring 16½ by 17 feet, it stands 12½ feet high from ground level to cornice and has walls approximately 10 inches thick. The building's most distinctive Scandinavian construction features can be found in its roof. Here, six purlins and a ridgepole rest on the log gable ends. In eastern Norway, including the Numedal region, where Fossebrekke had lived, this massive structural system ordinarily supported a slate or sod roof. The presence of these roofing characteristics suggest that sod may have been the building's original roofing material. Moved to its new museum setting, the Fossebrekke house, with its garden, fenced clearing, and crude animal shelter, accurately portrays the austere atmosphere that must have existed in its original primitive environment (Fig. 13-6).

The Anders Ellingsen Kvaale house is the focal point of a large, well-established, diversified Norwegian farmstead exhibit with six related outbuildings. Built circa 1848 and restored to its 1865 appearance, the dwelling originally stood in the south central Dane County town of Dunkirk. Unlike many of his fellow Norwegians, Kvaale could afford to construct a substantial house immediately upon his arrival. Built of tightly fitted logs, in the northern European log building tradition, the one-and-one-half story house measures 28 feet in length and 22 feet deep. An interior log wall divides the first floor into a kitchen and a living room; an unheated enclosed porch

Fig. 13-6 The Knud Crispinusen Fossebrekke house. Built in 1841, it has been carefully restored at Old World Wisconsin which is near Eagle, Wisconsin. (Photo by W. Tishler.)

(*svalgang*) runs along the front wall. Built as an integral part of the house, the latter contains a slightly wider storage chamber at one end and the staircase leading to the two upper sleeping rooms. The Kvaale house resembles the low, squat weatherboarded houses of Norway's west coast and the Sogndal Province where Anders had lived.[35]

Other buildings in the Kvaale farmstead ensemble were moved from Norwegian-American farms in southern Wisconsin and represent structures used on Norwegian farms around 1865. These include a log summer kitchen that had originally served as living quarters, a double-crib log barn with central drive-through that sheltered both horses and cattle, a granary—actually an American version of the Norwegian *stabbur* used for grain and farm storage as well as other seasonal needs including a summer weaving workshop, a small log animal shelter, a hewn-log corncrib, and a frame three-hole privy. Complimenting the two log farmsteads, and sited some distance away, is the Raspberry School. This plain, well-crafted, one-room log structure was used by students in Norwegian and Swedish families of northern Wisconsin's Bayfield County.

The Loft Cottage

Studies of Norwegian building in Wisconsin have indicated that, except in the Luther Valley settlement, wood was the predominant construction material used by immigrant Norwegian farmers and builders. From these studies, the early houses built by this ethnic group can be categorized into three basic types: timber structures, including the one-room cabin, the double-pen house, and the sval house; and two later types, combination timber and stone dwellings and stone structures. In addition to these dwelling types, several examples of another type, the loft cottage have been found (Fig. 13-7). An important folk building in Norway, it has a characteristic overhanging front upper gable. The loft area was used as a sleeping chamber, with the smaller, lower space traditionally used for storage, and later (as in most of the Wisconsin examples) as living quarters. These rare buildings represent Americanized simplifications of the medieval loft cottages of Norway, which frequently incorporated overhangs on three or more sides.

Conclusion

The architecture of Norwegian immigrants, as of most of the ethnic groups who settled in rural Wisconsin, often utilized the building technology and traditional vernacular forms of their homeland. Yet, as a culture group they quickly adapted their skilful northern European log construction methods to the demands of their new environment. Initially, the urgency of providing immediate shelter, combined with the less-skilled craftsmanship of farmers who had to double as builders and the difficulties of utilizing hardwood from the local oak forests, resulted in cruder forms of wood joinery and other more expedient construction innovations. On their farms, significant architectural changes resulted from adopting American agricultural practices that called for farmsteads with fewer and different buildings. Another decisive force for change was the penchant of Norwegian-Americans, as they achieved a higher standard of living, to quickly adopt

Fig. 13-7 A small loft cottage, built by a Norwegian immigrant near Stoughton, Wisconsin, in 1844. (Photo by W. Tishler.)

prevailing Yankee building styles and construction techniques. In settlements where traditional house forms were retained, most were visibly modified over time by frame additions and interior partitions or by the use of mass-produced lapped siding, sawn wood shingles, or double-hung windows when each became available. Thus a complex picture emerges of an architecture that sometimes reflected the ethnic group's Norwegian vernacular traditions but, where necessary, revealed a quick assimilation of the building ideas of their American neighbors. This dichotomy has made the analysis of Norwegian folk architecture in America a complex and multifaceted activity that provides many opportunities for future scholarly attention on both sides of the Atlantic.

14

Finns in the Lake Superior Region

Matti Enn Kaups

TRANSATLANTIC mass migration from Finland to the United States began just past the middle of the nineteenth century, in 1864. Slow at the outset, the movement gathered momentum in the early 1890s and reached its peak during the first decade of the present century. Its magnitude in the years prior to the onset of the restrictive quota laws of the 1920s has been the subject of speculation, various interpretations, and numerous conclusions. According to official U.S. statistics, 359,324 Finns landed at American ports between 1872 and 1920.[1] The fairly accurate figure on arrivals ought not to be equated with—nor taken to represent—the true size of Finnish immigration in these years, because it includes migrants who entered the country on more than one occasion and were counted each time as new arrivals. For example, 11.3 percent (17,189) of the 151,774 entrants during the years 1899–1910 had been in the United States previously. An untold number had crossed the Atlantic several times in quest of employment in the American labor market, in hopes of permanently improving their economic status at home with the dollars saved.[2]

Another reason for approaching the 1872–1920 statistics with caution is that a considerable permanent return migration to Finland existed. It is not surprising, therefore, that in 1920, when the foreign-born Finnish population reached an all-time high in the United States, only 149,824 individuals were enumerated in the federal census.[3] The difference between this total and the number of entrants during the period 1872–1920—a difference of nearly 210,000—represents arrivals (including repeaters), deaths from natural and accidental causes in the United States, and return migrations to Finland. Perhaps as many as 30 percent of the arrivals during the first two decades of the present century returned home to Finland permanently.[4]

From the early years of settlement, the location of the Finns showed a strong human ecological association with the primary sector economic activities—lumbering, agriculture, and especially mining. The relationship to mining dates from the very beginning of Finnish settlement, in 1864, when a group of about 20 Finns from northern Norway arrived at the copper mines of Houghton County on the Keweenaw peninsula of Michigan, and another small group came to Red Wing in southeastern Minnesota. Although three diminutive rural settlements were established in Renville, Wright, and Douglas counties, Minnesota, in the 1860s, the destination for the vast majority of Finns was the burgeoning mining districts in the Lake Superior region. The demand for common labor, first in the copper and iron ore mines of northern Michigan and subsequently in the Wisconsin and Minnesota mines, drew thousands of rural Finns, who were novices to mining but who needed employment. Indeed, unskilled wage labor in the mines was the vocational niche found by most early Finnish immigrants in the American economic structure, and mining locations and towns provided the setting for life in what was for them a novel environment. Once arrived in these settlements, they learned of employment opportunities elsewhere.

As early as the 1870s, Finns were present in the mines of the Black Hills in South Dakota, in the Rocky Mountain states, and in smaller numbers, in Pennsylvania and Ohio. In the lumber industry the Finns found employment as lumberjacks in logging camps and as laborers in sawmills in the Lake Superior region, the Pacific Northwest, and in Maine. At the same time, there were Finns who worked on railroads, as fishermen and stevedores along the Pacific Coast and the Great Lakes, in quarries here and there, and as factory hands primarily in New England towns. Few were the Finns who resided in the urban-industrial centers of the nation's manufacturing belt, and Finns were almost entirely absent from the South.

Agriculture was another primary sector of the economy that appealed to the Finns. As farmers and part-time farmers they established small rural settlements to the north of the Mason-Dixon line from Maine to California, with a marked concentration in the Midwest. More than two-thirds of the settlements founded during the seven decades of land taking (1860s–1920s) were located in northern Minnesota, Wisconsin, and Michigan, within an area which became the geographical and institutional heartland of Finnish America.[5]

The Lake Superior Area

One of the salient characteristics of the geographical distribution of the Finnish immigrants was their persistent concentration in the Lake Superior area. One-half (50.8 percent) of the nation's 62,641 foreign-born (born outside the United States) Finns tabulated in the federal census for the year 1900 inhabited the states of Minnesota, Michigan, and Wisconsin. They were most numerous in counties bordering Lake Superior, in which copper and iron ore mines were located. Twenty years later, when 149,824 Finns were enumerated nationally, the concentration remained unmoved, with 44 percent of the Finnish population residing in those three states at that time (Fig. 14-1).[6] The propensity for migration into the area has not gone unnoticed, and it has been suggested that deterministic environmental perception rather than employment opportunities and availability of land, was the causal link responsible for the concentration.[7]

It bears emphasis that, while the concentration of Finns in the Lake Superior area persisted from census to census, it was to some extent actually composed of many individual moves into and out of the mining areas, logging camps, sawmills, and towns, moves which do not appear in the decennial census reports. A relatively high degree of both seasonal and perennial geographical mobility resulted from fluctuating labor demand in the primary industries. The mining settlements in particular served as nodes of an

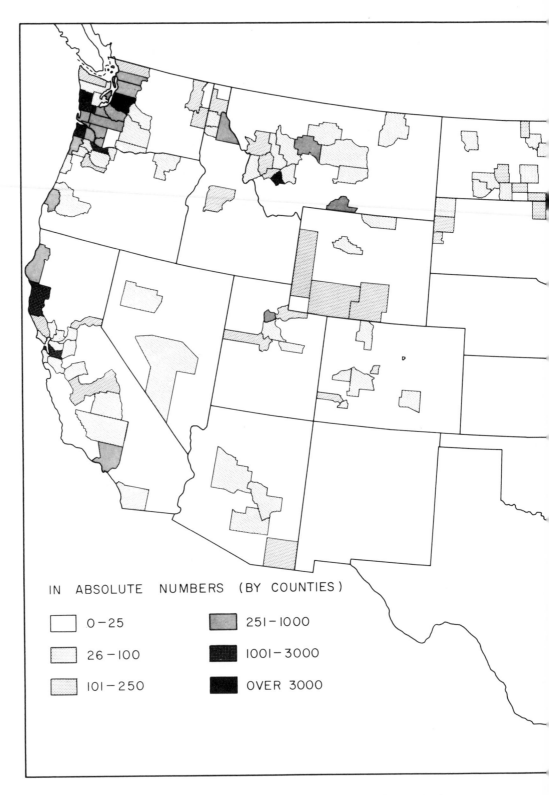

Fig. 14-1 Distribution in 1920 of Finnish immigrants to the United States.

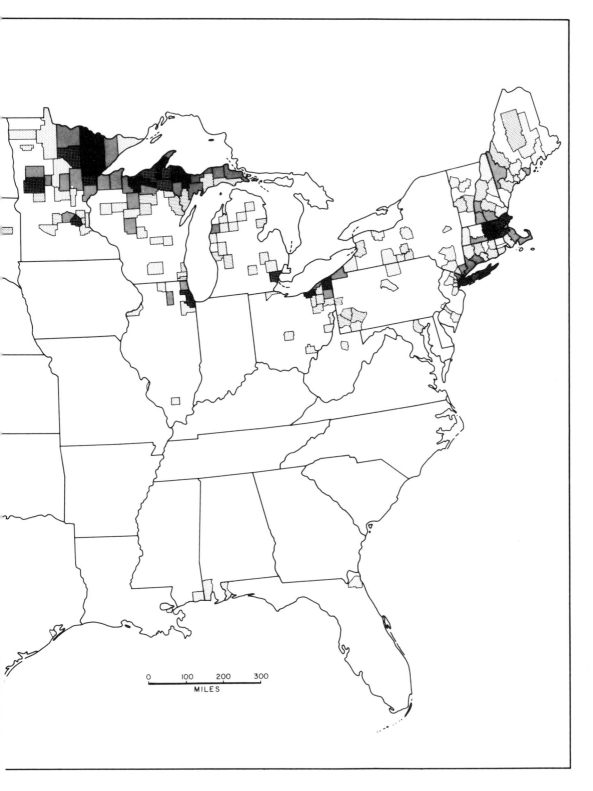

(From U.S. Census data. Map by M. Kaups.)

inter- and intraregional migration network. For the Finns, it meant moves from mine to mine, from mines to logging camps, harvest fields, fishing sites, sawmills, and back, and more importantly, from mines to the land.

With relatively few exceptions, the movement of Finns to the land represents a second-stage migration, which occurred after some capital had been accumulated for the purchase of essentials needed in incipient farming. Several factors facilitated the movement to land settlement. One was that the Finns were predominantly from rural backgrounds. Of the 274,000 who left Finland for overseas destinations between 1893 and 1920, 87 percent came from the countryside, and farming was an activity in which they had some experience.[8] Besides those who harbored a desire to own and work a parcel of land as a means of achieving some measure of economic security, there were Finns who settled on land because of widespread dissatisfaction with employment and living conditions in the mining settlements, such as hazardous working conditions, fluctuating labor demand, and periodic strikes. These and yet other motives, including the seemingly brighter prospect of preserving ethnicity in rural areas than in mining settlements, were discussed in the Finnish-language press that published in this country. Eventually these thoughts found their way into the offices of land companies and the minds of publicists who blithely employed, with some success, these themes in exploitative advertising campaigns aimed at luring Finns into buying and settling on land in the sparsely populated hinterland of Lake Superior, particularly after the turn of the century.[9]

Altogether 168 rural settlements of various sizes were established by the Finns in Minnesota, Wisconsin, and Michigan during the period 1865–1922 (Fig. 14-2).[10] Of the 152 settlement areas for which data on founding are available, 19.1 percent were established between 1865 and 1889, 66.4 percent in the following two decades (1890–1909), and the remaining 14.5 percent between 1910 and 1922. Provided the 16 undated settlements are added to the 1890–1909 category—and from the historical evidence there is reason for doing so—then almost 70 percent of all the settlements were established in those two decades, most during the first decade of the present century.

With some notable exceptions, the settlements were located within the so-called Cutover Area (see Fig. 14-2).[11] More than one-half (54.8 percent) of the settlements were located in Minnesota and nearly one-third (29.8 percent) in Michigan. In both states they formed ethnic islands, which had relatively small populations and were ethnically nearly homogeneous. These islands ranged in area from a fraction of a township to tens of square miles. The largest one, which had several service centers, measured somewhat in excess of twenty by forty miles. It was located in Otter Tail, Wadena, and Becker counties of Minnesota and was only partially within the Cutover Area.[12] Unlike certain rural settlements of the Swedes and Norwegians in the Midwest in which the settlers derived from a common village or small district in the home country, the Finnish settlements were composed of people with diverse geographical backgrounds. The common denominator of belonging was the Finnish language.[13]

The smaller of the widely separated settlements were not necessarily doomed to ethnic isolation. Frequently, such groups had access to the religious, economic, and social life in neighboring ethnic settlements of greater size. Obviously the population size and structure of a given settle-

Matti Enn
Kaups

246

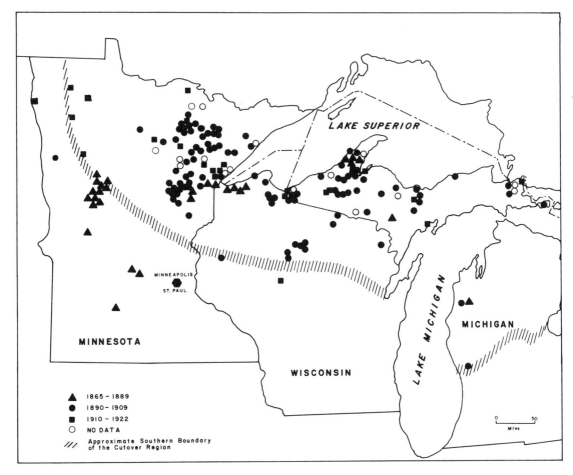

Fig. 14-2 Finnish rural settlements in the Lake Superior region, 1865–1922. (Map by M. Kaups.)

LEGEND:
▲ 1865–1889
● 1890–1909
■ 1910–1922
○ NO DATA
/// Approximate Southern Boundary of the Cutover Region

ment affected its organizational framework (see Chapter 22).

Although there were Finns who acquired land in the Cutover region by homesteading, most purchased it from railroad, lumber, and land companies in tracts generally ranging from 40 to 160 acres. The land, for which there was little demand, sold at from $5 to $15 an acre after the turn of the century, and it was available on long-term credit. According to an authoritative estimate, some 85 percent of the Finns in Wisconsin purchased their holdings; the percentage was probably somewhat lower for the Finns who settled in northern Minnesota and Michigan.[14]

Regardless of the size and the geometrical shape of the properties secured, the settlement pattern the Finns established was in large measure an expression of the Federal Rectangular Survey, which decades earlier had divided the land into townships and sections. Dispersed settlement with unit-block holdings was the norm throughout the area. The small size of the properties the Finns secured brought about, in some cases, a higher density of roads than was customary. In areas of 40-acre holdings (or a mixture of

247

40- and 80-acre holdings), auxiliary roads were constructed at one-half mile intervals through the middle of sections, in either north-south or east-west directions, in order to provide access to settlers on the interior forties, which were unreachable from the township roads spaced one mile apart. Such sections and townships had a higher population density than like units in areas where Finns had acquired larger properties.[15] The small holdings were expressions of economies of scale and should not be construed as an intentional replication of the Finnish landscape. After all, dispersed rural settlement in various densities, as well as farm villages, were common in nineteenth-century Finland.[16]

In describing the cultural landscape that the Finns fashioned in the Cutover Area, it is important to note that nearly two-thirds of the settlers came from the ranks of tenant farmers, small land holders, and landless agricultural laborers in Finland.[17] It was customary for men to supplement their income by working at nonagricultural chores seasonally, especially in logging operations during the winter months. Small-sized holdings and part-time farming became established in the Cutover Area.

While there were a number of bona fide and successful farmers amongst the Finns in the area, the majority ended their days as part-time farmers and others as nothing more than gardeners or horticulturalists, men who customarily had worked during the peak months in the mines, logging camps, and sawmills. In their absence, women minded the household and the part-time farm. Indeed, it is not an accident that many of the Finnish settlements were located in rather close proximity to places of seasonal employment. In the agricultural side of their lives the immigrants could implement and practice aspects of folk culture they had brought with them, while in places of employment they were wage earners, members of a non-Finnish industrial society. This duality, coupled with differences in the size and quality of land holdings and a new diversity of individual aspirations, left the imprint on the cultural landscape of a population coming from the periphery of northern Europe, moving from traditions once steeped in forest culture into those of industrial society.

The Finnish-American Cultural Landscape

One of the outstanding characteristics of the material landscape that the Finns shaped was the abundance of buildings constructed of horizontally stacked logs joined at the corners with notches and manifesting basic architectural concepts and techniques known for centuries in northern Europe. At the same time, some of the structures show evidence of alien practices, particularly in architectural detail. Although as a rule, small land holders, tenant farmers, and landless agricultural laborers still lived in log houses and constructed buildings out of logs, the time of emigration was a period of transition from folk to industrial culture in Finland, and models of different building types and materials than those traditionally used had been available in Finland for some time, especially to those residing in the western districts of the country.[18] Moreover, Finns were exposed to the architectural traditions current in the mining settlements and elsewhere in the United States where they settled. It is not surprising, therefore, to find old log structures built by Finnish immigrants in which traditional northern European concepts and "modernisms" are juxtaposed.

Though their numbers were relatively small, there were immigrant Finns who at the time of initial settlement in the rural Cutover Area built houses and other buildings of frame and board construction, even in localities with abundant stands of timber suitable for building with logs, but more commonly in places where logging operations had removed the supply. Vertical pole, fieldstone, and stovewood construction were also applied occasionally.

Not only tradition but also economic considerations influenced individual decisions in favor of building with logs rather than with more expensive processed construction materials, such as boards, two-by-fours, bricks, and sundries. Thus it follows that the kind and quality of standing timber were important in the selection of land for settlement. The immigrants certainly engaged in "environmental perception," provided that this hackneyed expression means that they evaluated the environmental potential of an area in terms of transplanted cultural perspectives. In general, the Cutover Area provided a positive environment for the implementation of known architectural practices.[19] At work was preadaptation, for, unlike the Scots-Irish, the English, and certain other European populations, the Finns did not have to learn the rudiments of log construction after arriving in America.

The assemblage of buildings on any Finnish immigrant landholding was a function of traditions, individual decisions, length of stay on the land, and kinds of economic pursuit. Besides the necessary house, the buildings that might potentially be included were privies, woodsheds, well houses, blacksmith shops, farmstead hay barns, saunas, houses for "drifters," barns for drying, threshing, and winnowing grain (riihi), summer kitchens, storehouse-granaries, chicken coops, smoke houses, pigsties, sheep barns, roadside garages, cow barns, stables for horses, implement sheds, milk houses, sub- or semisubterranean root cellars, and meadow or field hay barns.

Probably never were all of the structures present on any one immigrant holding. If a man was not versed at smithing then he had no need for a blacksmith shop, and in some traditions livestock and hay were housed under one roof rather than in separate buildings. Firewood could be stored in a lean-to attached to a house rather than in a woodshed, and there was not need for a storehouse in the early years, since small material accumulations were easily stored in the house. Nor were granaries essential in the first stages of farmsteading, since little grain was grown on the small acreage of cleared land, most of which was devoted to the production of hay. Although a few grain drying, threshing, and winnowing barns were built, they were not really needed in the Lake Superior area, where weather conditions during the harvest season were drier than in Finland. Other nonessential structures, for example summer kitchens, some Finns built, but others went without them, regardless of whether the structures were present or absent in their home areas in Finland. Finns also erected public buildings—churches, schools, co-op stores, and halls for various gatherings—some of which were of log construction. In addition, lumber camps and a small number of wind and waterpowered gristmills were built and operated by Finnish immigrants.

As a rule, in the early stages of settlement the holdings of immigrant farmers and part-time farmers had five buildings: a house, a sauna, a live-stock and hay barn, a privy (more often in the form of a lean-to), and a meadow hay barn. However, there were properties on which cows, horses, and hay were housed in three structures attached to one another lengthwise or in three free-standing buildings, bringing the number of units to seven. Each holding had a hand-dug well, and some of these were equipped with a well sweep for lowering and raising a bucket mechanically. Wooden and boulder fencing of types known in Finland, or barbed wire, enclosed garden plots, fields, and pastures.

The cultural landscape the Finns established in the Cutover Area was an evolving landscape. During the life span of immigrant settlers, buildings commonly increased in size and in number. Growing families and economic operations warranted more space, and the vanities of men demanded more ostentatious expression. Additions to existing structures, whether in lateral, longitudinal, or vertical direction, as well as separate new units, were in either log or frame and board construction. Functions that initially had been crammed into limited space, now found expression in separate buildings erected to accommodate them.

Of the many interesting material elements of the cultural landscape associated with the Finns, the timber construction technique for, and function of, houses, saunas, and meadow or field hay barns are most edifying.

Construction Techniques

Wherever the preferred pine and spruce were unavailable, the Finns built with logs of cedar, balsam fir, tamarack, jackpine, and occasionally even with hardwoods such as birch, poplar, and maple.[20] Construction employed essentially green logs in round or shaped (hewn) form that were stacked horizontally and interlocked at the corners with notches. Peeled or partially peeled, round logs, almost exclusively, were employed in the construction of hay barns and wood sheds. In these structures the logs were intentionally set apart, with an opening between each, to provide ventilation for the contents. Wall logs hewn on one side for the interior, and left round on the other for the exterior, and logs planked on all four sides, were used in a handful of woodsheds and hay barns. They constituted an insignificant minority and are mentioned here only to demonstrate the range of shapes of wall logs that was used.

Regardless of the shape of the wall face, logs in walls that needed to be tight, for heat retention or for other reasons—including those for houses, saunas, barns, storehouses—all had on the bottom a broad longitudinal groove cut the length of the log up to the notch. Round logs with groove joints were uncommon and were found only in some old saunas, pigsties, and barns. Walls with round logs, plank-shaped near corners in order to accommodate certain types of notching, had a somewhat greater distribution, occurring primarily in barns and stables. Logs that were plank-shaped on the sides were by far the most common type. They were hewn on both sides with a broadaxe, leaving a core measuring some 5 to 8 inches in thickness. The face of these logs varied considerably, as there was no need to make their surfaces uniform. The tops of these logs either were left in natural curvature or were shaped somewhat.

A *vara*, or scriber, a specialized tool fashioned by immigrant blacksmiths, helped attain a tight horizontal fit between logs.[21] Fill for the longitudinal groove, in the form of sphagnum moss or other materials, especially textiles, was placed on top of each log during construction of a wall. It functioned as insulation and should not be equated with the chinking found in the older type of central European log construction and the "American" log cabin. Although chinking with clay was practiced in Finland and in the Baltic lands in the early and middle Iron Age, the northern European technique using a vara and moss was introduced to Finland probably during the first millennium of our era. Lack of archaeological and historical data makes it imprudent to render an opinion at present regarding when the new technique superseded the older one entirely. The few nineteenth-century examples of chinking with clay to be found in the far eastern part of Finland probably represent isolated survivals. Chinking the exterior of walls with wooden strips is known for a few localities in western and northern Finland. It might be that the practice was brought to Finland from America in the late nineteenth and early twentieth centuries by returning immigrants, as probably was stovewood construction, present in a handful of buildings in south and central Finland.[22] However, it is certain that the Finns in the Cutover Area employed chinking, if only to a limited extent. Such chinking consisted of cement, mortar, clay, and strips of wood and was associated with houses, barns, and even saunas in which the wall logs would otherwise have had a poor fit because of substandard workmanship or differential drying because of the variety of woods used. Since, in nearly all the cases observed, the northern European technique had been applied, chinking in these instances is best regarded as having been added later.[23] However, in preparing walls for wallpapering, the indentations between logs were commonly filled with plaster or strips of wood. It was practiced to some extent in Finland in the nineteenth century and also by Finns in the Cutover Area. Moreover, uncovered interior walls could be provided with an "even look" by covering the indentations with wooden strips. Otherwise wall logs were left untreated and unpainted.

The idea of evening walls and the use of wallpaper were rather limited and later practices in peasant households in Finland (dating from the nineteenth century). It should not be equated with chinking, nor thought of as being a relic of a former practice. Lack of experience and time may have been responsible for poor wall construction, and the idea of chinking was probably borrowed from the building techniques of other nearby nationality groups. Moreover, the presence of chinked log structures on holdings owned by Finns does not, of course, mean that they were necessarily constructed by Finns. The Pelkie area on the Keweenaw peninsula of Michigan is a case in point. Here some Finns in the early years of settlement lived in chinked log structures that had been built earlier by French-Canadians. A few of these buildings are yet standing on properties owned by descendants of Finnish immigrants. Chinking the walls was an exception, for Finns built houses, barns, saunas, and other buildings that needed tight walls, according to the northern European timber construction tradition. Quite obviously, in the construction of hay barns and woodsheds, Finns followed another tradition, which they practiced, in Finland as well as in the Cutover Area, side by side with the northern European technique.

Notches

The horizontally stacked wall logs were interlocked at each of the four corners with notches in order to achieve structural stability. Significantly, the immigrants made use of only a fraction of the fifty-two different kinds of notches known in Finland. The single saddle notch, cut on the underside, was applied in the construction of nearly all buildings with walls of round logs, that is, hay barns, woodsheds. Only when logs of different girths were used did the larger ones require additional notching on the upper surfaces (Fig. 14-3). The round-log V-notch and the half hexagon notch are known from a small number of hay barns, and in some cases, they occurred with single saddle notching (Fig. 14-4). The saddle notch was also employed in the construction of the few saunas with round logs having longitudinal grooves. These notches were shaped with an axe.

The vertical-double and the full-dovetail notches were by far the dominant types in buildings with tight-fitting, plank-shaped logs or with round logs planked near corners to accommodate notching.[24] The tooth (Fig. 14-5),

Matti Enn Kaups

Fig. 14-3 An old pigsty, Baraga County, Michigan. Note the single and double saddle notching and the remains of the board roofing. (Photo by M. Kaups.)

Fig. 14-4 Round-log V-notching mixed with single saddle notching in the wall of a meadow hay barn, Carlton County, Minnesota. (Photo by M. Kaups.)

square, half-dovetail, and V-type notches were used infrequently. All of these notches were cut with ripsaws, and the outlined wood in tooth, vertical-double, and V-notches was removed with chisels and axes. Though not visible at corners, the wall logs have a longitudinal groove on the underside running the length of each, up to the notching. The shape of log heads or crowns may give no indication of the groove that is present (Fig. 14-6). Thus the shape of crowns cannot always be used as a reliable index to whether the wall logs are plank-shaped on tops and bottoms or whether they fit in a concave-convex manner (Fig. 14-7).

It bears emphasis that notches do not always correspond in detail to stereotyped illustrations found in the literature. For example, the full-dovetail notch in which two angular surfaces function to bind the wall logs comes in such variety of angular shapes that a case could be made for subtypes. Moreover, in some buildings two or more notch types occur. These may range from full-dovetail to half-dovetail to square notch, the latter requiring dowels or spikes for stability. In other buildings, the logs in an original wall may be fastened with vertical-double notching, while the logs in an upper addition to the building are held together with full-dovetail notching, implying that two different builders practiced their preference for a particular mode of notching. Furthermore, there are hay barns with logs fastened with a mixture of saddle, half-hexagon, and V-notches. Variations in notches are expressions of what Glassie labels *subtypifications* and demonstrate that there are rules for doing things and that in folk practice there are individual statements that wander from the rules, producing variations on themes.[25]

Finns in the Lake Superior Region

Fig. 14-5 Tooth or lock notching in plank-shaped wall logs with groove joint, Becker County, Minnesota. (Photo by M. Kaups.)

Dwellings

Although they did not match the spacious dwelling units of the Karelians and the large, two-story houses of the well-off farmers in Finland, the habitations built by Finnish immigrants in the Cutover Area were essentially like nineteenth-century Finnish rural houses. They generally were smaller and were simpler in architectural detail.[26] Blueprints and architects were not employed in raising these structures.

Besides the temporary shelters, five kinds of Finnish immigrant houses are distinguishable, in terms of floor plans, number of rooms, and horizontal and vertical dimensions (Fig. 14-8). These are: the one-room unit, the two-room house, the Nordic pair dwelling, the one-and-one-half–story house, and the two-story house. The basic unit was the square or nearly square one-room house, generally measuring some 14 by 16 feet on the exterior.

The most common dwelling was the one-story two-room house with bisected floor plan, which generally had a rectangular shape, though some were nearly square. These houses varied considerably in horizontal and vertical dimensions, the larger rectangular units measuring 16 by 32 feet. In

Fig. 14-6 Double notching of plank-shaped wall logs with groove joint, Price County, Wisconsin. (Photo by M. Kaups.)

these houses, with two more or less equal-sized rooms, the entry door led into the kitchen, which also served as a combination living room and bedroom. The other room functioned as a parlor/visitors' room (*sali,* in Finnish) (Fig. 14-9). However, with an increasing number of children, the parlor was, in some instances, turned into additional bedroom/living room space. If more living space was desired, then both the one-room and two-room houses were enlarged by adding one or two more or less equal-sized rooms in either a longitudinal or lateral direction. Thus, a one-room house became a two-room house or even a three-room house, though three-room houses were generally extensions of two-room houses. Dwellings with a trisected floor plan (see Fig. 14-8) took the form of an elongated rectangle or the shape of a T or an L. One-story square units with four rooms are unknown.

One-story houses often had small lofts or attics, which functioned as general storage space and sometimes as sleeping quarters for youngsters during the warm season. They were accessible only from the outside, by ladder through a gable door.

Significantly, the expansion of living space was not limited to the addition of rooms horizontally; some of the one- and two-room houses evolved vertically. This was accomplished by temporarily removing the roof, extending the walls and the gables upward, equipping one or both gables with a window, lengthening the chimney, flooring the upstairs, constructing a narrow and steep interior staircase, generally located in one of the kitchen corners, and then reattaching the roof. The upstairs functioned as a permanent sleeping and storage area. Commonly it remained unpartitioned and stoveless. The vertical expansion of one-story one- and two-room houses thus re-

Finns in the Lake Superior Region

Fig. 14-7 Shaping the underside of a log for a plank-shaped wall. Notice full dovetail notching. St. Louis County, Minnesota. (Photo by M. Kaups.)

sulted in one-and-one-half–story dwellings. Regardless of the materials used and the direction of the expansion, the additions represent secondary activity and not initial architectural statements on the part of the builders, and must be considered separately from the basic types.

Far more common than the few one-story, rectangular, trisected Nordic pair houses, with a central entrance hall located between the two rooms, were the bona fide one-and-one-half–story habitations (Fig. 14-10). These units varied considerably in size and commonly had either two or three rooms on the first floor and were constructed on a variety of floor plans. Some were built with bi- or trisected L- and T-shaped layouts, a few with a square plan of four rooms, and others with a bi- or trisected rectangular de-

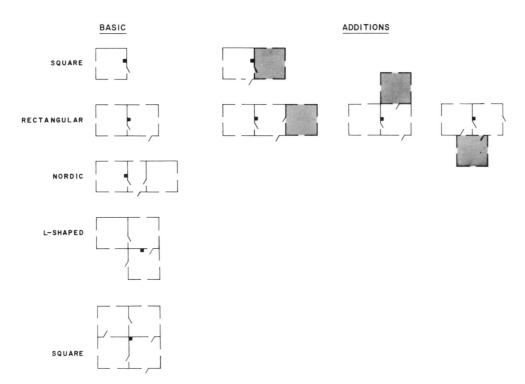

BASIC   ADDITIONS

SQUARE

RECTANGULAR

NORDIC

L-SHAPED

SQUARE

Fig. 14-8 Typical floor plans of Finnish houses. (Diagrams by M. Kaups.)

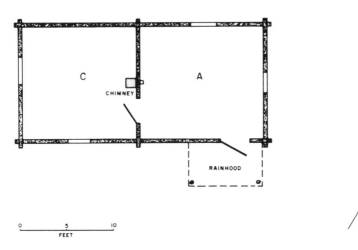

C   A

CHIMNEY

RAINHOOD

0   5   10
        FEET

Fig. 14-9 Floor plan of a one-story, two-room house in St. Louis County, Minnesota. The doorway is covered with a rainhood, and the door leads to the combination kitchen, living, and bedroom (A). The other room (C) was originally used as a parlor–visitors' room (*sali*). (Diagram by M. Kaups.)

sign. An interior staircase located in the kitchen provided access to the upstairs, which, except for flooring, in most houses remained unfinished, stoveless, and unpartitioned. As in smaller houses, it was used for storage and as sleeping quarters.

Fig. 14-10 A one-and-one-half–story house with covered porch, frame and board construction, and tar paper roofing, St. Louis County, Minnesota. (Drawing by M. M. Geib.)

Both in Finland and in the Cutover Area, some of the houses with one-and-one-half stories were constructed with one- or two-gabled dormers facing either the road or the yard. Although there were exceptions, the dormers the immigrants built were vertical continuations of the house wall and extended either some distance up the roof slope or all the way to the height of the ridge of the roof. Generally, the dormers were centrally located and had a window placed above the eave line or across it. The dimensions of the dormers varied considerably. In some houses they occupied the roof slope almost entirely, giving a square house the appearance of having four gables (Fig. 14-11).

The few two-story houses built by Finns had a square or a rectangular layout. The largest known example, which had a trisected floor plan, measured 21 by 53 feet and nearly 29 feet in height. Though a sizeable structure, this house measures less in length than the largest of the farm houses constructed in west central Finland in the nineteenth century. The larger one-and-one-half–story houses together with the two-story variety generally represent a second stage in house construction.[27] They were built some years after the initial settlement phase. On some land holdings the progression from a small one-story unit to a larger house may still be seen clearly.

Regardless of variations in dimensions and form, the houses the immigrants erected had a number of basic elements in common. They were free-standing units of simple design without full basements or indoor plumbing. Generally, the structures rested on glacial boulder foundations, but some were supported by cedar blocks or piers and a few were built directly on the ground. To reduce the draft beneath the floor, any open space between the lowest tier of logs and the ground was filled with loose rocks, pebbles, and soil, in some instances kept in place by vertically placed boards. Wooden pegs or dowels were used about doors and windows and in gables to provide struc-

Fig. 14-11 A nearly square, one-and-one-half–story dwelling in Baraga County, Michigan. The dormer and the gables are of frame and board construction. Note the soil pushed against the walls in order to eliminate draft beneath the floor. (Photo, early twentieth century, courtesy of Viano Heikkinen.)

tural stability. Eventually the interior face of the log walls was covered with sheets of newsprint, pressed paper board, metal sheeting, or wallpaper. In some houses the lower three to four feet of the wall was wainscoted. In time, the exteriors were generally, but not always, covered with tar paper, shingles, or with boards and painted, especially in the case of larger structures. Even galvanized metal sheeting was used on some exteriors.

Although brick was the most common material of chimney construction, some houses in the early years of settlement had chimneys of metal stovepiping. In most houses, chimneys were more or less centrally located, but in some structures they were situated along a side or gable wall. The brick chimneys were commonly wall mounted, with a stovepipe leading from the chimney to the wood burning cooking stove, of a common manufactured variety, which was the only means of heating the house. Manufactured double-hung windows and doors were already in general use in the early years of settlement. Generally the roof was supported by purlins and ridge-pole, all notched into the gable logs. The saddle or gable roof was by far the most common type. Other varieties of roof built by Finns were pyramid, hip, half-hip, and gambrel. Shingles were the dominant roofing material, followed by tar paper and overlapping boards placed in the direction of the roof slope. Also employed as roofing were hollowed logs (scoop roof) and birch bark kept in place with roof poles. Use of birch bark was more frequent in the early stages of settlement than later. Doorways were generally protected by enclosed porches of frame and board. These were built some years after the house and served also as storage areas for outdoor clothing and footwear.

Fig. 14-12 An abandoned one-room *savusauna,* Itasca County, Minnesota. (Photo by M. Kaups.)

The Sauna

Of all the free-standing structures the Finns raised on the landscape, none has received more attention than the sauna, or bathhouse (Fig. 14-12). It has been noted and described by American observers as well as by Finnish travelers, and geographers have utilized it as an index to Finnish rural settlement in the Cutover Area.[28] Indeed, the omnipresent sauna was an essential ingredient in the lives of immigrant Finns, an indispensable appendage to the rural dwelling. In more recent years it has enjoyed some measure of popularity among populations of various ethnic backgrounds, so its value as a diagnostic element of ethnic settlement has diminished in some localities. Moreover, changes have occurred in both the location and interior design of the sauna.

With the exception of those few situated about farmyards, the saunas that immigrant Finns first built were generally located some distance from dwellings, up to 150 feet and more, because, lacking connecting chimneys, they were regarded by some as fire hazards. Tradition also played a role in the choice of location. In construction characteristics, saunas closely paralleled houses, with tight-fitting, plank-shaped wall logs, notched at the corners, or frame and board construction. A handful of semisubterranean saunas built into hillsides are known in the Cutover Area.

The saunas in rural Finland and in the Cutover region in the late nineteenth and early twentieth centuries were of the traditional chimneyless, or smoke sauna (*savusauna*), type, of which the immigrants built two varieties, both known in the homeland. The simpler form consisted of one room only. Having a square to nearly square plan, these saunas commonly measured from 8' × 10' to 12' × 14'. The other variety was a larger, two-room oblong structure, measuring generally some 12 to 14 feet in width and from 16 to 20 feet in length. The larger of the two rooms was the sauna proper, while the smaller room functioned as a dressing room. Some of the one-room saunas were in time enlarged by the addition of a frame and board dressing room.

Both saunas and dressing rooms had small windows, though some one-room saunas were windowless. Windows were a source of light rather than ventilation. In a few of the one-room saunas the cantilevered roof provided a protective hood for the doorway and space for storing firewood. The sauna room generally was equipped with a step-up platform 3 to 4 feet above the floor, situated along one of the walls in a bleacher-type arrangement. In some instances there were only simple removable benches for sitting. Flooring consisted of boards, flatstones, or simply packed earth. A large stove (*kiuas*) constructed of unmortared igneous and metamorphic fieldstones heated the sauna. It occupied the space to one side of the door and measured 4 to 5 feet square and about 3 feet high. However, some saunas that were situated on sloping land were heated from outside, with the top of the stones reaching only a few inches above the floor level. Regardless of their location, the stoves had a doorless central fire chamber about 3 feet long and measuring about one foot square inside. From three to five hours of hardwood (primarily birch) firing was required to store sufficient energy in the rocks for continued heating of the sauna. Smoke escaped the sauna through a small wall vent located in the rear gable wall, through a board construction roof flue in those saunas equipped with them, and through the doorway. Once firing of the stove ceased, and after most of the smoke had cleared, the wall vent and the roof flue were closed with shutters, or, in their absence, the apertures were stuffed with old cloths or potato sacks, in order to prevent heat loss. Notwithstanding the water sprinkled on the stove to clear the air of noxious fumes, some smoke residue lingered in the sauna and was the cause of slight eye irritation to bathers.

Universally the principal objective of the sauna was to provide a place to bathe.[29] Perspiration was the basic component of this form of bathing so that a sauna bath was fundamentally a sweat bath. Also associated with it was steam (*löyly*) and the use of bath whisks (*vihta* or *vasta*), made of tied cedar, leafy birch, or other hardwood twigs. Although the sequence of bathing was an expression of individual or group preference, it generally started with exposure to dry heat, at temperatures near or above 200°F and the whisking of one's body with bath whisks. Steam was produced by throwing water onto the hot stones on top of the stove with the aid of a dipper. After some ten to twenty minutes, or more, of sitting on the platform or benches perspiring, one would leave the sauna and cool off, either in the dressing room or outdoors. If desired, the interval of cooling off was followed by more perspiring and whisking, and the routine could be repeated several times.

Regardless of the sequence, eventually there was washing with soap, rinsing, and cooling off before drying, then relaxing and dressing. Cooling was aided by rinsing with cold water. Since most rural dwellings, including saunas, were located some distance from lakes, rivers, or creeks, cooling by submergence in water was not a universal practice. Likewise, sitting or rolling in snow was an uncommon indulgence for the immigrants. It is worth noting that washing with soap was not always a concomitant of a sauna bath. Especially during the warm season of the year, when fields were plowed and harvested, the sauna was heated several times a week and the bath frequently consisted of perspiring, whisking, and rinsing. The use of soap was commonly reserved for the Saturday sauna, as it was during the winter months, when the sauna was heated only once a week, for the traditional Saturday evening bath. The duration of bathing varied but commonly lasted an hour and more.

Besides bathing, several other functions were served by the sauna, both in Finland and in the Cutover Area. The following list of functions is based largely on field interviews conducted beginning in the early 1960s with first and second generation Finns residing in the Cutover. Seldom, if ever, were all of the uses made of a single sauna, because regional traditions brought from Finland and individual preferences varied considerably. Savusauna were used by the immigrant Finns for drying berries, leaves, bark and grain; smoke-curing fish and meat; drying and shelling peas and beans; malting barley and wheat; making candles; distilling liquor; and washing clothes. Some saunas also functioned as maternity rooms, where midwives delivered children, and in the treatment of illness by means of traditional folk therapy, including massage and cupping. Both saunas and dressing rooms were sometimes used as sleeping quarters, especially by youngsters, during the summer months, for they provided a measure of relief from mosquitoes. In the few saunas that had an open, chimneyless fireplace in the dressing room, the room functioned also as a summer kitchen. There were a few saunas, too, which had a frame and board summer kitchen attached to one of the gable walls.

A bath in the sauna was a social event. News and gossip were exchanged when guests, neighbors, and at times even Finnish lumberjacks from nearby camps came over for a sauna. As a rule, men bathed first followed by women, and then children. Socializing continued over coffee and cake or rolls, served in the house of the proprietor. It was the traditional way of ending a Saturday evening bath. In some localities, a small group of rural families made up a so-called sauna neighborhood. Instead of each family preparing its own sauna on Saturday, especially during the winter months, each would take a turn and invite the others. Saunas also provided a measure of in-group social status for the immigrant males, who at times vied informally for the honor of being the local "steam man." A steam man could endure more heat than others in a sauna, a sure sign of superior manliness.

Meadow Hay Barns

One of the significant components of the cultural landscape that the Finns molded was the *niittylatos heinälato,* or meadow hay barn.[30] These freestanding units of log construction were located a considerable distance from the other farmstead buildings and served as sheds for the storage of dried, loose, wild, and cultivated hay (Fig. 14-13). Although nearly ubiquitous on immigrant holdings, there were other traditional options. The hay could be stored in haycocks or stacks (*heinäsuova*) in the meadows and adjacent to the

Fig. 14-13 A meadow hay barn with sloping walls, Carlton County, Minnesota. (Photo by M. Kaups.)

livestock barns. Hay was regularly stored in lofts of cow barns and stables and in hay barns, whether free-standing or attached to a cow barn, these hay barns might be located in the meadows or in the farmyard. The significance of hay in the forage economy and in the land use of immigrant farms and part-time farms is attested to by the fact that hay storage occupied by far the greatest proportion of building space on these holdings.

Meadow haybarns were constructed at two different kinds of sites. Some were situated along rivers and creeks, if the flood plain had a rather high water table, where various native grasses and sedges prevailed. But most barns were in the natural meadows on higher ground. Eventually, with clearing and plowing of land, these meadows became improved hay fields.

The hay barns were rectangular in floor plan, measured variously from 16′ × 19′ to 25′ × 32′, and some even larger. Heights varied from 10 feet to 20 feet from the bottom of the sill to the vertex of the roof. A few double-pen or crib barns with a central breezeway are known, the largest of these measured 21′6″ × 66′ overall.[31]

Except on flood plains, where they were supported by a framework of horizontally placed logs, the barns commonly rested unattached on field boulders set at the corners and, in larger units, also at intervals below the longitudinal sills. Besides certain vertical pole barns, the walls were built of round peeled or partially peeled logs, left untreated and unpainted. Commonly the logs were held together at the corners with single saddle notching, but double saddle notches, half hexagon notches, and V-notches also were employed, albeit sparingly, and at times mixed with the former. The logs were spaced a few inches apart to facilitate ventilation. Certainly the northern European log construction technique was not applied in raising hay barns, because tight walls were not required or desired for the storage of hay. The walls in the barns with horizontally placed wall logs were constructed

Fig. 14-14 A log meadow hay barn with modified roof and gable. The gambrel roof has sheet metal roofing remaining on one side. Note the large drop door in the gable, and the pulley and the rainboard above the door. The barn was in St. Louis County, Minnesota, but was recently demolished. (Photo by M. Kaups.)

according to two different attitudes. Some were built with straight, vertical walls, and others with oblique walls, that is, the walls slanted outward from the bottom of the barn on two opposite sides or on all four sides.

All the barns had a loose fitting, pole flooring with the end of the poles tapered so that they slipped into the interstices between the sill and the layer of logs immediately above. The flooring kept the dry hay from being spoiled by contact with the ground. The door openings generally were located in the gable walls and measured from 5′ × 5′ to 8′ × 10′ in the smaller barns. These could be closed with poles, each grooved at both ends so that they fitted into slots in posts on either side of the doorway.

The roofs were of the saddle or gable type and were supported by a ridgepole and purlins, all of round logs notched into the gable logs, or by rafters to which sheathing was attached. Roofing materials consisted variously of wood shingles, vertically placed overlapping boards, scooped-out logs, birch bark, and, to a lesser extent, straw or thatch. Both birch bark and thatch were weighted down by roof poles. In time, the original roofing in some of the barns was removed and replaced by tarpaper, composition shingles, or metal sheeting.

The haymaking complex transplanted by the Finns from their homeland changed during the life span of the immigrant generation as they accepted some of the available labor- and time-saving technologies that rendered hay production and storage less cumbersome. Generally, the changes accompanied an increase in hay acreage, and the expanding production required enlarged storage facilities. On some holdings larger barns, of frame and board construction, were built. On other holdings the demand was met

Fig. 14-15 A log horse stable with expanded hayloft of frame and board construction, Ontonagon County, Michigan. Note the privy attached to the gable wall. (Photo by M. Kaups.)

by the construction of additional log meadow hay barns. Some existing log barns were added lengthwise, while others were extended vertically. Gables of vertically placed boards and frequently gambrel roofs were built on to maximize space (Fig. 14-14). These additions and the newly built barns of frame and board construction, and even some of the older log barns, were equipped with pulleys, to make the transfer of hay into the barns less taxing than it was by pitchforks in the traditional manner. The employment of pulleys necessitated an opening in the front gable, commonly equipped with a trap door, through which most of the hay was brought in. These barns were generally built with a hood projecting from the ridge above the pulley termination. At the same time that the capacity of haylofts in log cow barns and stables was increased, the meadow hay barn holding capacity was enlarged in the same manner (Fig. 14-15). Large dairy barns of frame and board construction began to be built at this time.

Eventually the expanding space for storing hay in the modified and new livestock barns rendered the role of meadow hay barns less significant than it had been in earlier years of settlement. There were, however, exceptions, especially on larger holdings, where sizeable meadow hay barns remained important storage facilities well past World War II. Though a few meadow hay barns are yet in use for storing baled hay, most of them have disintegrated, been demolished and the wood used for other purposes (including firing wood burning sauna stoves), or are standing vacant on the landscape.

Summary

The cultural imprint of the Finns in rural areas is seen in aspects of material culture, land use, and language. Since the Finnish language was the primary medium of communication for the immigrants, it defined the group and its ethnic enclaves and set them apart from populations speaking other languages. However, the use of Finnish in everyday speech was ephemeral. Its decline followed the general pattern of linguistic retrogression observed amongst foreign groups in the United States, namely, from a monolingual first generation to a bilingual second generation to a monolingual third generation.

At the same time, a decline occurred in the number of immigrant-founded and supported organizations and businesses with a concomitant decrease in Finnish names and inscriptions on storefronts, churches, cemetery gateposts, township halls, and other institutional structures. Names on headstones in cemeteries and, more significantly, Finnish place names have a more durable place on the linguistic landscape and continue to define the area of Finnish-American culture (Fig. 14-16). Over two hundred landscape features, including schools, township halls, lookout towers, cemeteries, and churches in the Cutover Area bearing Finnish names appear on the topographic maps published by the United States Geological Survey.

The cultural landscape the immigrants established was in its basic form an extension of Finland to America, and as such included traditions that originated elsewhere in Europe. These included use of manufactured cooking stoves, milled doors, and double-hung and bay windows. In farming it embraced a transition from paleotechniques to neotechniques. But, with the exception of log construction, it was an extension in simplified form, which in time underwent selective transformation as immigrants borrowed and implemented ideas and technologies they encountered in the areas where they settled. In its fundamental characteristics the incipient material cultural landscape, composed largely of nonmanufactured local materials, was an organic landscape. Upon disintegration the various structures left little by way of permanent debris except some brick, metal, and glass. As symbolic landscapes, the settlements of the Finnish immigrants represent, to one degree or another, dissatisfaction with the American urban and corporate environments encountered in the mining towns and camps. They show a willingness to maintain ethnicity. Most Finns settled on marginal land at a time when the national migratory trend was from farms to cities.

In the Cutover Area countryside an undetermined number of log houses, now covered with siding and painted, that were built by immigrants are lived in yet by their descendants. Some saunas are now in basements, and free-standing saunas are of frame and board construction. They are in widespread use and remain to a large extent "the sign of the Finn" in rural areas, though not necessarily in suburbs or at lakeshore cottages. Finnish place names are the most lasting imprint on the landscape and will remain in everyday use long after the last vestiges of the immigrant-shaped material cultural landscape have vanished.

Matti Enn Kaups

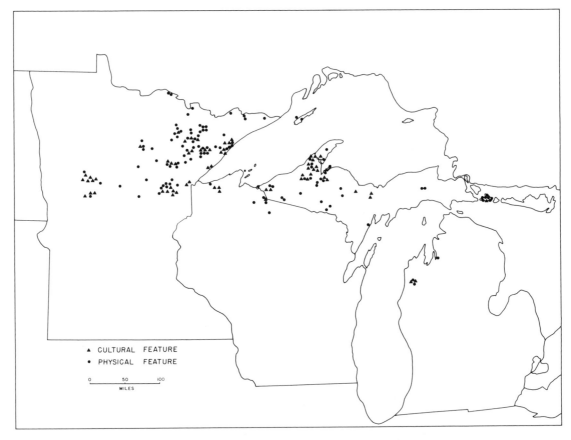

CULTURAL FEATURE
PHYSICAL FEATURE

0   50   100
MILES

Fig. 14-16 Landscape features bearing Finnish names, 1887–1977.
(Taken from U.S. Geological Survey maps.)

15

German-Russian Mennonites in Manitoba

Allen G. Noble

THE NINETEENTH CENTURY was almost three-quarters over before German-speaking Mennonites from Russia began to settle in Manitoba in two areas, one on either side of the Red River, south of Winnipeg Fig. 15-1). The establishment and settlement history of both areas have been extensively documented by Warkentin and others.[1] This study focuses upon the unique village form in the settlements and the morphology of the housebarns of the Mennonite settlers, the remarkable consistency of these forms, and the strength and tenacity with which traditional features have been retained by these people. At the same time, certain changes were accepted by the community and adopted, as evidenced by the modifications in the surviving housebarns.

The Mennonite Strassendörfer

Unlike most immigrants to North America, the German-Russian Mennonites established agricultural villages rather than settling on individual farmsteads in a dispersed pattern. They were able to do this because of a special provision in the Dominion Lands Act which permitted them to pool their allotments. The villages that the Mennonites established followed the traditional North German Plain form of the *strassendorf*, a form familiar to them from the northern Netherlands, the Vistula delta, and the Ukraine, all areas of earlier settlement by Mennonites.

Few traces of early strassendörfer can be found in the East Reserve (see Fig. 15-1), but a considerable number of them survive virtually intact in the West Reserve, where soils are better and agriculture more secure. Easily identified by their attenuated pattern on topographic maps, the Mennonite strassendörfer (Fig. 15-2) are unlike other Manitoban villages. They lack that core of commercial development around which other Canadian villages typically are organized, because these settlements are not budding towns but purely agricultural villages. Consisting of a single road or street, they often are not located at crossroads or intersections, and are always elongated, up to half a mile in length. These settlements do not function as trade centers and,

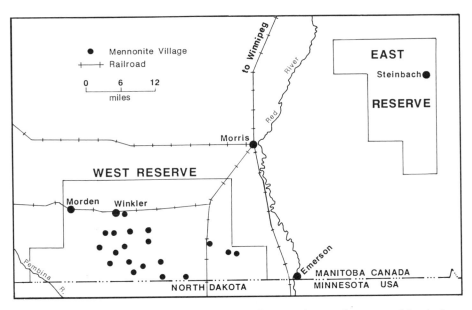

Fig. 15-1 German-Russian Mennonite settlement in southeastern Manitoba

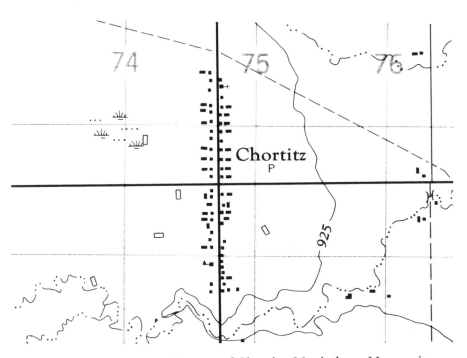

Fig. 15-2 On this topographic map of Chortitz, Manitoba, a Mennonite village, the housebarns appear as squares (houses) in front of rectangles (barns). Absence of houses or barns or combined structures is noticeable in the gaps breaking the regular pattern of the settlement. (Section of the Altona, Manitoba, Topographic Quadrangle 62 H/4.)

hence, have no commercial establishments. There are none of the stores, eating or drinking establishments, and facilities for care of automobiles that are so common in most towns. Whatever stores may originally have existed are long since gone, victims of the limited market that small farming villages provide and also of the increased mobility of the modern-day residents of those same villages. Inhabitants of the strassendörfer must travel to visit the few trade centers, such as Winkler, Altona, Plum Coulee, and Gretna, for shopping and services. Today, the Mennonite village consists of farmers' residences, a church (Fig. 15-3), and sometimes a school, although the function of the school may have been usurped by a larger, neighboring settlement and the original school building converted to use as a community center.

The village structures normally are along a single roadway, although a short cross street housing nonfarming community members is occasionally found.[2] There are no commercial intrusions along the main street. Here and there, however, the rhythm of the settlement is broken. Where formerly a housebarn had stood, there may be only an open field, as the village settlement gradually contracts. The arrangement of village agricultural lands, the rationale for property divisions, and the direction that modifications of the system have taken have been discussed by Warkentin and others and are not treated in this study.[3]

All of the strassendörfer are small, averaging only about 24 households. The arrangement of individual properties within the village is remarkably constant and regular. Houses are normally set back from the roadway about ninety feet and the lots are approximately one hundred feet wide. These

Allen G.
Noble

Fig. 15-3 The Mennonite church, Reinland, Manitoba, was constructed in 1876. It is the best maintained of the original churches. (Photo by A. Noble.)

standards do not vary much from one village to another. The single village street typically is lined with large cottonwood trees, which identify its location from far across the prairie. One of the most charming and perceptive accounts of these villages has been given in poetic form. Here is an excerpt from "Daut Darp" by Harold Funk:

> Linking buildings together is uniquely
> Adaptive to the Canadian Prairie physical environment.
> The idea originated in the Netherlands.
> Possibly for reasons of proximity,
> And for reasons of economics of space
> And building materials.
> In Russia the link served the all important factor
> Of security from wandering bandits.
> In Canada the link became the weapon
> That conquered the long, cold, harsh, blizzardous winters.
>
> Ironically, the concept of "linking,"
> Indigenous within the *Darp* architecture,
> Is also reflected within the concept of "community":
> Dependence of one building to another,
> Dependence of one community member to another.
>
> This proud architecture within each family unit—
> Having a long history inscribed deeply into its form,
> And having immigrated with the people
> To various parts of the world—
> Is repetitious throughout the village,
>
> On the narrow-long parcels of land, and
> Reinforces the sense of community,
> So obvious and beautiful.[4]

The Earliest Dwellings

Using sod block called *Kohlstein* for the upper walls and roof, the earliest Mennonite settlers frequently built partly excavated houses called *semlins* or *semeljanken,* because they were familiar with them from their Russian homeland (Fig. 15-4). Furthermore, such structures were cheap and easy to build with the limited construction materials available to them in Manitoba. In the area called the East Reserve, east of the Red River, some early log houses, often using a technique locally called Red River framing and consisting of horizontal logs held by tenons in upright posts, also were built, but few similar structures were erected in the West Reserve, west of the river. It has been suggested, at least by implication, that the use of this type of construction represents a cultural borrowing from neighboring French Canadian sources, where it is referred to as *pièces-sur-pièces* construction (see Fig. 2-3A).[5] While this possibility exists, it seems more likely that the method derives from contact in the Ukraine with Polish, Ukrainian, and Russian sources, all of whom used it for residential building. The open-air museum in Lvov, in the Ukraine, as well as similar facilities elsewhere in east central Europe, has several examples of this type of construction.

Fig. 15-4 The *semlin* or *semeljanken* (*left*) and the *serai* (*right*), the earliest German-Russian Mennonite house forms. (Drawing by M. M. Geib.)

Fig. 15-5 Close-up of a housebarn showing the details of timber frame construction, Chortitz, Manitoba. Note the heavy joist ends. (Photo by A. Noble.)

Allen G. Noble

272

Another Old World structure used in the earliest settlement period in Canada was the *serai* (Fig. 15-4). This was little more than a hipped-roof frame of poles covered with thatching and resting on the ground or slightly incised into the ground. None of the semlins or serais has survived, although a reconstruction of a semlin exists at the Mennonite Museum at Steinbach in the East Reserve and photographs of serais have been preserved in the Manitoba Archives.

Almost as early as they were building semlins, serais, and separate log houses, some Mennonites were constructing housebarns. In time, these structures became the standard dwellings in the strassendörfer. The semlin and serai were cultural transfers from Russia, but the housebarn had even earlier origins. It came from the original Dutch homeland of the Mennonites. The earliest of the housebarns were typically of hewn-timber frame construction (Fig. 15-5), although a few log housebarns were also built.

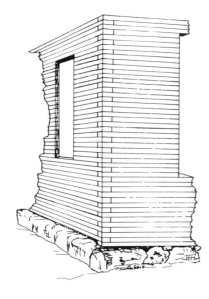

Fig. 15-6 Stacked lumber walls of 2″ × 6″ boards. (Drawing by M. M. Geib.)

Later, as dimension lumber became available at lower cost, the house walls frequently were formed of 2″ × 6″ boards laid one upon another (Fig. 15-6). The high cost of stacked lumber walls, because of their liberal use of lumber, was somewhat balanced by the houses' not needing additional wall insulation, an important consideration in the long, cold winters of Manitoba. The lumber pieces were carefully and truly sawn and tightly nailed together, so that no chinking was necessary between the boards to provide an air-tight structure. Often the lumber was faced with overlapping clapboards for decorative effect.

Stages in the Evolution of Housebarn Design

Three stages in the evolution of the Manitoba Mennonite housebarn can be discerned from surviving structures (Fig. 15-7). In the earliest period, the building was a single unit with an integrated roof. Observed from outside, the residential part of the structure is differentiated from the barn only by the presence of windows. Very few of these early-design housebarns remain. Much more common are structures of the second stage, in which the house and barn were independently framed but placed so that they abut one another on the gable, to give the external appearance of a unified building. The roof of the house was typically one to three feet lower than that of the barn and had a slightly lower pitch (Fig. 15-8). In a few instances, such as the John Ems housebarn in Reinland, the house roof line is higher than that of the barn (Fig. 15-9). In any event, the traditional orientation in both stage one and stage two is for the gable of the building to be presented to the roadway.

The third stage of development involved the greater separation of the house from the barn and the turning of the house 90° from its earlier orientation (see Fig. 15-7). Normally the house still was connected to the barn, but through a one-story intervening hallway. This stage represents the adoption

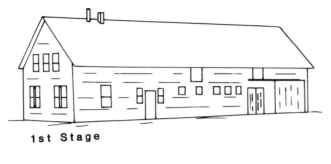

1st Stage

2nd Stage

3rd Stage

Fig. 15-7 Stages in the evolution of the design of Mennonite housebarns. (Drawings by M. M. Geib.)

of the concepts of the Canadian majority about house orientation and thus demonstrates partial Mennonite assimilation.

Some houses, one in Osterwick, one in Chortitz, one in Schanzenfeld, and perhaps others elsewhere, provide an interesting transitional orientation of house and barn of stages one and two, but the two sections are separated from each other by an intervening, single-story room, which is typical of the connecting hallways of the third stage.

Stage One: Housebarn Design

There is remarkable constancy among the house portions of the early housebarns, which makes the structure instantly recognizable as belonging to the Mennonite tradition. The structure is large, although always just one-and-a-half stories in elevation. The gable is invariably presented to the street and, since the door is on the side of the house, a certain aura of distance,

Allen G.
Noble

Fig. 15-8 An excellent example of a stage two housebarn, in the Mennonite Village Museum, Steinbach, Manitoba. (Photo by A. Noble.)

Fig. 15-9 Summer kitchen wing of a Mennonite housebarn. The John Ems housebarn in Reinland is one of the few structures in which the roof of the house is higher than that of the barn. (Photo by A. Noble.)

reserve, and restraint is created. This, plus the considerable width of the village street and the distance the houses are set back, enhances the feeling a stranger has of personal reserve and community restraint. Building orientation was constant, so main doors always faced either east or south, for climatic reasons. The doors of neighboring houses do not face one another. The house gable has two widely spaced windows on the first floor, usually complimented with wooden shutters. The wide spacing of these windows is one of the most distinctive design characteristics of the Mennonite house. Two evenly spaced, but much smaller and closer, windows admit light for the loft.

The side of the house that contains the front door usually also has three or four windows. Houses with three windows appear to be earlier in design evolution; and when four windows occur, the door usually is not symmetrically placed but is between the third and fourth windows from the street. Windows are usually of the four-over-four sliding sash type, but considerable later modification has taken place in existing structures. In a few instances, window openings on the north side of the house have been filled in and covered over with siding probably for better winter insulation.

The window and door arrangements do not reflect any particular architectural style but rather the internal room arrangement of the house. The plans of these houses reveal them to belong to a type of structure called *black kitchen houses,* which were common over the entire northern European plain from the Netherlands to Prussia.[6] The plan was transferred intact by the Mennonites to settlements in the Volga River region and then subsequently to Manitoba by Old Order Mennonites. Other more liberal groups of Mennonites settling both in Canada and the United States adopted North American types of houses or created new types, rather than holding on to traditional forms.

The typical house plan of early Manitoban Mennonite housebarns is illustrated in Figure 15-10. The main door of the dwelling opens from the driveway into a room measuring about 10′ × 14′ and traditionally called the *vorderhaus.* This room functions as a hallway and as an area for receiving visitors. Immediately behind the vorderhaus and connected to it by a door and small open passageway is a larger room (12′ × 16′) called the *hinterhaus,* because it occupies the back of the dwelling, as related to the house's main entry. The hinterhaus functions as a back hallway, a dining room, and often as a food preparation room. The hinterhaus is the most occupied and utilized room of the house.

Between the vorderhaus and the hinterhaus and roughly in the center of the structure, lies the small (5′ × 7′) kitchen with its built-in stoves and ovens, which expand its overall area considerably. Constructed of brick, the kitchen walls are pierced by opposed openings, which dissipate heat to both the vorderhaus and the hinterhaus rooms and which also admit light to the otherwise dark kitchen. A large brick stove/heater extends forward from the end of the kitchen and is the principal heat source of the house. Though designed primarily for house heating, the heater could be used for cooking and baking as well. Small vents, covered by adjustable iron doors permit the heat generated in this stove/heater to warm several other rooms. The smoke from the stove fire, as well as the smoke from the other open fires in the kitchen, is permitted to accumulate in the upper parts of the kitchen room,

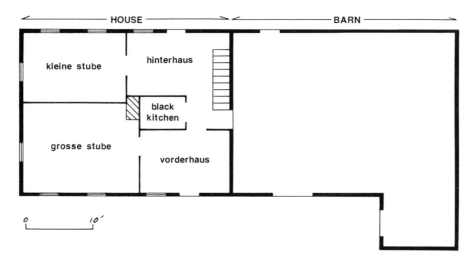

Fig. 15-10 Floor plan of a stage one Mennonite housebarn

which is built in the form of a great tapering chimney. It is usually black from years of use. Meats are hung high up on hooks or rafters to cure slowly.

The black kitchen is a feature common to housebarns all across the North German Plain, but the stove/heater is not. However, such a device is found in German-Russian houses erected in the American Great Plains by other immigrants[7] and in various parts of the prairie provinces of Canada, where they were built by Ukrainian settlers.[8] Consequently, the stove/heater of Mennonite housebarns has been considered a Ukrainian feature adopted by the Mennonites. However, at least one source providing housebarn plans, shows the stove/heater in early Mennonite housebarns in East Prussia, which would predate their move to the Ukraine and the Volga basin areas.[9] The balance of the Manitoban house plan is also typical of other North German Plain housebarns.

The largest room of the house, the *grosse stube,* measured 18' × 14' and was adjacent to the vorderhaus and toward the roadway. It was a multifunctional room, almost as busy as the hinterhaus. A center for entertainment (especially formal) and daily family activities, it might also contain a large bed for visitors or for neighbors from other villages inadvertently stranded by inclement weather.

The fourth room of the house, usually called the *kleine stube,* was the bedroom for the head of the household and his wife. It was essentially unheated and, given the long, bitterly cold winters of the Red River plain, must have tested the stamina of early Mennonites.

Stage Two: Housebarn Design

Most of the housebarns that have survived in the Manitoban Mennonite villages are of the second design period. During that period, the house and the barn, while still attached and located in proper reference to one another, underwent design modifications. The earliest stage two housebarns apparently had a unified system of framing and construction. However, in all of the housebarns to which I have managed to gain entry, the house and barn, although abutting one another, are, in fact, independently framed. The only direct connection is a common interior door on the main floor level. Uniformly, these housebarns are of timber frame construction and more elaborate in both form and plan than stage one housebarns. One feature of the framing is the use of a distinctive lap notch on sway braces (Fig. 15-11).[10] Otherwise, the framing follows standard German methods.

The elaboration of the house is revealed in the increasing subdivision of the plan into rooms of more specific function (Fig. 15-12). Thus the typical house of this period contains eight or nine rooms, depending upon whether the hallway (*gang*) to the barn is counted. Furthermore, the rooms received commonly accepted vernacular names, which persist to the present day. The vorderhaus became the *fae t'hues* in the low German dialect of the Mennonites and the hinterhaus the *alt t'hues*.

The grosse stube remains the largest room, serving a variety of functions, but it is popularly referred to as the *groote shtov*. More and more, however, it began to serve as a formal parlor and sitting room. Breaking the regularity of the room's plan is the back of the central oven/heater, which juts out from one interior corner. Into this irregular niche, was often placed a built-in, ceiling to floor, cupboard and chest called a *mauerschrank* or a *glauss shaup*. The most prized possessions of the family were kept and displayed in this traditional piece of furniture.

The kleine stube has been subdivided into the *ajck shtov,* occupying the corner of the house, and the *tjleene shtov,* the smaller bedroom. The latter was usually occupied by the younger children or, if the children were older, by female offspring; the older male children used a bedroom called the *somma shtov,* adjacent to the barn wall (Fig. 15-12). From this location, the boys could attend to early morning chores in the barn without disturbing the rest of the

Allen G. Noble

278

Fig. 15-11 The lap notch used on sway braces, distinctive to stage two Mennonite housebarns. (Photo by A. Noble.)

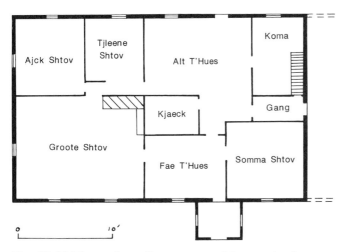

Fig. 15-12 Floor plan of a stage two Mennonite house

family. They also did not need to be so closely watched as girls did in traditional families, and thus could sleep at a greater distance from their parents.

Between the hinterhaus and the barn is a small pantry/storeroom. Squeezed into this area are stairways to the loft above and to a small root cellar beneath. The latter stairs are entered from the pantry, whereas the loft stairs open into the passageway (gang) that provides access to the barn.

The upper half floor of the house is an unfinished loft interrupted by the huge flue of the black kitchen. Originally this space was used primarily for grain storage. Indeed, today traces of grain can be found in many of these lofts. In June 1983, I was able to get into one of the lofts in a house in Chortitz which was being renovated. Although a few surplus household items had been tossed into the loft, its original function was betrayed by the numerous loose kernels of grain still lying about on the floor. Although the owner confirmed that "much earlier such lofts were always used for grain storage," most lofts today are used simply for general storage. Rarely have they been finished to expand the house's living space.

Within this design period, as time passed, the older houses themselves were modified. One such change was the addition of a wing at right angles to the main house building. This innovation may not be as radical as it initially appears, since many early housebarns had summer kitchens in similar locations, and these were sometimes connected to the house by intervening hallways. The summer kitchen shown in Figure 15-9 is still shuttered in early June from a winter of inactivity.

Another early but nontraditional expansion of the house was the addition of a dormer to provide both light and extra headroom in the upper half story. Although both shed roof and gable roof versions were built, this change is not very common. This modification signals the use of the loft for sleeping, which was not common before stage three. Much more frequently encountered is the addition of a small closed entryway that projects from the south or east side of the house. A similar entry structure is typical of Finnish houses,[11] and on Mennonite houses it may represent a cultural borrowing, since Finnish settlement is widespread and geographically nearby. Similar in

Fig. 15-13 Housebarn in Reinfeld with an unusual gallery. (Drawing by M. M. Geib.)

form but quite different in function is a small projection extending from the opposite side of the house, the north or west side. This extension incorporates a modern bathroom, replacing the original detached privy.

The addition of galleries or verandas is a twentieth-century phenomenon reflecting the late popularity of these features both in the Mennonite and in the larger North American community. In some instances, it was the orientation rather than the design of traditional houses that changed. In at least one case, a gallery provides a link from house to attached garage wing, giving an uncharacteristically modern aspect to the dwelling, which otherwise retains its traditional form (Fig. 15-13).

In barns of the middle design period, the barns are larger than the houses. Overall, the main part of the barns are 40 to 44 feet long and 26 to 32 feet wide, although considerable variety in size is encountered. The barn is divided basically into three functional areas. Closest to the house is the stable (*shtaull*) where the larger farm animals are housed, horses on one side and the few cattle on the other, with a central aisle between running to the back of the barn. The second section of the barn is called the *sheen*, and is divided into two parts. One is used for equipment storage and sometimes as a hay mow, and the other is an informal cross aisle connecting pairs of double wagon doors. This part was originally used for threshing grain. The third section of the barn is the lean-to shed, called the *ovesid*, which projects from one side of the barn (Fig. 15-14). The ovesid might be used for tool and gear storage, as a chicken house, or sometimes as a milk house. It is covered by an extension of the main barn roof, creating an off-center, unbalanced roofline. A few barns have a *sheua*, a shed-roofed extension at the rear of the barn.

Two exterior features of Mennonite barns are distinctive. The barn doors are always painted, even when the rest of the structure is not. Furthermore, the double doors are often braced on the outside with strips of lumber placed diagonally, forming decorative diamond shapes, and often painted to contrast with the door itself. A feature associated with smaller barn doors is the use of multiple diagonal braces, arranged in herringbone pattern, which provides support and at the same time allows rain water and melting snow to drain away quickly, thereby prolonging the life of the lumber.

Barn windows are also distinctively treated. Although a few double-pane, single-sash windows may be positioned at various locations in the barn walls, the most characteristic openings are a row of small, rectangular, closely

Fig. 15-14 An *ovesid* projects from the barn portion of a housebarn in New Bergthal. The pitch of its roof is lower than that of the barn roof. (Photo by A. Noble.)

Fig. 15-15 This housebarn in Sommerfeld has a traditional barn but a vernacular house, which is not from the German-Russian Mennonite tradition. (Photo by A. Noble.)

set windows placed about six feet high along the stable wall (Fig. 15-15). The narrow frames of these windows usually are painted to match the diagonal door braces and hence are highly visible hallmarks of the barn.

Houses are more likely to have disappeared or been replaced than are the barns, although the framing of the demolished house may still be traceable. Some houses have been converted to barn uses simply by covering the siding and windows with plywood sheeting. Such a conversion of a house to barn use reflects the trend toward larger farms, which is felt not only among Mennonites but by all Canadian farmers. When a house is dismantled or otherwise removed and a new house erected, the later structure is built in the same position as the earlier, sometimes even using the original foundations.

Stage Three: Housebarn Design

The third stage of housebarn design is the one in which the greatest break with tradition occurs. One of the factors encouraging change was the departure of many members of the original, very conservative Altkolonier, who fled to Mexico and elsewhere in an attempt to conserve their traditions and lifestyle from ever-encroaching Canadian culture. At the same time, their places were taken by Russlaenders, Mennonite refugees from the Russian Revolution, migrating directly from the Ukraine and elsewhere in Russia. These people were not as conservative as the Altkolonier and did not cling as tenaciously to traditional building methods.

The major modification to the house in the third stage was its turning 90° so that the side faced the street rather than the gable, as in the first two design stages. This single change enabled Mennonite houses thus to be more Canadian, since most houses elsewhere in Canada were oriented with a side to the street rather than a gable end. But the separation of house and barn and the turning of the house presented a new problem: how to connect the two frames of the structure to maintain its unity. A few structures built at the close of stage two offer the answer. In these structures, the house and barn retain their traditional orientation to one another but are independently framed and separated by a few feet. The intervening space is filled by a low hallway or passage and, in a few instances, by a more elaborate building serving as a summer kitchen. In this later event, the intermediate building, in its location and function, resembles the "back house" of the New England connected barn.[12]

Retaining an interior connection between house and barn, by means of which the farmer could avoid exposure to inclement weather, preserved one of the major advantages of the traditional building form. The separation of the two parts of the structure had the further advantage of moving the barn and its animal pollution farther from the dwelling. The greatest benefit, however, was the reduced risk to the farmer of losing all if a fire started in either the barn or the house. A few of the houses of this third stage, especially the earlier ones, retained the black kitchen fireplace and hearth in the center of the house.

Changing the orientation of the house required some modification of the floor plan, if the greatest efficiency was to be retained, since the connection with the barn was now with the back side of the house rather than the back gable (Fig. 15-16). The gang disappeared as a separate space within the house, and the connection to the barn was through a separately framed structure that opened into the alt t'hues or the tjleene shtov. The overall number of rooms was reduced to six, partially because the upper half story

Allen G. Noble

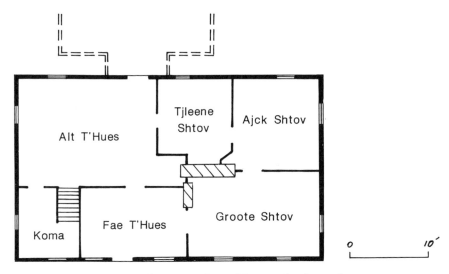

Fig. 15-16 Floor plan of a stage three Mennonite housebarn

of the house now was used for bedrooms. This shift was made possible by two changes in function of the loft. First, by this time, grain was being mechanically threshed and taken immediately to nearby elevators for storage, so the house lofts were no longer needed for this purpose. Second, the black kitchen was rarely built into stage three houses, and the upper smoke chamber was eliminated or, at times, replaced by smokehouses in the farm yard. The heating of the house was accomplished by furnaces, sometimes found in the location of the traditional oven/heater but more likely placed in a basement.

As these changes to the housebarn form became more acceptable in the late nineteenth and early twentieth centuries, the houses began to be more complicated in design, with extensions, bays, ells, and extra gables. In some cases, the houses, although vernacular, were not of the main Mennonite tradition, although the barns were and the traditional Mennonite location of house directly in front of barn continued to be observed (see Fig. 15-15). In one case, in the village of Osterwick, both the house and the barn are of nontraditional design; but, although the barn orientation is innovative, the locations, and even spacing, of both barn and house are "correct," and the two structures are connected by a one-story passageway.

Barns have been subject to some modification, although not to the extent or in the numbers that houses have. Their orientation is less subject to change also. Roof lines have been modernized, and some newer barns are not of the traditional type, although their placement usually follows traditional rules. In a very few instances, the barn may be gone entirely, sometimes as a result of fire and in other cases because the barn became redundant and hence not cost effective to maintain. The latter is most often the case when the property is occupied by elderly couples retired from farming or by young families who have either been forced out of farming or have been unable to gain entry.

Conclusion

Although the hand of tradition lies heavy upon the German-Russian Mennonite communities in Manitoba, evidence of modification and change is clear. Barns of traditional design disappear or, less often, are replaced by newer, more efficient structures. Houses are even more likely to be modified. But in the face of these relentless changes, the integrity of the settlement persists—a tribute to the tenacity of ethnic identity.

Allen G.
Noble

16

Czechs in South Dakota

John E. Rau

URING THE latter half of the nineteenth century, hundreds of thousands of immigrants came to the open prairies of the central United States from Europe, and occasionally Asia, bringing with them many Old World ideas. Along with the diverse groups of Amerindians and the established American stock of the eastern states, many of whom were migrating westward, these newcomers helped create a new cultural and ethnic mosaic on the landscape. South Dakota was a major stage for much of this migratory activity. A spacious but sparsely populated region, it became the home of many different ethnic groups who, for the most part, laid claim to their own little communities. Among the less well publicized immigrant groups to settle in this area were the Czechs of central Europe, who, since their arrival in 1869, have left a distinctive mark on the built environment of South Dakota. Though they were a relatively small group, making up less than two percent of the population of the state in 1930, they established a tightly knit, almost homogeneous, community in southeastern South Dakota. Remnants of their early settlement include folk buildings, vernacular churches and lodge halls, and iron cross grave markers, as well as a range of social customs still observed by many of their descendants. This chapter will explore the environment created by the Czech immigrants to South Dakota and especially will analyze their historic building stock.

Czech History in Europe

The modern history of the Czech people goes back to the fifth century, when they migrated westward into what is now central Europe. They conquered the land of the Boii, led there by a man named Cech. Since that time they have been known by the name *Bohemians*, a derivative of the name of their predecessors, or as Czechs, in honor of their ancient chief. They developed a dialect of the western Slavic language called Czech. Those who spoke this tongue soon occupied the areas of Bohemia, Moravia, and a small part of Silesia. Sandwiched between Germany, Austria, Slovakia, Hungary, and Poland, they were an integral part of the confederation of kingdoms, principalities, and duchies that made up the Holy Roman Empire. As such, they were always at the crossroads of Europe and its volatile political climate.[1]

In the fourteenth century Bohemia reached the height of its cultural

285

and political greatness when the Holy Roman Emperor Charles IV chose the Czech capital of Prague for his residence. By the next century, however, the influence of the Czechs had eroded under the reign of subsequent emperors. They were soon subjugated by the Hapsburgs of Austria, who were ardent German Catholics. An early Protestant movement, under the leadership of a teacher named John Huss, took root in Bohemia at about this same time. Branded a heretic, he was burned at the stake in 1415. A revolution resulted from his martyrdom that continued sporadically for two centuries and eventually culminated in the wanton bloodshed of the Thirty Years' War. Austria finally subdued the Czech resistance at the Battle of White Mountain in 1620, following which they severely punished many of the rebels. To avoid persecution, some members of the intelligentsia and religious leadership along with a few farmers and artisans emigrated to the United States, settling in North Carolina and Pennsylvania during the mid-seventeenth century. It would be two more centuries, however, before Czechs came to the New World in any significant numbers.

During these dark days of Austrian oppression, the native culture survived only among the peasants. German was the official language and Roman-Catholicism was the overwhelmingly favored religion. Prague University, started by Charles IV, was segregated into separate schools for Germans and Czechs, and censorship became an accepted government policy. Many Czechs forgot their heritage. After the successful American and French revolutions of the late eighteenth and early nineteenth centuries, monarchs did their best to suppress further insurrection; however, nationalist passions continued to spread throughout Europe. Czech historians, most notably Frantisek Palacky, urged the people to recognize their history and to demand a nation-state of their own. Incited by new revolutions in France in early 1848, Czechs once more broke into violence. Although eventually overcome, the rebels won some token reforms for people of Czech descent. As a result, those who still longed for more independence chose, and were allowed, to emigrate to America.[2]

Czech Culture in America

Between 1848 and 1914, some 350,000 Czechs came to America. Forty-five percent of them settled in the urban centers of New York City, Cleveland, and Chicago. In fact, after Prague and Vienna, Chicago was the third largest Czech-speaking city in the world during the latter half of the nineteenth century. Others came to the Great Plains to take advantage of the advertised large tracts of free land. A majority of these rural Czechs found their way to Nebraska, Wisconsin, Texas, Iowa, and Minnesota. Considerable numbers also came to the Dakotas, Michigan, Missouri, and Kansas. Although they lacked political freedom and social rank in Europe, most had been land-owners or craftsmen and as a rule were educated and highly skilled people. They brought their talents and limited financial means to both urban and rural New World settings. Often, Czech émigrés moved as entire family units and not as individuals; thus, they kept many of their European traditions alive simply through familial continuity.[3]

John E. Rau

Religious Factors

Czech-Americans were well divided on the subject of religion. Due to centuries of Austrian indoctrination, a large number of the immigrants remained at least nominally faithful to Catholicism. An equally large proportion shed their ecclesiastical bonds in favor of agnosticism. Often calling themselves freethinkers, they basked in the freedoms and independence, sometimes amounting to isolation, of the Great Plains. Still others affiliated themselves with Presbyterianism or the Czech Brethren sect originated by John Huss. In the new country, even Catholics were mostly indifferent about religion. Many preferred references to Czech history over those to church history. Thus, their edifices contain liturgical icons using Czech script and are often named to commemorate great national folk heroes of their pre-Austrian past. Czech immigrants regardless of religious conviction generally remained true to their national heritage.[4]

Social Organizations

The cornerstone of ethnic survival for early Czech-Americans was their affinity for fraternal societies. Providing a wide range of services, these clubs might be benevolent and insurance institutions, athletic organizations (*sokols*), or religious fraternities. In the lonely plains of America, the immigrants used these associations not only to provide security for individual members but also to restore the sense of community they remembered from the old country. Many of the groups published Czech-language newsletters, which kept alive their linguistic roots as well as encouraging migration of others still in the homeland. Most local societies were affiliated with one of the major national orders, such as the Czech-Slavonic Benevolent Society, the Union of Czech Women, Západní cesko-bratrská jednota (Z.C.B.J.)—later called the Western Bohemian Fraternal Association—the Czech Catholic Union, or the Catholic Workmen.[5]

Czech Settlement in Dakota Territory

Permanent settlement by Czechs in the region now called South Dakota began in 1869. During June of the previous year, a small contingent of Czech émigrés in Chicago founded the Czech Agricultural Society, for the express purpose of locating available land in the west and organizing group migrations of prospective settlers. In only a few months, 4,000 individuals joined the society. Enough money was raised through membership dues that in late 1868 and early 1869 society founders Frank Bem, Frank Janousek, and Edward Strausse traveled to Kansas and Nebraska in search of land suitable for colonization. Reporting that they had found such a place in north central Nebraska, they quickly assembled an expedition of nine eager migrant families, who in May 1869 left Chicago, bound via passenger train for Sioux City, Iowa. From there they set out for Niobrara, Nebraska, in wagons purchased at Sioux City. Upon arriving at their destination, the travelers were shocked by the sight of that mostly treeless, dry sandhill country. It seems that the scouting party had heard only reports about supposedly rich land west of

Niobrara and had not actually visited the site. Greatly discouraged and fearful of Indian attack, the party had turned back toward Sioux City, and possibly Chicago, when they encountered a young engineer from Dakota Territory named Charles Meyers. He told them about bountiful land west of Yankton, the territorial capital, and recommended that they inspect that area before returning home.[6]

Dakota Territory was organized in 1861 in the vast lands stretching west of Minnesota all the way to the Continental Divide; but drought, grasshopper plagues, and Indian scares discouraged early rapid settlement. It took a gold rush into the Black Hills, from about 1874 to 1879, to bring about the first major influx of settlers. Later, railroads, land speculators, and territorial officials advertised the opportunities for a new start in Dakota during the boom era that followed. The size of Dakota Territory was reduced until it was only that of present-day North and South Dakota. Both states were finally admitted to the Union in 1889.[7]

The Czechs, now escorted by only Frank Bem, entered Yankton, Dakota Territory on the Fourth of July, 1869. They found available parcels some eight miles or so west of the city and settled there. In the meantime, Janousek had returned to Chicago and started writing articles praising the virtues of land around Niobrara, which Bem countered with articles of his own boasting about his group's newfound homeland in Dakota. Amid this controversy and confusion, the Agricultural Society fell apart. Still, Bem continued to write stories for eastern newspapers, and by 1872, substantial numbers of Czechs from both New World and Old World locations were migrating to southeastern Dakota Territory (Fig. 16-1). Soon their community comprised much of western Yankton and eastern Bon Homme counties.[8]

In spring 1872, a group of these settlers founded a new town to serve as a nucleus for Czech immigration to Dakota. They named the town Tabor, after the Hussite radical capital in Bohemia. Located about twenty miles west of Yankton, Tabor was at the heart of the area being homesteaded by Czechs at that time (see Fig. 16-1). Yet, the town grew very little until 1900, when the Chicago, Milwaukee, and St. Paul Railroad ran one of its east-west lines into the city. The town, which was populated primarily by Roman Catholics, still has a large parish worshipping in its beautiful 1898 brick church. Religious and intellectual fraternities, sokols, and the Z.C.B.J. have had a welcome place in Tabor since its early days. Other towns of the immediate area that had predominate or large Czech populations included Yankton, Tyndall, Utica, Lesterville, Havlicek, Janousek, Lakeport, and Ziskov. The last four are no longer extant.[9]

Several distinct later phases of Czech migration to Dakota occurred. In 1871 and 1872, a few Wisconsin Czechs began settling in the Pembina region of the territory, which is now Richland County, in southeastern North Dakota. Eventually, there were small pockets of Czech-Americans scattered throughout northern Dakota. In southern Dakota, they began moving into Brule County and western Charles Mix County in 1879. After the Yankton Indian Reservation was opened to White settlement in 1895, a number of families took homesteads in eastern Charles Mix County. Beginning in 1904 with the opening of the Rosebud Reservation, many of them moved west of the Missouri River into Gregory and Tripp counties. By the turn of the century, Czechs could be found in all areas of North and South Dakota. Yet, as

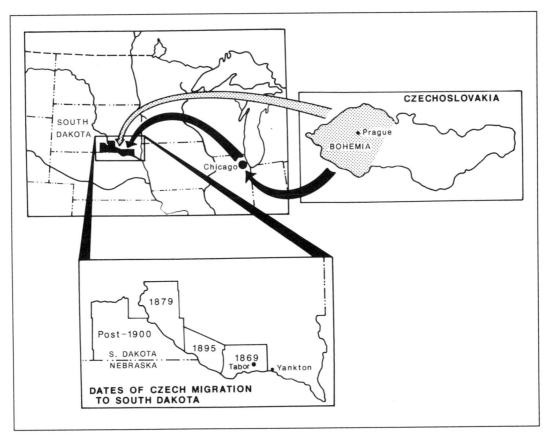

Fig. 16-1 The movement of Czechs to settlements in southeastern
South Dakota

late as 1910, 90 percent of their members in South Dakota lived in the five counties of Yankton, Bon Homme, Charles Mix, Gregory, and Brule. Sixty percent resided in the first two counties alone. Very few Czechs migrated to the United States after World War I; this was due in part to the creation the nation-state of Czechoslovakia. The number of all foreign-born residents of South Dakota diminished rapidly after 1920, and gradual assimilation into a mass culture ensued.[10]

Folk Buildings

Because the southeastern corner of South Dakota witnessed the earliest and greatest share of Czech immigration, it also contains most remaining Czech material culture. Although all ethnic groups make an imprint on the land, the Czechs of the Tabor area left an unusually high concentration of landscape features. Indeed, an abundance of folk buildings and other artifacts surrounds the town itself and bears witness to the technologies these people carried with them to their new homes. Actually, very few folk structures survive within the town of Tabor, but the encircling farms contain a plethora of resources. The discussion that follows is based on an in-depth

*Czechs
in South
Dakota*

Fig. 16-2 The Machecek house, near Utica, Yankton County, South Dakota, has clay brick, stone, and wood frame construction. (Drawing by M. M. Geib.)

field survey of that region, including firsthand analysis of surviving folk buildings. Constructed with a wide variety of both store-bought and indigenous materials, most of these structures are single-pile, rectangular, one-story houses or barns capped by gable roofs. Although there are numerous similarities and differences among Czech settlements in various surrounding states, the emphasis here is on those around Tabor.[11]

Masonry Technology

Czech builders had a profound knowledge of masonry technology from the old country. Consequently, of the building materials they employed in southeastern South Dakota, earthen materials predominated. They utilized stone or clay in some fashion in almost all the structures they erected. Even primarily wooden buildings often incorporated well-crafted masonry treatments. Early masonry work was done with mud-and-grass mortar, while later repairs and new construction, especially after 1890, were accomplished with Portland cement and concrete. With few exceptions, the Czechs covered the exterior facades of stone walls with a thick, smooth veneer of plaster or mud (Fig. 16-2). One of their favorite materials was chalkrock, a very soft sandstone usually of a light yellow color and found along the banks of the Missouri River, or at a few prairie outcroppings. Since it is prevalent around Yankton, many buildings of this material were, and still are, erected by people from a variety of backgrounds. In fact, early guidebooks published by territorial officials advocated use of the material by would-be homesteaders.[12] Therefore, its application is hardly limited to Czech builders, but their experience in masonry construction led them to be the principal users of chalkrock in this area.

Log Construction Technology

As for timber resources, trees are scarce in the Dakotas today and were even more so during the 1870s and 1880s. Except for conifers, in the moun-

John E. Rau

290

tainous Black Hills region, the only trees that early settlers found were along prominent streams such as the Missouri River. Like many of their Scandinavian immigrant neighbors, the Czechs had experience in log construction technology, which they employed frequently in the early days of their settlement in Dakota. In keeping with central European customs, they built their log structures of hand-hewn timbers, planked on at least two sides and fitted at the corners with full- or half-dovetail notches.[13] Although the dovetail is by far the most prevalent type of corner notch, several different notches have been found among the Czech-built log buildings in northern Nebraska. No variance from the dovetail cut has been seen on South Dakotan specimens. Interior partition walls are usually notched into the outer load-bearing walls. The interstices are filled with a mixture of mud, small stones, wedges of wood, and, later, cement. Most log buildings, soon after initial construction, were sided with clapboards. In some instances, a heavy layer of mud, presumably for insulation was packed between the load-bearing log walls and the siding.

Similarly, a few Czech houses of wood frame construction in both South Dakota and Nebraska exhibit an infill of clay or brick nogging between studs in the outer walls. Only rarely, however, did Czechs use earthen composition other than stone or, later, brick. Yet a few of them did expand the use of masonry to include puddled clay and clay brick construction. Very scarce today, most examples of these soft earthen structures that do survive in South Dakota are in extremely poor condition.

Old World Forms

Regardless of the material chosen, Czech folk buildings appear in forms distinctive to the group. Like other people from the central and northern portions of Europe, Old World Czech artisans often built in a linear, central chimney form, adding a room to either end when necessary. The most common such form is a three-bay plan with a main entrance in the center bay (Fig. 16-3). This central hall, called the *sin* in Czech, is generally not a through passage but only a common area between two living chambers. It

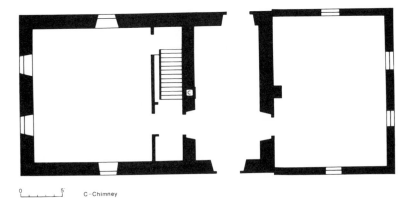

0   5'   C—Chimney

Fig. 16-3 Floor plan of a three-bay Czech house, the Jacob Sedlacek house, near Tabor, South Dakota

offered space for a kitchen or heating source and the stair to the loft. Flanking the sin are the *svetnice,* or sitting room, and the smaller *komora,* often a storage or bed chamber. Several central, northern, and eastern European groups used this form. A modification of this plan often employed by Czech builders is an L-shaped tripartite structure. Both forms in log and masonry construction are well represented in the few, but highly informative, published works that deal with the folk architecture of Czechoslovakia.[14]

Sometimes, a barn was attached to the gable end of the house. In fact, the European farmstead often consisted of a courtyard created by a series of connected single-pile units with gates controlling access to fields and to the public roadway. Ideally suited to that rugged, densely populated continent, this self-contained plan was of little use in the open plains of America. Yet some evidence of loosely arranged courtyard plans of mostly free-standing structures can be found on a few Czech-American farms.

South Dakota Forms

In South Dakota, several patterns for houses and barns developed in harmony with those established in the old country. Although greatly simplified, Americanized, and adjusted to life on the plains, these structures have plans and features very similar to those in Europe. Dramatically linear in form, the Czech houses in the Tabor area do not use interior lateral subdivisions. Each cell is a single room. Consequently, they are very narrow structures, making flow from one room to another somewhat awkward.

Single-Bay Houses in South Dakota

The simplest house built by Czechs in South Dakota is a single-pen dwelling (Fig. 16-4). In many instances these one-room houses were just the first of what would become several linear bays, connected to form a larger structure as the needs of the family grew. Still others were set aside in favor of a completely new house. The trend is, of course, not unique to the Czechs, nor is it a particularly European trait. Many different groups built in this

John E. Rau

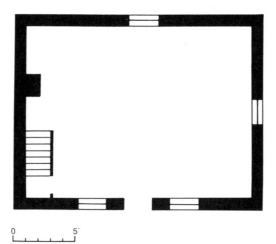

0 _____ 5'

Fig. 16-4 Floor plan of the J. Hruska log house, near Tabor, South Dakota

same manner, some of them probably influenced more by homestead laws than by tradition, yet the Czechs who built initial single-pen houses frequently incorporated many of their familiar building technologies into the structure. Most of them are log buildings using full-dovetail corner notches, masonry chinking, and an internal chimney. Many bear evidence of a masonry insulating layer between the log walls and any clapboard siding.

Various other small, single-bay folk structures were constructed around the farmstead, including granaries, smoke houses, chicken coops, summer kitchens, and stables. Each structure is unique to its farm site. Dimensions of both the one-bay houses and the outbuildings vary so widely that no pattern is apparent. Size and shape most likely depended strictly upon the needs of the individual farm.

At least one Czech-built log school is known to exist in the Tabor area. Completed by 1873, it was originally located in the newly founded village, but less than ten years later it was replaced by a larger American vernacular building, and the original was moved to a nearby farm for use as a dwelling. At that time, a wood frame section was added to the rear of the building. The log walls feature a combination of full- and half-dovetail notches and a doorway in the center of the front facade. Most other early schools from across the state utilize a somewhat standard gable-end entry, while this building conforms more closely to Old World domestic traditions. It is certainly one of the oldest extant school buildings in the state. In 1973, it was purchased by the Czech Heritage Preservation Society of Tabor for use as a museum and headquarters and was moved to a memorial park not far from its original location. Although it has suffered some unsympathetic alterations in recent times, its original form remains largely unchanged.[15]

Two-Bay Houses

Like its single-bay cousin, the two-bay dwelling was often expanded into a larger linear structure. In general, the two-room Czech house has one relatively narrow entry bay or hall and the larger chamber to either its right or left, in much the same manner as the hall-parlor plan of early America. The two cells are separated by a brick chimney and remain fairly independent of each other. This form resembles the Old World three-bay house, missing only one of the larger chambers. Dimensions again vary widely, but the ratio of gable lengths to axial lengths among measured buildings in both Nebraska and South Dakota runs fairly close from one example to another, ranging between .5:1 and .62:1.

Three-Bay Coaxial Houses

Hallmarks of early Czech occupation, traditional three-bay houses also are found in the Tabor vicinity. Many of these houses comprise the old country sin, svetnice, and komora described earlier, while others are linear single-pile sets of coaxial cells, nearly equal in size. A simple brick chimney rises from one of the interior partition walls. Among all measured specimens, the ratio of gable lengths to axial lengths differs from .35:1 to .48:1. The average is .42:1. Dimensions range from 14′ × 35′ to 15′ × 45′.[16] Both log and masonry specimens of this form are found in southeastern Dakota.

One particularly fine specimen of this Old World tripartite form is the Frantisek Pechan house in Yankton County (Fig. 16-5). It is perhaps the most

Fig. 16-5 One of the best surviving Czech folk houses in South Dakota, the Frantisek Pechan house displays an Old World tripartite form and is of log construction. It is located in Yankton County. (Photo by Rolene R. Schliesman, courtesy of the South Dakota Historical Preservation Center.)

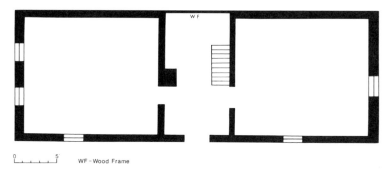

WF - Wood Frame

Fig. 16-6 Floor plan of the Pechan house, Yankton County, South Dakota

John E. Rau

undiluted example of Czech folk housing in South Dakota. Built in the early 1870s by Frantisek Pechan and his father Joseph, who were members of the first Czech settlement party, from Chicago, it is a three-bay log house measuring 15′4½″ × 42′8″. Its log walls, clad with clapboard siding, rise from a loose, unmortared stone foundation. The corners are fitted using full-dovetail notches. The house is capped by a gable roof covered with wooden shingles. A simple brick chimney projects upward from the left interior wall (Fig. 16-6). Except for the sin, which exhibits bare log walls, interior wall surfaces are covered with standard lath and plaster and a short wainscot. Of some mystery is a wood frame section comprising the whole rear wall of the sin. The reasons for, intentions of, and history of this component are unknown. Like so many of the folk buildings in the Tabor area, the condition of the Pechan house is deteriorating fast, yet it remains an important example of centuries-old building traditions.

L-*Shaped Three- and Four-Bay Houses*

The L-shaped dwelling is yet another very interesting house form that Czechs used in Dakota (Fig. 16-7). Many of these ells are only perpendicular extensions of preexisting one- or two-bay houses. They consist usually of three, but sometimes four bays and frequently employ different building materials for each addition. Dimensions vary widely. Because they were constructed in distinct phases, sometimes separated by several years, more than one chimney is common.

Also surrounding Tabor is a peculiar collection of folk dwellings that seem to have been conceived and built originally as L-shaped structures. These masonry buildings, usually of cut chalkrock, are strikingly similar in orientation, dimensions, and floor plans (Fig. 16-8). Most are situated nearly identically, with gables facing south and east. Stairways generally appear between the northwest and the northeast bays, while a few examples have stairways placed between the two western bays. Although the number and placement of entrances to these structures are quite irregular, doors usually face east or south. Often, an open, sometimes crudely fashioned, L-shaped porch shades the east and south facades. Dimensions of these buildings differ very little from one to another, averaging 18′ × 35′. It is not known whether or not a single area builder influenced or even directed construction of these fairly uniform structures, but a remarkably large concentration of them is

Fig. 16-7 The three-bay Martin Honner house, a typical L-shaped Czech folk house, near Tabor in Bon Homme County, South Dakota. Walls are of chalkrock masonry construction. (Photo by Rolene R. Schliesman, courtesy of the South Dakota Historical Preservation Center.)

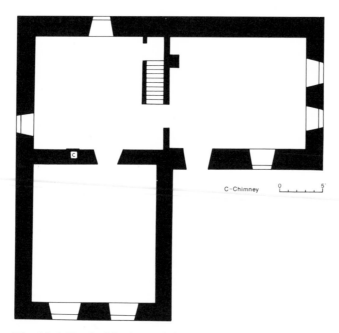

Fig. 16-8 Typical L-shaped floor plan, the Joseph Herman house, near Tabor, South Dakota

found around Tabor. Proported construction dates, some of them as late as the 1890s, indicate that this form might be a relatively late manifestation or derivative of older forms.

Other Constructional or Design Features

Besides materials and form, other features of these folk houses appear in distinguishable patterns. For instance, all of the buildings are capped with moderately pitched gable roofs usually covered with wooden shingles. Roof systems are almost always composed of common rafters built from store-bought precut materials. Many times, the rafters are secured at the roof peaks with collars or other transverse braces. Occasionally, lateral wind-braces are used to stabilize the roof. Rafter spacing is not uniform. The inside ledge along the wall plate between each rafter, no matter whether the building is a log or masonry structure, is packed with a mixture of mud and grass or with plaster. Frequently, iron straps or rods, extending from the middle of axial walls up to the plate, are employed in an effort to anchor the roof to the rest of the structure. These New World roofs are in stark contrast to European models, where steeply pitched thatch roofs were still quite common during the nineteenth century. No evidence—neither physical artifacts nor historical documents and photographs—has been found that indicates any use of thatch by Czechs in South Dakota.[17]

Likewise, chimneys follow American lines rather than more traditional configurations. In many European folk houses, particularly those located further east from Bohemia and closer to the Ukraine, the rear half of the sin

John E. Rau

296

was subdivided to provide space for a massive earthen oven or black kitchen. Such heating/cooking facilities do not seem to have been brought to the new country by Czechs settling in South Dakota. No evidence of ovens or black kitchens has been uncovered at those sites examined by the author, despite the fact that the Czechs' German-Russian neighbors in Hutchinson County did transplant that technology to the plains of Dakota. (Chapter 15 contains a discussion of such stoves in the German-Russian settlements of Manitoba.) It seems likely that the Czechs who came to South Dakota and surrounding states stopped using these ovens a generation or so before coming to America. Instead, their chimney systems, regardless of house form or building materials, are simple unadorned brick towers, similar to those built by most other homesteaders. The chimneys typically rise from about the midpoint of an interior partition wall. Very frequently, a built-in cupboard was installed below the chimney.

As implied earlier, the masonry buildings that Czech builders put up were not simply crude piles of indigenous materials but were carefully engineered structures using stones cut precisely, to provide an attractive and weather-tight fit. The Czechs' high degree of skill and experience with masonry construction is most evident in their design and treatment of windows. The openings in the walls were tapered to allow maximal solar lighting and heating of the interior space. Heavy wooden sills, measuring the full depth of the outside walls, were frequently embedded into the stone. The crowning element, however, is the finely crafted jack arches over both windows and doors. These near-textbook examples of ancient structural arches usually were fashioned out of the soft chalkrock material often chosen for the rest of the load-bearing walls (Fig. 16-9). Jack arches are found on practically all stone masonry buildings built by Czech immigrants, and their use sets Czech masons apart from their less adept immigrant neighbors.

Another distinctive element of the Czech craftsmanship is the use of a one to one-and-a-half foot high *knee wall* on both log or masonry buildings. The so-called knee wall is a vertical extension of the load-bearing walls above the ceiling joists. The rafters are set atop or embedded into this wall above the floor of the loft (Fig. 16-10). This device allows a higher roof and thus greater interior space in the upper sleeping chamber. It may also provide better insulation; however, very little is really known about the impetus for this design feature. While it is quite common in Czech folk buildings in South Dakota, its use in that state is certainly not unique to the Czechs. Oddly, however, the knee wall does not seem to have been used by Czechs in northern Nebraska.

Interior colors of the Czech houses were similar to those of other immigrant groups on the plains. Favored hues were light blue, medium blue, medium green, dark green, and white. Some of these colors may have been made by mixing natural and household dyes.[18] The earliest houses had a layer of whitewash beneath the first layer of paint. Little evidence has been found of the fancy hand-painted decoration characteristic of folk houses in the old country. Colors for trim work include gray, brown, and red. Some houses exhibit several layers of wallpaper. Exterior colors seem to have been generally quite light, perhaps shades of white and beige.

Fig. 16-9 Example of a jack arch. The Tiebel-Sykora rubblestone masonry born, Tabor vicinity, Bon Homme County, South Dakota. (Photo by Rolene R. Schliesman, courtesy of the South Dakota Historical Preservation Center.)

Czech Barns in South Dakota

In addition to houses, several sites contain distinctive masonry barns that incorporate Czech building traditions. The most common folk barn in the Tabor area is a medium-sized rectangular rubblestone or chalkrock structure with a gable roof (Fig. 16-11). Typical of barns on the American agricultural landscape, these buildings include at least one large gable-end door, a feature not usually found in European settings (Fig. 16-12). Yet, construction technologies, materials, and interior features demonstrate Old World folk traditions. Depending upon the needs of the individual farm, dimensions vary considerably, ranging from 27' × 48' to 30' × 80'. Recorded heights of the barns at their peaks range from 17 feet to 26 feet. The height of masonry walls ranges from 8½ feet to 10 feet. If the builder desired a taller peak and therefore more loft area, a wood frame wall up to 3 feet high was placed atop the masonry wall. The rafters, then, rested on a plate at the top of the frame wall. Some evidence exists of this same barn form applied to early timber frame construction. No matter what material is used, these barns seem to be a combination of American vernacular agricultural forms with older Czech folk traditions.

John E. Rau

Fig. 16-10 Knee wall construction raises the rafter base above the joist supports. This example is from the Pechan house, Yankton County, South Dakota. (Photo by Rolene R. Schliesman, courtesy of the South Dakota Historical Preservation Center.)

Fig. 16-11 The Teibel-Sykora rubblestone barn, Lincoln Township, Bon Homme County, South Dakota. (Photo by Rolene R. Schliesman, courtesy of the South Dakota Historical Preservation Center.)

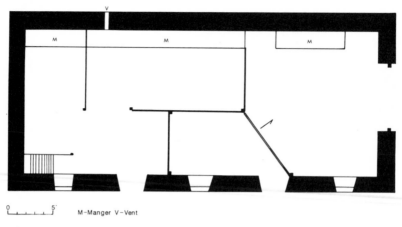

Fig. 16-12 Floor plan of a gable-entry Czech barn

Fig. 16-13 A South Dakotan Czech barn. (Drawing by M. M. Geib.)

Several of the barns feature ventilation ports in the side walls, but occurrence and placement of these ports is not uniform. Interior finishing is never more than a simple plaster veneer and whitewash or white paint. Other characteristic features of the barns include handmade ladders, mangers, or tack hangers as well as heavy exposed joists. Windows are usually placed quite high on the wall, with sills tapered to allow more light to enter the barn (see Fig. 16-12). Jack arches usually cap each window or door opening. Doors, as well as door and window frames, were frequently handmade, but used store-bought hardware.

A second type of folk barn found on Czech farms in South Dakota is a long rectangular form with entrances primarily along the side walls (Fig. 16-13). Some of these structures appear to be housebarns; however, their use as dwellings has been long abandoned and is in some cases difficult to verify. These barns utilize the same materials, techniques, and features discussed above, but their overall form is different. The long dimensions and linear design resemble Old World barns (Figs. 16-14 and 16-15). Length varies from

John E. Rau

300

Fig. 16-14 A rare example of a linear form barn, the John and Katherine Merkwan housebarn, Tabor vicinity, Bon Homme County, South Dakota. (Photo by Rolene R. Schliesman, courtesy of the South Dakota Historical Preservation Center.)

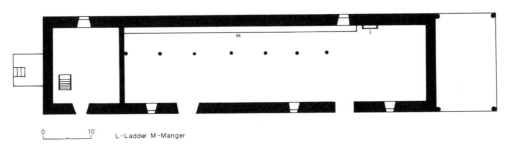

0   10'   L–Ladder M–Manger

Fig. 16-15 Floor plan of the Merkwan barn

44 feet to an extreme of 160 feet. The latter figure is from the John Frydrych barn, which has a heavy timber frame, a rubblestone bank, and several side openings. One of these openings, located on the banked side of the barn, is a second-story drive-in door for loading hay, a characteristic not uncommon to the American vernacular farm landscape. The Frydrych barn also incorporates one large gable-end entrance on the ground story.

Another good example of this linear barn is the Charvat-Straka housebarn, recently relocated to a memorial park in Tabor. The barn was constructed of cottonwood logs using traditional Czech building technology, including full-dovetail notches. Its exterior was originally covered by a clay veneer and then sided over with clapboard. However, when the structure was moved to town, the exterior cladding was removed, exposing the bare logs. Despite these changes, the basic form of this rare housebarn combination still survives.

Churches

As with many other immigrant groups, the central focus of the Tabor community was the church; therefore, early vernacular churches of this predominately Catholic settlement are an important part of the Czech landscape (Fig. 16-16). Throughout the state, early Catholic churches were generally simple structures with little ornamentation. Second generation churches, however, were usually designed by an architect following the stylistic preferences of the parish priest. In South Dakota, German Gothic Revival or Romanesque Revival styles show up most frequently.[19]

As early as 1872, Tabor Catholics were working on an edifice of chalkrock, which was used by the parish until the present church was constructed in 1898. Little information about the earlier church remains. Its successor, a brick structure measuring 132' × 42' with a tall bell tower and steeple, dominates the skyline of the tiny town. Called St. Wenceslaus, after the patron saint and murdered tenth-century duke of Bohemia, it is situated on a slight rise in the center of the village. The simple nave-plan building utilizes Gothic-arched window and door openings and Latin crosses at the corners of the bell tower and at the peak of the steeple. In many ways it is typical of early Catholic churches in Dakota, except that on the interior it displays numerous Czech influences. Captioned Stations of the Cross and stained glass windows with biblical passages written in Czech script adorn the side walls.

Adjacent to the church is a cube-shaped brick rectory built in 1910. A cemetery, with grottoes, statues, and several iron cross grave markers, extends to the east and north of the church. Located across the street to the

John E. Rau

Fig. 16-16 The Church of Saint John the Baptist, Yankton County, South Dakota. (Photo by Scott Gerloff, courtesy of the South Dakota Historical Preservation Center.)

southeast, the old parish house is a very simple Italianate two-story structure built in 1878 of soft local bricks. Taken together, this entire complex illustrates the dominant presence of Czech Catholics in Tabor.[20]

Not far to the east of Tabor stands a small, austere chalkrock church next to a modern farmstead. This building marks the site of the town of Lakeport, which, except for the church, has long since vanished from the landscape. Built in 1884, the church replaced a wood frame building that had been located a few miles away and was reportedly the first Czech Catholic church in Dakota. So much controversy evolved from the decision to construct the new stone edifice that several members dissolved their bonds to both the parish and to the Roman Catholic Church. Although they did not formally call themselves Freethinkers, as Czech agonistics elsewhere did, a few of these families have remained churchless for three or more generations. Named the Church of Saint John the Baptist, the Lakeport church is a blocky rectangle constructed of native chalkrock with a fieldstone foundation (Fig. 16-16). Carefully handcrafted Gothic-arched windows pierce the walls. A tiny wooden cross rises from the peak of the roof. At some point, the exterior walls were covered with a concrete veneer scored to look like smooth ashlar stone. Most of this surface covering had eroded before the remainder of it was manually removed in 1987 by a local stone mason. The building features an unadorned interior of deteriorated plaster walls and a reconstructed wooden balcony. The faded stained wood, hand-carved altar is from the original chalkrock church at Tabor. Restoration of the church is under way by a group of area citizens many of whom are descendants of the founders.[21]

Iron Cross Grave Markers

As at St. Wenceslaus, the churchyard at Lakeport is dotted with iron cross grave markers. These mortuary symbols are fairly common in pioneer Catholic or Lutheran cemeteries throughout the Dakotas, particularly those of either German or Czech background. They were sometimes handmade by local artisans using various symbols to represent both death and life. Among Czech grave markers, the heart motif occurs frequently. The inscriptions on these monuments are generally written in Czech. Later, precast and stamped metal markers ordered from catalogs were employed, in an effort to continue the tradition after the old cross markers had themselves left this world. Although today granite markers are most common, the Tabor area still abounds with small rural cemeteries that gleam in the sunlight because of the large number of reflective metal markers they contain. In South Dakota, some limited systematic survey of iron cross grave markers has been conducted, and several general surveys of historic sites in all parts of the state have turned up numerous examples of these artifacts; yet, a great deal more research is needed. In North Dakota, a major statewide thematic survey of iron crosses has been conducted and a thematic National Register of Historic Places nomination recently has been completed.[22]

Lodge Halls and Other Structures

Czech fraternal organizations have had an important and far-reaching role in all Czech-American communities, and many such institutions were established in Dakota. As late as 1937, there were still twenty lodges of the

Fig. 16-17 The lodge hall of the Západní cesko-bratrská jednota, a Czech fraternal organization, in Tabor, South Dakota. (No longer extant.) Note the lunette-shaped parapet. (Drawing by M. M. Geib from a photo in South Dakota Historical Preservation Center.)

Z.C.B.J., four of the Czecho-Slovak Society of America, and five local units of the National Sokol in South Dakota.[23] Today, however, the venerable Czech lodges have all but faded from memory. Many of the old lodge halls are no longer extant, and the few that do survive in Dakota seldom bear any ethnic marks. Most of these buildings are plain frame or brick structures of an American vernacular form, yet one very subtle traditional element can be spotted at a few of the public meeting halls. That is the use of the lunette-shaped front parapet (Fig. 16-17). Even the Tabor town hall exhibits this treatment, which shows up with even greater frequency in northern Nebraska. Perhaps the builders were simplifying the stylistic effect of the Renaissance Revival and Baroque public buildings they remembered from their homeland. There, a much more elaborate rounded parapet is common. Whatever the influence, it nevertheless remains one of the rare and forceful elements of the Czech-American built environment.

Preserving the Czech Heritage

The social environment is another lasting legacy of these people. Every summer since 1941, the townspeople of Tabor have sponsored a celebration of their heritage called "Czech Days." During two days in June, the normally sleepy little town attracts thousands of people from all over the state and nation for street games, pageants, dances, and parades. Festivities always include traditional Czech music, food, dress, and dance, intermixed with the attractions of modern small town celebrations, such as a midway and beer gardens. Over the years, the ability of the small community to support such an event has dwindled because the number of Czech descendants willing to participate has declined, yet it continues with a good deal of popularity.

In the 1970s, a Czech Heritage Preservation Society was incorporated, to

John E. Rau

304

encourage the furtherance of heritage institutions in the community—to take up the mission of the bygone fraternal societies. One of the proudest accomplishments of this group has been the slow but steady creation of a memorial park, to which many Czech pioneer buildings have been moved to save them from demolition. This park, located in the center of town, has become the focal point for the annual celebration. In addition, the society sponsors regular membership meetings, historical programs and plays, group trips to Czechoslovakia, and Czech language courses. The spirit of the founders lives on in Tabor largely because of the efforts of this society.

Conclusions

What then can be said, in summation, of the environment around Czech-American Tabor? How important is it in our understanding of the immigrant forces in the Midwest and Great Plains? Within South Dakota, it is a unique landscape not so much for its topography but for what humankind has built there. The land form is generally flat, interrupted by a few deep riverine trenches left by ancient glaciers. The most prominent of the streams is the Missouri River. Early Czech settlers were adept stone masons by tradition and were able to use that skill on the native materials of southern Dakota. Some also utilized the scarce timber resources, often combining them with some kind of masonry construction. The Tabor landscape retains its Czech-American legacy. Other parts of the state that are blessed with the same natural resources, but that were not populated by people with such strong masonry traditions, do not display such a concentration of native stone buildings. A quick comparison of regions reveals the strength of the Czech impact on the Tabor community. No matter what material is used, forms and special details of the early folk buildings and other artifacts found there are noticeable and distinct. They reflect central European architectural trends.

The forces of assimilation are also evident. Czech settlers around Tabor influenced, and were influenced by, their neighbors. Despite the pride they had in their European roots, most Dakota immigrants felt equally honored to be Americans. They quickly adopted the general trends of middle-American mass culture. Much of the early folk building stock was soon replaced by or supplemented with American vernacular and patternbook structures.

Despite this Americanization, Tabor Czechs still managed to retain their European identity. As late as 1942, the use of the Czech language in routine affairs in Tabor was commonly heard in the streets.[24] Sermons at St. Wenceslaus were often conducted in Czech until the early 1960s.

The landscape around Tabor is changing rapidly as farm operations become larger and fewer, making many small farmsteads obsolete and expendable. Thus, most remaining pioneer folk houses and barns lie decaying on abandoned, often forgotten farmyards. Members of the community usually refuse to actively demolish parts of their past; although in many instances they do allow the buildings of their grandparents to deteriorate into oblivion, they will not tear them down. Some even openly admit that they really

*Czechs
in South
Dakota*

should stabilize and save the crumbling artifacts of their ancestors' toil. As long as the structures stand there is some hope for preservation. Still other descendants utilize them in day-to-day farming activities. Many masonry barns are used for calving, hog feeding, or storage. Few residents fail to understand or appreciate the interest of the scholar in these buildings. Nevertheless, their folk architectural resources are diminishing and in danger of becoming extinct.

John E. Rau

Part V

Western
North America

17

Ukrainians in Western Canada

John C. Lehr

OR OVER two decades before the outbreak of the First World War, immigrants from the western Ukrainian lands of the Austro-Hungarian Empire settled vast tracts of territory on western Canada's homestead frontier. Collectively their settlements mirrored the geographies and cultural landscapes of their homelands in the two provinces of Galicia (Halychyna) and Bukovyna, situated on the Carpathian slopes in the peasant heartland of central Europe[1] (Fig. 17-1).

Immigration into Canada from the Austrian western Ukraine did not commence until 1891, when two peasants from the Kalush district of Galicia traveled to Canada to inspect opportunities for securing free homestead land in districts settled earlier by ethnic Germans (Völksdeutche) from the same district.[2] A year later a slow trickle of Ukrainians, almost all from the village of Nebyliw in Kalush, and mostly related by blood or marriage, began to settle in Alberta, taking up homesteads around Star, some 40 miles from the railhead in Edmonton but only a few miles from the Völksdeutche settlement of Josephburg.[3]

Until 1896 all Ukrainian immigrants into Canada came from the province of Galicia. Virtually all were from Kalush, mostly from the village of Nebyliw and environs.[4] All who settled on the land took homesteads in the Star district of Alberta. In 1896 the character of the immigration changed, for besides increasing dramatically in volume it expanded geographically to include emigrants from the province of Bukovyna. For the first time, Ukrainians began to take homesteads outside of the existing colony at Star in Alberta. Guided by officials of the Department of the Interior, some chose lands in Saskatchewan and Manitoba, laying the foundation of the distinctive geography of Ukrainian settlement, which had clearly emerged by 1900 and which was consolidated and expanded, until the outbreak of war in continental Europe in 1914 put an end to emigration.[5] By then, a discontinuous arc of blocks of solid Ukrainian settlement had been established across the northern margins of the aspen parkland in Alberta, Saskatchewan, and Manitoba, with a few, relatively small, settlements below the international boundary, in southwest North Dakota (Fig. 17-2). In these Canadian block settlements, some 170,000 Ukrainians occupied thousands of square miles of agricultural land, virtually all of it obtained under the homestead and preemption provisions of the Dominion Lands Act.[6]

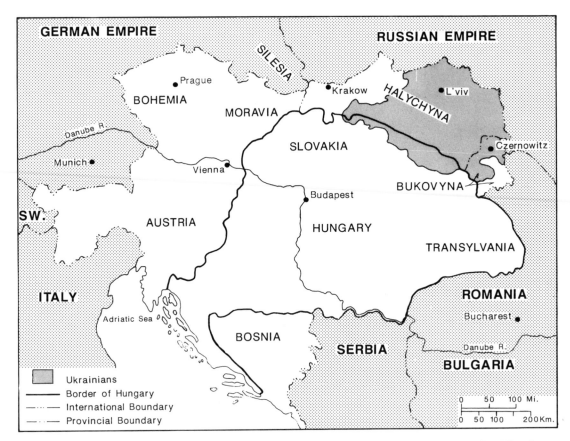

Fig. 17-1 Galicia (Halychyna) and Bukovyna, the source areas for Ukrainian immigrants to Canada between 1891 and 1914

The Ukrainians arrived in Canada as independent settlers; they did not come as part of a tightly organized group to occupy lands reserved for their exclusive settlement, as did the Mennonites, Icelanders, and Doukhobors, nor did they have the benefit of a strong central leadership, as did the Mormons. Nevertheless, the process of settlement, whereby individual settlers sought out homesteads adjacent to friends, kinfolk, and compatriots, and the connivance of the Department of the Interior in channeling the arriving immigrants into a limited number of settlement nuclei, created a remarkable degree of ethnic integrity within the Ukrainian blocks. Other ethnic groups emigrated to Canada from the same districts of Austria-Hungary as the Ukrainians: Poles came from Galicia, Romanians from Bukovyna, and Völksdeutsche and Jews from both provinces. Their numbers were only a small fraction of the Ukrainian migration, and the Germans, Poles, and Romanians all tended to settle separately from the Ukrainians, keeping adjacent to them but seldom placing themselves amongst them. With few exceptions, Jews gravitated to the burgeoning urban centers of the prairies and industrial east.

Ukrainian immigrants to Canada before 1914 were mostly peasant farmers bent on securing farmland in the West. In the early years of immi-

John C. Lehr

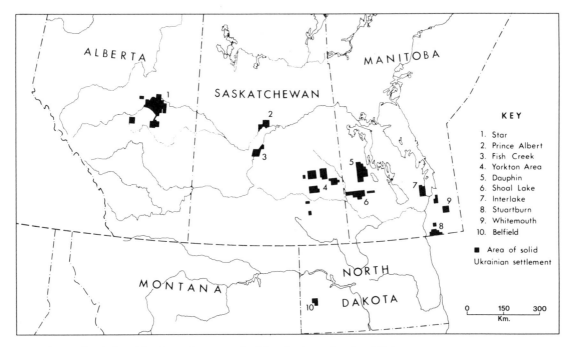

Fig. 17-2 Ukrainian block settlements in North America by 1914

gration, before the turn of the century, a high proportion of immigrants were illiterate, and the majority were poor on arrival. They were by no means a homogeneous group, for they included members of many ethnographic Ukrainian subgroups, such as Hutsuls from the Carpathian highlands, Lemkos from Zacapathia, Boykos from the eastern Carpathians, and Podolyaks from Podillia. Those who hailed from Galicia were mostly adherents of the Greek Catholic (Uniate) Church, while those from Bukovyna were virtually all adherents of the Greek (Russian) Orthodox Church. Both were sufficiently mutually suspicious that it affected the process of settlement. Government officials quickly became aware of their mutual antipathy and directed them to separate areas within the Ukrainian blocks.[7] The end result was the recreation of the former social geography of the homeland in microcosm: the replication of family, village, and provincial old country groupings in Canada,[8] a phenomenon that naturally had important ramifications in terms of the transference of folk culture, especially those material elements that had a high visibility in the landscape: domestic and religious architecture.

The Framework for Settlement

Like most immigrants seeking land on the agricultural frontiers of western Canada, the Ukrainians sought out the free homestead lands on the edge of the settlement frontier, where they faced a wilderness of unbroken land and uncleared bush. But the wilderness was deceptively ordered, for the onrush of settlement had generally been preceded by the crews of the Dominion Land Survey. Section lines had been driven through the bush

Ukrainians in Western Canada

311

with geometric precision, dividing the land into townships of 36 square miles, each further divided into one mile square sections, each again quartered into the 160 acre units available for homestead claim by any settler able to pay a $10 entry fee and fulfill basic requirements of cultivation and residence.[9] This order was more apparent to the administrators than to the new arrivals, but those sections open for homesteading could be identified and distinguished from those set aside for the railway land grants, school lands, and the Hudson's Bay Company land settlement.

The checkerboard system of land division had a number of immediate effects upon the settlement of all groups who settled in the West. Since, in an average township, at least 91 of 144 quarters were reserved from homestead settlement (Fig. 17-3), the density of settlement was kept low, and farmsteads were widely dispersed across the landscape.

In order to obtain full title (patent) to a homestead, every settler had to fulfill the Dominion Lands Act requirement that he reside upon the claimed homestead for at least six months of each year for three years. This requirement and the checkerboard division of land precluded settlement in a village format if one were homesteading and ordained the single isolated farmstead as the norm across the West. Some groups, notably the Mennonites (see Chapter 15) and Doukhobors, settled on lands reserved specifically for their settlement and were privileged to settle in villages and fulfill the residence requirement away from the claimed land. The Ukrainians received no such exemption, although they too were a people accustomed to village settlement and anxious to secure the social benefits of close association that only agglomerated settlement could provide.

Despite that the requirements of the Dominion Lands Act militated against close settlement, Crown agents involved in the colonization process sometimes attempted to mitigate this by securing permission for groups of Ukrainians to homestead on odd-numbered sections normally reserved for railway land grants or as Crown lands set aside for later preemption. Even

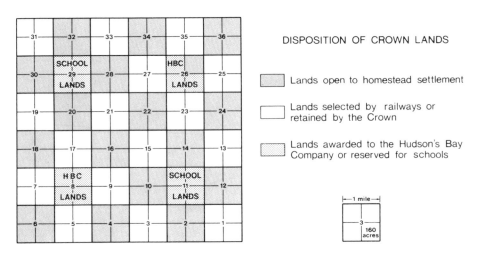

Fig. 17-3 Hypothetical Canadian township, showing lands available for disposition during the period 1891-1914

when this did occur—and it was by no means a frequent occurrence—the settlement density nowhere approximated that of village settlement, and the typical Ukrainian pioneer farmstead remained always the *einzelhof,* the single isolated farm.

Taking Root

The new arrivals made little impact upon the landscape initially. They were few and were dwarfed by a vast land. Pressures of survival, the need to clear timber, break land, and even to secure work at distant mines, railroads, or farms, prevented the settlers from immediately marking the landscape with a strong cultural signature. In their first years many lived with their "established" relatives; others, less fortunate, overcame the pressing need for shelter by resorting to cavelike dwellings in riverbanks,[10] but more usually by building a temporary shelter, often a sod-roofed dugout termed a *zemlyanka* or *burdei,* or a small one room log hut, a *buda.*[11] The latter were strongly reminiscent of the chimneyless *chorna khata* (black houses) that had been common in the Carpathian region in the eighteenth century but were seldom encountered by the time of emigration. The dugout was similarly modeled upon the largely defunct form of the Carpathian mountain hut, or *staya,* of the Hutsul shepherds.[12]

Occasionally, these temporary dwellings were occupied for several years, although most were inhabited for only a few months, pending the construction of a more substantial house invariably built in the traditional style. The temporary dwelling was then relegated to the role of root cellar, store house, summer kitchen (*komora*), or animal shelter. As such, many survived for decades.[13]

Although the second dwelling, located in the clearing so painstakingly hacked out of the pervasive bush, constituted the first major element of Ukrainian material culture to be placed in the new landscape, other elements also emerged, all of which bespoke European influences. Farm layout, fence types, water drawing arrangements, design of animal shelters and hay storage were all transferred from the western Ukraine, though few of these survived for more than a decade or so. For example, the traditional fence type of the western Ukraine, a woven willow fence, was initially used to protect kitchen gardens; but in the wooded lands settled by Ukrainians, split logs or sawn boards were cheap and barbed wire soon became available, and so the old laboriously constructed willow fences faded from the landscape.

Farm layout also reflected the changed realities of agriculture in the new land. In the old country, and on many early farmsteads, buildings were arranged in a quadrangle formation, the buildings enclosing a yard. The Hutsul building groupings called *hrazhda,* found in the Carpathian highlands, even had all buildings joined by a stockade wall, but this form was not transferred to Canada by Hutsul settlers.[14] The quadrangle arrangement survived on many pioneer farmsteads, although economic progress and acquisition of draft animals and farm machinery soon changed the traditional layout of the farm. As turning circles of machinery widened and as the shelter area necessary for draft animals grew, it became evident that an arrangement of buildings suited to an operation using herded stock and hand-sown and -harvested grain was inappropriate for one based on team-drawn implements, and was totally inadequate for fully mechanized operations.

Even crop types reflected the new economy of western Canada. Hemp, widely grown for its fiber and seed oil in the old country, soon lost its importance, as cheap and superior commercial products replaced homemade rope and home-pressed cooking oil.[15] Rye, a popular crop in the western Ukraine but never widely grown in Canada, was quickly replaced by the early maturing wheats, which gave the pioneer the preferred and, in the peasant view, high status wheat bread. After two years of settlement in the Stuartburn district of Manitoba, only 2 acres of rye were in cultivation by Ukrainian pioneers, compared to 49 acres of wheat and 32½ acres of barley. Increasing use of horses as draft animals, replacing the oxen often used in the early years, was reflected in the increasing cultivation of oats, grown for feed.[16]

Kitchen gardens maintained a stronger link with the past. In them the pioneer women cultivated vegetables and herbs brought across the ocean, among them the poppy, cultivated for its seed, from which was made a sedative for fractious infants.

Some elements of the cultural landscape, such as the *zhuravel'*, or well sweep, did survive for many years—into the 1980s in some instances. The utility of the well sweep was not compromised until the introduction of electricity enabled water to be piped into houses and barns. The traditional hay storage cradle, however, had no place in North American agriculture and, if present at all, survived only briefly on the pioneer margins.

Traditional Architecture

Apart from the churches, with their Byzantine domes and separate bell towers, it was the family dwelling that proved to be both the most enduring and the most obvious element of Ukrainian material culture in the pioneer landscape (Fig. 17-4). It will not outlast the church as a landscape symbol, but it was the one element of material culture which most effectively created a sense of place and imparted much of the distinctive ambience remarked upon by early visitors to areas of Ukrainian settlement:

> We entered a district as typically Russian as though we had dropped into Russia itself. Here and there beside the winding trail loomed groups of buildings, low browed, and usually thatched. These always faced south. The houses were all of rough logs, rough hewed and chinked with a mortar made of clay and straw. Some were plastered on the exterior, and almost all had been limewashed to a dazzling whiteness.[17]

Within the variation in building detail that reflected the settler's region of origin, these pioneer homes had a unity of form, design, and decorative element, of which the most evident were a southward orientation, a single-story rectangular plan, a basic two- or three-room configuration, a central chimney, a gable, hipped-gable, or hipped roof, and very frequently an exterior both plastered and limewashed (Fig. 17-5).[18]

As in the home regions of Galicia and Bukovyna these houses were constructed of local materials: wood, mud, straw, fieldstone, lime, and animal dung.[19] Surprisingly, the move to the new land had little effect upon which materials were used in construction. They remained virtually unchanged,

Fig. 17-4 Ukrainian pioneer house, Sirko, Manitoba. Note vertical timbering construction. (Photo by J. Lehr.)

save for the substitution of aspen, white pine, spruce, balsam poplar, and tamarack for the oak that was widely used in the Carpathians. Though pine and spruce were often readily available for building in areas settled by Ukrainians, poplar was generally the preferred building material. This may have been a reflection of its ubiquity. However, while, as Wonders and Rasmussen point out, it tends to rot faster than other species, the Ukrainians' preference for this timber may have been based only on the fact that it looked most like their former building materials. It possessed other properties of immediate attraction: a light weight, lack of heavy gums, and easy workability.[20]

In roofing, slough grass often replaced rye straw for thatching, but otherwise the ancillary materials used by the peasant builder were frequently as accessible to the Ukrainian settler on the agricultural frontiers of western Canada as they were to the peasant in a small village in the western Ukraine.

Log Construction Methods

In Galicia and Bukovyna, methods of building in wood varied according to the price and availability of building timbers within and between regions. In the nineteenth century, two methods of log building predominated: horizontal log construction and "frame and fill." The former was employed in areas of mature forests and low timber prices. Where timber prices were kept high by transportation costs or control of forests by landowners, the more economical frame and fill method was more common, since expensive mature timber was required only for building the frame and cheaper inferior logs could be used for infill within the load-bearing frame.[21]

On the Canadian frontier of settlement the nature of the timber on the

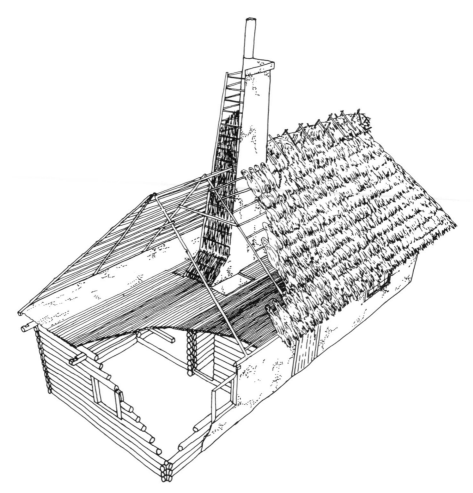

Fig. 17-5 Fedoryshyn cottage. Isometric view showing construction details.

homestead or available within the immediate locality was the prime determinant of construction method. In most areas settled by Ukrainians, timber—usually poplar—of sufficient diameter to permit corner notching or dovetailing, and hence horizontal log construction, was available. In Alberta, this method was universally employed, although elsewhere in the West, particularly in parts of southern Manitoba, frame and fill (known locally as Red River frame) was also widely used. It is evident that the type of construction employed was a direct reflection of the quality and size of building logs available to the pioneer builder; it had no discernible relationship to the geographic origin of the settler.[22] In parts of southern Manitoba, for example, Ukrainian immigrants took up homesteads in marshy areas that had been ravaged by bushfires less than twenty years earlier; what little mature timber had been present was destroyed. Hence, in building they were restricted to using immature trees and so resorted to placing the logs vertically, thereby avoiding the need even for the larger-diameter load-bearing timbers necessary for frame and fill. Logs were placed upright on a wooden sill, topped by a horizontal log, and braced at each corner to keep the wall in line. Although the method permitted poor, immature logs to be used, and the resulting walls were easily built, this type of log building was not widespread. In western Canada it is encountered infrequently and principally in the more marginal areas of southeastern Manitoba (see Fig. 17-4). One major drawback associated with the technique is that, in contrast to horizontal or *pièces-sur-pièces* log construction, aging or shrinkage will not lead to compaction of the log wall but to gaps between the logs. In consequence, some kind of plastering is necessary to provide an airtight wall.

On the open grasslands of North Dakota and on the woodland margins in Manitoba, scarcity of timber led Ukrainian settlers to use wattle and daub techniques.[23] Significantly, the settlers in the Dakotas who used this method were from the same district of the western Ukraine (Borshchiv) as were the settlers in the Tolstoi-Senkiw district of Manitoba, who uniformly constructed log houses, mostly of saddle-notched horizontal logs or Red River frame, which suggests that New World conditions, not Old World traditions, were paramount in deciding the form of house construction.[24]

Occasionally, pioneer houses would display an eclectic mix of log building types. This occurred mostly in additions to a horizontal log house. To maintain the same building method posed problems in joining logs; hence, an extension, or lean-to, of either frame and fill or vertical log construction, more easily integrated with existing construction, was added to the building.

Log Notching

The type of corner notching used to interlock horizontal logs showed wide variation. Most common was the conventional saddle notch, usually with the notch carved in the top of each log, although the type where the underside of the log was notched was also quite frequently used. Most expert log builders eschewed the former method, since that joint favors the retention of water and thus is more prone to rot. This was not a consideration for the builder intending to sheath the logs with a protective plaster, and since it was sometimes more convenient to fashion notches in situ, the Ukrainians showed no hesitation in using the topside notch. Examination of numerous houses built in this mode did not reveal any instances of this type of notching leading to rotting of the logs.

Dovetailing was less widely employed, since it required a high degree of skill and experience in working with wood, together with timber of a size that afforded the opportunity to execute dovetail joints. Not surprisingly, this type of joint was found most commonly among those settlers who came from the Carpathian highland areas and who settled in areas of the West where stands of mature softwood timber were available, as, for example, in the Pakan and Smoky Lake areas of Alberta.

Wall Plastering

A high proportion of Ukrainian houses in the West were sheathed both inside and out with limewashed mud plaster (Fig. 17-6). Indeed, among both contemporary and later observers this practice was invariably remarked upon, and taken to be a unique characteristic identifying all Ukrainian pioneer building.[25] In fact, it was a technique used by other ethnic and indigenous groups, such as the Metis and, moreover, was one which was by no

Fig. 17-6 Ukrainian pioneer house, Elk Island, Alberta. Note horizontal log construction, limewashed plastering, flared cornice brackets, and roof projection at the eaves. (Photo by J. Lehr.)

means universal among the Ukrainians.[26] Those whose origins were in the Carpathian highlands, in areas where good mature timber was available, seldom plastered the exterior of their buildings (Fig. 17-7). If they did so at all it was only around the points where windows and door frames abutted the log frame.[27] In Canada, wherever these settlers found timber of suitable maturity and quality they continued their homeland practices, otherwise they resorted to overall plastering. Plastering enhanced insulation and, one suspects, appeased aesthetic sensibilities, for it both sealed the wall and concealed the uneven nature of a poor log surface. In many cases walls needed little preparation prior to the application of plaster since undulations in the logs gave it better purchase. For squared, or partly squared, logs, and on vertical logs, additional purchase was given by attaching wood lathes or, less commonly, short hardwood pegs, to the wall. The lathes were spaced from four to six inches apart and were always angled at 45° from the vertical.

House plastering was traditionally women's work, but on the frontier it was frequently a communal effort, with a *toloka*, or "bee," being held for that purpose.[28] The plaster was made by mixing clay and water, then pounding it with the feet or under the hooves of oxen so as to break down the clay.[29] Horse or cow dung and finely chopped straw, were added, the fibrous material preventing the plaster from cracking upon drying. A viscous clay-straw-dung mixture was applied, smoothed roughly, then further finer coats of mud and dung were added, ultimately topped by a mixture of active lime and water. Skim milk or washing blue was added to this final coat to bring out the brilliant whiteness of the lime.

John C. Lehr

318

Fig. 17-7 House built by settler from Galicia in Gimli, Manitoba, ca. 1905. (Drawing by M. M. Geib.)

The lime served to both decorate and protect the clay from rainwash.[30] The wall was often embellished with geometric designs in blue, a relatively simple operation that involved only the addition of extra washing blue to the limewash before application.

At the base of the mud-plastered log wall of the house facade, a low clay embankment (*pryspa*) about 6 to 8 inches high and 12 to 24 inches wide was constructed.[31] This slanted downwards away from the house and deflected rainwater from the base logs. It enhanced the insulative properties of the wall base, as well as serving, along the sunny southern facade, as a convenient seat.

Roofs and Floors

In the early days, many Ukrainian houses had thatched roofs (Fig. 17-8). These ranged from the proficient to the slapdash, for not all settlers had the time or experience necessary to construct a neatly trimmed thatched roof. In the western Ukraine, rye straw was the usual thatching substance; in Canada, little rye was grown, so slough grass was substituted.[32] Practical considerations meant that thatched roofs were steeply pitched, to enhance their ability to shed water (Fig. 17-9). Hipped or hipped-gable roofs were also easier to thatch than straightforward gable roofs and hence were favored.

Although well-crafted thatch can provide a good roof for up to forty years, it needs attention and it is always a fire hazard. Even in the homeland, thatch had fallen into official disfavor and sheet iron roofing had begun to make an appearance by 1908,[33] so it is not surprising that in Canada many thatched roofs were soon replaced by hand split shingles, and in later years, by the ubiquitous asphalt shingles (Fig. 17-10). Furthermore, in many areas

Fig. 17-8 Thatched roof house, Stuartburn, Manitoba, 1922. (Ukrainian Cultural and Educational Centre, Winnipeg, Professor Iwan Boberskyj Collection.)

Fig. 17-9 Ukrainian structure formerly a dwelling, now used as a storage shed, ca. 1935. (Manitoba Archives.)

Fig. 17-10 Ukrainian farmhouse, Manitoba, ca. 1915. (Manitoba Archives.)

of the western Ukraine, most houses had been roofed with hand-split wooden shingles, so when settlers from these areas had the capability to create their own shingles, they employed them from the beginning, never thatching their roofs.[34] Replacement of thatch with shingles was almost invariably accompanied by a restructuring of the roof, lowering the pitch and perhaps adopting a more simple gable conformation. The result was a radical change in the profile and appearance of the building, with much of the obvious bucolic spirit and picturesque flavour of the pioneer house being eliminated.

Initially, many, if not most, pioneer Ukrainian houses had dirt floors. Dirt was packed down to the level of the fieldstone house foundation, smoothed over with clay and water and regularly washed over with a mixture of cow or sheep dung and water. This imparted a shiny appearance to the floor and kept dust down. According to all informants this process did not create any odor and, rather surprisingly, given the obvious lack of hygiene, it apparently did not have any adverse effects upon the occupants.[35]

Although some houses were built with wooden floors in place, for most it was some years before the wooden floor was added. At that time a small cellar was usually excavated, to serve for winter storage of potatoes and other vegetables.

Floor Plans and Interior Space

Floor plans of Ukrainian pioneer houses were remarkably consistent. In terms of house dimensions and wall ratios there was little variation between the pioneer houses and those left behind in the Old World. Typically, the long wall would be between 26 and 30 feet and the side wall between 12 and 17 feet, though front to side wall ratios ranged from 1:1.4 to 1:2.5, normally being in the order of 1:1.8.[36]

The Ukrainian house derived much of its distinctive external appearance from the internal arrangement of space. Such spatial patterns were determined by the placement of the large clay stove (*pich* or *pietz*), in the center of the house, and by long-established patterns of social behavior within the building. The house revolved around a basic threefold division of space based on two rooms and a central hallway (see *A* in Fig. 17-11). The western half of the house was usually subdivided into an entrance hallway (*siny*) and living room (*mala khata*—literally, *little house*), which contained the stove and hence served as the focus of all family activities. In the early years of settlement the huge pich, built of clay over a willow framework, took up a good proportion of the room's area. The pich was used for heating and cooking, and a large shelf built into its flat top was a prized winter sleeping place, as its bulk enabled it to store heat well and to radiate it long after the fire had died.[37] Unfortunately, the size of the pich reduced the living space, and its weight exerted great physical stress on wooden floors, factors which expedited its demise. By the end of the first decade of settlement, usually coincident with the building of a wood floor, the pich was replaced by a conventional manufactured iron stove. The presence of the stove maintained the

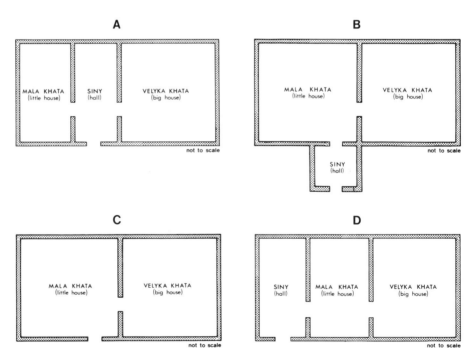

John C. Lehr

Fig. 17-11 Variants of basic floor plan in Ukrainian houses in western Canada

mala khata's pivotal role within the life of the Ukrainian family.

Use of the larger east room (*velyka khata,* big house), across the hallway, was restricted to formal occasions, dining on saints' days, guest accommodation, or, in larger families, as the parents' sleeping quarters.

This tripartite division of space was fundamental to all Ukrainian pioneer architecture and had direct antecedents in the western Ukraine. Although the general arrangement of rooms is described above, variations upon the basic pattern were numerous, both in the old country and in the Canadian West. In Canada four major variations of the basic design were present (see Fig. 17-11). It has been argued that these floor plans may be associated with specific regions in the western Ukraine, but Bilash has suggested that this is unlikely, for in both the western Ukraine and on the Canadian frontier the internal arrangement of space within the house was always evolving. Many two-room houses in Canada were simply later modifications of the three-room variant, a concrete reflection of a need for greater living space, accomplished by removing the most westerly internal wall of the house, eliminating the hallway, and enlarging the mala khata.

In a detailed study of a single Ukrainian house built by a Bukovynian settler in east central Alberta, Hohol catalogues its evolution from a standard three-room house—mala khata, siny, velyka khata—in 1918, to a two-room house with a truncated siny in the early 1920s, with a further modification, to give it its final two-room configuration—mala khata, velyka khata—made in 1928[38] (Fig. 17-12). According to the Ukrainian ethnologist T.V. Kosmina, parallel changes were occurring in three-room dwellings in the Ukraine at the opening of the twentieth century,[39] suggesting that this pattern of modification was actually a continuation of a long process of house plan evolution rather than an aberration triggered by emigration and exposure to the pressures of acculturation.

In most pioneer houses the interior was furnished and arranged in traditional fashion. Apart from the pich in the mala khata, the usual furnishings would be "a couple of wide bunks built of rough lumber, a small table fashioned of the same and a stationary bench along one side of the room."[40] In the absence of closets a wooden rail (*zherdka*), suspended from the ceiling, ran the length of the north wall, and from it implements and apparel could be hung.[41] This furnishing corresponded to that of the average peasant household in the western Ukraine at the end of the nineteenth century.[42] The austere decor was relieved by the placing of flowering plants in the curtainless windows and the placing of icons and religious calendars on the eastern wall of the velyka khata: "Clustering around the picture [icon] there was sure to be some cunningly devised flowers, fashioned of tissue paper as gaudy in hue as were the pictures themselves. Since the walls of the rooms were limewashed the pictures, against the glistening whiteness, proved very effective."[43]

Ceilings, if not limewashed to the whiteness of the walls, were colored blue, done simply by adding extra washing blue to the limewash. Wooden trim around the windows and the wooden door was left unpainted in the early years, but when commercial paints became available, it was painted, with a remarkable degree of uniformity, in green or sky blue.[44]

Ukrainians in Western Canada

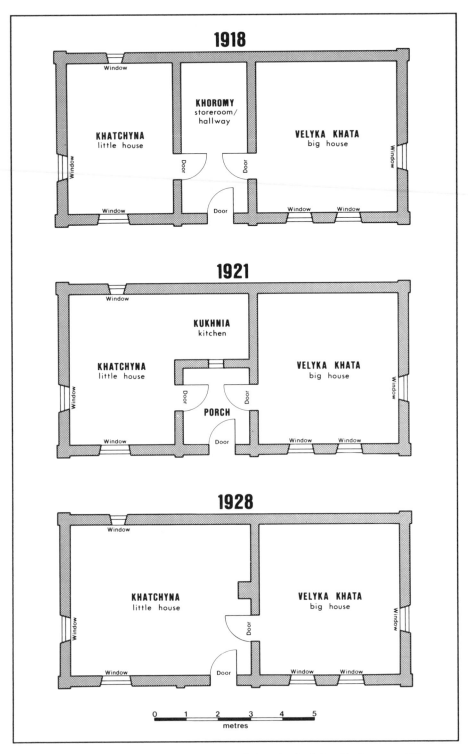

Fig. 17-12 Evolution of the floor plan of the Grekul family house, Alberta, 1918–1928. (After Hohol.)

Stylistic Variation

Ukrainian settlers in western Canada came from a wide array of districts in both Galicia and Bukovyna. In their homeland areas buildings bore a distinctive appearance associated with their locality. These local peculiarities, fine nuances of decor, intricacies of design and form, were frequently obscured in the turmoil of migration, the shock of settlement, and the pressures of survival in a raw frontier environment (Fig. 17-13). Nevertheless, the process and pattern of Ukrainian settlement in the West, whereby some areas were settled almost exclusively by immigrants from one particular district, even village, in the Ukraine, created an opportunity for these local characteristics to be transferred to the new landscape. The extent to which this was done has been the subject of some debate, centering principally on whether one can distinguish stylistic variation among Ukrainian houses in Canada based upon the province of origin in the Ukraine. Although a stylistic identification of a Galician and a Bukovynian design, based on field observations, was made in the 1970s, Bilash has recently argued that this is essentially unsatisfactory, since it divides the community purely on the basis of an Austrian administrative boundary that ignored the realities of regional ethnographic divisions.[45]

Nevertheless, in areas settled by immigrants from Galicia or Bukovyna, certain respective stylistic characteristics appeared in their dwellings with sufficient frequency that, even in the 1980s, it is possible to determine with reasonable accuracy the pioneer's province of origin. Whether some of the features of house design or form are truly a reflection of the regional types

Fig. 17-13 The structures, the house and granary of J. Mihaychuk, Vita, Manitoba, 1915, illustrate the retrenchment of building style caused by emigration. The house (*on right*) is smaller and more functional than the original Ukrainian house. It lacks the flamboyance and intricate decoration typically found in more established areas.

found in the old country or whether these apparent differences were simply manifestations of the generally later settlement of the Bukovynians and their occupation of more remote and marginal territory and consequent tendency to retain aspects of traditional folk culture, is a moot point.

In areas settled by Bukovynians, houses with heavy hipped or hipped-gable roofs with wide overhanging eaves were frequently encountered. This eave projection was always especially pronounced along the southern facade of the house, where it was often supported by a number of pillars so as to form a porch. This roof overhang was up to 3 feet on the sides and rear and 5 feet at the front, although a more common projection was of about 2½ feet on the front facade, slightly less on the other walls. To support the heavy roof overhang, the topmost wall logs were frequently flared outwards towards the roof edge to form a cornice bracket (see Fig. 17-5). Most were in the form of a smooth outward, slightly convex curve; others were stepped.[46]

These elements also appeared on houses in areas settled by immigrants from Galicia, but far less frequently. On the odd occasion when they did appear, they were of a more restrained style than those on Bukovynian houses. Since in these Galician-settled areas houses did not have the extensive overhang on the roof, the cornice bracket, if present, was not a prominent feature. The gable roof appeared to predominate,[47] and the use of a pent extension on the gable at eave level became a distinctive feature (Fig. 17-14). These were placed so as to deflect rain away from the mud plaster on the wall immediately below the gable.

A further element that, in the Alberta block settlement at least, appeared to be most commonly associated with the houses built by Bukovynian settlers was the "eyebrow vent" on the roof's front slope (see Fig. 17-5). According to

John C. Lehr

Fig. 17-14 Abandoned Ukrainian pioneer house, Tolstoi, Manitoba. Frame and fill (Red River frame) construction that was covered with limewashed mud plaster. (Photo by J. Lehr.)

informants, these predated the building of the chimney, at one time being used as a means of smoke dissipation, but were kept after the chimney was constructed and then used as a means of attic ventilation.[48]

A further difference observed between surviving pioneer houses in areas of Galician and Bukovynian settlement was the greater predominance of the three-room house in Bukovynian areas, the two-room variant being more commonly found in Galician areas. This difference has been ascribed to a homeland regional stylistic difference, although no hard evidence to support this supposition has been documented. Bilash has argued against the apparent association of house plans with either group.[49] In light of Hohol's documentation of the evolution of one Bukovynian house from a three- to two-room plan, it might well be argued that the prevalence of one type in any district is a reflection of the rate of economic progress and cultural adaptation and that those who came from Galicia simply adapted the basic folk design more readily than did the Bukovynian immigrants, thereby creating in the landscape a pattern that had little to do with homeland antecedents.

One of the more minor elements of the domestic landscape, the use of color in decorative trim, has remained as a cultural element closely connected to regional group. Urban immigrants, who had little avenue for the expression of their material culture in their tract housing, distinguished themselves by their color preferences in trimming their houses.[50] In the rural areas these preferences were equally pronounced. Among the Galicians blue was a favored trim color, whereas among the Bukovynians green enjoyed a wide popularity. This largely unconscious perpetuation of group preferences or habits has survived. In many instances it has been transferred to modern architect-designed or mass-produced houses.[51]

The Sacred Landscape

Within a few years of settlement, as soon as the immigrants felt a degree of security, they began to build their churches, invariably in the styles of the homeland as they were remembered. The architectural influence most evident was seldom the ancient style of the Carpathian Mountains but the Russified Byzantine architecture, which had begun to replace the older forms in the western Ukraine.[52] In the pioneer environment, communities seldom had the expertise, capital, or time, to construct lavish church buildings. Indeed, many churches were simple in form and waited several years before the addition of the ornate pear-shaped *banyas* (Byzantine cupolas) that had become so closely associated with the Ukrainian church that they served as a symbol of ethnic identity.[53] Ukrainian churches were, and still are, distinguished by their separate bell towers and by their plan, generally being divided into three sections on an east-west axis, with the central section slightly larger than the adjacent two.[54] In the early years most churches were constructed in the same fashion as the houses; most were of log, some even had thatched roofs, and all were built by local craftsmen from materials gathered locally.

The introduction of larger churches, often of frame construction and carrying the hallmarks of professional architectural design, marked the passing of the pioneer era.[55] In most areas of the Canadian West, this did not take place until the 1920s, 1930s, or later. Since this passage was dependent upon the degree of acculturation and economic progress within the locality, it was by no means a simultaneous event, even within the broader Ukrainian blocks of settlement. More so than that of the house, the form of the church was highly resistant to forces of assimilation and acculturation. In both the (Ukrainian) Greek Catholic [Uniate] Church and the (Russian) Greek Orthodox, the church functioned as a guardian of cultural and ethnic identity, fulfilling the role of a national state in promoting ethnic heritage, linguistic survival, and spiritual awareness. This unique role buffered it from the many acculturative influences that gradually came to pervade the Ukrainian settlements. Until the sense of national consciousness had faded in the Ukrainian-Canadian community, to build a church in accordance with Anglo-Canadian tastes was unthinkable.

The Ukrainian Landscape in the 1990s

For the wider rural landscape there was no such protective screen. The demands of adapting to a mechanized and highly capitalized market-oriented farming economy ensured the rapid encroachment of Anglo-American elements on farm operation. Barns, stock shelters, and implement sheds in the traditional design became either inadequate or inefficient and so saw rapid modification or replacement by popular North American designs that owed nothing to the folk tradition. Indeed, within his peer group the Ukrainian farmer derived prestige from mechanization and modernization, the two forces that speeded abandonment or replacement of the traditional in the landscape.

Within the house and its immediate environs, the authority of the woman provided a measure of protection from acculturation, for she was usually more conservative, accepting change more slowly, judging the need for change and being judged by her peers on the maintenance of domestic skills and adherence to aesthetic traditions based squarely upon the deep-set patterns of Old World peasant society. She was less exposed than her partner to the alien tastes and fashions of Anglo-American society, whether in the adoption of North American dress, incorporation of English into her lexicon, or the alteration of the physical space within which she functioned. Virtue lay in the familiar; those elements of the domestic landscape in her charge changed slowly, and changed little until a new Canadian-born generation saw fit to adopt styles more expressive of their perception of their role in Canadian life.

When it came, change to the domestic landscape was often dramatic. Whereas incremental adaptation of the interior of the house was seldom evident from the exterior, the decision to build a new dwelling generally signaled a sharp parting of the ways with the traditional. Modern Anglo-American design was clearly emblematic of progress, the adoption of a new role in mainstream society, and at least a partial assumption of the aesthetic tenets of Brittanic culture (Fig. 17-15). Nevertheless, hints of the traditional still remained in the new buildings in the choice of colors for interior and exterior decoration, in the patterns of use developed within a reorganized interior, in the methodology of construction, and in the orientation of the dwelling. Occasionally, ethnic hybrids appeared in the developing rural service centers, when conventional false fronts were married to traditionally constructed buildings.

Today, a century since the first Ukrainian settlers set foot in western Canada, much of their impress upon the landscape has become blurred and is fading quickly. Farm consolidation, rural out-migration, and retreat from the agricultural margins have all combined to speed farm abandonment and

Fig. 17-15 First and second houses, Stuartburn district, Manitoba, 1921. (Ukrainian Cultural and Educational Centre, Winnipeg, Professor Iwan Boberskyj Collection.)

Fig. 17-16 Ukrainian Orthodox graveyard, bell tower, and church, Sirko, Manitoba. (Photo by J. Lehr.)

the physical decay of pioneer artifacts. In most areas of Ukrainian settlement the white-sided cottages may still be seen scattered across the landscape. Most are abandoned and yearly become increasingly screened by the unchecked growth of the sheltering trees and bushes planted by their builders. Others have descended the social scale and serve as granaries or as livestock shelters. A few remain as farm dwellings, disguised with modern siding and roofs of asphalt shingles. More prominent are the often imposing churches of the Ukrainian Catholics and Ukrainian Orthodox, for even their modern buildings retain elements of the ethnic tradition in Byzantine cupolas and distinctive separate bell towers. Alongside lie the graveyards where weathered wooden crosses with faint Cyrillic lettering mark the graves of the pioneers (Fig. 17-16), while glossy slabs of black granite with English lettering denote those of their descendants, a metaphor for the wider ethnic landscape.

John C. Lehr

18

The Navajo in the American Southwest

Stephen C. Jett

THE NAVAJO (*Diné* in the Navajo language) are an Apachean-speaking tribe now living in an area comprising some 25,000 square miles in northwestern New Mexico, northeastern Arizona, and southeastern Utah.[1] Their Athapaskan ancestors migrated southward from somewhere in present-day western Canada, arriving in northernmost New Mexico between A.D. 1000 and 1400 (Fig. 18-1). The numbers of these pre-Navajo were probably not great, and they may have arrived in several small independent bands.[2] Although it is possible that during their southward drift the Diné learned the rudiments of agriculture from Plains or Colorado Plateau tribes, it is generally believed that upon their arrival in the Southwest they still subsisted largely on wild plant and animal foods, leading a nomadic existence in the mountains and foothills.

Historical Background of Navajo Settlement in the Southwest

History and archaeology place the earliest known territory of these people in the upper San Juan and Chama drainages in the present New Mexico–Colorado border country, not far northwestward of the Pueblo Indians of the Rio Grande Valley. This old homeland, though largely abandoned today, is still referred to as *Dinétah* (Navajo Country). Contact and trade with Puebloans, and the receipt of occasional Puebloan fugitives fleeing the Spanish conquerors after A.D. 1598, led to adoption of some of their plants and farming techniques and certain political offices, but few other Puebloan cultural traits. A combined farming-gathering-hunting strategy seems to have allowed rapid population growth and the establishment of extensive floodwater farms in the lower-elevation areas; about 1629, the Spaniards began applying the term *Navahuu*—Tewa Puebloan for "valley fields" or "to take from the fields"—to this group of Apaches. Despite adoption of the horse from the Spanish, the proto-Navajo's emphasis on farming led to a more sedentary existence, although seasonal moves to hunting and gathering areas continued to be usual.

In 1680, the Puebloans successfully revolted against the Spanish, who fled southward. However, following the reconquest of New Mexico in 1692,

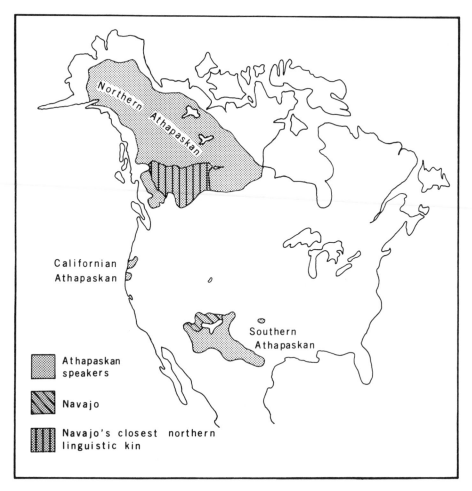

Fig. 18-1 Distribution of Athapaskan speakers. (From Jett and Spencer 1981, 3.)

Spanish reprisals caused considerable numbers of Puebloans to flee to Dinétah. This influx was crucial to Navajo cultural history, for it resulted in a fusion of Puebloan practices such as weaving, Pueblo-style dress, clans, complex ceremonialism, painted pottery, and certain building methods, with the Northern Hunter culture and Athapaskan language of the Apacheans.[3] The Puebloans also introduced certain crops they had adopted from the Spanish, and, more importantly, livestock; the raising of goats and sheep was to have a fundamental impact on this new hybrid people, the true Navajo.[4]

Stock provided a movable but controllable alternative to game as a source of meat. When the Ute and Comanche obtained horses and firearms in the mid-eighteenth century and their raids (and later those of the Spanish) drove the Navajo from most of Dinétah, the Navajo from that region were able to move into areas to the west and southwest and to adopt a settlement strategy of dispersal, mobility, and concealment.[5] Farming, along with gathering and hunting, continued on a reduced scale, but sheep and goats

Stephen C. Jett

became a linchpin of subsistence; and the horse provided a vehicle for human locomotion.[6]

The Navajo in the Nineteenth and Twentieth Centuries

The westward expansion of the Navajo continued through much of the nineteenth century, accelerated by Anglo-American punitive expeditions against the tribe from the time of the Mexican War (1846–1848) until near the end of the Civil War.[7] The year 1864 saw the beginning of a four-year deportation of most of the Navajo to a small reservation at Ft. Sumner in eastern New Mexico. Their experience at Bosque Redondo Reservation taught them both the futility of further fighting and the utility of many Anglo tools and techniques.[8]

At the end of their confinement, in 1868, the Diné returned to their homelands, both from the Bosque and from the western wilds adjacent to the Colorado River, to which some had fled to escape captivity. Numbers of eastern and central Navajos moved into the more westerly areas as well.

Peace, plus the coming of the railroad in 1881, allowed both the renewed growth of farming, encouraged by irrigation projects, and the partial entry of the Navajo into the national economy, through the trading of wool (raw and as hand-loomed rugs) for commercial foodstuffs and drygoods. The burgeoning sheepherding economy, however, was brought low in the 1930s and 1940s by government-mandated stock reduction designed to conserve the deteriorating range. Postwar economic collapse on the reservation also led to further flock reductions as animals were consumed for survival.[9]

Service by many Navajos in the armed forces and in field and factory during World War II greatly increased the Navajo's familiarity with modern Anglo ways, including housing. Postwar cultural change was rapid, accelerated by stepped-up government programs, including education, and by improved transport. Wage work and welfare far outstripped farming, sheepraising, and rug weaving as sources of subsistence.[10]

Navajo Settlement Patterns

The pre-Navajo hunters had brought with them from the North a pattern of dispersed settlement and seasonal migration that, in modified form, continued to serve them well in the Southwest, in the context of small, scattered farms and mobile livestock resources. The basic socio-territorial group was the extended matrilocal family, or homestead (residence) group, which operated as an economic unit, sometimes cooperating with one or more related neighboring homestead groups as resident lineages (coresidential kin groups). Local bands, comprising a number of homestead groups, evolved into communities, which came to be focused on specific trading posts. Only occasionally did the premodern Diné act at the level of the tribe as a whole.[11]

Land was not ownable, according to Navajo thinking, but use rights to farm land could be obtained, maintained, and inherited (usually matrilineally) as long as those rights continued to be more or less regularly exercised. Originally, pasturelands were open to all, but population growth and herd expansion gradually led to the evolution of "customary-use areas," in which one family would retain grazing privileges; this was formalized, during the mid-twentieth century, into a grazing-permit system ultimately tied to traditional-use areas.[12]

Various patterns of seasonal movements developed, according mainly to local differences in the relative importance of herding versus farming. Where farming opportunities were reasonably good, families might establish summer homesteads in the valleys, near their floodwater fields; after the harvest, they would move to their winter homestead, in the intermediate elevations, where pinyon pine and juniper provided plenty of winter firewood. During the summer, a few family members might also take the flocks to a "sheep camp" amid the glades and meadows of the highlands.

A different pattern characterized many areas where pastoralism predominated. Although smaller lowland fields might be planted in the spring, only a few, or no, family members would remain to tend them. Most of the group would move the goats and sheep into the higher country, to exploit the summer grazing opportunities. They would return to the valleys for the fall harvest and remain in the lower, less snowy country through the winter.

Until the establishment, in the twentieth century, of numerous stock ponds and windmills, large areas of (usually sparse) pasture were usable only when winter snows or mid-summer rains provided some seasonal water. Seasonal movements involved longer distances in the past than at present. Shrinking family land-use territories resulting from population growth, plus the development of new water sources, have reduced mobility.[13]

These transhumant movements involve the establishment of two or more homesteads with permanent dwellings, plus, in some cases, scattered, temporary sheep camps. The number of dwellings in these homesteads varies according to how many individuals reside there, which, in turn, is influenced by local resource (and, today, employment) availability. A traditional homestead might include the dwelling of the parents and their unmarried children and one additional dwelling for each married daughter and her husband and their offspring. If there are single adult relatives or a particularly large number of children, an additional dwelling or dwellings may be erected for them to live or sleep in. There will be a summer shade or *ramada*, a sheep corral, a horse corral, and perhaps other, minor structures, including animal sheds and shelters, storage structures, outdoor fireplaces and bread ovens, a sudatory, and, today, a privy. The homesteads of two or more groups that form a resident lineage may be located near each other for social reasons and to facilitate economic cooperation.

Dwellings have always been located with plenty of elbow room between them, and with little or no discernible pattern of arrangement. Until after World War II, multiroom dwellings were almost nonexistent; if more people needed to be housed, additional, separate, one-room units would be built, rather than adding rooms to existing structures.[14]

This traditional Navajo pattern of settlement pertained (and, to a considerable degree, still pertains) over some 16 million acres, mostly on the Navajo Indian Reservation but also on the mixed-ownership checkerboard area to the east and on the Ramah, Cañoncito, and Alamo reserves in New Mexico. There are perhaps 175,000 Navajos today, and they are anything but a minority group in their own territory. They completely surround the

Stephen C. Jett

334

Hopi reservation and are bordered by Anglo-Americans to the north, west, and southwest and by Anglos, Hispanos, and Puebloans to the east and southeast.

Early Evolution of the Hogan

Canadian Athapaskans traditionally lived in conical structures consisting of a tripod framework of poles, against which other poles were leaned; the exterior was covered with hides, bark, brush, or boughs, held in place by additional poles. In the case of the Beaver Athapaskans—linguistically closely related to the Navajo—the three main poles were forked, and interlocked at their upper ends. Northern Athapaskans also constructed brush- and bough-covered single and double lean-tos.

Archaeological and documentary evidence of the dwellings of the proto-Navajo Dinétah phase (circa 1400–1696) in northwestern New Mexico is limited, but it suggests that the northern-type conical dwelling, with a tripod framework of interlocked forked poles, was used.[15] Whether or not these structures were earth-covered, as were later hogans (circular or polygonal one-room Navajo dwellings) is not certain. However, it seems quite likely that application of an earthen covering was one consequence of the Pueblo Revolt of 1680 and its aftermath.

When the Spanish reconquered New Mexico in 1692, many Puebloans (especially Jemez) fled to Dinétah and joined the Apaches de Navahuu there. The resulting intermixing gave rise to a hybrid culture, distinct from both Apache and Puebloan but containing a blend of both. The Diné were now a distinctive society—the Navajo—and had entered a new era of their history, the Gobernador phase (1696–1770). In the West, the less Puebloized culture of the period is called the del Muerto phase.

The Puebloan refugees introduced many of their building types and techniques. One of these was the stone-and-adobe masonry *pueblito:* a multi-room, rectilinear defensive and habitation structure with flat, earth-covered horizontal-beam roofs. It is believed likely that at this time the Puebloan practice of covering the roof poles with juniper bark and earth was applied to the Athapaskan tipiform brush- or bark-covered dwelling. Thus was created the conical forked-pole hogan, the classic Navajo hogan, the form that was the most common Navajo dwelling type in most areas until early in the twentieth century (Fig. 18-2).[16] The earth covering was probably also applied to the lean-to dwelling during this period, creating another, though minor (and now obsolete) type of shelter, the lean-to hogan (Fig. 18-3).[17]

In addition to serving as dwellings, forked-pole hogans seem to have become the new substitute for the Puebloan *kiva*, or ceremonial chamber. For the larger, more elaborate ceremonies, another kind of structure was created. The Puebloan shade, or ramada—four or more vertical forked posts supporting a bough-covered flat roof—had its roof and leaning-pole sides covered with bark and earth, to form the leaning-log hogan.[18] As described below, this initially uncommon ceremonial form ultimately evolved into a common dwelling type.

Another hogan form emerged early in the Gobernador phase. Employ-

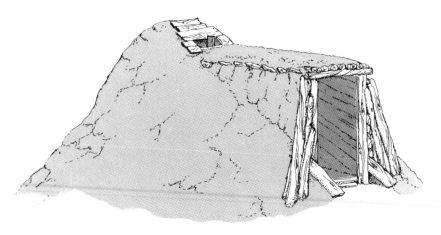

Fig. 18-2 Conical forked pole hogan with extended entryway, Navajo Mountain, Utah, 1970. (Drawing by S. Leyba.)

Fig. 18-3 Hypothetical reconstruction of a double lean-to-hogan. (Drawing by S. Leyba.)

ing a rare construction technique, which had a long history in the Anasazi (Basketmaker and Pueblo) Southwest, this dome-shaped dwelling involved logs piled in even-tiered fashion. A number of logs would be laid in a rough circle; a second tier, of somewhat shorter logs, would be laid from center to center of the logs of the first tier. Addition of more tiers, juniper-bark chinking, and earth, resulted in creation of a corbeled-log hogan (Fig. 18-4).[19] This round structure was considered "female" as opposed to the pointed, "male," conical forked-pole hogan.[20] At or near the summit of all hogans was a smoke hole.

Finally, Puebloan stone masonry building techniques began to be applied to the circular hogan form, and stone hogans—first with flat roofs, later with corbeled-log ones—came to be the most often built type in the treeless San Juan Basin of northwestern New Mexico (Fig. 18-5).[21]

Thus, most of the common hogan types had evolved by the end of the first quarter of the eighteenth century, probably all under strong Pueblo-refugee influence. Each of the forms (except the lean-to hogan) persisted through the nineteenth century and up to the present day.

Fig. 18-4 Earth-covered corbeled-log hogan near Rainbow Lodge, Arizona. (Photo by R. Farber, 1970.)

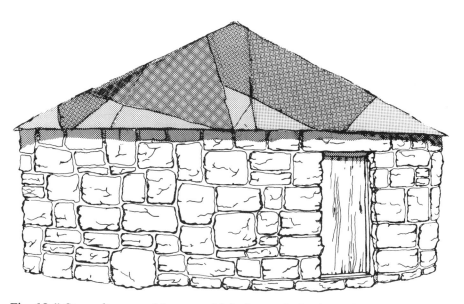

Fig. 18-5 Stone hogan with pyramidal plywood plank roof, St. Michaels, Arizona, 1968. (Drawing by S. Leyba.)

Dispersal, Revivalism, and a New Hogan Form

By 1770, Dinétah had been largely abandoned, because of Ute, Comanche, and Spanish incursions; and the Navajo from that area were entering a new phase, the Cabezon (1770–1864), characterized by a shift in emphasis from a more sedentary farming economy and settlement to a more mobile livestock-raising pattern based mainly on goats and sheep. The corresponding phase in the West, the de Chelly, continued to be freer of Puebloan influences. Maximum dispersal and concealment came to characterize Navajo settlement.

Early in this period, or perhaps even in the latter Gobernador phase, Athapaskan cultural values seem to have reasserted themselves, in reaction to the threat of excessive Puebloization by the refugees. Blessingway, the central ceremony of Navajo religion, may have arisen at this time. Blessingway expressly rejects Puebloan dwellings and painted pottery; the latter ceased to be made, and the building and use of rectilinear, multiroom pueblitos either terminated or evolved toward a merging with the stone, single-unit, circular hogan form.

Continued harassment by Utes and Spaniards led to greater and greater dispersal of the people, as did the search for new pasture. Many eastern Navajos moved west of the Chuska Mountains and into Arizona, taking their more hybrid culture to the western Navajo. Perhaps for the first time, Navajos began to occupy the areas north and west of the Hopi pueblos.

Although conflicts between Navajo and Spaniard had erupted periodically through the latter half of the eighteenth century, relations notably deteriorated following Mexican independence in 1821. Navajos raided Hispano holdings for livestock, and Hispanos raided for slaves and in reprisal. But this interaction also led to some cultural exchange. The latter may have inspired a new hogan type, one that eventually was to become the most popular form over wide areas—the cribbed-log hogan (Fig. 18-6).

In early colonial times, German-speaking Silesian miners had been brought to central Mexico. It was apparently they who introduced there the cribbed-log house-building technique, employing odd-tiered horizontal logs whose ends interfinger.[22] The same technique was also employed in later colonial times in eastern North America. Whatever its immediate source, cribbed-log construction was established in the Santa Fe, New Mexico, area

Stephen C.
Jett

Fig. 18-6 Cribbed-log hogan with earth-covered corbeled-log roof. (Drawing by S. Leyba.)

by the mid-eighteenth century and became a common Hispano building method in the wooded mountains.[23]

Presumably it is due to observing this building method, perhaps while being held as slaves, that a few Navajos had, by the 1840s, taken the small step from corbeling to cribbing in hogan construction. Possibly with occasional exceptions,[24] these early cribbed-log hogans, unlike Hispano cribbed-log structures, did not employ corner-timbering (notching); corner-timbering requires a certain skill, and is difficult with aboriginal stone axes. It was not until the end of the nineteenth century that this hogan form was to begin to come into its own.

The Earlier Reservation Period (1868–1899)

After 1868, when the Navajo were released to their own country from Bosque Redondo, warfare all but ceased, permitting a more sedentary, if still transhumant, existence. In 1881, the railroad arrived at the borders of the new reservation. Even before this time, numbers of steel axes had been distributed by the government; but they became much more readily available after that date. Sedentariness and the availability of better axes encouraged the construction of larger, more substantial hogans; they also changed the frequency of occurrence of various types of hogans and led to certain alterations in these types.

The leaning-log hogan—square in plan, with rounded corners—had, up to this time, been erected essentially only for ceremonial use, for which the usual conical forked-pole hogan was often too small. The cutting and hauling of many more logs was required for construction of a leaning-log hogan, a significant task when stone axes were used. But the cutting of timbers became markedly easier with steel axes, and sub-rectangular or circular leaning-log hogans began to overtake the forked-pole type in areas where sufficient timber was available, beginning about 1890.[25] The squarish ones usually carried flat roofs, the round ones, domical corbeled-log roofs.[26] The round form—more Navajo in plan and easier to heat—came to predominate.

In the meantime, government policy was to encourage Navajos to build rectangular, "civilized" log or stone houses (which they had rarely done),[27] and a certain number of leaders, among others, did so. A knowledge of corner timbering (mostly, saddle notching) seems thus to have been gained, and appears to have been transferred to the heretofore rare cribbed-log hogan, perhaps in the early 1880s. Long timbers could be notched with steel axes and stacked to make a solid and roomy polygonal structure with a corbeled-log roof.[28] But these hogans were hard to heat with an open wood fire and seem to have been used initially mainly for ceremonial purposes.

The Middle Reservation Period (1900–1945)

Increases in the efficiency with which dwellings were heated seem to have contributed importantly to an increase in the size of hogans. The first innovation in heating was the flue, usually a ramshackle device made from old cans, kettles, buckets, sheet metal, and the like, suspended by wire and sometimes attached to adobe or stone-slab fireplaces. The draw that these tubes provided resulted in faster, more complete combustion of firewood;

the increased quantities of wood consumed could be felled and split with the now-common steel axe. Use of such flues became widespread around the turn of the century.

Flues were followed by stoves made from cut-off oil drums, with stove-pipes rising from them to the smokehole. Such stoves are still in use, but commercially made cast-iron cooking and heating stoves became increasingly common.[29] Stoves further improved heating efficiency; and for the first time, it became practical to have large hogans for winter as well as summer residence. This paved the way for the wide diffusion of the capacious round leaning-log hogan as a dwelling and, somewhat later, the ascendency of the cribbed-log hogan.

In many ways, the Navajo of the first half of the twentieth century had a way of life equivalent to that of frontier Anglo-Americans of the first half of the nineteenth century. Anglo-Americans then were, for the most part, long beyond the log cabin stage and, even in rural areas, were rapidly shifting to gas and oil stoves for cooking and heating; the use of electricity was spreading. The Navajo, on the other hand, had barely begun to build cribbed-log cabins, or even cribbed-log hogans; were only then getting wide access to metal axes and farm tools; had no electricity, running water, or telephones; and were just in the process of acquiring wood-burning stoves. Even the trading posts—largely a railroad-era phenomenon—were only then becoming general stores, adding a variety of products to their meager range of flour, sugar, coffee, tobacco, utensils, and drygoods.[30]

The rectangular log house (in a form more Hispano than Anglo) first became somewhat common among the Navajo in the 1890s, because of governmental encouragement to build that type and because of exposure to the form in governmental buildings, trading posts, railroad section houses, and the like. However, neither the cribbed-log house nor the stone house (built particularly in treeless areas) ever approached dominance among dwellings of the Navajo. What did occur was the widening application of the corner-timbered cribwork technique to the hogan form—as nearly as this could be done, for long, horizontal logs produced not a circular plan but a polygonal one (most often, with six or eight sides). But a polygonal plan was deemed a sufficient concession to circularity to make the dwelling Navajo, to make it a *hogan,* not a foreign, rectilinear *house;* as such, the cribbed-log hogan was suitable for ceremonies.

A minor and rather recent type of hogan is the abutting-log hogan, in which stacked logs are unnotched and even-tiered, their ends nailed to vertical corner posts.[31]

It seems likely that the earliest corner-timbered, "modern" cribbed hogans were built near Indian agency headquarters at Fort Defiance, Arizona. At any rate, once axes and heating devices permitted, this structure, initially built for ceremonies, rapidly became the preferred ordinary dwelling over a wide area, and by mid-twentieth century had diffused throughout most of the central part of the Navajo Country, where appropriate timber (ponderosa and pinyon pine) was available.

In regions where only scrub timber (especially, juniper) or no timber at all was available, and in better-timbered areas distant from the center of diffusion of the cribbed-log hogan, older dwelling forms persisted. In the west, north, and far east, leaning-log and corbeled-log types predominated, while in the tree-poor San Juan Basin, the stone hogan continued to be the usual kind. All of these older forms waned in the central area as the cribbed-log hogan waxed in popularity; and everywhere, particularly from the Chuska Mountains eastward, the old conical forked-pole hogan became rare or obsolete.

The distribution patterns of hogan types came directly and indirectly to reflect the degree of influence from the outside (e.g., axes, corner-timbering, stoves) as well as to reflect the local availability of building materials. Another acculturative factor was the development of a road system and Navajo acquisition of buckboard wagons—while the rest of the country was buying automobiles. Wagons allowed the hauling of construction timbers some distance from their source. The limits even of this new transport medium continued to be reflected in the pattern of different types of hogans.

During the early twentieth century, two developments probably encouraged another evolutionary trend in hogan construction, the employment of vertical walls. These developments were the use of wooden doors and the adoption of Anglo-American manufactured or homemade furniture such as beds, tables, shelves, and bureaus. In some hogans, the entryway extended from the side of the hogan and had a vertical doorframe, from which hung the door covering, consisting of hides, a blanket, or a mat (see Fig. 18-2). Of course, the diffusing cribbed-log technique allowed for vertical doorways without any extension. But in areas far from wood suitable for long timbers, or from the most intense acculturative influences, the trend toward verticality of walls and doors manifested itself in the evolution of the palisaded hogan (Fig. 18-7) from the leaning-log hogan. This new vertical-post form usually employed eight or ten uprights upon which the corbeled-log roof was placed. Then, instead of leaners, a more or less vertical palisade of shortish timbers would be set in a trench, the tops of these timbers abutting the

Fig. 18-7 Palisaded hogan with earth-covered corbeled-log roof, Black Mountain area, Arizona, 1970. (Drawing by S. Leyba.)

The
Navajo
in the
American
Southwest

341

undersides of the lowest tier of roof logs. This form became, and remains, the most common hogan type in most of the west and north of the Navajo Country.

Palisading is a small step from the leaning of logs, but this transition in hogan building was certainly facilitated by previous familiarity with the same technique in house construction. New Mexican Hispanos had long utilized this method of construction, particularly at intermediate elevations where scrub timber, but not long logs, was available.[32] Some buildings at the early forts, and some early trading posts, employed palisading, and the method was adopted by Navajos erecting small houses at Fort Wingate in the late 1880s,[33] and possibly earlier.[34] Although never becoming particularly popular, palisaded houses have temporal precedence over palisaded hogans, which seem to have developed only about the turn of the century and to have become widely used by the 1930s. Unlike Hispano palisaded buildings, Navajo ones do not involve fitting tenonned log ends into grooves in head plates.

Navajo Building in the Latter Twentieth Century

In cultural terms, the Navajo Country began definitively to enter the twentieth century in the 1950s. The prolonged off-reservation experience of many Navajos during World War II, plus accelerated governmental and tribal programs in education, employment, welfare, and other social services, escalated the rate of acculturation. So, too, did a major road-building and -paving program that began in the early 1960s, and, somewhat later, the extension of electrical power lines along many of these roads, allowing use of televisions.[35]

Experience in construction work during and after the war made many Navajos familiar with frame and cinder block construction. The first manifestation of this was a proliferation of polygonal plank-sided hogans. In the West, boards were sometimes employed like leaning logs, to create circular leaning-plank hogans; these usually carried corbeled-log roofs. Much more common in the central areas were post-and-plank hogans, in which boards were nailed horizontally to lumber corner posts set into the earth. And a few dwellings were true frame hogans, employing both head and sill plates (Fig. 18-8). These last two types depended entirely on contemporary Anglo house-framing techniques, dimension lumber, and nails. They employed pyramidal or hipped frame roofs covered with mineral-surfaced roll roofing. Such roofs also came to be applied to some cribbed-log hogans. These polygonal plank dwellings probably first developed around the government-operated and tribal sawmills near Fort Defiance in the 1930s, but they gained popularity only in the 1950s and 1960s. Much of the lumber was obtained gratis or at low cost from the mills. The usual practice was to cover the building with tarpaper, chicken wire, and stucco; glazed windows were standard.[36] Planks and stucco have very poor insulation qualities compared to logs and earth, so wintertime habitability of plank hogans depended on the use of stoves.

Knowledge of frame construction techniques, plus accelerating acculturation, doomed the plank hogan to a brief period of importance in certain areas. It, along with hogan building in general, was quickly and largely

*Stephen C.
Jett*

342

Fig. 18-8 Frame hogan, near Wheatfields, Arizona. (Photo by R. Farber, 1970.)

superseded by small, owner-constructed versions of Anglo-American frame houses, usually stuccoed.[37] A minority of houses were built of masonry, using modern materials instead of the stone that had formerly been used. Thus, cinder-block houses (and a few adobe-brick and fired-brick houses) came to be built during the post-1950 period. A very few cinder-block hogans and even fewer adobe-brick and poured-concrete hogans were also erected.[38]

Summary

Over the centuries, Navajo housing has evolved from simple brush- or bark-covered tipi-form or lean-to shelters into a proliferation of more substantial hogan forms. Much of this involved a fusion of Apachean, basically Northern Hunter, building styles, with Puebloan construction techniques, from the late 1600s through the mid-eighteenth century. During the following century, major migration southward and westward out of Dinétah plus much greater dependence on mobile livestock resulted in wide dispersal of these dwelling forms (Fig. 18-9).

Hispano and Anglo influences on construction were apparently first felt as early as the 1840s but began to become significant only with the military defeat of the Navajo in 1864, their confinement at Bosque Redondo from 1864 to 1868, and the coming of the railroad in 1881. The availability of steel axes, the influence of Euro-American log cabin corner-timbering techniques, and improved heating efficiency consequent upon adoption of flues and, later, stoves, and the availability of wagons for transportation of logs all contributed to a flowering of certain capacious hogan types in the late 1800s, forms which spread widely, though at different rates, through the mid-twentieth century.

From World War II on, massive outside influences, increased wage work,

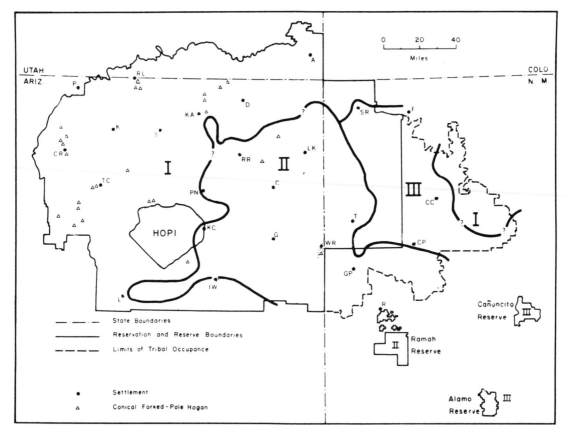

Fig. 18-9 The Navajo Country, showing areas of dominance of various traditional hogan types, circa 1970 (modified from Jett and Spencer 1981, 213.) Numbered zones show areas where different types of hogans dominate as follows: I = vertical-post/corbeled-log, II = cribbed-log, III = stone. The letters on the map represent principal settlements.

and influxes of welfare money and other assistance, pulled the majority of the tribe out of the nineteenth century mode and into that of the twentieth century. By the late twentieth century, frame houses had become by far the predominant Navajo owner-built dwelling, with mobile and modular homes also becoming increasingly common. Even so, old hogan types persisted as ceremonial structures and as dwellings, particularly in more remote areas; this author even observed, in 1985, a brand new conical forked-pole hogan in the Tall Mountain area of the northwestern part of the Navajo Indian Reservation. As a supplemental dwelling, a storage structure, and a ceremonial site, the hogan seems destined to remain for a long time as a symbol of Navajo identity in the landscape of the Southwest.[39]

Stephen C. Jett

19

Spanish Americans in New Mexico's Río Arriba

Alvar W. Carlson

NEW MEXICO'S Río Arriba (upper Río Grande Valley) located in Rio Arriba, Sandoval, Santa Fe, and Taos counties, is one of the oldest and most identifiable European-settled rural cultural regions in the United States (Fig. 19-1). After a small number of Spaniards had made exploratory forays into New Mexico, don Juan de Oñate in 1598 established a Spanish colony in the Río Arriba at the confluence of the Río Grande and the Río Chama.[1] The colony was moved in 1610 to the site of present-day Santa Fe, which became Spain's northernmost colonial capital. Spain's colonizing efforts went awry when the Pueblo Indians revolted in 1680. All of the estimated 2,500 Spanish residents fled southward to El Paso and beyond, and remained there until some returned during the reconquest led by don Diego de Vargas in 1692.[2] Despite the Pueblo Revolt, the Spanish government in Mexico had retained its interest in the Río Arriba, if for no other purpose than the religious conversion of the Pueblo Indians; but it probably valued the region more as a buffer, to provide protection for its Mexican mining settlements.[3]

This region—with Spanish settlement found mostly between Albuquerque on the south and Taos on the north, the Jeméz Mountains and the Río Chama on the west and the Sangre de Cristo Mountains on the east—in time became the Spanish Americans' cultural core and homeland, from which many of their descendants migrated to surrounding counties.[4] (Los Alamos County, location of the world-renowed atomic energy research facilities, was created in 1949 from Sandoval County and is not considered as a part of the Spanish Americans' rural homeland.)

In order to achieve effective and permanent occupation of this portion of the Río Grande's watershed, Spanish colonial officials and colonists again assessed the Río Arriba's physical resources and relative isolation in combination with their own customs and perceptions. Their decisions produced not only distinctive settlement and field patterns but also a distinctive vernacular material culture—aspects of both are still dominant components of the region's rural landscapes.

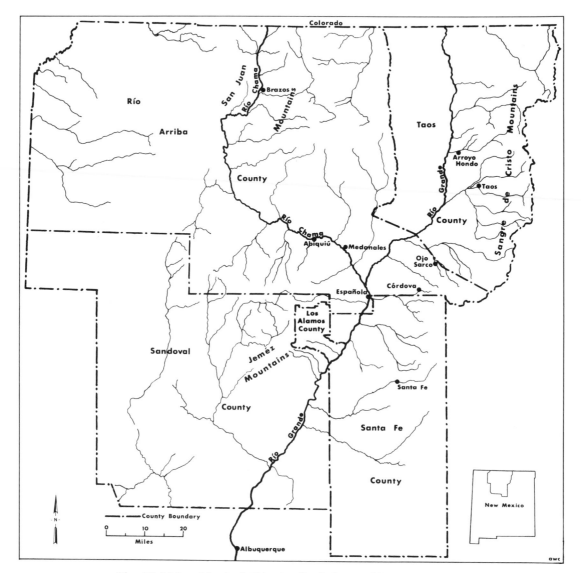

Fig. 19-1 New Mexico's Río Arriba is located largely from the Colorado border south to Albuquerque and from the Sangre de Cristo Mountains west to the Jeméz and San Juan mountains, encompassing the Río Chama and Río Grande valleys.

Spanish and Mexican Land Grants

Alvar W. Carlson

All colonial governments implemented plans in America that allowed their colonists to acquire and settle land. Agriculture was needed for sustaining the colonial population, and by its nature as a form of extensive land use it was ideal for aiding in the establishment of political control of territory. Prior to the Pueblo Revolt, the Spanish government awarded *encomiendas*, large land areas to be used for grazing livestock, primarily to military of-

346

ficers. Holders of these lands, *encomenderos*, also had the right to require labor of and to collect tributes in kind from the increasingly disenchanted Pueblo Indians.[5] A small number of *peonías* and *caballerías* (smaller land units) were given to other military personnel. These land parcels consisted of approximately twenty acres and one hundred acres, respectively.[6] After the reconquest, the Spanish colonial government decided not to issue the controversial encomiendas but to implement a land delivery system that included private and community land grants (*mercedes*). The community land grants, in particular, left the greatest and most lasting imprint upon the region's settled landscape, so they will be analyzed here in some detail.

Spanish agrarian planning, like the Spanish town colonization scheme, considered the characteristics of the physical environment.[7] The upper Río Grande watershed is dominated by rough terrain, high elevations, and aridity, the last stemming from annual precipitation ranging from ten to twelve inches and relatively high evaporation. The surrounding Sangre de Cristo Mountains to the east and the San Juan and Jeméz mountains to the west receive more than twenty inches of precipitation annually. Surface run-off and meltwater from these mountains give rise to a limited number of short but perennial streams whose waters flow ultimately into the Río Grande (see Fig. 19-1). Because of the region's relatively short growing season, it is imperative that adequate irrigation water be readily available at times critical for crop production.[8] The Río Arriba's physical environment is similar to that of Spain and northern Mexico, which were the sources of its colonial officials and colonists.[9]

The isolated Río Arriba offered few economic incentives that could attract large numbers of colonists. To expedite permanent settlement in the region, the Spanish colonial government gave land grants to groups of landless settlers—ten families or at least twelve adults—who were to become farmers, dependent upon the subsistence production of crops and livestock. Initially, all land outside of the Indian pueblos was presumed to be vacant and therefore in the royal domain, *tierras realengas y baldías*, according to the Spanish codified laws and instructions for colonization, the *Recopilación de leyes de los reynos de las Indias*.[10] The potential recipients of community land grants would normally file a petition for land with the local ranking official, who was the justice of the peace (*alcalde*). Because alcaldes were knowledgeable of local environmental conditions and prior land claims in their area, they were required to review the petitions and to inspect the proposed locations of each land grant. The colonial government was thereby given assurances that successful settlement could be maintained by colonists possessing, in particular, sufficient irrigable cropland to sustain themselves and future population growth and that no claims would arise from third parties, such as the Pueblo Indians and adjacent settlers. This information was forwarded to the colonial governor in Santa Fe, who was charged with approving all land grants in the Río Arriba.

Upon the governor's approval, the appropriate alcalde took the petitioners to their land grant. Upon arrival, his first task was to point out the grant's boundaries, which were set by the metes-and-bounds cadastral system. Prominent landscape features, such as mountain ridges and arroyos, were used in outlining the boundaries and corner points. Normally, a community land grant incorporated a microbasin or portions thereof, which consisted of a small elongated floodplain along a perennial stream. The alcalde's next task was to divide the floodplain's bottomland (*joya*) into small tracts (*suertes*), which the grantees took possession of by drawing lots.[11]

Suertes extended from the contemplated community irrigation canal or ditch (*acequia madre*), which was to be dug along a line above the floodplain, across the valley to the stream. This layout enabled irrigation water to flow from the canal or ditch by gravity into lateral ditches on the floodplain and eventually to drain back into the stream. The widths of the suertes were assigned by the alcalde, who considered the extent of the floodplain and the number of settlers. His assessment could also include a person's marital status, the size of a family, and a settler's ability to cultivate land. Generally, attempts were made to provide each grantee with the same amount of bottomland. The width of most suertes measured between 100 and 150 *varas* (one vara equals approximately thirty-three inches). Additional varas of bottomland were given to those settlers who drew lots at the narrow ends of the floodplain. These individually owned irrigable tracts were measured by their widths rather than by their lengths, resulting in indefinite measurements.[12]

Because most of the suertes, especially those in the broader portions of the floodplains, were considerably longer than their widths, they resembled long lots, consisting in many cases of fewer than ten acres (Fig. 19-2). These long lots appear to be similar to those found on the French *seigneuries* laid out first in the 1630s in Canada's St. Lawrence watershed and later on French settlements in Illinois, Indiana, Louisiana, and Mississippi[13] (see Chapter 8). Riverine long lots developed independently in the Río Arriba, however, without French influence, as they did in the Spanish colonies of lower Texas.[14] For instance, in 1695, more than forty settlers received small tracts of land, measured simply in widths, on a land grant in the Santa Cruz Valley, east of present-day Española.[15] Many of these tracts were presumably fashioned as long lots. This settlement and others occurred long before any of the French fur trappers and traders who came to the region had appeared, and there is no Spanish term for long lot to indicate antecedents in Spain. Undesignated bottomland was left for the growth of the community, and it was also divided lengthwise. This land often served temporarily as the community's commons (*ejido*), where the settlers could graze some of their livestock, especially milch cows.[16]

Colonial officials encouraged colonists to settle in clusters for mutual protection from raids by marauding Indians, notably the Comanches, Navajo, and Apaches. A defensive arrangement was accomplished by the way the colonists settled on their suertes. The farmsteads, built above the floodplain so as not to consume valuable irrigable land, formed line villages, *rancherías*. Another arrangement was promoted by Governor Pedro Fermin de Mendinueta, who complained in the 1760s that the settlers should live together within walled *plazas*.[17] Consequently, settlers occasionally were assigned small house sites, *solares*, arrayed in such a way that they could build continuous-walled dwellings that would enclose an open space or plaza.[18] The plaza could be used as a corral for livestock and as a mini-fortress for defense against Indian attacks. These colonists also received suertes on a nearby floodplain. This arrangement was used, for example, in 1796 in the settling of the don Fernando de Taos Grant.[19] In most cases, once the Indian

Fig. 19-2 Aerial photo of long lots in the Spanish-American community of Arroyo Hondo on the Arroyo Hondo Grant, Taos County, settled in 1815. (United States Department of Agriculture, Agricultural Stabilization and Conservation Service, Salt Lake City, Utah, aerial photos DXG-4CC-78 and DXG-4CC-2, October 11, 1962.)

349

menace was brought under control the colonists in time moved to their suertes.

Besides having bottomland, each community land grant was laid out to include large portions of upland and woodland, both designated as communal land. The uplands were to be used as pastures, *dehesas,* for the livestock, mostly sheep. Pasturage was also available in the mountainous woodlands, which were largely of piñon, juniper, and ponderosa pine and which supplied the colonists with building materials, domestic fuel, and game animals.

Although Spain's control of the Río Arriba ended in 1821, Mexican officials carried on essentially the same land policies and continued to issue land grants in the region. More of them, however, went to private individuals than to communities. Heretofore, most of the private land grants had been in the area south of Albuquerque in the Río Abajo, where there were fewer perennial streams with arable floodplains and more pronounced aridity, conditions less suitable for colonization and more suited to extensive pastoralism. After the United States acquired New Mexico from Mexico in 1848, as a result of the Mexican War and the Treaty of Guadalupe Hidalgo, it made preparations to implement its own system of alienating land in the public domain. First, American officials needed to know the extent of the public domain. This led to the controversial adjudication proceedings that determined the validity of 176 land grant claims in the Río Arriba and the extent of the 76 claims that were eventually approved and patented.[20] These proceedings were concluded in 1904.[21]

Approximately one-third of the Río Arriba's patented land grants were definitely community land grants, according to their original petitions. They included approximately one-third (1,450,000 acres) of the total acreage in the patented land grants (4,500,000 acres), which amounted to about one-half of the region's land area. Ranging in size from several thousand acres to nearly 200,000 acres, the community land grants possessed most of the region's many microbasins. Furthermore, some of the private land grants became, in essence, community land grants as the original petitioners sold parcels or allowed settlers to reside on them. For instance, the Cristoval de la Serna Grant in Taos County was given to an individual and his family in 1715, but by the 1870s it had over three hundred residents, many of them landowners.[22]

When land grant claims were rejected and they involved settlements, the Court of Private Land Claims Act of 1891 protected the many settlers who lived on small tracts of land, by giving them ownership of their tracts in fee simple. There was no mass eviction of settlers. In these cases, much of the irrigable bottomland was claimed in parcels that resembled long lots. This was also true of the thousands of small parcels of land the Spanish Americans acquired within the boundaries of the region's Pueblo Indian land grants. The Spanish government had laid out small land grants, averaging 17,000 acres, surrounding the different Indian pueblos, to protect, in particular, their irrigable land from encroachment by Spanish settlers. By the 1850s, however, encroachment had already taken place on many of the Indian land grants. Spanish-American settlement intensified within the Pueblo Indian land grants because both the Mexican and American governments considered the Pueblo Indians to be citizens, thus allowing them to alienate land within their land grants under the presumption of legality.

Fig. 19-3 Spanish-American communities of Chamita, San José, and Hernández, within the San Juan Pueblo Indian Grant. (Río Grande Project, 1936, National Archives, Washington, D.C.)

Thousands of Spanish Americans acquired, by purchase, barter, or as squatters, strips of land that extended from a major irrigation ditch or canal to a stream, including the Río Grande (Fig. 19-3).[23] The non-Indian (Spanish) occupants assumed communal use of the remaining portions of the Pueblo Indian land grants. These occupants were given titles to most of their claims in the latter 1920s and the 1930s, after a review board, the Pueblo Lands Board, was established in 1924 to evaluate the legal conveyance and settlement of each non-Indian parcel.

Spanish Americans had not only settled nearly all of the available irrigable land in the Río Arriba, but they had also implanted an agrarian system that accommodated hundreds of families in a region with limited agri-

Spanish Americans in New Mexico's Río Arriba

cultural resources. If many had not moved onto the Pueblo Indian land grants and migrated in the mid-1800s to adjacent areas, such as the upper Pecos River Valley and Colorado's San Luis Valley, the Río Arriba's growing population would have been confronted with far more serious shortages of irrigable cropland than was actually the case during the 1800s. Although the Spanish Americans experienced a very high infant mortality rate, their numbers grew because of their high birth rates and limited out-migration. The Río Arriba's Spanish-American population doubled from an estimated 20,000 in 1850 to 40,000 in 1900. Spanish-American villages provided bonds of kinship, egalitarianism, and familiarity that resulted in a sense of security for a population that spoke only Spanish in a region that was gradually being engulfed by Anglo-American settlers and their culture. Residents found themselves mired in subsistence agriculture that was further facilitated by the custom of partible inheritance whereby the parents' land was bequeathed equally to their children rather than by primogeniture. Consequently, long-lot farms and other rectangular tracts were partitioned lengthwise to continue to provide irrigable land for each heir, resulting in further intensification of the system of ribbon-shaped parcels.[24] The custom of partible inheritance declined in the early 1900s as seasonal employment increasingly provided an alternative to dependence upon subsistence agriculture and as slow, but permanent, outmigration reduced the number of heirs who needed land.

These methods of acquiring small tracts of land, in conjunction with the use of communal lands, allowed Spanish Americans the opportunity of entry into agriculture with little or no accumulated wealth. In essence, these land units formed the basis for the establishment and the endurance of the Spanish-American culture core and homeland. On the other hand, they also facilitated dense populations, in fact overpopulation, within microbasins that had limited resources. Unfortunately, the Río Arriba emerged during the 1900s as a clearly identifiable region of endemic rural poverty within the American economic system.

Small Farms and Endemic Poverty

The abnormally high percentage of small farms with traditional agriculture and low farm incomes plagued this rural region. For instance, three-fourths of its peak number of farms (8,845 in 1935) averaged twelve acres in size. Over forty percent of all the farms averaged slightly more than five acres. Although the number of farms had declined by 1954, to 4,544, more than forty percent of them averaged about five acres.[25] Some irrigable tracts were reportedly only one-eighth to one-tenth of an acre. In an example of approximately one hundred tracts containing a total of 158 irrigated acres in the 1960s on the Nuestra Señora del Rosario San Fernando y Santiago Grant (Córdova, Rio Arriba County), only fourteen tracts had more than two acres. Tracts averaged about one acre. Many of the grant's landowners had more than one tract, but none owned more than a total of seven acres.[26] The Nuestra Señora land grant had a total of 14,787 acres. The livestock grazing capacity for the Río Arriba's uplands and mountains, because of scanty vegetation, is generally between fifty and one hundred acres per cow for six

Alvar W.
Carlson

months, which further illustrates the meagerness of the region's resources for agriculture.

In 1982 one-fifth of the region's 1,943 farms averaged only four and one-half acres; two-thirds of these included an average of only 3.9 irrigated acres. Farms of under ten acres (389) represented less than one percent of the region's total farm acreage,[27] but many small tracts were undoubtedly not included in the agricultural censuses because they did not meet the combined requirements of minimum acreage and sales of agricultural products that until 1974 defined a farm in the censuses. After 1974, farms were defined as land units having sales of $1,000 or more regardless of size. Then, too, many land units had become residential only and saw at most only part-time farming. In fact, in 1982 ten percent of the region's cropland lay idle.

In many cases, Spanish Americans no longer own the communal portions of their patented land grants. Some of these lands were sold to the United States government during the Depression and the drought of the 1930s and thereafter, and others were forfeited because of tax delinquency. Communal lands were also sold to ranchers, but in nearly all cases the residents of these land grants retained their small irrigable tracts. Moreover, they were able to continue to use most of their communal lands, because they were returned to the public domain and in large part placed under the management of the U.S. Forest Service, which permitted grazing on them.

For many decades, the region's small farms provided Spanish Americans with per capita incomes dependent upon an acre or less. After World War II agricultural sales from the Río Arriba's farms, still characterized by traditional methods and little mechanization, ranked the lowest in New Mexico. In Taos County, average farm product sales in 1945 were under $600 and over seventy percent of the farms produced less than $1,000 in agricultural products. A similar situation existed in the mid-1950s when the majority of the region's farms had average sales of less than $1,200.[28] In 1960, three of the region's counties (Rio Arriba, Sandoval, and Taos) were ranked among the poorest rural counties in the United States.[29] In 1978, one-half of the region's farms were owned by Spanish Americans, and only two out of five of those farms had sales of $2,500 or more. Rio Arriba and Taos counties, which today are home to most of the region's Spanish-American small farmers, had the lowest average farm sales in 1982 of all counties in New Mexico.[30] General welfare assistance of all kinds dating from the 1930s has sustained a large number of the region's rural Spanish Americans.

Aspects of the Vernacular Landscape

As Spanish Americans acquired land in the Río Arriba, they developed and established a vernacular material culture that has remained to a considerable degree intact, especially in the case of buildings.[31] It was not unusual for settlers on America's agricultural frontiers to use initially available cheap building materials. In time, and as settlers accumulated wealth, most abandoned, for instance, their small log cabins and sod houses for larger and more substantial frame houses with large windows and ridge or gable roofs—reflecting their acceptance of the housing styles used by Anglo-Americans. Although the Spanish Americans had resided in the Río Arriba for nearly two centuries, they did not become fully aware of Anglo-American building styles, techniques, and materials until the influx of homesteaders and the arrival of railroads in the late 1800s. Isolation was undoubtedly a factor in the maintenance of the region's vernacular material culture. Moreover, just as being able to acquire small land units had enabled the Spanish Americans to enter agriculture with little capital, their traditionally simple building styles allowed them to construct dwellings despite having few if any financial resources.

Upon arriving in the upper Río Grande Valley, the Spaniards found that the indigenous Pueblo Indians had built multitiered structures (*pueblos*) of small cells enclosed by thick walls of puddled clay mud or adobe.[32] This type of construction was similar to that found in Spain, where the Moors had influenced building styles by using adobe. Unlike the Pueblos, the Spaniards strengthened their adobe by mixing into it straw or grass as a binding material and placing it within forms to create molded bricks. They likewise built small, but separate, houses from the local clay, so the region's built landscape continued to have an earthen appearance. Anglo-Americans, when they arrived considered these mud structures to be inferior and indicative of the residents' economic plight, although they viewed the Indian pueblos with considerable fascination.

Adobe Houses

The earliest Spanish houses were narrow one- and two-room structures of one story (*ranchitos*). Adobe bricks formed walls that were often more than one-and-one-half feet thick, normally placed upon a crude stone foundation to prevent settling and erosion. Each room had an exterior door and one or two small windows. The width of the rooms was determined largely by the manageable lengths (thirteen to fifteen feet) of the horizontally placed ceiling beams (*vigas*), usually made from the straight trunks of the ponderosa pine, by the strength of the *vigas*, and by the weight of the materials used to cover the flat roof (*azotea*). By interlacing peeled saplings and branches (*latias*) in a herringbone pattern between the round or crudely hewn vigas, the roof could be covered with a combination of dirt, mud, brush, and twigs; it was tapered toward the back to provide drainage via wooden troughs (*canales*). Although a room's width was somewhat limited, each room (*sala*) could be fairly long, resulting in a linear structure.

These houses could be enlarged easily by building rooms at either end to extend the straight line of the house or to create an L- or a U-shaped structure. When rooms were built perpendicularly to the original room or rooms, the house began to enclose a small open area that resembled the private courtyard (*placita*) common to houses in Spain. All of the exterior doors and windows opened onto the placita, leaving solid rear walls that gave the appearance of a small fortress and facilitated defense against Indians.[33] Placitas were frequently characterized by the presence of outdoor ovens (*hornos*) and a wellhouse (Fig. 19-4).[34]

Many of the L- and U-shaped structures came about because, under the Spanish-American patriarchal system, a landowner's married sons and their families remained at home and additions were built onto the house, resulting in family compounds. Architectural historian Roland F. Dickey describes

Fig. 19-4 A *placita* on a farmstead in Córdova, Rio Arriba County. Note the *horno* in the left foreground. (Photo February 15, 1939, National Archives, Washington, D.C.)

the process: "Beginning with a single room, the house grew like a game of dominoes. As each son brought home his bride, he added a room to one end of the paternal dwelling. Every room had its own outside door, and the system solved the in-law problem by giving privacy to the married couples of the family."[35] This practice occurred particularly where the landowner had sufficient land to provide subsistence for several families. On occasion, walls were built from these houses to join the outbuildings, resulting in an enclosed *casa-corral*.[36] In general, adobe houses were built largely in the lower elevations, especially in the Río Grande trough, where their thick walls provided the desired insulation during the hot summers and cold winters, and where, also, there was not an abundance of usable timber for building with logs.

Pole and Log Houses

Cultural geographer Charles Gritzner has pointed out there is a lingering opinion that nearly all Spanish-American houses were built of adobe, when, in fact, wood poles and logs were used extensively in the construction of walls, especially in the microbasins found in or near the forested elevations of the mountains.[37] Gritzner maintains that "it is possible that highland areas of northern New Mexico have the greatest concentration of historic log buildings remaining today anywhere in the United States."[38] His assertion is certainly true, for if one were to analyze all of the region's houses that appear to be of adobe construction, one would find that many were built of log walls and covered with an adobe plaster.

It was not uncommon for Spanish settlers in higher elevations to initially

Spanish Americans in New Mexico's Río Arriba

Fig. 19-5 *Jacal* construction and horizontal log with corner notching construction are incorporated in a house near Medanales, Rio Arriba County. Adobe plaster was applied to some of the walls, while others were merely chinked with adobe. (Photo by A. Carlson.)

build small, one-story, flat-roofed houses of a room or two by placing unhewn poles or logs from short juniper and piñon trees vertically into the ground to form palisaded walls. Known as *jacales,* these houses were usually associated with the poorest settlers. Many in time were enlarged to several rooms and often took on an L shape. Spaniards had used this building technique in Mexico; its antecedents can be traced to Spain and to other European countries.[39]

Other Spanish settlers in the Río Arriba used the techniques of horizontal-log construction and corner notching in building houses that were also one story with flat roofs. Although horizontal-log construction is associated primarily with the early housing of northern European colonists, Spaniards also used it, in Spain and in their colonies. They did not, however, use the corner-notching techniques that allowed for a tighter fit of the logs. It appears that the Spaniards learned the technique of saddle corner notching from German miners, who employed it in Mexico during the 1500s. The practice diffused throughout central Mexico, where it was in common use by the 1800s.[40] Presumably it was introduced into the Río Arriba by Spanish settlers from Mexico. Some researchers have suggested that the Río Arriba's Spanish settlers may have adopted corner notching from the Anglo-Americans who entered the region in the first half of the 1800s because of their involvement in trade along the Santa Fe trail.[41]

The spaces between the logs on both horizontal-log houses and jacales were at least chinked with mud or adobe, but it was more common to cover the exterior walls entirely with an adobe plaster (Fig. 19-5). Both house types were, for the most part, as narrow and elongated as those in adobe houses, and probably for the same reasons. These common features also characterized the region's small number of stone houses, built of sedimentary rock from local outcroppings, especially in western Sandoval County.

The Anglo-American Influence on Spanish-American Houses

Although Anglo-Americans knew about New Mexico, as a result of trade activity on the Santa Fe Trail, not many settled in the territory until the opening of its public domain for homesteading. Most Anglo-Americans arrived in the Río Arriba after 1880. Some built log and even stone houses, but they normally did not plaster the exteriors with adobe and they did not build adobe houses. Most chose to build their familiar frame two-story structures, using milled and planed lumber obtained from local Anglo-American–operated sawmills. In any case, Anglo-Americans used the gable or ridge roof that allowed for an attic, occasionally with dormers, and for a wider roof span, which facilitated houses that had larger rooms and were more than one room deep. They were in many cases covered with corrugated metal over tar paper. Wood trim embellishments around the doors and the relatively large windows made for a finished appearance. In addition, a porch (*portal*) or a veranda was added to the front of Anglo-American houses. All of these features contributed to creating the more elaborate houses that characterized what became known as New Mexico's territorial architecture (Fig. 19-6).

Spanish Americans adopted certain aspects of Anglo-American hous-

Fig. 19-6 The Río Arriba vernacular landscape. The house in *center* displays elements of territorial architecture. Brazos, Rio Arriba County. (Photo by A. Carlson.)

ing. In particular, those who were able to afford lumber began to build adobe houses with gable roofs that extended beyond the walls to provide protection for the bricks and plaster. Many owners of older adobe houses merely built ridge roofs over their flat roofs. These new roofs provided attics (*altos*), used largely for storage, with entries by way of exterior ladders or stairways. Seldom was there entry to the attic from within the house as in Anglo-American houses. Speculation exists that the Spanish-American one-and-one-half–story dwelling with an alto may have had antecedents in Spain or in Mexico and that it existed in the Río Arriba before the arrival of the Anglo-Americans. It must be pointed out, however, that these houses in general had altos built of milled lumber, which strongly indicates that the alto was a modification influenced by Anglo-American building techniques.[42] In addition, Anglo Americans may have influenced Spanish-American construction by introducing the practice of building frame walls filled with packed earth. This type of construction in the Río Arriba has not been studied in detail.

Spanish Americans used largely local resources to finish the interiors of their houses. Walls were normally plastered with fawn-colored dirt (*tierra bayeta*) or beige-yellow dirt (*tierra amarilla*), both of which contained particles of mica. Whitewashes, made from *caliche* or a mixture (*yeso*) containing gypsum (*tierra blanca*) and wheat paste, were applied to the walls to lighten the rooms. Little natural light entered the dwellings, as there were only one or two small windows per room and the panes were made from translucent sheepskins (*pergamino*), mica, or selenite. Spanish-American house interiors were distinct in that they were heated by an adobe quarter-round, corner fireplace (*padercita*) rather than by a fireplace placed in the middle of a wall (*fogón*) or a room. The padercita was used also in Spain.[43] The floors were merely of packed earth and, consequently, basements (*soterranos*) were rare. Anglo-Americans also brought change to the interiors of Spanish-American dwellings, by introducing plank floors, glass windows, and cast-iron stoves.

Barns, Gristmills, and Moradas

Because Spanish-American farmers were not dependent upon dairying and their agricultural operations were relatively small, there was no need for a large farmstead with large barns and sheds for sheltering animals and storing hay. Most Spanish Americans had only a few livestock. Sheep, in particular, were generally kept outdoors in winter, even, in some cases, on the range, in the lower elevations. Consequently, small outbuildings (*fuertes*) were characteristic of the farmsteads.[44] Outbuildings in the higher elevations were mostly of one-and-one-half stories, had pitched roofs over small hay lofts, and were built largely of poles and logs (Fig. 19-7). In the lower elevations, adobe bricks were used in the construction of outbuildings. Ridged roofs were often added later. Some farmsteads had small storehouses (*trojas* or *dispensas*) in lieu of house basements.

Aside from these house types and outbuildings, two other buildings distinguished the rural vernacular landscape developed by the Río Arriba's Spanish Americans. One was the gristmill (*molino*), which was located on streams and large irrigation ditches. It was not the gristmill housing that was different from most European mills but the fact that the water wheel turned

Alvar W. Carlson

358

Fig. 19-7 A type of outbuilding known as a *tapeiste*, located in Los Cordovas, Taos County. Hay was placed on top of a platform to keep it from the animals and to provide shelter for livestock. (Photo December 1941, National Archives, Washington, D.C.)

horizontally, rather than vertically, and in a counterclockwise direction. This peculiar placement and direction of the water wheel followed a practice found in the gristmills of Spain.[45] The second building was the meeting-house (*morada*) of the region's Penitentes (Los Hermanos de Jesús), found in nearly every rural community by 1900 (Fig. 19-8).[46] The Penitentes were a religious group peculiar to the Spanish-American southwest. To maintain secrecy, chapters of the brotherhood built moradas, in secluded sites on the periphery of their villages if possible, especially in their early years when, allegedly, there were sanguinary activities associated with the reenactment of the crucifixion of Christ and penitential flagellation during Holy Week. (Some activities of the Penitente brotherhood can be traced to those used by Spain's confraternities [*cofradías*] prior to New World colonization.)[47] Building the morada on the edge of the village often placed it near a hill, which was designated *Calvario.* Moradas began to appear more frequently in the Río Arriba after 1850, largely in response to criticism of the Penitentes by the hierarchy of the Roman Catholic Church and by Protestant Anglo-Americans. Constructed initially as a one-room meeting house, moradas were enlarged to include a chapel (*oratorio*), characterized by the Death Cart (*carreta de la muerte*), holding the allegorical Angel of Death (La Doña Sebastiana), located near the altar, and a storage room and frequently a kitchen. The placement of these additions to the meeting room frequently created an L- or a U-shaped structure. Others were built in a T configuration to resemble a cross. No one building plan was used, probably because none was deter-

Fig. 19-8 One of the two linear Penitente *morada* in Abiquiú, Rio Arriba County. The flat roof was replaced in 1982 with a gable roof. Note the use of stone in the bell tower and the weathered adobe plaster. (Photo by A. Carlson.)

mined by the brotherhood's hierarchy.[48] Moradas were constructed of the same building materials and with the same types of roofs as the Spanish-American houses.

A Persistent Vernacular Landscape

The Spanish-American vernacular landscape in the Río Arriba has persisted largely intact longer than has any other landscape settled by a particular European population. Nevertheless, out-migration during the 1900s, particularly after World War II, has led to considerable abandonment of the old densely settled villages. After more than two centuries of subsistence agriculture, rural poverty emerged as a deeply entrenched characteristic of the region's economic system. This problem can be attributed partially to the Spanish colonial land policies that produced small individually owned units of irrigable land, which were further reduced in size by partible inheritance, a means of accommodating a growing population that could not afford to settle elsewhere. The resultant long lots were ideal for providing cropland for settlers in a region of limited environmental resources but impractical for expanding the scale of agriculture to keep pace with a modern cash economy. At first, in the late 1800s and early 1900s, these conditions helped to push Spanish Americans into the wage economy as seasonal laborers and introduced them to out-migration—although it was slow, because of the many bonds they had with their villages. Military service and the need for

Alvar W. Carlson

laborers in industry during World War II eventually pulled many Spanish Americans from the Río Arriba.

Steady in-migration by Anglo-Americans, to Santa Fe, for instance, and out-migration by Spanish Americans, especially from the relatively isolated rural villages, left the latter group by 1980 a minority population in the Río Arriba. Spanish Americans represented only forty-two percent of the region's total population of nearly 160,000. They continued, however, to be the numerically dominant rural population, particularly in Rio Arriba and Taos counties. Many rural Spanish Americans remain largely dependent upon some form of general assistance to offset their continued poverty.[49] Like the Anglo-Americans who came to the region, some have settled in Santa Fe and Albuquerque, while others have migrated to cities in Colorado, southern California, and elsewhere in the West.

Because those who remain in the rural villages are largely poor, and in many cases elderly, they cannot afford new and modern houses. Therefore, many continue to inhabit dwellings dating back to the eighteenth and nineteenth centuries. Although farming has declined significantly, farmstead outbuildings are sometimes used for nonfarming purposes. Even moradas are still used in many communities but the Penitente brotherhood's membership has declined greatly. Thus, the distinctive Spanish-American vernacular landscape has been retained to a relatively large degree, despite the fact that the housetrailer has become the modern alternative form of cheap housing for the younger generation. Anglo-Americans have acquired old Spanish-American dwellings and restored them, for the sake of preserving an aspect of the Spanish colonial past. Chronic poverty, however, is probably the major reason for the remarkable retention of much of the Río Arriba's vernacular landscape.

20

Germans in Texas

Gerlinde Leiding

THE CULTURAL LANDSCAPE of Texas bears the imprint of people from many nations. Spaniards and Mexicans colonized the land primarily during the eighteenth century. Beginning in the early years of the nineteenth century, southerners from the United States were attracted to Texas by land grants offered to promote population of the Mexican province. Cultural and economic growth gained momentum when European settlers began to arrive after the Texas revolution in 1836. The Germans were the largest group of European immigrants to settle in nineteenth-century Texas. Those who settled in the eastern region of Texas were encouraged to emigrate through the efforts of one individual, Friedrich Ernst; they represent the earlier migration. Those who settled in the western region came later, mainly as organized groups under the patronage of the Verein zum Schutze Deutscher Einwanderer in Texas (Society for the Protection of German Immigrants in Texas). The history of this migration, the expression of German settlement in the landscape, German cultural practices in Texas, and these immigrants' building endeavors will be discussed as separate but parallel regional developments.

The History of German Settlement in Texas

The beginning of German settlement in Texas can be dated to the arrival in 1831 of Friedrich Ernst, former head gardener for the Duke of Oldenburg, who had obtained a "league and labour" of land (variously defined as 4,000 or 4,600 acres) located near the colonial capital of San Felipe in Stephen F. Austin's colony. Individuals, like Stephen F. Austin and Henri Castro (mentioned below) received large land grants from Mexico (several leagues) to act as impresarios—agents—to colonize the Texas territory. Ernst became a "sub-colonizer," and it is not clear how big his league—received from Austin—was. Ernst was ill-equipped for pioneering. He did not know how to build a cabin, hated guns, and had brought none of the necessary equipment for life on the frontier. Still, he had an abounding love for this new country. His enthusiasm was expressed eloquently in a letter to a friend in Oldenburg urging him to come to Texas. The letter was published throughout northern Germany and started the first steady stream of German migration to Texas. Two hundred eighteen Germans were listed as residents of the republic by the Texas census of 1836.

In 1842 a group of German noblemen, interested in overseas colonization for both philanthropic and economic reasons, met at the castle of the Archduke of Nassau to found the Society for the Protection of German Immigrants in Texas. The society had obtained the right to settle Germans on a vast tract of land in west-central Texas known as the Fisher-Miller grant. The society brought 7,380 Germans, primarily Hessians, to the "Paradise of North America" between 1844 and 1846. Poor planning and mismanagement forced the society to declare bankruptcy in 1847.

Though the society was no longer aiding emigrants, its influence continued to persuade many Germans to go to the western frontier to be near friends, relatives, and countrymen. Politically discontented, better-educated city dwellers—professionals, merchants, craftsmen—followed on their own initiative in substantial numbers into the late 1850s.

During the period of 1847 to 1861 the German population in Texas was increased not only by immigrants coming directly from Germany but also by approximately 7,600 who came to Texas after stopping in New Orleans. By 1860 the German population in Texas exceeded 30,000, and a massive emigration period had ended. After the Civil War and through the 1880s, German individuals and families continued to depart their homeland, not to be pioneers on the frontier, but in search for a higher standard of living. Their numbers were substantial. Another 14,200 Germans came to Texas via New Orleans during the period of 1865 to 1886. One more colonization effort has to be mentioned to complete an account of German migration to Texas. In 1844 impresario Henri Castro settled 2,134 German-speaking people from Alsace, Baden, Swabia, and German Switzerland in the areas west of San Antonio now known as Medina County.[1]

The German migration to Texas was substantial enough to create two areas of dense settlement (Fig. 20-1). The eastern and south-central rural communities founded by followers of Friedrich Ernst and the south-central and western colonies established through the efforts of the Society for the Protection of German Immigrants in Texas together formed a broad belt of German settlement deep into the state.

The German Cultural Landscape in Texas

From the rolling prairie landscape of east and south-central Texas to the undisputed hunting grounds of Plains Indians on the fringes of the Hill Country, a broad but fragmented belt of German settlements had been created by 1850. All major features of settlement were established, and were strengthened and expanded by the later influx of immigrants.

The Anglo-Americans who settled in east and south-central Texas between the Brazos and Colorado rivers during the early years of the nineteenth century adhered to the scattered farmstead settlement form, which was dominant throughout the rural South. Ernst, the German newcomer, however, laid out a townsite on his property in 1838. It became the village of Industry. Ernst offered building lots measuring 50' × 150' for twenty dollars, claiming that he was not a speculator who desired to turn German

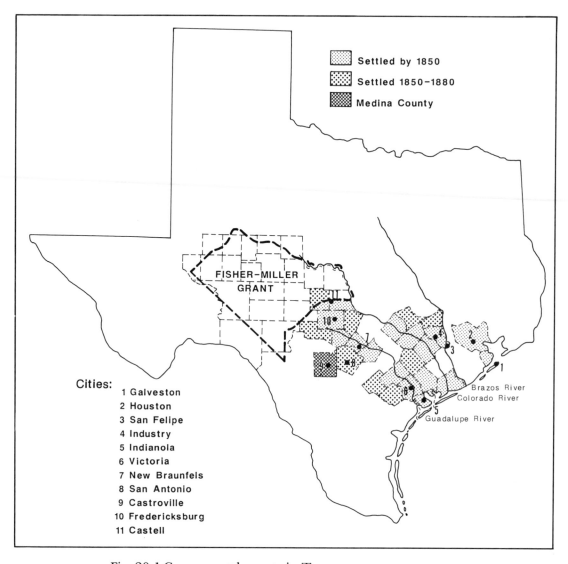

Key:
- Settled by 1850
- Settled 1850–1880
- Medina County

FISHER–MILLER GRANT

Cities:
1 Galveston
2 Houston
3 San Felipe
4 Industry
5 Indianola
6 Victoria
7 New Braunfels
8 San Antonio
9 Castroville
10 Fredericksburg
11 Castell

Brazos River
Colorado River
Guadalupe River

Fig. 20-1 German settlements in Texas

immigration to his advantage, but that he wanted to attract educated fellow-countrymen to his town.[2] The tradition of loose agglomerations of farmsteads in northern Germany, the source area of most of Ernst's followers, and the cheapness of land led to the founding of islandlike German rural communities among the more numerous and widely distributed Anglo-American settlers. Although free land was given by immigration agents to colonists during the 1830s and early 1840s, these grants lay in regions too remote for immediate settlement. Instead, the immigrants purchased small tracts of land from a pioneer settler and stayed in his vicinity for a number of years, "commencing a series of improvements, pursuing them patiently, 'til completion," as an English writer observed.

A fragmented German belt along the Brazos, Colorado, and Guadalupe

Gerlinde Leiding

364

rivers came into existence without a concerted plan. The belt was strengthened by additional land purchases until it filled out to the extent that the second generation and later immigrants had to push north and south in their search for new land.[3] Those Germans brought from 1844 onward by the Society for the Protection of German Immigrants occupied the unsettled land north and west of San Antonio. The western end of the German belt was defined between 1844 and 1885. Here the Germans were pioneers, not second settlers. The first footholds were made at Castroville in 1844, New Braunfels in 1845, and Fredericksburg in 1846.

The Society for the Protection of German Immigrants in Texas promised free passage, land, a log house, farm implements, and urban amenities to prospective settlers of the Fisher-Miller grant. In return the colonists had to pay a small per person fee and promise to occupy and cultivate at least fifteen acres for three years. Prince Carl von Solms-Braunfels and, later, Baron von Meusebach supervised the colonization beginning in 1844. The first emigrants, most of whom were Hessians, left via sailing vessel for Galveston and thence to Indianola, the society's port. Instead of leading these Germans through the established areas to the land they were to colonize, the prince chose the wilderness path, to avoid American contact. However, the realization that the Fisher-Miller grant lay too far inland to reach without a layover resulted in the founding of New Braunfels as a way station. The location was chosen because it was equidistant between the coast and the land to be settled; the proximity to San Antonio, a trading center, also was important (see Fig. 20-1). Fredericksburg, eighty miles to the north of New Braunfels, became the second way station on the route to the Fisher-Miller grant. The society succeeded in founding only four minor settlements on the southern edge of the vast land grant before its collapse in 1847. Thousands of Germans brought by the society found themselves stranded along the immigrant road from Indianola to the grant settlement of Castell on the Llano River. Most settled along the road, others stayed in port cities or scattered among the existing German communities of the eastern region of German settlement.

The immigrants of the 1850s either pushed farther westward or settled in established German communities; they increased the German population substantially in cities and towns such as Galveston, Houston, Indianola, and San Antonio. The Anglo-American frontiersmen avoided the rugged hills to the west of the Balcones escarpment for fear of Indian attack. Not until the late 1850s did Anglo-Americans occupy areas adjacent to Germans in the Texas Hill Country.[4]

Ethnic culture was expressed in farming practices and choice of crops raised by the settlers. The belief in the validity of the German rural heritage held by the noblemen who patronized German settlement led to the imposition of a farm village concept on Texas soil. Travelers to Texas frequently reported the German influence on the landscape: "The more settled and thrifty the appearance of the country . . . indicates the approach to a German settlement"; "the Germans left an impress of industry, order and economy on the section"; and "fields are fenced and plowed" were typical comments.

The Anglo-American farmers in the eastern region of Texas differed greatly from their German neighbors. The former had larger landholdings and more livestock, often had slaves, and knew what to produce on a large scale for a cash crop: for example, corn and cotton. Because of the economic and physical hardships suffered by the German immigrants, they could afford only small tracts of land. However, operation on a small scale was a familiar condition of the German rural heritage; with the barest minimum of farm tools, German settlers accepted the challenge of the unknown and began to raise cotton as well as corn to make a living. In the intensive care required by tobacco culture Germans felt they had an advantage over the large-scale American farmer. Market gardening and the easily adopted practice of raising cattle on the open range became further sources of livelihood.

The deep fertile soil along the river and creek beds in south-central Texas and the oak-forested uplands recalled parts of the homeland in northern Germany. The geography and the humid, subtropical climate gave promise of success for farming. Through motivation, patience, and determination, together with agricultural diversification among cattle, cotton, and tobacco, with white and sweet potatoes as cash crops, German farmers soon became competitive with their Anglo-American neighbors.

The picturesque Hill Country is marked by fertile basins and valleys interspersed with the prominent heights of eroded remnants of the Edwards Plateau. The appearance of the landscape, with cedar and pecan trees, and the hot semi-arid climate are far removed from the European homeland experience. German pioneer farmers in the West had to rely on recommendation and experimentation to provide for their livelihoods. Corn was recommended to be planted as a first crop. It proved not only to be good for raising cash, but its sweet variety became a new dietary staple, which lasted past the pioneer years. The planting of European grains, particularly wheat, was a successful experiment, as the proliferation of gristmills during the 1850–1860 decade attested. From the very first, the western settlements were characterized by numerous kitchen gardens with a great variety of vegetables as well as fruit trees. However, only the peach offered possibilities for the establishment of large orchards. Since many settlers came from wine-producing areas in Germany, the establishment of viticulture as a commercial undertaking seemed feasible, but winemaking—from wild grapes—thrived only as a hobby.

The basic livelihood for the German settler, however, came from ranching. On their journey from Indianola to the posts on the western rim of European settlement, the immigrants observed the suitability of the land for large-scale cattle ranching. Since cattle graze selectively, German ranchers in their homeland had kept sheep to "clean up" the pasture. They did so also on the open range in Texas. The practice of raising a combination of cattle and sheep was introduced by the German rancher and proved very profitable. Before 1850, swine foraged in the bottom lands of rivers and creeks around New Braunfels. German sausage and cured ham became famous throughout Texas.

Unlike the Germans in the eastern Texas settlement, those pioneer Germans on the western frontier could not rely on an established economy. Therefore, diversity of crops and livestock was essential, and the extent of its achievement by the German pioneers of the western frontier is impressive.[5]

The source areas from which the protection society's and Empresario Castro's colonists came had farmsteads clustered together in unplanned, ir-

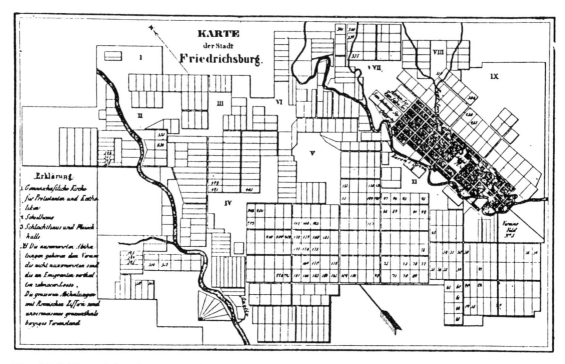

Fig. 20-2 Plat of the German colony of Fredericksburg, from a folder of instructions issued in 1851 by the Society for the Protection of German Immigrants. The settled town is shown shaded, claimed or available immigrant land is shown in rectilinear lots, areas with Roman numerals represent land not yet surveyed. (As reproduced in Biesele 1930.)

regular villages. The founders of New Braunfels, Castroville, and Fredericksburg attempted to establish similar farm villages on Texas soil.[6] Early settlers in the society's towns were granted town lots of one-half acre and outlying farms of ten acres. The Castro settlers were given one-third acre town lots and twenty to forty acres for farming. It was assumed that the colonists would locate house, barn, and garden in town and go to the fields to work, as was traditional in Germany. Since all three settlements were also intended to be market towns, the streets and lots were laid out in a rectangular grid pattern with an open central square reserved for the market (Fig. 20-2). Only a few years after the founding of New Braunfels and Fredericksburg, many settlers moved from town to their farms, leaving behind what in Fredericksburg came to be called "Sunday houses," tiny structures for weekend use only.

This relocation of dwellings resulted in scattered farmsteads and extended family communities, much like the settlements in the eastern counties. Establishment of the farm village concept in Texas failed because the natural grazing grounds in the vicinity of the towns became exhausted, the desire to increase farm size rose while land prices remained low, and, last but not least, the influx of new immigrants pushed the perimeter of the settlements farther from town, making daily journeys to the field impractical.

The Germans in the western counties commenced farming on a very

Germans in Texas

small scale—10 acres in 1845, but by 1850 the average farm size had grown to 166 acres. The Old World meticulousness employed in working gardens and fields, together with larger-scale planting and ranching methods, led to success. Within thirty years the pioneers had overcome their initial deficiency of capital and had become the largest operators in the Hill Country. Endless stone fences criss-crossing the landscape are remnants left by the German settlers of their hard work and pride of land ownership.[7]

Some Early German Intellectual Communities

One of the most interesting early settlements was the Bettina colony on the edge of the Fisher-Miller grant. "The Forty," consisting of professional men, artists, and musicians, who were all young, idealistic university scholars, established a settlement along communal lines.[8] The venture soon failed: "too many chiefs and not enough Indians."[9]

Latium, in Washington County, was a community of intellectuals where classical Latin was spoken regularly in debates.

Sisterdale, in the New Braunfels vicinity, is another settlement of classicists. Tiling observed: "A library of ancient and modern classics was to be found in almost every house. The latest products of literature were eagerly read and discussed in weekly meetings held at the schoolhouse. As comfort and taste was found in the homes, one could also hear real drawing room conversation on the frontier of civilization."[10]

While melting into the general pattern of Texas life, the German immigrants held on to native customs and traditions. Clubs devoted to agriculture, singing, literature, gymnastics, shooting, and mutual aid abounded in rural German areas. Each town had at least one German-language newspaper, and German was the language used in church services.

The Vernacular Architecture of Texas German Colonists

Most early colonists had little knowledge of building techniques, let alone of which type of house construction was best suited to the climate. The immigrants to the eastern settlements were quick to observe and adopt the American custom of building a rough log cabin as a first dwelling. Stone piers 12 to 15 inches above grade formed the foundation, upon which rested a sill and horizontally laid timbers, notched to one another at each corner, forming the walls of the structure. A 45-degree gable roof without a ridge pole spanned the one-room interior and projected over the south side, covering the porch. These pioneer cabins were small, windowless shelters, hastily erected by minimally skilled workers. The logs were left round and with bark attached and were laid with ample chink or gap between them to compensate for timber variance, warping, and lack of skill in building. The chinks were filled with mud, mixed with grass or animal hair, to keep the weather out. Frequently these cabins were built directly on earth, which served as the floor. To the European, this house was a temporary affair to be dispensed with as soon as possible. It made little use of more sophisticated German log building techniques.

The immigrant with means could afford to have a log house built by experienced craftsmen. The differences between cabin and house were carefully hewn timbers that were neatly notched, with sawn-off flush corners, and tightly chinked; a wooden board floor resting on sleepers; windows; a fireplace with an exterior, preferably free-standing, masonry chimney; and a gable roof covered by wooden shingles or shakes.

Ferdinand Roemer describes the plantation Nassau, which was founded in 1843 by Count von Boos-Waldeck.

> The manor house lies on a hill covered with oak trees and is sepa-
> rated from the other farm buildings. It is one of the best con-
> structed and most comfortable houses . . . nevertheless, it is only a
> log house. . . . The whole house is built of rough-hewn oak logs
> carefully grooved, lying horizontally over each other. It is separated
> into two parts . . . forming in the center an open, covered passage,
> which offers the inhabitants a cool, pleasant resort in summer. The
> two longer sides of the house face north and south, so that the pre-
> vailing south winds in summer can circulate freely through the hall.
> On these two sides the roof projects about ten feet and is supported
> by wooden pillars forming galleries, whose floors are two feet above
> the ground. On each end of the house is a fireplace built of ashlar
> stones reaching several feet above the top of the house which gives
> to the whole building a stately appearance.[11]

The common German log houses in the eastern settlements were usually one-room structures of 16′ × 16′ or 18′ × 18′, one-and-one-half stories high. The sleeping loft for the children was reached by a boxed-in, corner stair located next to the fireplace. The interior finish allowed for distinctions to be made reflecting means, values, and origin of the builder or owner.

Once the pioneer stage had passed, cabins were demoted in function to serve as stalls and coops and were replaced as dwellings by frame structures. The more substantial frame houses eventually were enlarged and decorated to offer comfort and pleasure. Rudolph Melchoir, an immigrant artist who was working in Texas in 1853, painted and stenciled colorful designs on the walls and ceilings of many large houses of prosperous German settlers in the lower Brazos area (Fig. 20-3).

The enlargement of a log house typically consisted of adding a second room of similar size and a covered breezeway of approximately ten feet width. The floor plan was converted from a one-pen to a double-pen or dog-trot type. The porch was extended over the entire length of the building. Entries, and often a single-run stair, were located in the open central hall (Figs. 20-4a and 20-4b).[12]

Fachwerk

Additions to German log houses in the eastern Texas settlements were usually executed in *Fachwerk,* or half-timber construction. Throughout Europe Fachwerk had a long history. A building skeleton of heavy timbers, mortised and tennoned together, created "fields" or *Fächer,* which were filled with brick or wattle and daub or sometimes stone (Figs. 20-5a and 20-5b). The settlers from northern Germany were accustomed to Fachwerk structures of impressive dimensions, some dating back to the sixteenth century. The frame timbers emphasized horizontal rectilinear or square fields. Diag-

Fig. 20-3 Drawing of the painted ceiling in the Lewis house, Winedale, Fayette County, Texas. (Historic American Buildings Survey.)

onal braces were kept to a minimum. The strong, dark, timber frame work contrasting with the whitewashed fields gave the buildings a neat and stately presence in the landscape. Quite a few German house additions in east Texas reflect their builders' architectural heritage, but only up to a point. The tradition of sheltering men, harvest, and animals under one roof, however, was never introduced to Texas. Furthermore, each nonresidential function was housed in a separate structure—kitchen, smokehouse, barn. Their location and proximity to the house were determined by convenience, not by adherence to a traditional plan.

Just as log construction had a social stigma among Germans (it was a symbol of frontier backwardness and deprivation) Fachwerk construction was an expression of national origin. The east Texas Germans, though not convinced until after 1856 that the Anglo-American frame building technique could provide a lasting, sturdy home, felt it inappropriate to display their construction heritage. Thus, log houses and Fachwerk additions were, if means permitted, covered up with horizontal or vertical siding.

Ferdinand Roemer, in 1846, recorded his impressions of an early German frontier settlement:

> The city, or correctly stated, the hamlet New Braunfels is laid out according to a regular plan [Fig. 20-6]. All streets cross at right angles and the principal streets converge at the market square. This plan was not much in evidence when I arrived in New Braunfels because the houses, instead of adjoining one another, appeared to be scattered at irregular distances over the entire plain. Only the principal street, the so-called Seguin Street, could be distinguished

Gerlinde Leiding

370

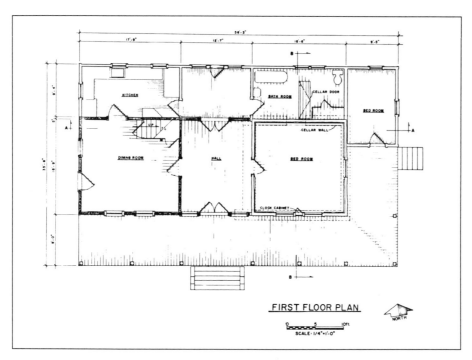

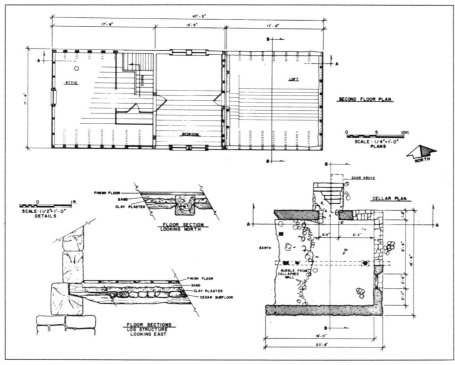

Figs. 20-4a and 20-4b Plans for first floor (4a) and second floor (4b) of the Zimmerscheidt-Leyendecker house near Frelsburg, Colorado County, Texas. A fine example of a single-pen log house expanded to a double-pen structure. (Drawings by Brad Flink (4a) and Madison Graham (4b), Historic American Buildings Survey.)

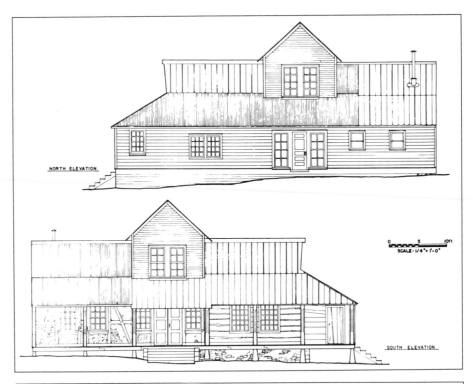

NORTH ELEVATION

SOUTH ELEVATION

0   5   10ft.
SCALE · 1/4" = 1'-0"

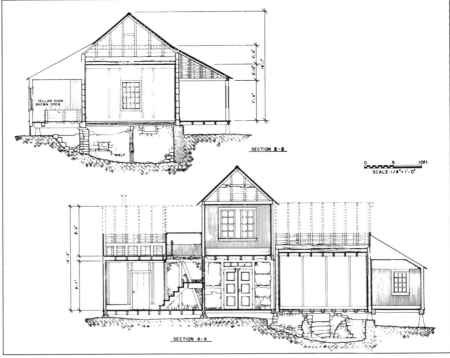

CELLAR DOOR
SHOWN OPEN

SHELF

SECTION B-B

0   5   10ft.
SCALE · 1/4" = 1'-0"

SECTION A-A

Gerlinde
Leiding

372

Figs. 20-5a and 20-5b The Zimmerscheidt-Leyendecker house near Frelsburg, Colorado County, Texas: (5a) exterior side views, (5b) cross-sectional end and side views, showing use of Fachwerk construction. (Drawings by Diane Proctor (5a) and Madison Graham (5b), Historic American Buildings Survey.)

Fig. 20-6 Modified from a plat of the German colony of New Braunfels, from a folder of instructions issued in 1851 by the Society for the Protection of German Immigrants. (As reproduced in Biesele 1930.)

quite well, for although houses were not built on both sides, still the town-lots, containing about one-half acre each, were enclosed by fences. The houses were of diverse architecture as everyone was allowed to follow his own taste and inclination. Besides, most people had no idea as to which particular type of construction was most suited to the climate. As a result, some houses were of logs, some were of studding framework filled in with brick, some were frame while others were huts with walls made of cedar posts driven vertically into the ground, like the posts of a stockade. The roofs, instead of being covered with the customary wooden shingles found throughout America, were covered with tent canvas or a couple of oxhides. Most of the houses followed the American style of roofed-in porch. . . . Most of the houses lacked a fireplace . . . since most were built in the summer time, the need for heating was remote. In addition to this, the building of a suitable fireplace required a dexterity which the German colonists did not possess. At the time of my arrival . . . there were probably eighty to one hundred such houses and huts . . . Several families were packed into one house, no matter how small it was. The interior of such a house, where men, women, and children were cooped up with their unpacked chests and boxes, often looked like the steerage of an immigrant ship.[13]

Floor Plans and Interiors

Adjusting to crowded conditions required little sacrifice for emigrants from central Germany. A typical basic Hessian farmhouse had one room called the *Herdraum* (room with stove) and one tiny chamber. Only if means permitted was a distinction made between living room and chamber or chambers. In any event, the Herdraum was the hub for all activities and provided access to the chamber and other rooms. The tight floor plan, low ceiling height, exposed joints, summer beams, small built-in cabinets and clock all added to the "essentials only" interior atmosphere.

Exterior Variations

Instead of demonstrating formality and strict adherence to an architectural tradition, the exterior treatment of the house reflected the character of its inhabitants and the manifold landscape from which they had come. Lean-to additions, projecting bays, dormers, open or covered entry stairs, and many diagonal and curved braces in the Fachwerk structure, all are defining elements for the architecture of Hesse.

The colonists sponsored by the Society for the Protection of German Immigrants in Texas were promised a log house upon arrival at the Fisher-Miller grant. But since New Braunfels and Fredericksburg were way-stations only and the society funds ran low, the pioneers were left to fend for themselves in providing shelter. Carpenters were in short supply among the first colonists, forcing many settlers to try their own hand in the unfamiliar technique of building with logs. Lack of experience, coupled with the diminishing number and size of trees in the western region of Texas, led to a distinctively German log cabin to be found in the hill country only. The 12′ × 12′ single-pen cabin showed wide chinks filled with hewn blocks of local limestone and mortar, giving it a horizontally striped appearance, looking half stone and half log (Fig. 20-7).

Gerlinde Leiding

Fig. 20-7 A basic Fredericksburg log house with additions and barn. (Drawing by G. Leiding.)

On the other hand, the Swiss and Alsatian settlers in Castro's colony had a long history of building with logs or planks. They had perfected the art of laying squared timbers on top of one another without the need for chinking. Only in Medina County, of all the areas in which Germans settled, can unchinked log structures be found. As in the eastern counties, log cabins were abandoned or added on to as soon as possible. In 1847 a visitor to New Braunfels noted that the old clumsy huts had disappeared and a number of neat permanent houses had been built.[14]

Fachwerk structures or additions abounded in the western settlements, but the love of using many diagonal or curved bracing members and the creation of irregular fields did not transfer from the homeland. A Hessian tradition was adhered to in the enlarging of a house. A room was added behind the original one, making the house two rooms deep. Another Hessian mark can be seen in the broken roof line, which resulted from treating the porch and additions as lean-tos with shallow-pitched shed roofs. Thatch covered many roofs in the western settlements, and the fireplace found in Anglo-American homes remained absent. Instead, a stove pipe was drawn from the center of the space to a chimney in the gable wall. Cellars for cold storage of garden and dairy products are seldom found in Texas. In the source area of the immigrants, barns, stalls, coops, and house formed an enclosed yard; not so in the new land, where freedom of choice and greater availability of land were evidenced in the scattered location of these structures.

Later Developments in the German Settlements

In 1850 New Braunfels was the fourth largest city in Texas. Only Galveston, San Antonio, and Houston exceeded it in population. Only eight Anglo-American families resided among the 3,500 Germans.

In 1855 Frederick Law Olmsted observed that the main street of New Braunfels, which was three times wider than Broadway, in New York, was thickly lined on both sides for a mile with small, low cottages of no pretentions, yet looking neat and comfortable. Many were furnished with verandas and gardens and the greater part were painted or stuccoed. There were many workshops of mechanics and also small stores.[15]

By 1860 a variety of industrial establishments were located in town— brick kilns, flour and grist mills, saw mills, breweries, soap and candle houses. The quantity of building products produced attests to a building frenzy, which aimed at the creation of durable, comfortable homes.

Since the pioneers of central Texas had no local building precedents to follow, it is not surprising that they remained loyal to their heritage, but it is remarkable that they quickly adjusted to new conditions (Figs. 20-8a and 20-8b). Fachwerk construction was abandoned as the builders discovered that the local limestone and sandstone were structurally sound building materials. In 1847 Fredericksburg had two stone structures. By 1856 only stone houses were being built, featuring one-and-one-half stories, covered front porches, outside stairs, and low-pitched roofs—structures uniform in appearance with Galveston, Indianola, Victoria, and other towns through which the Germans passed en route to their new homeland.

After the Civil War, larger stone houses were built and fewer imported construction methods and building elements are evident. These solid build-

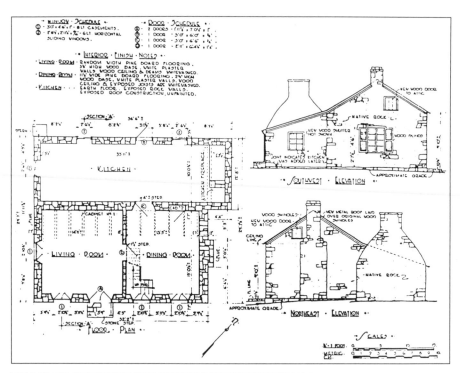

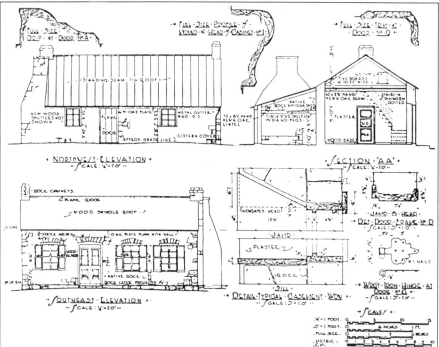

Gerlinde Leiding

Figs. 20-8a and 20-8b The John Peter Tatsch house in Fredericksburg, Gillespie County, Texas. A fine example of houses found in the western German settlements and reflecting the Hessian origins of the builder. (Historic American Buildings Survey, Anton Heisler, Jr., delineator.)

Fig. 20-9 A single-pen Fredericksburg log house to which was later added a second pen, executed in ashlar masonry, and a detached Fachwerk structure with lean-to and fireplace. (Drawing by G. Leiding.)

ings were executed in ashlar masonry, with particular care given to details. Style and organization of the house reflected the taste of the time. Gingerbread (fancy wooden fretwork) decorated eaves and balcony or porch railings and provided a playful contrast to the smooth stone walls. After the mid-1880s the Germans abandoned stone construction also and erected frame buildings.

The first assimilation of the American way of building—log cabins and houses—was only a temporary one, followed, after only five to ten years, by a cultural rebound, as evidenced by the increased use of Fachwerk and stone construction, casement windows, exterior plastering and whitewashing, and thatched roofs (Fig. 20-9). Careful choice of architectural elements from the Old World and integration of these as demanded by the new environment reflect a spirit and intellect capable of building a new world. It was the second generation of Germans in the United States that dispensed with their cultural heritage through complete assimilation of a new lifestyle and architecture based on frame construction, expediting their passage into the new society of Texas.

Conclusion

In 1960 over 400,000 persons of at least half German descent were estimated to be living in Texas. In many fields of endeavor, German Texans have contributed heavily to the state's general prosperity.[16] Their distinctive vernacular architecture still dominates the landscape in a large area of central Texas. The meandering stone walls that enclosed many settlers' entire property add to the picturesqueness of the Texas Hill Country. The collective charm of the small ethnic buildings in New Braunfels and Fredericksburg, together with frequent festivals to celebrate German customs and traditions attract visitors year-round. At the Oktober-, Wurst-, and Schützenfesten, sauerkraut and sausage and baked goods, not to mention beer, still delight the palate of many, while oompah bands provide an invitation to dance. Old German songs—Studentenlieder and Wanderlieder—are still being sung by Männerchören, and a bastardized German can occasionally still be heard on the streets of Texas. During World War I and World War II, pride in the German heritage and culture was noticeably subdued. In recent times, however, preservation of the German cultural element in Texas is enjoying a marked resurgence.

Gerlinde
Leiding

21

Basques in the American West

William A. Douglass

THE BASQUES are sometimes called the mystery people of Europe. The reference is to the conundrum posed by their origins. Speaking a language that is unrelated to any other and manifesting a blood type profile radically different from that of any other European population, the Basques were clearly occupying their Pyrenean homeland prior to the invasions by Indo-European peoples (ca. 2000 B.C.) that established the ethnographic makeup of the continent as we know it today.[1]

The Basque Country straddles the French-Spanish frontier where the western spur of the Pyrenees meets the Cantabrian seacoast. Taken together, the four traditional Spanish Basque regions and three French Basque regions are tiny by any definition (approximately one hundred miles across on both north-south and east-west tangents). At present this Basque homeland has fewer than three million inhabitants; prior to the industrialization of parts of the area in the late nineteenth century the population was less than a million.

The Impetus for Emigration

Its minuscule territorial extent and modest demographics notwithstanding, the Basque Country has been one of Europe's pronounced source areas for trans-Atlantic emigration. As the continent's earliest whalers, from a region geographically well situated to serve as one of Iberia's doorways into the North Atlantic trade routes, Basques were famed mariners. They were, therefore, ideally postured to participate in Spain's voyages of discovery and subsequent colonization of vast stretches of the globe.

Several centuries of Basque emigration was fueled by a land-tenure system in the peasant villages of the interior. Given the scarcity of arable land in the difficult mountainous terrain, the region had long been characterized by a system of impartible inheritance. A single heir to the farm was selected in each generation and the other siblings were required to leave (or remain celibate and subordinate to the authority of the heir). A disinherited sibling might marry the designated heir of another rural household or profess religious vows, but the majority were forced to seek their fortunes elsewhere.[2]

It is, therefore, scarcely surprising that Basques became major players in the Spanish imperial drama and came to constitute an ethnic elite within the ranks of the Old World commercial, civil, and ecclesiastical hierarchies. Nor was Basque emigration to the New World interdicted by the Latin American independence movements of the early nineteenth century. Rather, many of the new nations required settlers and encouraged the immigration of kith and kin from their former metropole. During the nineteenth century the Basque area experienced a population explosion, leading to periodic famine and epidemics, and was thrice ravaged by war—in the Napoleonic campaigns and the two Carlist wars. Thousands of Basques, therefore, opted to leave, particularly for the River Plata region of southern South America. By the 1830s and 1840s Basques were well ensconced in urban occupations in Buenos Aires and Montevideo and as sheepmen on the Argentine pampas and the plains of Uruguay.

Basque Sheepherders in Western North America

When gold was discovered in California, the peoples of southern South America were geographically advantaged in the race to El Dorado. Many Basques, and particularly those resident in South America, entered the ranks of the gold seekers. Like most of their fellow argonauts, they failed, and turned their attention elsewhere. For the South American Basques the vast open ranges of California offered the opportunity to replay the southern South American sheep-raising scenario. By the late 1850s several Basque sheepmen were established in the ranges of southern California, leasing land from the California *dons* and/or roaming about the unclaimed public lands of the interior (Fig. 21-1).

A pattern of transhumance quickly emerged in which the sheep bands grazed during the winter in the deserts and valleys and were then trailed to the high country of the Sierra Nevadas for summer pasturage. It was a unique opportunity for a thinly capitalized immigrant, since a man could herd sheep for a few years for an established fellow Basque, take his wage in ewes, which he ran with those of his employer, and then eventually hive off to seek range of his own. Such sheep outfits were truly nomadic, requiring neither a home base nor an investment in land. Rather, a man and his dog, along with his burro to transport supplies, bedroll, and tepee tent, could roam at will about the public lands, or at least until he bumped up against the claims of others.

In this fashion Basque sheepmen spread rapidly throughout the western United States. By the 1860s they had entered California's central valleys. By the 1870s they had expanded eastward into Nevada, Arizona, and New Mexico. By the 1890s they were penetrating eastern Oregon and southern Idaho. Indeed, by the first decade of the twentieth century they were ubiquitous throughout the open-range districts of all thirteen states of the American West (see Fig. 21-1). By then, to say *Basque* was to mean *sheepherder*, and to refer to a desired employee of the Basque- and non-Basque-owned sheep outfits alike. At the same time, the Basque nomadic bands, "tramps" to their detractors, were anathema to the settled livestockmen of an increasingly crowded range. While access to the public lands was theoretically open to all on a first-come basis, irate ranchers pressured their local, state, and federal representatives to exclude the itinerants from the range. The anti-alien, pro-property bias of the legislation that created both the U.S. Department of Ag-

William A. Douglass

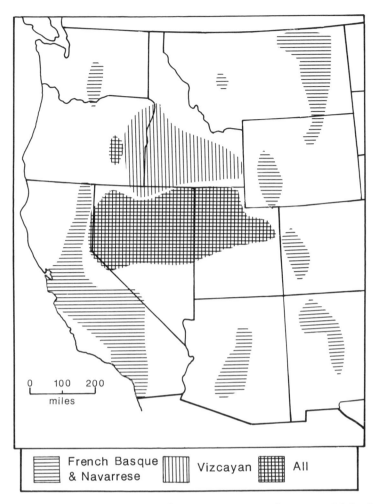

Fig. 21-1 Basques scattered over vast areas of western United States. Horizontal lines identify areas of predominantly French Basque and Navarrese settlement; vertical lines locate areas of predominantly Vizcayan population.

riculture's national forest system and the U.S. Department of the Interior's grazing districts was pointedly, though not exclusively, inspired by the campaign to rid the range of tramp sheep operators. With the passing of the Taylor Grazing Act in 1934, signaling the end of open access to grazing on the public lands, the era of the nomadic sheep outfit was over. Some of the former Basque itinerants acquired land and became U.S. citizens, thereby becoming part of the establishment. Others found employment on ranches or in small towns; many simply returned to Europe.[3]

The Emergence of the Basque-American Community

From the outset, in the early 1850s, few Basques entered the United States with the intention of remaining. Whether seeking a fortune in golden nuggets or in "golden fleeces" they saw themselves as sojourners in an alien land. The Basque who wished to emigrate permanently was much more likely to select a Latin American destination, where his familiarity with the Spanish language reduced his sense of isolation and broadened his range of opportunity.

Eventually, however, some Basque sheepmen in the American West changed their minds about returning to the old country. They either sent back, or went back, to Europe for a bride. A few, very few indeed, married non-Basques, usually women from other Roman Catholic immigrant groups, such as the Italians of central California. In this fashion, a Basque-American community emerged. While probably an underestimate of those who are of Basque descent, the 1980 U.S. Census lists 43,130 individuals who identified themselves as being Basque to some degree. The largest concentrations were in California (15,530), Idaho (4,332), and Nevada (3,378).[4]

Finding the Cultural Landscape of the Basque

If we pose the question of what kind of ethnic mark the Basque-American community has implanted upon the architectural landscape of the American West, the answer must be, practically none. The reply is not meant to be facetious, a kind of bad joke of the shaggy-dog variety that would call into question the relevance of the present article to this volume. I would argue differently, since there is a sense in which it is important to ask how an ethnic group could persist for more than a century throughout a vast region without having a greater impact upon its domestic and public architecture. The seeds of the answer have already been planted in the foregoing discussion.

First is the issue of the selective nature of Basque immigration into the United States, viewed against the backdrop of the global Basque diaspora. Those who entered this country were recruited primarily from the peasant villages of the Old World Basque regions of Vizcaya, northern Navarra, and Basse Navarre, for the specific occupation of sheepherding under frontier conditions. Most who left the Basque Country were semiliterate single men in their late teens or early twenties. Conversely, Basque professionals— medical doctors, lawyers, engineers, and even architects, emigrated as well, but inevitably to Latin America, where they could pursue their careers with a minimum of disruption, their professional credentials being recognized much as an educated British national had little difficulty in becoming certified in Australia, Canada, or in the United States. This meant that the U.S. Basque-American community lacked its intelligentsia in the past. To the extent that it has developed one *in situ*, it is constituted of U.S.-born individuals who have little or no knowledge of Old World Basque culture, and particularly its architectural traditions.

Second, Basques moved into more (or less) than a country, in the abstract, when they entered the United States. Rather, more than most other immigrant groups, Basques entered a specific occupational niche. Sheepherding was a specialized activity that subjected its practitioners to a unique set of circumstances, many of which had architectural implications (Fig. 21-2).

William A. Douglass

Fig. 21-2 The simple, portable, ephemeral dwelling of the Basque sheep-herder, Elko County, Nevada. (Photo by José Mallea, courtesy of the Basque Studies Program, University of Nevada-Reno.)

The Domestic Architecture of the Basque

The most obvious place to begin is with consideration of the lack of Basque domestic architecture in the United States. The majority of Basques who entered the country did so as young single men who then became employed as sheepherders. There were also a few married men, but they inevitably left the established family behind in Europe, because the nature of sheepherding was antithetical to family life. Whether working for an established sheepman or herding his own band as an itinerant owner/operator, the herder was a true nomad, with no need for a permanent dwelling. The cycle of transhumance between winter and summer range might take him on an annual trek covering as much as five hundred miles. From late spring through early fall the herder's shelter was the canvas cocoon of the tepee tent, while in the winter months his "home" was the sheep wagon (Fig. 21-3). The watchwords were *portability* and *mobility,* since the herder moved his camp every few days in search of a fresh grazing area for his charges. In the rugged high country the entire outfit had to be transported on the back of a donkey or mule, whereas the winter sheep wagon was drawn across the desert flats by horses, or more recently, by a pickup truck.[5]

Such was the domestic architecture of the herder. It is not that it could not be discerned on the western landscape but rather that it had an ephemeral or phantomlike quality, something that a casual visitor might stumble across and contemplate for the moment but surely not rediscover should he

Fig. 21-3 Basque herder with his wagon. (Photo courtesy of the Basque Studies Program, University of Nevada-Reno.)

return to the same spot a week later. Nor was there anything peculiarly Basque about these minute domestic outposts in their wilderness settings. The tepee tent (see Fig. 21-2) was generic throughout the American West, in both its ranching and mining economies, and available through the general stores of any rural town. The sheep wagon was likely descended from the covered wagons or prairie schooners of the nation's westward trek, an alternative use for an otherwise useless item once its original mission was completed.

Minor Landscape Features

There was, however, something that was physically distinctive and lasting about the Basque presence on the western ranges. It involved the attempt of the herders to combat the psychological dangers of one of the world's most socially isolating occupations. Deprived of human contact, excepting the periodic (possibly weekly) brief visit of his camptender and the chance encounter with a hiker, hunter, or fisherman, time and solitude were a man's greatest enemies. The herders have their own vocabulary of madness to describe the man who adjusts only too well to life without human contacts. He is referred to as being "sagebrushed" or "sheeped." Each herder, then, confronted the challenge of maintaining personal sanity in the face of near total solitude; the trick became how to humanize, in at least some small fashion, an otherwise unrelentingly natural world. The herders resorted to two strategies in this regard, each of which has left its legacy in the western environment.

William A. Douglass

384

The first was construction of rock cairns on bare, windswept hillsides and promontories (Fig. 21-4). Carefully stacking stones into durable monuments might seem a means to simply while away the hours, as indeed it was, but the expression used by the herders themselves to refer to the cairns is revealing. In Basque they are called *arri mutillak,* or stone boys.

The groves of aspen trees along mountain streams, the favored campsites while on the summer ranges, provided a second opportunity to personalize one's surroundings. By serrating the bark of young saplings with a knife blade, the germ of future words and images could be implanted. As the tree matured the scar widened, revealing the carver's intent. In this fashion, aspen groves throughout the sheep-raising districts of the American West have been converted into both message banks and living art galleries, linking the solitary herder with both his predecessors and successors (Fig. 21-5). Some of the carvings simply document the passage of an individual by recording his name and possibly the date. Others exalt a man's homeland, "Viva Navarra" or "Gora Euskadi" (Basque for "Long Live the Basque Country"), and thereby underscore his homesickness. There are denunciations of the exploitative employer, yearnings for the girl left behind in Europe, and the not-so-tender longing for the prostitutes of the nearest town. The figurative art ranges from subtle depictions of sheepdogs, horses, and the Old World church or farmhouse to crass pornography. As a body of information, the tree carvings provide our best first-person documentation of the travails and sorrows of the herder's lot. Their tone is purgatorial, and totally lacks the romanticism with which an urbanite might vest the spectacular scenery and lovely sunsets of the western range. Indeed, the herders seem to be kindred souls to the prisoner or the young soldier impatiently biding his time in some godforsaken outpost.[6]

There is one other physical trait of the sheepherding lifestyle that may be mentioned, if only as a sort of footnote. On a few Basque-owned ranches

Fig. 21-4 Typical rock cairn. (Drawing by M. M. Geib.)

Fig. 21-5 Basque tree carving, Thomas Creek Canyon, western Nevada. One carving states, "Aqui estoi [*sic*] pescando," or "Here I am, fishing." (Photo by José Mallea, courtesy of the Basque Studies Program, University of Nevada-Reno.)

there are free-standing, beehive-shaped ovens modeled after those found on farmsteads in the Basque Country. There a camptender might fashion large round loaves of "sheepherders' bread," with which to resupply his herders. However, such structures are unusual, since many of the outfits baked their bread by digging holes and burying the dough in dutch ovens covered with hot coals.

If sheepherding is antithetical to family life, and hence to elaboration of domestic architecture, not all Basques remained in herding. Those who did not return to Europe either acquired their own ranches or moved into the small towns of the sheep districts of the American West. Such individuals were likely to establish families. Few, however, built their own dwellings. Rather, it was common for the settled Basque family to acquire an existing ranch house when purchasing a ranch, or to rent or buy an existing home in town. There are, therefore, no external features to distinguish Basque domestic design from generic ranch and town architecture throughout the American West. The same is not entirely true of internal decoration, however.

The living room of a Basque-American home is likely to contain unmistakable symbols of the owners' ethnic origins. There may be a few books about Basque topics casually or formally displayed. A photograph or painting of an Old World Basque scene is likely to grace one of the walls, as may an escutcheon of the seven Basque provinces and/or the family name. Old World Basque bric-a-brac may decorate a coffee table surface or wall shelf.

William A. Douglass

The owner's pride in his ethnic heritage may be further underscored by the bumper sticker on his car in the driveway which proclaims "Basque is Beautiful" or even "Basque Power."

The Basque Hotel

From an architectural standpoint, considerably more distinctive than the dwelling is the Basque hotel, or boardinghouse, which emerged throughout the open-range districts of the American West. Each was the local node in a larger network, including establishments in Bordeaux, Le Havre, Liverpool, New York, Salt Lake City, San Francisco, and Los Angeles, which facilitated the movement of the potential sheepherder from his peasant farm to his final destination on a ranch in the American West (Fig. 21-6). Most were started by ex-herders, oftentimes married to a local Basque-American woman, who provided the fluency in English necessary for a town enterprise.

The hotel served many purposes in addition to the obvious one of providing temporary food and shelter to Basques in transit either from or to the old country.[7] It was an employment agency for the local ranchers and a source of information about employment prospects in other parts of the American West. It was a town address for the local herders, a place where they could collect mail and leave a set of town clothes while out on the range. If a herder returned to Europe to visit his family or in search of a bride, he might store his saddle, bedroll, and rifle in the room designated for the purpose in his favorite Basque hotel.

Fig. 21-6 Hotel Vasco, a Basque hotel in San Francisco, ca. 1900. (Photo courtesy of the Basque Studies Program, University of Nevada-Reno.)

The nature of herding was such that few of the men learned any English. The hotel was, therefore, an ethnic haven in an otherwise unfamiliar world for the herder who was in town for a week's vacation or for medical treatment. The hotelkeeper, or more likely his wife, served as interpreter should the herder need to shop or transfer funds back to Europe through a bank. Similarly, it was the hotelkeeper who served as translator for both the court and the herder should the latter be accused of trespass or some other offense. Above all, the hotel provided the unemployed herder with room and board on credit over an extended period of time. This was of utmost importance, since it was the nature of herding that after the lambs were shipped in the fall, two sheep bands were consolidated into one for the winter months. This meant that almost half the labor force annually faced the prospect of a layoff that could last for several months. During such periods the hotel was as much a home as a hostelry. The domestic atmosphere of the establishment was further enhanced by its population of permanent boarders—retired single herders with no desire to return to the old country after decades in the American West.

The hotel was equally important for the local Basque-American community. It provided a point of reference and reunion where American-born Basques could learn at least something about their heritage as well as practice their faltering Basque, Spanish, and French language skills. Basque feast days were celebrated in the hotels, as were baptisms, weddings, and funerals. Indeed, the hotel generated many of the marriages that it hosted, since it was there that the young herder might meet his future Basque-American or Old World Basque spouse. The latter union was made possible by the practice of providing employment in the hotels to single women from the Basque Country. Few remained spinsters for very long after arriving in the American West, which meant both a high turnover and strong infusion of young married couples into the fledgling Basque-American community.

The hotel, then, was the single most important social institution of the Basques of the American West. It had several distinctive physical features. First, ideally, although not invariably, it was situated within view of the local train station (Fig. 21-7). This was to facilitate the arrival of the semiliterate, frightened, Old World neophyte. When put on the train by an agent of Valentin Aguirre's Basque hotel in New York, possibly with the name of his town of destination pinned to his lapel, the young man was told that when he got off the train the Sante Fe Hotel, for example, would be in plain sight. Indeed, several communities of the American West had multiple Basque hotels clustered near the train station.

As with private dwellings, the hotels were not constructed by their proprietors, since Basques were seldom among the original settlers in any particular area. The prospective hotelkeeper would therefore purchase an existing bar, boardinghouse, or small hotel and then refashion it to his specifications. The ground floor contained a bar and an ample dining room where the boarders took their meals family style (Fig. 21-8) at long tables that could also be arranged to serve a wedding or baptismal banquet for a local Basque-American family, or shoved against the wall to reveal a makeshift dance floor. The second story consisted of small, spartan, but clean, rooms, with bathroom facilities at the end of the hall. The lack of decoration or embellishments, the bare walls, and the exposed light bulb hanging from the

William A.
Douglass

Fig. 21-7 Basque hotels in Elko, Nevada, located adjacent to the railroad tracks. (Photo by Bill Belknap, courtesy of the Basque Studies Program, University of Nevada-Reno.)

ceiling were consistent with a clientele made up exclusively of single males. Yet, curiously, the hotels have an air of permanence, or at least they lack a sense of transience. They seldom attracted the overnighter, and, indeed, many of the hotels refused to rent rooms to non-Basques even when the rooms were available. It was as if the entire second floor were one big dormitory, the special territory of its occupants, where a man could leave his toothbrush and razor in the common lavatory.

An ethnic feature that further distinguished some Basque hotels was the *fronton*, or handball court (Fig. 21-9). *Pelota* was, and still is, the Basque national sport. Consequently, a particularly enterprising hotelkeeper with enough space might append a handball court to his operation, thereby making his business the preferred Basque establishment in a particular area.

Fig. 21-8 Dinner time in a Basque hotel. Family style service was typical. (Photo by Bill Belknap, courtesy of the Basque Studies Program, University of Nevada-Reno.)

This feature underscores another aspect of the demographic profile of the clientele, namely its youth and exuberance. While some Basque-Americans learned the game as well, the viability of pelota depended upon the infusion of a steady stream of fresh, Old World–born herders. Once the stream became a trickle, or dried up altogether, and the local established colony began to age, the frontons quickly fell into disuse, although some still survive as storage areas and a few continue to be used for competition.

The demise of the frontons was just one aspect of the evolution of the original Basque boardinghouses into something else. Over time, they began to cater to a wider audience, which shared the herders' table and their potluck. At first the hotels did not advertise, but their reputation for wholesome, abundant, inexpensive meals served family style in an exotic atmosphere, spread by word of mouth. By the 1960s the Basque hotels were becoming a favored, though still semi-secret, place to eat for an ever-expanding group of

Fig. 21-9 Handball court (*fronton*) Elko, Nevada. (Drawing by M. M. Geib.)

cognoscenti. America's binge with ethnic revivalism further enhanced the latent tendency to commercialize Basque ethnicity.[8] By this time the competition over the western ranges was a thing of the past, and Basques had gained the respect of their immediate neighbors as a hardworking, frugal, and honest people. For the wider public, the Basques were an object of curiosity.

This growing interest in the Basque heritage coincided with a decline in Basque immigration. Sheep populations throughout the American West plummeted during the 1970s and 1980s, in part because of unfavorable economic conditions and in part because of the successful efforts of environmentalists and governmental agencies to reduce livestock grazing on public lands. Europe's, and particularly Spain's, economic recovery diminished the attraction that sheepherding in the United States held for Old World Basques; desperate sheepmen turned to Peru and Mexico for herders. It is scarcely surprising, then, that the Basque hotels shifted their emphasis from the sleeping rooms upstairs to their bar and dining room downstairs.

By the early 1970s practically all the Basque hotels of the American West depended upon an American clientele for their survival. It became commonplace to remodel the public areas to display, in rather ramshackle fashion, Old World Basque artifacts, paintings, photographs, maps, musical instruments, and other items.

The Basque Restaurant

Over the past two decades another kind of Basque establishment has emerged—the Basque restaurant. These are posh dinner houses with no second floor, likely owned by a Basque-American rather than by an exherder, where the ethnic decor is studied, and the diner orders from a menu, featuring a number of Basque dishes, and sits at his own private table. The proprietor himself, or his hired bartender, is likely to be decked out in Basque folk costume, as are waitresses in the dining room, thereby themselves becoming props in the staging of Basque ethnicity. In addition to serving drinks or food, the staff are expected to answer questions about the mysterious origins of the Basques, the uniqueness of the language, or the herder's lot. The new Basque establishment, whether evolved from the former hotel or of more recent vintage, is now a part of its host community's local color, touted by the visitors' bureau, the chamber of commerce, and advertised in newspapers, on billboards, and through radio and television.

The Basque Festival Cycle

The dwelling and the hotel are both privately owned contexts in which Basque ethnicity may be displayed. However, there is a public arena as well. Throughout the American West, beginning in May and ending in early September, there is a Basque festival cycle. Wherever Basques have concentrated in relatively large numbers there is likely to be an annual festival hosted by a local Basque club. Usually lasting over a weekend, festivals attract a minimum of five hundred persons, some as many as three thousand. Typically, the festivals include a Basque-language Mass and sermon, provided by a California-based Basque chaplain who travels throughout the West, Old World athletic competitions that include weight lifting and woodchopping events, and folk dancing by both the local club's dancers and groups from distant clubs.

A public dance and huge outdoor barbecue provide Basques and Basque-Americans, many of whom have traveled hundreds of miles, with the occasion to visit. The festivals are open to the public and are therefore another means of both projecting and commercializing Basque ethnicity.

In and of themselves, these festivals do not leave lasting architectural marks upon the landscape. An exception is the handball court built in a park in Elko, Nevada, for the national Basque festival. However, the festivals have become an integral part of the mental map of the American West, and particularly that of its Basque-American residents. Like the sheep camps, the festivals are ephemeral. However, for the weekend, the celebration transforms the local community, particularly in the smaller towns, where the Basque festival may be the most spectacular annual event.

The Basque social clubs, which sponsor the festivals, can be found wherever there is a concentration of Basques. There are currently nineteen clubs in the American West, primarily in California, Nevada, and Idaho. In addition to sponsoring a festival and possibly a folk dance group, the clubs hold members-only picnics, dinners, and dances. Some stage handball competitions and *mus* tournaments (a Basque card game similar to poker).

Few clubs have a physical locale. There are, however, notable exceptions. Since 1949, Basques in Boise, Idaho, have had a club facility (Fig. 21-10); and in 1982 the San Francisco colony inaugurated its Basque Cultural Center. Next to the Boise Basque Center there is a small museum, a transformed Basque boardinghouse, which conveys to its visitors the themes central to both Old World and New World Basque culture.

William A. Douglass

Fig. 21-10 The Basque Center, Boise, Idaho. (Drawing by M. M. Geib.)

Monuments and Memorials

Until quite recently there was no monumental Basque architecture in the United States. However, in August, 1989 a monument to the Basque sheepherder was inaugurated in Rancho San Rafael Park in Reno, Nevada. The project was initiated by the Society of Basque Studies in America. An international committee headed by Nevada's former U.S. senator Paul Laxalt, himself the son of a Basque sheepherder, and the governors of California, Idaho, and Nevada raised more than $350,000 in the Basque Country and all fifty United States. Noted contemporary Basque sculptor Nestor Basterretxea submitted the winning design. The monument included a focal, abstract sculpture in bronze of the lone figure of a Basque shepherd carrying a lamb (Fig. 21-11). The figure dominates a raised platform that includes a map indicating the location of concentrations of the Basque population of the United States. To one side is a wall with donors' plaques and commemorations of deceased family members, many of whom were pioneering sheepherders in the American West. Other plaques placed along a walking trail inform the visitor about the Basques and their collective experience in the New World.

Summary and Prospects

Such, then, is the architectural legacy of the Basques and their American descendants. Few in numbers, dispersed over a tremendous area, derived from modest Old World origins, and closely linked to an occupation that required few architectural supports, the Basques contributed little to the United States landscape in the form of bricks and mortar. The architecture they influenced reflects work and play rather than worship and shelter.

The reverse was true in Latin America, which, as we have noted, received a more varied influx of Basques, who upon arrival entered a broad range of occupations. Therefore, in places like Mexico City, Lima, Santiago, Buenos Aires, Montevideo, Caracas, and Havana, Basques have left a more visible mark upon the urban landscape. Some domestic architecture in these cities suggests, without mirroring, Old World Basque architectural styles. There are dozens of Basque centers or social clubs in Latin America, many with their own physical facilities. Several clubhouses are constructed in the form of the Basque farmhouse or *baserria,* a palpable symbol of Old World Basque culture and object of nostalgia for its New World representatives.

Fig. 21-11 The national monument to the Basque sheepherder, dedicated in August 1989 in Reno, Nevada. (Photo courtesy of the Basque Studies Program, University of Nevada-Reno.)

Several Latin American cities have important Basque monuments, such as that in Buenos Aires to Juan de Garay, founder of the city, or the ubiquitous monuments to Simon de Bolivar, the Basque-descended liberator of the South American continent. Then there are truly impressive charitable institutions such as the Colegio de las Vizcainas, founded in the eighteenth century in Mexico City to prevent Basque orphan girls from going astray, or Euskal Echea, built in Buenos Aires in the late nineteenth century to shelter and educate needy Basques. All stand in stark contrast to the modest architectural efforts of the United States' Basques.

What are the prospects of the Basque-Americans? There are consider-

Fig. 21-12 Appropriately, a lamb motif decorates tombstone of a Basque couple. (Photo courtesy of the Basque Studies Program, University of Nevada-Reno.)

able grounds for pessimism. Basque immigration to the United States remained, throughout its history, intimately intertwined with sheep husbandry. Currently, the open-range sheep industry of the American West is all but moribund, and it is difficult to foresee positive changes. Today there are fewer than one hundred Basque sheepherders in the entire region, and practically no Basques enter the country to replenish their ranks. Indeed, the effort to commemorate the Basque sheepherder in bronze and stone is itself eloquent testimony to his passing from the scene (Fig. 21-12).

The handful of Basques who enter the United States annually to work as milkers in the dairies of southern California or gardeners in the San Francisco Bay area is hardly sufficient to renovate and energize the region's several Basque colonies. Those colonies, in turn, are aging and assimilating. One might, therefore, suspect that the recent flurry of interest by Basque-Americans in their cultural heritage has more breadth than depth. Unless some unforeseen series of events in both Europe and the United States creates the conditions for renewed Basque immigration, we may well be witnessing the dying embers and ultimate demise of Basque-American culture.

Part VI

Conclusion

22

The Immigrant Experience in the Nineteenth Century and Afterwards

Allen G. Noble

ALL THE immigrant groups discussed in this volume have formed, to a greater or lesser degree, unified and cohesive communities. Of course, the ultimate necessity for the immigrants was to be able to support themselves. The level of support acceptable to these immigrants could be quite low—in fact, just above bare subsistence in some instances, enabling them to partially substitute social support for economic support. The natural inclination on the part of immigrants was to head for those areas where their folk already resided, other economic considerations being essentially equal.

If unoccupied land was available, as it usually was up to the end of the nineteenth century, it proved to be an irresistible magnet, since most migrants had been rural-dwelling peasants in Europe. The chain of communication between pioneer settlers and kinsmen left behind in Europe, as well as the concentrated and concerted efforts of railroad land and settlement agents operating in specific locations among a restricted ethnic community, ensured more or less homogeneous settlement of ethnic groups in many parts of the New World.[1] This was true in the United States, where ownership of land not reserved for railroads and government use was open to all settlers, regardless of place of origin. In Canada, group settlement was, in fact, encouraged by government reservation of blocks of land to accommodate particular nationalities. In both countries, clearly defined rural ethnic islands arose, although in some instances, these settlements bordered one another.[2] In other cases, the ethnic islands were surrounded by a sea of mixed settlement of various immigrants and longer-term residents.

The Persistence of Rural Ethnic Islands

An intriguing question still to be answered is why some ethnic islands have persisted to the present day, with many of their traditional cultural characteristics intact, while others have disappeared as their members were assimilated into the larger surrounding Canadian and American cultures. For all of the groups discussed in this volume, original numbers were great enough for the community to have a chance at preservation of their group identity. Yet some have survived, others did not, and still other groups are well along in the process of assimilation or acculturation.

Some answers have been suggested in earlier chapters. Strength of religious convictions certainly has been important for some groups such as the Welsh, the Belgians, and the German-Russian Mennonites. The persistence and extent of poverty has been another significant factor, as in the cases of the Irish and the Spanish-Americans. Perhaps the most dominant and critical relationship is that of the timing of settlement. This is expressed as "the principle of first effective settlement." Those groups first on the scene are likely to have the greatest influence and longest-lasting impact in determining the cultural landscape of an area. The significance of such early settlement is clearly demonstrated by the Germans in Texas and the Scots-Irish throughout Appalachia. The Danes in Iowa and Minnesota and the Norwegians in Wisconsin illustrate the same situation but from the opposite perspective. Other, earlier-arriving groups had the greater effect.

This difference in ethnic tenacity has intrigued numerous scholars. At least three theories have been advanced: (1) The melting pot theory proposes that ethnic groups ultimately lose their identity, submerged into a larger American culture. (2) The cultural pluralism theory postulates the continued independent survival of immigrant groups, although often in a modified character. (3) The ethnic revival theory views the acculturation process as much like the swing of a clock's pendulum. The first generation is completely ethnically oriented; the second is uncertain and insecure and "thus prone to compliance with the demands of Americanizers" and the rejection of ethnicity; the third generation has none of these insecurities and can explore its ethnic heritage with confidence. Thus, in the ethnic revival theory, if the ethnic community is large enough, many essential, or even peripheral, elements of the group's culture may ultimately be preserved.[3]

None of these theories, which address primarily the results of acculturation or assimilation, takes sufficient account of the processes involved, especially the operation of important geographical factors, which are often overlooked or deemphasized in these studies. Before examining the influence of geographical factors in the migration and settlement process, the basic relationship between assimilation and settlement needs to be explored.

The Relationship of Settlement and Assimilation Processes

Very little research has been devoted to the questions of what effect size of settlement and density of settlement (or degree of ethnicity, to express it another way) have upon the persistence of tradition in immigrant communities. A closely related concern is the effect that accessibility has on the success with which an ethnic community will be able to maintain its individuality. These questions all impinge upon the issue of cultural assimilation. Assimilation has been defined as "a social and cultural process involving, on the one hand, the fusion of cultural heritages and, on the other, the modification of sentiments and attitudes and the gradual incorporation of the strangers into the [dominant] cultural groups."[4]

Accessibility must be evaluated not merely on the basis of geographical proximity and the ease of reaching a settlement location from outside, but also on the facility with which the workings of the ethnic immigrant commu-

Allen G.
Noble

nity can be penetrated. To give just one example by way of illustration, the Amish settlements in many locations in eastern United States are quite geographically accessible, yet their society remains largely impenetrable. The closeness and congeniality of the colony is a hindrance to assimilation, since the members prefer to associate with their own group and to avoid outside contacts as much as possible. Consequently, their traditional culture continues mostly intact.[5]

Each ethnic community is subject to conflicting pressures. It hopes to maintain its identity by preserving its culture, as much as possible, but the stress of adapting to a new environment and situation may prove overwhelming. At the same time, the community is under pressure to assimilate—to adopt those cultural characteristics of the larger community that will ensure the ethnic group's continuity and its successful competition with other groups, both immigrant and native. In part, this process involves making the particular ethnic group "acceptable" to the majority. This is especially important in urban areas, where the economy may be largely in the hands of other groups.

An ethnic group made up of only a few individuals or families rarely has much impact or identity, even locally. In fact, its members are often not easily recognized by outsiders and the group has little or no sense of community. To some extent, the small size of an ethnic community may be compensated for by a high density of settlement, if that results in homogeneity. Such homogeneity produces a material cultural landscape that is easily recognizable by members of the community itself and, with instruction and exposure, to members of the larger surrounding society. The presence of a distinctive material cultural landscape is a major factor in promoting group consciousness in rural areas, and it has an effect even in urban areas, where it may be expressed mostly by signs being in a vernacular language and by distinctive church architecture. How effectively the group occupies the land is the most important consideration. In humid areas and in areas having great soil fertility or some other important resource, the population numbers must be high, to repel competition from other groups. In less well-endowed regions, the numbers in the ethnic group may be much smaller, as long as they effectively dominate the settlement area.

Mormon Settlement

The Mormons may be used as a case in point. The members of this religious community possess other cultural traits besides religious affiliation which characterize or identify them as a distinct ethnic group. They effectively occupy the Great Basin of the western interior of the United States, where population densities are low because of climatic conditions. While the number of non-Mormons is lower than that of Mormons in the Great Basin, the clear Mormon imprint on the landscape is primarily the result of the group's almost universal employment of certain material cultural traits, such as grid-plan villages with exceptionally wide streets, distinctive brick homes, Mormon ward chapels, in-town barns and granaries, hay derricks, and rows of poplar trees. This imprint has been analyzed in several studies.[6] In the Great Basin, it is how effectively the Mormons shaped the cultural landscape rather than their absolute numbers which enables them to be identified by

The Immigrant Experience

401

non-Mormons. In a different environment, if other groups had been competing for the land, larger numbers might have been required to create so clear an imprint. In fact, the original Mormon settlement strategy was to seek a location beyond the frontier of settlement, a place not desired by other groups. The Mormons also recognized that a continuing influx of like-minded new settlers would ensure the perpetuation of their settlement. Thus, throughout the latter half of the nineteenth century, American and European converts received assistance from the Mormon church to help them settle in the Great Basin.

In other ethnic communities that developed recognizable settlements, a similar process of renewal was going on in the nineteenth century. The basic difference was that cultural conditioning occurred in the Mormon community *after* settlement, as a result of the strict discipline of the community and its isolation from its Anglo-American neighbors, whereas the conformance to cultural norm among immigrant ethnic communities elsewhere in the United States took place *before* settlement. The continual arrival, year after year, of new immigrants strengthens the traditional and ethnic elements of the settlement and prevents or delays assimilation.

A Model of the Migration and Settlement Process

The processes of migration, settlement, and acculturation or assimilation, which have been touched upon above, are all parts of a human continuum which may be expressed in terms of a descriptive model (Fig. 22-1). The model attempts to organize the continuum within the framework of three categories: movement factors, acculturation barriers, and immigrant community adjustments.

Movement Factors

Each of the conditions which impelled movement from Europe to North America may be placed under one of two headings: push factors and pull factors. Two other sets of movement factors, inertia and return migration, worked to discourage or dilute migration.

Under one interpretation, the push factors may be viewed essentially as negative phenomena that encouraged migration by establishing situations within the European milieu which were unconducive to development. They include such situations as political or religious repression, rigid social class distinctions, discrimination against various minorities on several levels, compulsory military training or conscription, land fragmentation, economic stagnation, or actual decline in standards of living and family income over a period of time. By creating negative situations and environments, the push factors created an economic and social climate in which the traumatic decision to migrate was made considerably easier than would otherwise have been the case.

Operating in the same direction, but having quite different origins, were the pull factors. These functioned as magnets drawing the migrants to North America, rather than encouraging them to leave Europe as the push factors did. Prominent among the pull factors was the availability of fertile agri-

Allen G.
Noble

402

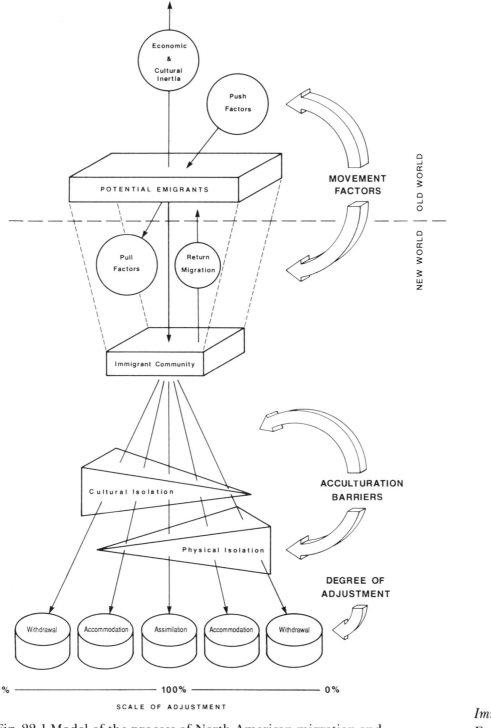

Fig. 22-1 Model of the process of North American migration and settlement

cultural land at almost unbelievably low cost. Furthermore, this land was often available for purchase in large blocks. Another pull factor was the presence of a society in which class restrictions were largely absent and in which upward mobility was possible. Thus, the immigrants, who usually were forced to enter at the lowest level of society, might expect to gain in social as well as economic status; if not they themselves, their children were likely to be able to make advances. Although the upward social and economic mobility provided by the "American dream" has been greatly exaggerated as a realistic model of American social development, it contained enough truth to make it a goal for many to strive toward. In actuality, it was often only the most talented and persistent of migrants or their children who could overcome the disadvantage and initial stigma of their backgrounds, especially as they were critically reviewed by their American associates.

Political and religious tolerance was another pull factor, but it operated with considerable limitation. Individuals might be allowed great latitude in their personal political and religious views, but organized groups and movements were not as welcomed, probably because they represented a potentially much more disturbing force. Nevertheless, the great size of both North American countries and their low population densities provided room for diverse religious and political expression by both immigrant and long-resident groups and individuals.

Still another pull factor of great importance to immigrants was the strength of the North American economy, which, except for brief periods, such as the Panic of 1873, usually was buoyant and growing during the nineteenth century. An expanding economy offered the promise of support to impoverished European rural peasants and urban workers.

The pull and push factors were powerful forces propelling the European migrants toward the New World. But a group of opposing forces were working simultaneously to discourage many Europeans from making such a momentous journey. Collectively, these forces may be referred to as the inertia factors. They are more difficult to describe and assess, because they are more complex. Migrants had to be willing to endure hardships and in many instances to face real dangers during both the voyage and the early process of settlement. Exactly what the new environment offered was often impossible to ascertain, and this introduced an element of uncertainty that intimidated many prospective immigrants. In any event, the necessity to leave family and the security of home place, however modest the level of the support it offered, often proved an insurmountable obstacle and prevented migration.

Even after migration, some individuals succumbed to homesickness or became discouraged by slow progress in improving their economic or social status. A few had problems in adjusting to the demands of a changing culture in the New World environment. Still others were never dedicated to migration and remained in North America only long enough to accumulate some savings that could be used to permanently improve their status back home in Europe. These movements collectively are a fourth movement category, which can be termed the return migration factors.

All four groups of factors, operating independently but simultaneously, determined the size and composition of the actual immigrant group, that is, the segment of the potential migrant population who actually journeyed across the Atlantic Ocean and stayed.

*Allen G.
Noble*

Acculturation Barriers

Once the immigrants had arrived in the United States or Canada, the process of settlement and adjustment began immediately. This process was controlled by the presence or absence of two types of barriers: physical or geographic and cultural or ethnic. These barriers impinged differently upon different ethnic groups.

Some deliberately sought, or accidentally found, physical isolation, which enabled them to maintain most of their culture for relatively long periods. The Waloon Belgians of the Door Peninsula in Wisconsin are an example. The Door Peninsula is a cul-de-sac, and once established in that area, the Belgians existed off the track of movement and thus out of touch with other groups, and competition from them. Consequently, the Belgians have been able to maintain their identity well into the twentieth century.

On the other hand, the Germans in Ohio had no such geographical isolation. Settling in a state across which ran several major paths of migration, their assimilation was rapid and virtually complete. By the middle of the twentieth century, the overt elements of German material culture in Ohio were few and difficult to identify readily.

Cultural isolation represents a different kind of barrier to acculturation, one which may be self-imposed in a conscious attempt to preserve the separate identity of the ethnic group involved.[7] Language and religion are commonly the most important elements in cultural isolation. The group must make serious and sustained efforts to preserve its cultural characteristics, recognizing that failure to do so will ultimately result in the group's disappearance or loss of identity. The conflicting pressures are often felt most severely by the children of the group, torn between the admonitions of elders and discipline enforced by parents on the one hand and the cultural seduction offered by non-ethnic playmates and acquaintances on the other. Similarly, for adults the social rewards for conformity to group are often overbalanced by the greater economic benefit associated with assimilation.

Cultural Adjustment

Both geographical and cultural barriers help to determine the adjustment of immigrant ethnic groups to the majority culture. The degree of cultural adjustment can be divided into three levels: assimilation, accommodation, and withdrawal.

Assimilation represents the complete adjustment of the minority culture to that of the majority. In the process, the minority group loses, or suppresses, most of its cultural traits and substitutes those of the majority. The minority effectively loses its identity over time. In the matter of material culture, only a faint and imperfect imprint of the group's original culture remains on the landscape.

Accommodation represents an equilibrium. The minority group maintains its identity by readily accepting some majority cultural traits, objects, and practices, but successfully preserves others of its own origin. The minority ethnic group is able to maintain itself as an independent entity, but its culture is modified in the process. Although it is not the same culture that migrants brought with them initially from their European source region, it is recognizably different from that of the majority group.

Finally, some groups, because of geographical or cultural isolation, or a combination of both, assume a position of withdrawal. Such withdrawal may be forced upon the group by the circumstances of its isolation, in which case the condition of withdrawal is not likely to last very long. Alternatively, withdrawal may be a consciously adopted strategy for the preservation of the group and its culture. In these cases the success of the strategy depends upon the discipline of the minority group.

Conclusion

The melting pot conception of the end result of the immigrant settlement process in North America is only partially true. Although most immigrant groups lost most of their ethnic identity through assimilation with the majority American and Canadian cultures, a few especially resistant or culturally vibrant groups were able to maintain separately recognizable cultures. For most peoples, however, some degree of reconciliation was necessary. Regardless of the degree of adjustment, each ethnic group contributed elements of material culture which have been incorporated into the mosaic of American and Canadian life, thus enriching it.

Allen G.
Noble

Glossary

Batten. A thin and narrow piece of wood placed vertically to cover any gaps in weatherboarding. Use of battens is especially common in Gothic Revival houses, where their verticality contributes to the design effect. The term also may refer to a strip of wood that functions as a brace.

Board-and-batten. A type of construction in which battens cover gaps in weatherboards.

Cantilever. A construction technique in which upper floors extend over lower floors, the overhang being unsupported by posts or pillars or walls.

Chimney pile. The entire structure, usually of bricks or stone, that encloses the heating and cooking facility of a house, consisting of fireplace and flues.

Cornice. The exterior horizontal plank that is at the top of a house's side wall and upon which rest the rafters. It should not be confused with the *plate* which lies behind it and which carries the weight of the roof and wall.

Crib. Originally, a single-room structure built of logs. Sometimes called a *single crib* to differentiate it from two-room or four-room cribs or *four-crib* buildings.

Dimension lumber. Wood cut by circular saw to precise standard widths and thicknesses, as opposed to *timbers,* which are cut with axe and adze and which vary somewhat in their dimensions.

Elevation. An architectural term that refers to the vertical organizational element of a structure, as *plan* refers to the horizontal.

Facade. The front exterior or face of a building.

Gable. The triangular part of the end wall of a building having a roof that slopes away on either side from a central roof ridge line. Sometimes the term is applied to the entire end wall of such a building.

Galerie. A French term for a verandah that is roofed and supported by posts. Properly, the *galerie* must extend across the entire side of a structure.

Headers. Bricks laid up with a short end exposed. (See stretchers.)

Mortise and tenon joints. A type of nailless joint that was used in timber frame buildings. The tenon is a rectangular projection cut in the end of one wooden member. The mortise is a corresponding groove in another member into which the tenon fits. The joint can be locked by a wooden peg running through it.

Nogging. Brick in-filling of a timber frame wall.

Notching. Refers to a wide variety of cuts that can be made in logs to fasten them together. Among the more prevalent types of notches are saddle, V, and half-dovetail.

Pen. Similar to *crib,* but usually restricted to describing dwellings.

Plan. Short for *floor plan,* the horizontal organizational element of a building.

Purlin. A horizontal roof member running at right angles to the rafters. The purpose of the purlins is to provide horizontal support to the rafters.

Quoins. Large blocks, usually of stone, laid up in an interlocking fashion at the corners of a wall to greatly strengthen a masonry, stone, or brick wall.

Stretchers. Bricks laid up with a longer side exposed. (See headers.)

Summer beam. A major structural member extending from one end or gable wall to the other. In a central-chimney house, two summers are usually employed, one on either side of the chimney.

Notes

Chapter 1:
Migration to
North America

1. Stella 1975, p. 3.
2. Newton 1974, pp. 143–54.
3. Jordan and Kaups 1989.
4. Harris and Warkentin 1974, p. 66.
5. Davie 1949, pp. 69–70.
6. Ibid., p. 10.
7. Walker 1968, p. 19.
8. Olson 1979, pp. 67–68.
9. Woodham-Smith 1962, p. 207.
10. Davie 1949, p. 64.
11. Woodham-Smith 1962, pp. 207–8.
12. Golab 1977, p. 12.
13. Woodham-Smith 1962, pp. 209–10.
14. Mannion 1974, pp. 15–32.
15. Davie 1949, p. 2.
16. Lindal 1967.
17. Ledohowski and Butterfield 1983.
18. Krissdotter 1982, p. 9.
19. Ledohowski and Butterfield 1983, pp. 18–27.
20. Ibid., p. 34.
21. Noble 1985, p. 250.
22. Noble 1984c, pp. 142–44.
23. Davie 1949, p. 54.
24. Billington 1949, pp. 722–42.
25. Gilkey 1968, p. 45.
26. Scott 1968, p. 11.
27. Elkins 1968, p. 89.
28. Dinnerstein and Reimers 1975, p. 43.
29. Briggs 1978, pp. 112–14.
30. Jones 1964, pp. 203–6.
31. Przybycien n.d., p. 42.
32. Ward 1971, pp. 106–7.
33. Briggs 1978, p. 142.
34. Bergman and Pohl 1975, p. 30.
35. Olson 1979, p. 219.
36. Gilbert 1989, pp. 181–84.
37. Fox 1970, p. 58.
38. Wytrwal 1961, pp. 110–11; 122–29.
39. Fox 1970, p. 59.
40. Pierson 1968, p. 56.
41. Golab 1977, p. 36.
42. Dinnerstein and Reimers 1975, p. 47.
43. Kantowicz 1984, pp. 214–38.

Chapter 2:
Acadians in
Maritime Canada

1. Clark 1968; Harris and Warkentin 1974, chap. 2; Harris 1987.
2. Clark 1968, passim.
3. Harris and Warkentin 1974, pp. 28–29.
4. Clark 1968, pp. 344–52.
5. Only one complete passenger list including Acadian settlers is known—one from a crossing of the *Saint Jehan* in 1636—and from it only about ten percent of Acadian origins can be determined. Passengers on the *Saint Jehan* appear to have come from the towns located south and west of Tours in the old province of Poitou. It is likely that most Acadians were recruited from the west-central regions of France within about two hundred kilometers of La Rochelle, the principal port serving the colony. d'Entremont 1978, p. 71.
6. Moogk 1977; Gauthier-Larouche 1974.
7. Diereville 1969, p. 9.
8. Clark 1968, p. 105.
9. Ibid., pp. 137–38.
10. Ibid., p. 214.
11. I am indebted to the expertise of Yvon LeBlanc of Fortress Louisbourg for the analysis of Acadian building techniques.
12. Richardson, et al. 1984.
13. Bourque 1971; Brun, Le Blanc, and Robichaud 1988.
14. Brunskill 1971; Gailey 1984.
15. Carson et al., 1988; Cummings 1979; Glassie 1968; Glassie 1975; Herman 1985; Isham and Brown 1986, pp. 149–58; Man-

nion 1974; Wilson 1970, pp. 21–28.

16. Bourque 1971, passim.

17. A good example of this genre is Arsenault 1965. Perhaps the best recent fictional examples of this romanticization are the writings of Antoine Maillet 1971 and 1979.

18. Dupont 1977; Tremblay and Laplante 1977.

19. Brun, Le Blanc, and Robichaud 1988, Chapter 16.

20. Ennals and Holdsworth 1981, pp. 86–106; Ennals 1982, pp. 5–21.

21. Allen 1974, pp. 32–66.

Chapter 3:
The Irish, English and
Scots in Ontario

1. Reaman 1957, p. 133; Hall 1829, pp. 341–43.

2. *Census Report of the Canadas 1851–1852.*

3. While place of birth is not necessarily an indicator of ethnicity, it is assumed that the major proportion of settlers were in fact Scottish, English, or Irish.

4. Cowan 1961, pp. 45–46.

5. Ibid., pp. 69–73.

6. Guillet 1933, p. 31.

7. Cowan 1961, p. 67.

8. Ibid., p. 289.

9. Ibid., p. 289.

10. *Census Report of the Canadas 1851–1852.*

11. Mills 1971, pp. 146–47.

12. Ibid., p. 150.

13. Ibid., p. 161.

14. Mannion 1974, p. 146.

15. Ibid., p. 138.

16. Ibid., p. 159.

17. Cowan 1961, p. 289.

18. Ibid., p. 289.

19. Ibid., p. 289.

20. Guillet 1963, p. 36.

21. Cowan 1961, pp. 19–20.

22. Howison 1821, p. 173.

23. McKenzie 1967, p. 19.

24. Humphreys 1974.

Chapter 4:
Germans in Ohio

1. Zelinsky 1973.

2. Wilhelm 1982.

3. Wilhelm 1981, pp. 1–10.

4. Wittke 1962, pp. 3–14.

5. Faust 1909.

6. Noble 1984a, pp. 18–29.

7. Brown 1984.

8. Wilhelm and Miller 1974, pp. 43–51.

9. Brown and Niekamp 1980.

10. Ibid.

11. Fitchen 1968; Sloane 1956; Sloane 1967.

12. Brown and Niekamp 1980.

13. Noble 1984a.

14. Beck and Webb 1977.

15. Woodsfield [Ohio] Chamber of Commerce 1969.

16. Wilhelm 1986b.

17. Glassie 1965a, pp. 21–30; McIlwraith 1981; Sloane 1956; Sloane 1967.

18. Wilhelm 1986a.

19. Becker and Daily 1982, pp. 75–88.

Chapter 5:
The Welsh in Ohio

1. Edwards 1899, p. 16.

2. Hartmann 1967.

3. Ibid.

4. Ibid.

5. Noble 1984a, p. 21.

6. Edwards 1899, p. 200.

7. Conway 1961, pp. 211–12.

8. Hartmann 1967, p. 70.

9. Wilhelm 1982.

10. Hartmann 1967.

11. Ibid.

12. Ibid.

13. Mildred J. Bangert, personal interview by M. Struble, Oak Hill, Ohio, September 10, 1988.

14. Struble 1989, pp. 21–28.

15. Hartmann 1967.

16. Olwen and Blodwen Williams, personal interview by M. Struble, Centerville, Ohio, September 17, 1988.

17. Bangert interview, 1988.

18. Davis 1938.

19. Edward G. Hartmann, telephone interview by M. Struble, January 8, 1989.

20. Phillips G. Davies, telephone interview by M. Struble, January 8, 1989.

21. Anne Knowles, telephone interview by M. Struble, January 13, 1989.

22. Evans 1896.

23. Ibid.

24. James A. M. Hanna, personal interview by M. Struble, Oak Hill, Ohio, September 10, 1988.

25. Brunskill 1974, p. 86.

26. Noble 1984c, p. 39.

27. Brown 1989, pp. 49–50.

28. Jones 1946.

29. Elizabeth F. and Evan E. Davis, personal interview by M. Struble, Maesglas (Green Meadows), near Oak Hill, Ohio, March 11, 1989.

30. Stout 1933, p. 72.

Chapter 6:
The Scotch-Irish
and the English
in Appalachia

1. Moody, Martin, and Byrne 1982, pp. 222–65; Dunaway 1944, pp. 4–15, 28; McWhiney 1988, pp. xxi–xlii.

2. Dickson 1966, pp. 23–64.

3. Graham 1956, pp. 185–88.

4. Hanna 1968, vol. 1, pp. 83–84.

5. McDonald and McDonald 1980, pp. 179–99; Purvis 1984, pp. 85–101.

6. Akenson 1984, pp. 102–19.

7. Purvis 1984, p. 98.

8. McWhiney 1988, p. xxi.

9. Hanna 1968, vol. 2, pp. 60–93; Campbell 1969, pp. 22–49; Dunaway 1944, pp. 50–71.

10. Dunaway 1944, pp. 72–85.

11. Hanna 1968, vol. 2, pp. 25–30.

12. Davidson 1946, pp. 167–81.

13. Ibid., pp. 149–66.

14. Campbell 1969, pp. 28–29.

15. Dykeman 1955, pp. 36–49; Davidson 1946, pp. 182–215.

16. DeVorsey 1966; Campbell 1969, pp. 38–39.

17. Raulston and Livingood 1977, pp. 39–75.

18. Mitchell 1972, pp. 470–72.

19. Zelinsky 1973, pp. 109–40; Mitchell 1978, pp. 66–89; Wilson and Ferris 1989, pp. 533–41; Gastil 1975, p. 26; Kurath 1949.

20. Newton 1974, pp. 143–53; Zelinsky 1951, pp. 172–78.

21. Newton 1974, pp. 150–53.

22. Campbell 1969, pp. 8–18; Raitz, Ulack, and Leinbach 1984, pp. 9–33; Ford 1967, pp. 1–8.

23. Kniffen 1965, p. 551.

24. Meinig 1986, pp. 240–42; Johnson 1976, pp. 25–26; Thrower 1966, pp. 25–29, 118, 127.

25. Glassie 1986, pp. 76–77.

26. Kniffen 1969, pp. 1–8; Kniffen and Glassie 1966, pp. 40–66.

27. Evans 1974, pp. 53–64; Brunskill 1978, p. 201.

28. Hanna 1968, vol. 1, pp. 519–31; Naismith 1985, pp. 20, 24.

29. Hanna 1968, vol. 2, pp. 25–27.

30. Forman 1967, pp. 9–13, 15.

31. Glassie 1975, pp. 124–25; Morrison 1952, pp. 135–39.

32. Jordan and Kaups 1989, pp. 135–78; Jordan 1985, pp. 3–14; Wright 1958, pp. 109–17; Mercer 1926; Weslager 1969, pp. 148–202.

33. Kniffen and Glassie 1966, p. 59; Glassie 1978, pp. 538–39; Bucher 1962, p. 14; Wertenbaker 1938, pp. 298–303.

34. Jordan and Kaups 1989, pp. 135–78; Jordan 1985, pp. 41–48.

35. Kniffen and Glassie 1966, pp. 58–59; Glassie 1978, pp. 538–39; Wertenbaker 1938, pp. 298–303.

36. Wilson 1970, pp. 21–28; Wilson 1975, pp. 26–31.

37. Wilson 1975, p. 77.

38. In 1978 and 1979, John Morgan, Joy Medford, Vincent Ambrosia, Neal Cyganiak, and I conducted comprehensive surveys of structures built before 1930 in Grainger County and Union County for the Tennessee Historical Commission, which are reported in Morgan and Medford 1980, p. 137–58.

39. Morgan and Medford 1980, pp. 152–56.

40. Ambrosia 1979, pp. 14, 10.

41. Smith 1979, pp. 89–165.

42. Addy 1898, pp. 17, 66–69.

43. Forman 1967, pp. 9–13, 15.

44. Glassie 1978, pp. 543–45; Glassie 1963, p. 9; Wilson 1971, pp. 9–10; Wilson 1975, pp. 54–55.

45. Glassie 1978, pp. 529, 543–53.

46. Wilson 1975, pp. 27–28.

47. Morgan and Medford 1980, pp. 152–56.

48. Ambrosia 1979, p. 10.

49. Morgan and Medford 1980, pp. 152–56.

50. The term *Cumberland house* was coined by Riedl, Ball, and Cavender (1976) and is used by Jordan (1985, pp. 24, 28, 146–49; Jordan and Kaups 1989, pp. 209–10).

51. Wilson 1975, p. 78.

52. Morgan and Medford 1980, pp. 137–58.

53. Smith 1979, pp. 89–165.

54. Kniffen 1965, p. 561; Carlisle 1982, pp. 46–76.

55. Wilson 1975, p. 79.

56. Ambrosia 1979, p. 14.

57. Smith 1979, pp. 89–165.

58. Carlisle 1982, pp. 51, 46–76.

59. Montell and Morse 1976, p. 21.

60. Jordan and Kaups 1989, pp. 179–96, 249; Jordan 1985, pp. 146, 149; Wright 1958, pp. 109–17; Scofield 1936, pp. 229–40.

61. Kniffen 1965, pp. 561–63.

62. Wilson 1975, pp. 32–43.

63. Hulan 1975, p. 42.

64. Glassie 1968, pp. 88–89.

65. Kniffen 1965, pp. 553–57; Jordan 1985, pp. 30–31; Glassie 1968, pp. 64–69; Francaviglia 1979.

66. O'Malley and Rehder 1978, pp. 904–15.

67. Kniffen 1965, p. 555.

68. O'Malley 1972, Chapter 3; O'Malley 1977.

69. Rehder 1989.

70. Ambrosia 1979, p. 14.

71. Smith 1979, pp. 89–165.

72. Kniffen 1965, p. 555.

73. Jordan 1985, p. 149.

74. O'Malley and Rehder 1978, pp. 904–15.

75. Noble 1984c, pp. 1–14.

76. Jordan 1985, pp. 146, 149; Jordan and Kaups 1989, pp. 183–84, 188.

77. Jordan 1985, pp. 113, 149.

78. Moffett and Wodehouse 1984, pp. 14–17.

79. Ensminger 1980, pp. 68–71; Jordan 1985, pp. 35–37, 98–101, 149.

80. Rehder, Morgan, and Medford 1979, pp. 75–83.

81. Moore 1975.

82. Gillenwater 1972.

83. Jordan and Kaups 1989.

Chapter 7:
American Indians in the
Eastern United States

1. Porter 1986.

2. Williams 1979.

3. McNickle 1962.

4. Dozier, Simpson, and Yinger 1957, pp. 157–65.

5. Sutton 1975.

6. Berry 1960, pp. 51–52.

7. Stevens and Kent 1943, p. 232.

8. Morse 1822, p. 31 and appendix, p. 2.

9. James and Jameson 1913, p. 115.

10. Chateaubriand 1969, p. 175.

11. Rafinesque 1832, p. 128; Mead 1832, pp. 127–28; Losing 1877, p. 452; Lewis 1897.

12. Porter 1986.

13. Berry 1963; Greissman 1972.

14. Berry 1963.

15. Cohen 1974; Montell 1970; Stern 1952, pp. 157–225; Porter 1979b, pp. 325–45; Rountree 1972, pp. 62–96.

16. Beale 1957, pp. 187–96.

17. Kawashima 1974, pp. 10–16.

18. McIlwaine 1928, pp. 363–64.

19. Robinson, 1959, pp. 49–64.

20. Porter 1979a, pp. 175–92.

21. Jennings 1982.

22. Salisbury 1974, pp. 27–54.

23. Nash 1978, pp. 3–8.

24. Brainerd 1746, pp. 1–2, 102–3, 135, 153.

25. Sheehan 1973.

26. Porter 1982, pp. 41–48.

27. *Federal and State Indian Reservations and Indian Trust Areas* 1974; Taylor 1972.

28. Mochow 1968, pp. 182–219.

29. Redfield 1947, pp. 293–308; Redfield 1955.

30. Porter 1982, pp. 41–48.

31. Porter 1979b.

32. Speck 1915, pp. 289–305.

33. Speck and Eiseley 1939, pp. 269–80.

34. Harte 1963, pp. 369–78.

35. Harte 1963. The students of Thomas J. Harte, at the Catholic University of America, extensively investigated the Brandywine (Piscataway Indian) community of southern Maryland. See Desmond 1962, Sawyer 1961, Yap 1961, and Sullivan 1962.

36. Porter 1984.

37. Dial and Eliades 1975; Blu 1980.

38. Willoughby 1902, pp. 31–32. For a more detailed and unbiased point of view see McMullen 1982, pp. 1–9 and Porter 1985, pp. 25–45.

Chapter 8:
French Creoles on the Gulf Coast

1. Toledano et al. 1974, pp. 26–27.

2. Dominguez 1979, pp. 24–25.

3. Winsor 1895, p. 64.

4. de Charlevoix 1870, p. 37.

5. Crousse 1966, p. 2; Besson 1929, p. 3.

6. Besson 1929, p. 3.

7. Leyburn 1966, p. 289.

8. Margry ca. 1974, pp. 4, 13–14, iii.

9. Du Pratz 1758, p. 17.

10. De Langlez 1935, pp. 2–3.

11. Roark 1984.

12. Conrad 1969.

13. Rushton 1979, p. 212.

14. Oszuscik 1981.

15. Oszuscik 1983, p. 53.

16. Professor Jay Edwards, Louisiana State University, has been concerned with the origins of the French Creole cottage as part of his scholarly investigation of Louisiana plantations. We have shared ideas about the theories of plan development that reach back to Caribbean and medieval Norman origins.

17. Oszuscik 1985.

18. du Ru 1934, pp. 47–51.

19. Oszuscik 1986, p. 63.

Chapter 9:
African-Americans in the American South

1. The author wishes to thank the University of South Alabama Faculty Research Committee, which granted funds to further his field work in the Southeast, including part of the research needed in writing this chapter.

2. John Vlach, personal interview by P. Oszuscik, Austin, Texas, 1981.

3. Vlach 1987.

4. Ibid.

5. Hall 1982.

6. du Ru 1934, p. 77.

7. Vlach 1975.

8. Vlach 1976, part 2, pp. 66–69.

9. Ibid., p. 61.

10. Leyburn 1966, pp. 42–48.

11. Vlach interview, 1981.

12. Vlach 1976, part 1, p. 54.

13. Vlach 1976, part 2, p. 57.

14. Vlach 1976, part 1, p. 51.

15. Biloxi, Mississippi, [City of] 1976, p. 28.

16. Manucy 1962, pp. 19–22.

17. Glassie 1968, pp. 101–7.

18. Merritt 1984, pp. 12–15.

19. Vlach 1987, p. 135.

20. Merritt 1984, p. 16.

21. Vlach 1987, p. 136.

22. Jeanton and Duraffour 1935.

23. Vlach 1987, p. 133.

Chapter 10:
Cajuns in Louisiana

1. Dorman 1983, pp. 33–52; Del Sesto and Gibson 1975, pp. 3–11.; Tentchoff 1975, pp. 87–109.

2. West 1986, pp. 8–12.

3. Lauvriere 1924; Leblanc 1932; Leblanc 1966; Winzerling 1955; Arsenault 1966.

4. Winzerling 1955.

5. Comeaux 1972, pp. 11–12.

6. Comeaux 1978, pp. 142–60.

7. Lounsbury 1955, pp. 347–58.

8. Robin 1966, p. 124.

9. Fontenot 1976, p. 194.

10. Comeaux 1972, p. 19.

11. Trewartha 1948, pp. 169–225.

12. Newton 1967.

13. Edwards 1986; Edwards 1988; Heck 1978, pp. 161–72; Kniffen 1936, pp. 179–93; Knipmeyer 1956, pp. 66–131; Newton 1971, pp. 1–18; Newton 1985, pp. 179–89; Phillips 1964, pp. 155–58; Post 1962, pp. 83–91; Robison 1975, pp. 63–77; Rushton 1979, pp. 163–90.

14. Comeaux 1989.

15. Konrad 1982, pp. 22–36; Bourque 1971, pp. 92, 135.

16. Knipmeyer 1956, pp. 133–34.

17. Post 1940, pp. 183–91.

18. Post 1962, p. 76.

19. Robin 1966, p. 124.

20. Oszuscik 1983, pp. 49–58.

21. Brackenridge 1834, p. 24.

22. Knipmeyer 1956, p. 139.

23. Mather and Hart 1954, pp. 201–13; Knipmeyer 1956, p. 140.

24. Post 1962, p. 96.

25. Ibid., p. 94.

26. Ibid., p. 91.

27. Knipmeyer 1956, p. 142.

28. Cothran 1973, p. 72.

Chapter 11:
Belgians in Wisconsin

1. Holmes 1948.

2. Defnet et al., 1986.

3. Hill 1942.

4. Ellis 1969, pp. 346–71; Hart 1984, pp. 192–217.

5. Namur Belgian-American District 1987; Henderson 1968.

6. Calkins and Laatsch 1979, pp. 1–12.

7. Laatsch and Calkins 1986, pp. 117–28.

8. Jean Jeanquart, personal interview by W. Laatsch, Namur, Wis., Aug. 12, 1976.

9. Grace LeMense, personal interview by W. Laatsch, Rosiere, Wis., July 19, 1978.

10. Weynes, Josef 1963.

11. Jule Vandertie, personal interview by W. Laatsch, Rosiere, Wis., Aug. 17, 1978.

12. Campbell 1962.

13. "Catholic Roadside Chapel" 1984, p. 7.

14. Kahlert 1978, part 2, p. 1.

15. Randy Vincent, personal interview by W. Laatsch, Brussels, Wis., Aug. 21, 1981.

Chapter 12:
Danes in Iowa
and Minnesota

1. Hvidt 1976, p. 232.

2. Hale 1984, pp. xv–xvii.

3. Plumbe 1839, p. xv.

4. Ibid., pp. iv, 8–9.

5. Ibid., pp. 25–41.

6. Ibid., p. 11.

7. Parker 1855, p. 91.

8. *Biographical History of Shelby and Audubon Counties, Iowa* 1889, p. 232.

9. Sklenar 1955.

10. Christensen 1952, pp. 66–69.

11. Andrews 1915, p. 68.

12. Ibid., p. 232.

13. Ibid., pp. 232–33.

14. Christensen 1952, p. 71.

15. Ibid., pp. 72–77.

16. Ibid., pp. 77–78.

17. Mortensen 1961, p. 7.

18. *Dannevirke* 1886.

19. Holger Nissen, personal interview by S. Betsinger, Jacksonville, Iowa, 1969.

20. Steensberg 1949, p. 37.

21. Lena Brodersen, Elk Horn, Iowa, and Mrs. Thomas Thomsen, Kimballton, Iowa, personal interviews by S. Betsinger, 1969.

22. Ibid.

23. Steensberg 1963, pp. 459–60, 470.

24. Amanda Herskind, personal interview by S. Betsinger, Kimballton, Iowa, 1969.

25. Ibid.

26. Ibid.

27. Palma Sornsen, personal interview by S. Betsinger, Kimballton, Iowa, 1969.

28. Ibid.

29. Amanda Boelth, personal interview by S. Betsinger, Kimballton, Iowa, 1969.

30. Ibid.

31. Betsinger 1986, p. 15.

32. Noble 1984b, pp. 122–23.

33. Carl T. Hansen, personal interview by S. Betsinger, Tyler Minn., ca 1983.

34. Nielsen [196–].

35. Clara Sorensen, personal interview by S. Betsinger, Tyler, Minn., 1980.

36. Sorensen n.d.

37. Betsinger 1986, p 30.

38. *Tyler Herald* 1907.

39. Olga Strandvold Opfell, letter to S. Betsinger from Torrance, Calif., ca. 1985.

40. Medora Petersen, personal interview by S. Betsinger, Askov, Minn., 1985.

41. Helge Thomsen, personal interview by S. Betsinger, Edina, Minn., 1985.

42. Ibid.

43. This chapter exists also as paper no. 15567 (unpublished) of the scientific journal series of the Minnesota Agricultural Experiment Station. The research for it was supported in part by the station.

Chapter 13:
Norwegians in Wisconsin

1. Munch 1980, p. 750.

2. Wyatt 1987, p. 5-1.

3. Krueger 1945, p. 159.

4. Blegen 1940, p. 38.

5. Clausen 1982, p. 73.

6. Clausen 1951, p. 42.

7. Clausen 1982, p. 107.

8. Helgeson [1915?], pp. 220–23.

9. Halvorson [1939?], pp. 22–23.

10. Helgeson [1915?], pp. 220–23.

11. Johansen and Bache 1949, pp. 46–47.

12. Blegen 1979, pp. 53–54.

13. Stortroen 1932, p. 364.

14. Ibid., p. 367.

15. Fapso 1977, p. 27.

16. Selkurt 1973.

17. This research resulted in several informative in-house reports, especially Knipping and Fapso 1978, and Fapso and Knipping 1975.

18. Tishler and Koop 1984; Tishler 1986.

19. Selkurt 1973, p. 74.

20. Ibid., p. 125.

21. Tishler 1984, p. 16.

22. Holand 1928, p. 33.

23. Tishler and Koop 1984, p. 7.

24. In a study of homestead documents for Coon Valley, 43 percent of the structures reported a 16-foot length or width and 89 percent had dimensions that fell into a range of from 14 feet to 18 feet, see Tishler 1986, pp. 24–27.

25. Holand 1928, pp. 36–37.

26. Perrin 1960–1961, p. 12.

27. Stewart 1953, p. 47; Perrin 1960–1961, p. 12.

28. Bjerke, 1950, pp. 259–69; Stewart

1953, pp. 31, 46, 50, 52; Kavli 1958, pp. 78–82; Lloyd 1969, pp. 33–42.

29. Stewart 1953, p. 46.

30. Lloyd 1969, p. 39.

31. Stewart 1953, p. 50.

32. Stortroen 1932, p. 360.

33. Bugge and Norberg-Shulz 1969, p. 11.

34. Nels Chrispensen, interview by *Beloit* [Wisconsin] *Gazette,* as quoted in Fapso and Knipping 1975, p. 48.

35. Knipping and Fapso 1978, p. 107.

Chapter 14:
Finns in the
Lake Superior Region

1. U.S. Bureau of Statistics 1893, p. 42; U.S. Department of Commerce and Labor 1904, p. 423; U.S. Department of Labor 1921, pp. 458–60.

2. U.S. Immigration Commission 1911, p. 104.

3. U.S. Department of Commerce 1922, p. 48. Of the total, 11.8 percent (17,721) were Swedish-speaking Finns, that is, Swede-Finns (vol. 2, p. 980).

4. Hoglund 1960, p. 8.

5. Kaups 1975, pp. 55–89.

6. U.S. Department of Commerce 1922.

7. Kaups 1971, pp. 77–91.

8. Suomen 1922, p. 74; Toivonen 1963, pp. 27–29.

9. Kolehmainen and Hill 1951, pp. 33–69.

10. Not all the settlements or population groupings constituted communities. The information on these groupings derives from Kolehmainen and Hill 1951; Wasastjerna 1957; Holmio 1967.

11. Zelinsky 1973, pp. 118–19.

12. Wasastjerna 1957, pp. 155–219.

13. On the diverse geographical background of the early Finnish settlers in the New York Mills area see Ilmonen 1923, pp. 200–218. Also consult Alanen 1977, pp. 190–97.

14. Kolehmainen and Hill 1951, p. 46.

15. Kaups and Mather 1968. (Note that the map by Leonard S. Wilson on page 58 has an incorrect scale.)

16. Rikkinen 1977, pp. 14–36.

17. Suomen 1922, pp. 72–73. The data are for the years 1893–1920. If we add domestics and working and unattached emigrants—who came primarily from the ranks of peasants—then 80 percent had a rural-peasant background.

18. Erixon 1938, pp. 207–30; Vuorela 1975, p. 5.

19. Although selective logging had either removed, or was in the process of removing, stands of economically profitable trees, the Cutover Area had not been reduced to a treeless state when the Finns settled on the land. The numerous log structures the settlers raised is evidence thereof.

20. Kaups 1983, p. 7.

21. Kaups 1981, pp. 138–41.

22. Valonen 1975, p. 204.

23. Herman 1985, pp. 155–75.

24. Kaups 1983 pp. 8–11. On log construction, including notch types, in America, see Jordan 1985 and Noble 1984b, pp. 110–22.

25. Glassie 1975, pp. 35–40.

26. Kaups 1983, pp. 13–24.

27. However, some of the rectangular, trisected one-and-one-half-story houses with dormers were initially built on a bisected plan. Later the third component was added, some of which were of frame and board construction.

28. Mather and Kaups 1963, pp. 494–504.

29. Kaups 1976, pp. 11–20. Much of the discussion in this section is based upon the author's unpublished field notes, 1964–1986.

30. The description of meadow hay barns is based on the author's unpublished paper "Economies and Buildings on Finnish Immigrant Farms in the Upper Middle West," presented at the Scandinavian Immigration Conference, Luther College, Decorah, Iowa, October 1985.

31. One of the double-crib barns was equipped with sliding doors.

Chapter 15:
German-Russian Mennonites
in Manitoba

1. Warkentin 1959, pp. 342–68; Redekop 1969; Epp 1974.

2. Butterfield and Ledohowski 1984, p. 84.

3. Warkentin 1959.

4. Funk 1970, p. 129.

5. Butterfield and Ledohowski 1984, p. 90.

6. Burcaw 1979.

7. Petersen 1976, p. 26.

8. Lehr 1976, pp. 21, 23, 32.
9. Rank 1962.
10. Butterfield and Ledohowski 1984.
11. Kaups 1983, pp. 2–26.
12. Noble 1984c, pp. 37–39.

Chapter 16:
Czechs in South Dakota

1. Freeze 1980, pp. 261–72; Thompson 1943, passim; Roucek 1967, pp. 7–14, 21–30; Capek 1915, pp. 17–113; Capek 1920, passim.
2. Pech 1969.
3. Freeze 1980, pp. 261–66; Bicha 1970, pp. 145–46.
4. Roucek 1967, pp. 30–38; Hrbkova 1919, pp. 145–46.
5. Freeze 1980, pp. 266–67.
6. Dvorak 1980, pp. 20–23; Vondracek 1963, pp. 7–11.
7. Schell 1975, pp. 79–222.
8. Dvorak 1980, p. 24; Vondracek 1963, p. 11.
9. Dvorak 1980, pp. 39–50; Vondracek 1963, pp. 12–14; Johansen 1937, p. 24; Chladek 1921, pp. 38–42.
10. Dvorak 1980, pp. 14–15; Johansen 1937, p. 25; Elanic 1913, pp. 63–66; Sherman 1983.
11. The balance of this chapter is based on field surveys conducted by the author in the summer of 1985 and subsequent analysis. The initial project was funded and coordinated by the South Dakota State Historical Preservation Center (SHPC) under a subgrant from the National Park Service (NPS). A National Register of Historic Places multiple property nomination entitled "Czech Folk Architecture of Southeastern South Dakota," (National Register of Historic Places nomination form, Bon Homme and Yankton counties, South Dakota) was completed by the author and accepted by NPS in 1987. Original data forms, field notes with measurements, and research files are housed at SHPC, 3 East Main, P.O. Box 417, Vermillion, South Dakota 57069.
12. Foster 1870, p. 59.
13. Jordan 1985, pp. 116–55.
14. Murphy 1986, pp. 112–17; Frolec 1974; Mencil 1980; Vavrousek 1925; Clark 1913.
15. "Tabor Log Schoolhouse" 1983.
16. Measurements have been rounded off to the nearest foot for clarity.
17. Some use of braided grasses by Czech immigrants is found in north central Nebraska, where woven reed interior ceilings can be found on rare occasions.
18. Samples taken from surveyed buildings were matched to color chips in the *Munsell Book of Color*. Greens that matched samples included: 10 GY 8/4, 7.5 GY 5/2, 2.5 G 5/4, and 7.5 G 5/4; blues: 10 BG 8/4, 2.5 PB 7/2, and 10 B 8/4. This very simple comparison of paint chips did not account for fading or distortions. A thorough professional paint analysis should be conducted to determine the original colors.
19. Erpestad and Wood n.d., pp. 1–16.
20. Dvorak 1980, pp. 125–28; "St. Wenceslaus Church and Parish House" 1987.
21. "Old Catholic Church" 1980.
22. Vrooman and Marvin 1982.
23. Johansen 1937, pp. 26–27.
24. Vondracek 1963, p. 53.

Chapter 17:
Ukrainians in
Western Canada

1. Lehr 1985, pp. 207–19.
2. Oleskow 1985, p. 35.
3. Goresky 1975, pp. 17–37; Czumer 1981, pp. 10–28.
4. Kaye 1984, pp. 21–344.
5. Lehr 1977, pp. 42–52.
6. Darcovich and Yusyk 1977.
7. Speers 1897; McNutt 1924, pp. 731–32.
8. Lehr 1985, p. 208.
9. Richtik 1975, pp. 613–28; Martin 1973.
10. Farion 1978, p. 86.
11. Nahachewsky 1985.
12. Zvarych 1962, pp. 151–53; Kaye 1964, p. 139.
13. Lehr 1975, pp. 25–29.
14. Samojlovych 1972, p. 30; Kusela 1963, pp. 303–7.
15. Personal communications by J. Lehr with Ivan Dolynchuk (Caliento, Manitoba, 1974), Fred Kraynyk (Sirko, Manitoba, 1976), and John Pamachuk (Arbakka, Manitoba, 1975).
16. "Report on the Stuartburn Colony" n.d.
17. Elston 1915, p. 532.
18. Lehr 1976; Lehr 1973, pp. 9–15.
19. Samojlovych 1972; "Architectural and Artistic Peculiarities of Ukrainian

National Dwelling" 1973, pp. 63–75; Kosmina 1980.

20. Wonders and Rassmussen 1980, p. 210.

21. Samojlovych 1972, pp. 14–16.

22. Lehr 1980, pp. 183–96.

23. Martin 1986; Palanuk 1974, p. 3; Sherman 1983, p. 9.

24. This conclusion is based largely on field research, recording over 100 surviving Ukrainian pioneer dwellings, undertaken in the Star–Smoky Lake–Vegreville area of east central Alberta and the Tolstoi-Vita-Sirko area of southeastern Manitoba, during the period 1971–1976.

25. Parfitt 1941, pp. 132–33.

26. Powter 1977; Elston 1915, p. 532.

27. Samojlovych 1972, fig. 4.

28. Lehr 1976, pp. 18–19.

29. Hohol 1985, pp. 84–87.

30. Although numerous informants in Alberta and Manitoba mentioned the practical benefits of plastering and liming the exterior of dwellings, Zenon Kusela has suggested that the entire process was strictly nonutilitarian and aesthetic. Kusela 1963, p. 303, fn. 14.

31. Hohol 1985, pp. 78–80.

32. Olynyk, Lausman, and Oram 1980, pp. 33–37.

33. M. Krykalowich, H. Konchorada, and F. Krill, personal communication by J. Lehr, Beaverhill Pioneer Home, Laurent, Alberta, 1972.

34. Kusela 1963, p. 303; Hohol 1985, pp. 97–103; Lehr 1973, p. 12.

35. Hohol 1985, pp. 80–82; Lehr 1973, p. 11.

36. This contention is based on the results of field research in east central Alberta and southeastern Manitoba.

37. Humeniuk [1979?], p. 52.

38. Hohol 1985, pp. 123–35; Olynyk, Lausman, and Oram 1980, pp. 14–17; Lehr 1982, p. 101; Ledohowski and Butterfield 1983, pp. 55–60.

39. Kosmina 1980, pp. 48–52.

40. Elston 1915, p. 532.

41. Hohol 1985, pp. 96–97.

42. Kusela 1963, pp. 306–7.

43. Elston 1915, p. 532. For a critical view by a nativist writer see Hardy 1913. A more balanced and accurate portrayal is given in MacGregor 1969, p. 253.

44. Lehr 1981, pp. 203–6.

45. Bilash 1986.

46. Hohol 1985, pp. 87–89.

47. Kusela attributes the popularity of the gable roof in parts of the Ukraine to German influences. These were probably greatest in Galicia at the end of the nineteenth century and might account for the predominance of the gable in areas of Galician settlement. Kusela 1963 fn. 14, p. 303.

48. Lehr 1976, pp. 22–33.

49. Bilash 1986.

50. "How Foreigners Became Canadian" 1907.

51. Lehr 1981, pp. 203–5.

52. Bilachevsky 1911, p. 24.

53. Manitoba Historic Resources Branch 1981, pp. 5–7.

54. Ibid.

55. Kotecki and Rostecki 1984, pp. 102–4.

Chapter 18:
The Navajo in the
American Southwest

1. Goodman 1982, pp. 10–11.

2. Aschmann 1970, pp. 79–97; Haskell 1987.

3. Brugge 1968, pp. 14–20, Jett 1987.

4. Bailey 1980.

5. Kemrer 1974.

6. Hester 1962, pp. 75–85; Brugge 1983, pp. 489–501.

7. McNitt 1972.

8. Bailey 1964; Bailey 1980; Thompson 1976; Shinkel 1965.

9. Kluckhohn and Leighton 1962; Roessel 1983, pp. 506–23; Bailey and Bailey 1986; Aberle 1983, pp. 641–58; White 1983.

10. Underhill 1956, pp. 241–73; Aberle 1983, pp. 644–57; Bailey and Bailey 1986, pp. 197–204, 217–88.

11. Jett 1978a, pp. 353–58; Aberle 1981, pp. 21–36.

12. Haile 1954, pp. 1–6, 15–17; Kelley 1986, pp. 11, 13–14, 45–47, 116, 168.

13. Hoover 1931, pp. 429–45; Jett 1978b, pp. 65–75; Henderson 1983, pp. 279–306; Kelley 1986.

14. Landgraf 1954, pp. 47–52; Jett 1980, 101–18; Jett and Spencer 1981, pp. 7–13, 22; Spencer and Jett 1971, pp. 162–63, 168–69, 172–73.

15. Reed and Horn 1990.

16. Mindeleff 1898a, pp. 489–93; Haile 1942, pp. 39–56; Brugge 1968.

17. Kluckhohn, Hill, and Kluckhohn 1971, p. 152; Mindeleff 1898a, p. 495.

18. Mindeleff 1898a, pp. 513–14.

19. Coolidge and Coolidge 1930, pp. 81–82.

20. Hubbard 1977, p. 1.

21. Corbett 1940, pp. 104, 106; Kluckhohn, Hill, and Kluckhohn 1971, pp. 152–53.

22. Winberry 1974, pp. 54–69.

23. Gritzner 1971b, pp. 54–62; Gritzner 1974a, pp. 514–24.

24. Warburton 1985.

25. Coolidge and Coolidge 1930, pp. 82–83.

26. Ward 1968, pp. 136–42.

27. Warburton 1985, pp. 164, 247.

28. Wilmsen 1960, pp. 15–16; Noble 1984b, p. 77; Thomas, Johnson, and Yazzie 1974.

29. Francisan Fathers 1952, pp. 11–12.

30. Kluckhohn, Hill, and Kluckhohn 1971; Bailey and Bailey 1986; McNitt 1972, pp. 65–66, 314, 340.

31. Page 1937, pp. 47–49.

32. Gritzner 1974a, pp. 25–39.

33. Shufeldt 1889, pp. 279–82.

34. Correll 1979, p. 37.

35. Goodman 1982, pp. 10–16, 80–81; Harris 1974.

36. Spencer and Jett 1971, pp. 166–67, 169; McAllester and McAllester 1980, pp. 21, 23, 27, 73.

37. Tremblay, Collier and Sasaki 1954, pp. 187–219; Spencer and Jett 1971, pp. 166–67.

38. Jett and Spencer 1981, Jett 1987, and on Native American architecture in general, Nabokov and Easton 1989.

39. Crumrine 1964.

Chapter 19:
Spanish Americans
in New Mexico's Río Arriba

1. Hammond 1952, pp. 321–30; Jones 1979, p. 110; Quinn 1979, pp. 437–86.

2. For background information on the Pueblo Revolt see: Hackett 1911, pp. 93–147; Hackett and Shelby 1942, vol. 8, pp. xxix–lii, and vol. 9, pp. 3–16; Simmons 1980–1981, pp. 11–15. Diego de Vargas's reconquest is discussed in Bailey 1940, pp. 10–36 and 88–93; Espinosa 1939, pp. 443–63.

3. Espinosa 1944, pp. 83–84; Scholes 1935, p. 96.

4. The description *Spanish-American* is preferred by most of the region's His-

panic residents. Lopez 1974, pp. 2–3; Marquez 1985, p. 73; Metzgar 1974, pp. 50–51. For a definition of the homeland, see Carlson 1990, pp. xiv, 129, 203.

5. Anderson 1985, pp. 353–77; Bloom 1928, pp. 366–69; Bloom 1939, pp. 366–417; Chamberlain 1939, pp. 23–53; Simpson 1950; Weeks 1947, pp. 155–59; Zavala 1943, pp. 69–92.

6. A small number of *peonías* and *caballerías* were also given to military personnel. These land parcels amounted to approximately twenty acres and one hundred acres, respectively. Twitchell 1919, p. 8.

7. Crouch, Garr, and Mundigo 1982, pp. 9, 13, 74; Haring 1947, pp. 159–61; Stanislawski 1947, pp. 94–105; Twitchell 1919, pp. 5–7.

8. Carlson 1983, pp. 75–80; Tuan, Everard, and Widdison 1969.

9. Chávez 1954a, pp. xii–xv, 1–114, 119–335; Twitchell 1919, pp. 29–39.

10. Schmidt 1851; Vassburg 1974, pp. 383–401.

11. The duties of the *alcalde* and the stipulations for bestowing land grants are discussed in Bowden 1969, pp. 272–808, 811–1031, 1035–1214, 1225–1478; Bradfute 1975, pp. 9–11; Morrow 1923, pp. 15–17; White, Koch, Kelley and McCarthy 1971, pp. 10–11.

12. Carlson 1975a, pp. 593–94; Carlson 1975b, pp. 48–57.

13. Burns 1928, pp. 570–71, 574–77; Gentilicore 1957, pp. 285–97; Hall 1970, pp. 11–13, 36, 40; Harris 1966.

14. Houston 1961, pp. 206–7; Jordan 1974, pp. 71–74, 82.

15. Twitchell 1919, pp. 24–25.

16. Carlson 1967, pp. 115–19.

17. Swadesh 1974, pp. 134–35.

18. Stilgoe 1982, pp. 40–43.

19. U.S. Bureau of Land Management, 1905, report 149, file 152, reel 48, frames 134, 150.

20. Bowden 1969, pp. 272–808 (Santa Fe County), 811–1031 (Taos County), 1035–1214 (Rio Arriba County), 1225–1478 (Sandoval County); Diaz 1960; Records of Private Land Claims, 1855–1890; Records of Private Land Claims, 1891–1904.

21. For discussions of these controversial proceedings, see, for example: Bandelier 1886, pp. 70–71.; Bradfute 1975; Ebright 1980; Julian 1887, pp. 17–31; McCarty 1969; Westphall 1983.

22. Bowden 1969, pp. 980–85.

23. Carlson 1975c, pp. 95–110; Collier 1923, p. 469; Renehan 1923.

24. Carlson 1975b, pp. 55–56; Libecap and Alter 1982, pp. 184–200.

25. U.S. Department of Commerce 1936, pp. 865–66; U.S. Department of Commerce 1956, pp. 51–52.

26. Diecker 1971, p. 49.

27. U.S. Department of Commerce 1983, pp. 143–44, 146–47.

28. U.S. Department of Commerce 1946, pp. 61, 70, 76–78; U.S. Department of Commerce 1956, pp. 53–54.

29. U.S. Department of Commerce n.d.; U.S. Department of Agriculture n.d.; U.S. Department of Commerce 1975, p. 77.

30. U.S. Department of Commerce 1981, pp. 153, 299; U.S. Department of Commerce 1983, pp. 130–34, 151–52, 251.

31. For a discussion of the literature on the cultural landscapes of northern New Mexico, see Gritzner 1983, pp. 116–20.

32. Jackson 1953–1954, pp. 20–25; Keech 1934, pp. 49–53; Mauzy 1937, pp. 21–30; Mindeleff 1898b, pp. 111–23.

33. For discussions of Spanish-American architecture, see Bunting 1970, pp. 13–50; Bunting 1962a, pp. 16–26; Bunting, Booth, and Sims 1964; Bunting and Conron 1966, pp. 14–49.

34. Chávez 1977, pp. 28–33.

35. Dickey 1949, p. 42.

36. Conway 1971, p. 6; Noble 1984b, p. 85.

37. Gritzner 1974a, pp. 25–39.

38. Gritzner 1979–1980, p. 21.

39. Torrez 1979, pp. 14–18.

40. Winberry 1974, pp. 62–69.

41. Ahlborn 1967, pp. 21–22; Gritzner 1974a, p. 37; Winberry 1974, pp. 59, 67.

42. Conway 1951, pp. 20–21.

43. Boyd 1958, pp. 219–24.

44. "A Catalog of New Mexico Farm-building Terms" 1952, pp. 31–32; Gritzner 1990, pp. 21–33.

45. Gritzner 1974b, pp. 514–24.

46. Chávez 1979; Chávez 1954b, pp. 97–123; Henderson 1937; Weigle 1976.

47. Barker 1957, pp. 137–38; Foster 1953, pp. 10–19.

48. Ahlborn 1968; Bunting 1962b, p. 15; Bunting, Lyons, and Lyons 1983, pp. 31–80; Carlson 1990, pp. 147–50; Kubler 1972, p. 142; Tate 1966, p. 27.

49. U.S. Department of Commerce 1982, pp. 12, 112–16, 121; U.S. Department of Commerce 1983, pp. 11, 259–60.

Chapter 20:
Germans in Texas

1. Jordan 1966, pp. 40–59. In addition, Jordan verifies population numbers cited in Biesele 1930, Bracht 1849, and Olmsted 1857, and correlates these accounts with U.S. census data.

2. Biesele 1930, p. 46.

3. Ibid., pp. 42–55.

4. Ibid., pp. 66–110 describes the activities of the *Society for the Protection of German Immigrants in Texas*.

5. Jordan 1966, pp. 60–191 spells out in great detail agricultural practices and yields.

6. Biesele 1930, pp. 111–38 and 139–52.

7. Jordan 1966, pp. 167–69.

8. University of Texas, Institute of Texan Cultures 1970.

9. Biesele 1930, pp. 154–57.

10. Ibid., pp. 171–72.

11. Roemer 1935, p. 163.

12. Jordan 1978.

13. Roemer 1935, pp. 93–94.

14. Biesele 1930, p. 132.

15. Olmsted 1857, pp. 142–43.

16. University of Texas, Institute of Texan Cultures 1970.

Chapter 21:
Basques in the American West

1. Caro Baroja 1971, passim; Gallop 1970, passim; Veyrin 1955, passim.

2. Douglass 1975, pp. 43–49; Ott 1981, pp. 46, 52–53.

3. Douglass and Bilbao 1975, pp. 203–325.

4. Douglass 1985, pp. 289–96.

5. Douglass and Lane 1985, passim.

6. Douglass 1973, pp. 28–39.

7. Douglass and Bilbao 1975, pp. 370–84; Echeverria 1989, pp. 297–316; Osa 1989, pp. 317–23.

8. Douglass 1980, pp. 115–30.

Chapter 22:
The Immigrant Experience in the
Nineteenth Century and Afterwards

1. Dinnerstein and Reimers 1975, pp. 18–22.
2. Noble 1985, pp. 241–57.
3. Kivisto 1989, pp. 11–21.
4. Davie 1949, p. 498.
5. Smith 1970, p. 181.
6. Francaviglia 1970, pp. 59–61; Jackson 1980, pp. 82–95; Noble 1984c, pp. 157–63.
7. Jones 1976, p. 108.

References

Aberle, David F. 1981. "A Century of Navajo Kinship Change." *Canadian Journal of Anthropology* 2.

Aberle, David F. 1983. "Navajo Economic Development." In *Handbook of North American Indians*. Vol. 10, *Southwest,* Alfonso Ortiz, ed. Washington, D.C.: Smithsonian Institution.

Addy, Sidney O. 1898. *The Evolution of the English House.* London: Swan Sonnenschein.

Ahlborn, Richard E. 1967. "The Wooden Walls of Territorial New Mexico." *New Mexico Architecture 9.*

———. 1968. *The Penitente Moradas of Abiquiu.* Washington, D.C.: Smithsonian Institution Press.

Akenson, Donald H. 1984. "Why the Accepted Estimates of the Ethnicity of the American People, 1790, Are Unacceptable," *William and Mary Quarterly,* 3rd Series, 41.

Alanen, Arnold R. 1977. "Back to the Land! Rural Finnish Settlement in Wisconsin." *Transactions of the Wisconsin Academy of Sciences, Arts, and Letters* 65.

Allen, James P. 1974. "Franco-Americans in Maine: A Geographical Perspective." *Acadiensis* 4.

Ambrosia, Vincent G. 1979. "Log Architecture in Union County, Tennessee: Dwellings, Outbuildings, and Notching Types." Department of Geography, University of Tennessee, Knoxville. Unpublished manuscript.

Anderson H. Allen. 1985. "The Encomienda in New Mexico, 1598–1680." *New Mexico Historical Review* 60.

Andrews, H. F. 1915. *History of Audubon County, Iowa: Its People, Industries, and Institutions.* Indianapolis: B. F. Bowen.

Arsenault, Bona. 1965. *Histoire et généalogie des Acadiens.* 2 vols. Quebec: Universite Laval.

———. 1966. *History of the Acadians.* Quebec: Conseil de la vie française en Amérique.

Aschmann, Homer. 1970. "Athapaskan Expansion in the Southwest." *Yearbook of the Association of Pacific Coast Geographers* 32.

Bailey, Garrick, and Roberta Glenn Bailey. 1986. *A History of the Navajos: The Reservation Years.* Sante Fe: School of American Research Press.

Bailey, Jessie B. 1940. *Diego de Vargas and the Reconquest of New Mexico.* Albuquerque: University of New Mexico Press.

Bailey, Lynn R. 1964. *The Long Walk: A History of the Navajo Wars.* Los Angeles: Westernlore Press.

———. 1980. *If You Take My Sheep: The Evolution and Conflicts of Navajo Pastoralism.* Los Angeles: Westernlore Press.

Bandelier, Adolf F. A. 1886. "Why New Mexico Does Not Flourish." *Nation* 42.

Barker, George C. 1957. "Some Aspects of Penitential Processions in Spain and the American Southwest." *Journal of American Folklore* 70.

Beale, Calvin. 1957. "American Triracial Isolates." *Eugenics Quarterly* 4.

Beck, Robert, and George W. Webb. 1977. "Barn Door Decorations in the Boundary Junction Area of Indiana, Michigan, and Ohio: The Case of the Painted Arch." Professional paper no. 10, Department of Geography and Geology, Indiana State University, Terre Haute.

Becker, Carl M., and William H. Daily. 1982. "Some Architectural Aspects of German-American Life in Nineteenth-Century Cincinnati." *Bulletin of the Historical and Philosophical Society of Ohio* 20.

Bergman, Edward F., and Thomas W. Pohl. 1975. *A Geography of the New York Metropolitan Region.* Dubuque, Iowa: Kendall-Hunt.

Berry, Brewton. 1960. "The Myth of the Vanishing Indians." *Phylon* 21.

———. 1963. *Almost White: A Study of Certain Racial Hybrids in the Eastern United States.* New York: Macmillan.

Besson, Maurice. 1929. *The Scourge of the Indies: Buccaneers, Corsairs, and Filibusters.* Trans. Euerard Thorton. New York: Random House.

Betsinger, Signe T. Nielsen. 1986. *Danish Immigrant Homes: Glimpses from Southwestern Minnesota.* Miscellaneous publication 38, Agricultural Experiment Station, University of Minnesota.

Bicha, Karel D. 1970. "The Czechs in Wisconsin History." *Wisconsin Magazine of History* 53, no. 3.

Biesele, Rudolph L. 1930. *The History of German Settlements in Texas, 1831–61.* Austin: University of Texas Press.

Bilachevsky, N. 1911. "The Peasant Art of Little Russia (The Ukraine)." In *Peasant Art in Austria and Hungary,* Charles Holme, ed. London: The Studio.

Bilash, Radomir. 1986. "Early Twentieth-Century Parallels in the Ukrainian Architecture of East Central Alberta and of Galicia and Bukovyna." Paper presented to the Society for the Study of Architecture in Canada, Winnipeg.

Billington, Ray Allen. 1949. *Westward Expansion: A History of the American Frontier.* New York: Macmillan.

Biloxi, Mississippi [City of]. 1976. *The Building of Biloxi: An Architectural Survey.* Biloxi, Miss.

Biographical History of Shelby and Audubon Counties, Iowa. 1889. Chicago: W. S. Dunbar.

Bjerke, Gunnar. 1950. *Lands-Bebyggelsen I Norge.* Oslo: Dreyers Forlag.

Blegen, Theodore C. 1940. *Norwegian Migration to America: The American Transition.* Northfield, Minn.: Norwegian-American Historical Association.

———. 1979. *Frontier Parsonage: The Letters of Olaus Fredrik Duus, Norwegian Pastor in Wisconsin, 1855–1858.* New York: Arno Press.

Blomberg, Belinda. 1983. *Mobility and Sedantism: The Navajo of Black Mesa, Arizona.* Research paper 32, Center for Archaeological Investigations, Southern Illinois University at Carbondale.

Bloom, Lansing B. 1928. "A Glimpse of New Mexico in 1620." *New Mexico Historical Review* 3.

———. 1939. "The Vargas Encomienda." *New Mexico Historical Review* 14.

Blu, Karen. 1980. *The Lumbee Problem: The Making of an American Indian People.* Cambridge: Cambridge University Press.

Bourque, J. Rodolphe. 1971. *Social and Architectural Aspects of Acadians in New Brunswick.* Fredericton, N.B.: Historical Resources Administration.

Bowden, J. J. 1969. "Private Land Claims in the Southwest." Master's thesis, Southern Methodist University.

Boyd, E. 1958. "Fireplaces and Stoves in Colonial New Mexico." *El Palacio* 65.

Bracht, Viktor. 1849. *Texas in Jahre 1848.* Elbersfeld, Germany: Julius Baedeker.

Brackenridge, Henry M. 1834. *Recollection of Persons and Places in the West.* Philadelphia: J. Kay, Jr. and Brother.

Bradfute, Richard W. 1975. *The Court of Private Land Claims: The Adjudication of Spanish and Mexican Land Grant Titles, 1891–1904.* Albuquerque: University of New Mexico Press.

Brainerd, David. 1746. *Mirabilia Dei inter Indicos, or the Rise and Progress of Grace Amongst a Number of the Indians in the Provinces of New Jersey and Pennsylvania.* Philadelphia: William Bradford.

Briggs, John W. 1978. *An Italian Passage: Immigrants to Three American Cities, 1890– 1930.* New Haven: Yale University Press.

Brown, Mary Ann. 1984. *Architecture of Cultural Settlements in Western Ohio.* Background information for a video-tape script. Ohio Historic Preservation Office, Columbus, Ohio. (Prepared with the support of the Ohio Arts Council.)

———. 1989. "Barns in the Black Swamp of Northwestern Ohio." *Material Culture* 12.

Brown, Mary Ann, and Mary Niekamp. 1980. "Marion Mosaic, Facet II, Marion Township, Mercer County, Ohio." *Ohio Historic Inventory.* Columbus: Ohio Historic Preservation Office.

Brugge, David M. 1968. "Pueblo Influence on Navajo Architecture." *El Palacio* 75, no. 3.

———. 1983. "Navajo Prehistory and History to 1850." In *Handbook of North American Indians.* Vol. 10, *Southwest,* Alfonso Ortiz, ed. Washington: Smithsonian Institution.

Brun, Regis, Bernard LeBlanc, and Armand Robichaud. 1988. *Les Batiments anciens de la Mer Rouge.* Moncton, N.B.: Michel Henry.

Brunskill, R. W. 1974. *Vernacular Architecture of the Lake Counties.* London: Faber and Faber.

———. 1971. *Illustrated Handbook of Vernacular Architecture.* London: Faber and Faber.

Bucher, Robert C. 1962. "The Continental Log House." *Pennsylvania Folklife* 12, no. 4.

Bugge, Gunnar, and Christian Norberg-Shulz. 1969. *Early Wooden Architecture in Norway.* Oslo: Byggekunst Norske Arckitekters Landsforband.

Bunting, Bainbridge. 1962a. "The Architecture of the Embudo Watershed." *New Mexico Architecture* 4.

———. 1962b. "The Penitente Upper Morada, Arroyo Hondo." *New Mexico Architecture* 4.

———. 1970. "An Architectural Guide to Northern New Mexico." *New Mexico Architecture* 12.

Bunting, Bainbridge, Jean Lee Booth, and William R. Sims, Jr. 1964. *Taos Adobes: Spanish Colonial and Territorial Architecture of the Taos Valley.* Santa Fe: Museum of New Mexico Press.

Bunting, Bainbridge, and John P. Conron. 1966. "The Architecture of Northern New Mexico." *New Mexico Architecture* 8.

Bunting, Bainbridge, Thomas R. Lyons, and Margil Lyons. 1983. "Penitente Brotherhood Moradas and Their Architecture." In *Hispanic Arts and Ethnohistory in the Southwest,* Marta Weigle, Claudia Larcombe and Samuel Larcombe, eds. Santa Fe: Ancient City Press.

Burcaw, George E. 1979. *The Saxon House.* Moscow, Idaho: University Press of Idaho.

Burns, Francis P. 1928. "The Spanish Land Laws of Louisiana." *Louisiana Historical Quarterly* 11.

Butterfield, David K., and Edward M. Ledohowski. 1984. *Architectural Heritage: The MSTW Planning District.* Winnipeg: Historic Resources Branch, Department of Culture, Heritage and Recreation.

Calkins, Charles F., and William G. Laatsch. 1979. "The Belgian Outdoor Ovens of Northeastern Wisconsin." *P.A.S.T.: Pioneer America Society Transactions* 2.

Campbell, John C. [1921] 1969. *The Southern Highlander and His Homeland.* Lexington: University of Kentucky Press. Originally published by the Russell Sage Foundation.

Campbell, Mrs. Melvin (Irene). 1962. Letter to Mr. and Mrs. Jule Vandertie. November 30. Located in the Vandertie Chapel, Door County, Wisconsin.

Capek, Thomas. 1915. *Bohemia under Hapsburg Misrule.* New York: Fleming H. Revell.

———. 1920. *The Czechs (Bohemians) in America.* New York: Houghton Mifflin.

Carlisle, Ronald C. 1982. *An Architectural Study of Some Folk Structures in the Area of the Paintsville Lake Dam, Johnson and Morgan Counties, Kentucky.* Huntington, W.Va.: U.S. Army Corps of Engineers.

Carlson, Alvar W. 1967. "Rural Settlement Patterns in the San Luis Valley: A Comparative Study." *Colorado Magazine* 44.

———. 1975a. "Commentary: Long-Lots in the Río Arriba." *Annals of the Association of American Geographers* 65.

———. 1975b. "Long-Lots in the Río Arriba." *Annals of the Association of American Geographers* 65.

———. 1975c. "Spanish-American Acquisition of Cropland within the Northern Pueblo Indian Grants, New Mexico." *Ethnohistory* 22.

———. 1983. "Environmental Overview." In *Borderlands Sourcebook: A Guide to the Literature on Northern Mexico and the American Southwest,* Ellwyn R. Stoddard, Richard L. Nostrand and Jonathan P. West, eds. Norman: University of Oklahoma Press.

———. 1990. *The Spanish-American Homeland: Four Centuries in New Mexico's Río Arriba.* Baltimore: Johns Hopkins University Press.

Caro Baroja, Julio. 1971. *Los Vascos.* Madrid: Istmo.

Carson, Cary, Norman F. Barka, William M. Kelso, Gary Wheeler Stone, and Dell Upton. 1988. "Impermanent Architecture in the Southern American Colonies." In *Material Life in America, 1600–1860,* Robert Blair St. George, ed. Boston: Northeastern University Press.

"A Catalog of New Mexico Farm-Building Terms. 1952. *Landscape* 1.

"Catholic Roadside Chapel Donated to Park." 1984. *Heritage Hill Intelligencer.*

Census Report of the Canadas, 1851–1852. 1852. Quebec.

Chamberlain, Robert S. 1939. "Castilian Backgrounds of the Repartimiento-Encomienda." *Contributions to American Anthropology and History.* Washington, D.C.: Carnegie Institution of Washington.

Chateaubriand, François A. R. 1969. *Travels in America.* Trans. Richard Switzer. Lexington: University of Kentucky Press.

Chávez, Fray Angelico. 1954a. *Origins of New Mexico Families.* Santa Fe: Historical Society of New Mexico.

———. 1954b. "The Penitentes of New Mexico." *New Mexico Historical Review* 29.

———. 1979. *My Penitente Land.* Santa Fe: William Gannon.

Chávez, Tibo. 1977. "In Search of the Horno." *New Mexico Magazine* 55.

Chladek, Mrs. F. F. 1921. *History of Bon Homme County from Early Settlement until 1921.* Tyndall, S.D.: Privately printed.

Christensen, Thomas Peter. 1952. *A History of the Danes in Iowa.* Solvang, Calif.: Dansk Folkesamfund.

Clark, Andrew H. 1968. *Acadia, the Geography of Early Nova Scotia to 1760.* Madison: University of Wisconsin Press.

Clark, Francis E. 1913. *Old Homes of New Americans: The Country and People of the Austro-Hungarian Monarchy and Their Contributions to the New World.* New York: Houghton Mifflin.

Clausen, Clarence A. 1951. *A Chronicle of Old Muskego: The Diary of Soren Bache, 1839–1847.* Northfield, Minn.: Norwegian-American Historical Association.

References

———. 1982. *A Chronicle of Immigrant Life*. Northfield, Minn.: Norwegian-American Historical Association.

Cohen, David S. 1974. *The Ramapo Mountain People*. New Brunswick, N.J.: Rutgers University Press.

Collier, John. 1923. "The American Congo." *Survey* 50.

Comeaux, Malcolm L. 1972. *Atchafalaya Swamp Life: Settlement and Folk Occupations*. Baton Rouge: School of Geoscience, Louisiana State University.

———. 1978. "Louisiana's Acadians: The Environmental Impact." In *The Cajuns: Essays on Their History and Culture*, Glenn R. Conrad, ed. Lafayette: University of Southwestern Louisiana.

———. 1989. "The Cajun Barn." *Geographical Review* 79, no. 1.

Conrad, Glenn. 1969. *First Families of Louisiana*. Baton Rouge, La.: Claitors.

Conway, A. W. 1951. "A Northern New Mexico House-Type." *Landscape* 1.

———. 1971. "Southwestern Colonial Farms." *Landscape* 1.

Conway, Alan, ed. 1961. *The Welsh in America: Letters from the Immigrants*. Minneapolis: University of Minnesota Press.

Coolidge, Dane, and Mary Coolidge. 1930. *The Navajo Indians*. Boston: Houghton-Mifflin.

Corbett, John M. 1940. "Navajo House Types," *El Palacio* 48, no. 5.

Correll, J. Lee. 1979. *Through White Men's Eyes: A Contribution to Navajo History* 6. Window Rock, Ariz.: Navajo Heritage Center.

Cothran, Kay L. 1973. "Pines and Pineywoods Life in South Georgia." *Proceedings of the Pioneer America Society* 2.

Cowan, Helen I. 1961. *British Emigration to British North America*. Toronto: University of Toronto Press.

Crouch, Dora P., Daniel J. Garr, and Axel I. Mundigo. 1982. *Spanish City Planning in North America*. Cambridge: MIT Press.

Crousse, Nellis M. 1966. *The French Struggle in the West Indies, 1665–1713*. New York: Octagon Books.

Crumrine, N. Ross. 1964. *The House Cross of the Mayo Indians of Sonora: A Symbol of the Ethnic Identity*. Anthropological Papers no. 8. Tucson: University of Arizona.

Cummings, Abbott Lowell. 1979. *The Framed Houses of Massachusetts Bay, 1625–1725*. Cambridge: Harvard University Press.

"Czech Folk Architecture of Southeastern South Dakota." 1985. Nomination by Bon Homme and Yankton Counties, South Dakota, to the National Register of Historic Places.

Czumer, William A. 1981. *Recollections about the Life of the First Ukrainian Settlers in Canada*. Trans. Louis T. Laychuk. Edmonton: Canadian Institute of Ukrainian Studies.

Dannevirke. (Danish-language newspaper published in Cedar Falls, Iowa.) September 1, 1886.

Darcovich, William, and Paul Yusyk, eds. 1977. *A Statistical Compendium of Ukrainians in Canada, 1891–1976*. Edmonton: University of Alberta Press.

Davidson, Donald. 1946. *The Tennessee: The Old River*. Knoxville: University of Tennessee Press.

Davie, Maurice R. 1949. *World Immigration*. New York: Macmillan.

Davis, Dan T. 1938. *Early History of Horeb Church*, Oak Hill, Ohio. Privately printed.

De Charlevoix, Peter Francis Xavier. [1870] 1962. *History and General Description of New France*. Vol. 1. Chicago: Loyola University Press.

Defnet, Mary Ann, Jean Ducat, Thierry Eggerickx, and Michel Poulain. 1986. *From Grez-Douceau to Wisconsin: Contribution à l'étude de l'émigration wallonne vers les États-Unis d'Amérique au XIXème siècle*. Brussels: DeBoeck Université.

De Langlez, Jean. 1935. *The French Jesuits in Lower Louisiana, 1700–1763.* Washington, D.C.: Catholic University of America.

Del Sesto, Steven L., and Jon L. Gibson. 1975. "The Culture of Acadiana: An Anthropological Perspective." In *The Culture of Acadiana,* Steven Del Sesto and Jon Gibson, eds. Lafayette: University of Southwestern Louisiana.

d'Entremont, Rev. Fr. C. J. 1978. "The Acadians and Their Genealogy." *French Canadian and Acadian Genealogical Review* 5.

Desmond, Ellen Mary. 1962. "Mortality in the Brandywine Population of Southern Maryland." Ph.D. dissertation, Catholic University of America.

DeVorsey, Louis, Jr. 1966. *The Indian Boundary in the Southern Colonies, 1763–1775.* Chapel Hill: University of North Carolina Press.

Dial, Adolph L., and David K. Eliades. 1975. *The Only Land I Know: A History of the Lumbee Indians.* San Francisco: Indian Historian Press.

Diaz, Albert J. 1960. *A Guide to the Microfilm of Papers Relating to New Mexico Land Grants.* Library series 1. Albuquerque: University of New Mexico Press.

Dickey, Roland F. 1949. *New Mexico Village Arts.* Albuquerque: University of New Mexico Press.

Dickson, R. J. 1966. *Ulster Emigration to Colonial America, 1718–1775.* London: Routledge and Kegan Paul.

Diecker, Jimmy C. 1971. "Culture Change in Cordova, New Mexico." Master's thesis, University of Oklahoma.

Diereville, Sieur de. 1969. "Relations du voyage du Port Royale de l'acadia ou de la Nouvelle France." (Amsterdam, 1710.) In *The Acadian Deportation: Deliberate Perfidy or Cruel Necessity,* N. E. S. Griffiths, trans. and ed. Toronto: Copp Clark.

Dinnerstein, Leonard, and David M. Reimers. 1975. *Ethnic Americans: A History of Immigration and Assimilation.* New York: Dodd, Mead.

Dominguez, Virginia Rosa. 1979. "Behind the Semantic Curtain: Social Classification in Creole Louisiana." Ph.D. dissertation, Yale University.

Dorman, James H. 1983. *The People Called Cajuns: An Introduction to an Ethnohistory.* Lafayette: University of Southwestern Louisiana.

Douglass, William A. 1973. "Lonely Lives under the Big Sky." *Natural History* 82.

———. 1975. *Echalar and Murelaga: Opportunity and Rural Depopulation in Two Spanish Basque Villages.* London: C. Hurst and Co.; New York: St. Martin's Press.

———. 1980. "Inventing an Ethnic Identity: The First Basque Festival." *Halcyon* 2.

———. 1985. "Ethnic Categorization in the 1980 U.S. Census: The Basque Example." *Government Publications Review* 12.

Douglass, William A., and Jon Bilbao. 1975. *Amerikanuak: Basques in the New World.* Reno: University of Nevada Press.

Douglass, William A., and Richard H. Lane. 1985. *Basque Sheepherders of the American West.* Reno: University of Nevada Press.

Dozier, Edward P., George E. Simpson, and Milton J. Yinger. 1957. "The Integration of Americans of Indian Descent." *Annals of the American Academy of Political and Social Science* 311.

Dunaway, Wayland P. 1944. *The Scotch-Irish of Colonial Pennsylvania.* Chapel Hill: University of North Carolina Press.

Dupont, Jean-Claude. 1977. *Heritage d'Acadie.* Ottawa: Lemeac.

du Pratz, Antoine Simon Le Page. [1758] 1975. *The History of Louisiana.* Baton Rouge: Louisiana State University Press.

du Ru, Paul. 1934. *Journal of Paul du Ru, Missionary Priest to Louisiana.* Ruth Lapham Butler, trans. Chicago: Caxton Club.

Dvork, Joseph A., comp. 1980. *Memorial Book: History of the Czechs in the State of Dakota* [1920.] Laddie E. Kostel, trans. Tabor, S.D.: Czech Heritage Preservation Society.

Dykeman, Wilma. 1955. *The French Broad.* Knoxville: University of Tennessee Press.

Ebright, Malcolm. 1980. *The Tierra Amarilla Grant: A History of Chicanery.* Santa Fe: Center for Land Grant Studies.

Echeverria, Jeronima. 1989. "California's Basque Hotels and Their Hoteleros." In *Essays in Basque Social Anthropology and History,* William A. Douglass, ed. Reno: University of Nevada, Basque Studies Program Occasional Papers Series, no. 4.

Edwards, Ebenezer. 1899. *Welshmen as Factors in the Formation and Development of the U.S. Republic.* Utica, N.Y.: Thomas J. Griffiths.

Edwards, Jay. 1986. *Louisiana's French Vernacular Architecture: A Historical and Social Bibliography.* Monticello, Ill.: Vance Bibliographies.

———. 1988. "Louisiana's Remarkable French Vernacular Architecture 1700–1900." Baton Rouge, La.: Dept. of Geography and Anthropology, Louisiana State University.

Elanic, William H. 1913. "Bohemians in Richland County." *Collections of the* [South Dakota] *State Historical Society* 4.

Elkins, Stanley. 1968. "African Negroes to the Americas." In *World Migration in Modern Times,* Franklin D. Scott, ed. Englewood Cliffs, N.J.: Prentice-Hall.

Ellis, William S. 1969. "Wisconsin's Door Peninsula: A Kingdom So Delicious." *National Geographic Magazine* 135.

Elston, Miriam, 1915. "The Russian in Our Midst." *Westminster.*

Ennals, Peter. 1982. "The Yankee Origins of Bluenose Vernacular Architecture." *American Review of Canadian Studies* 12.

Ennals, Peter, and Deryck Holdsworth, 1981. "Vernacular Architecture and the Cultural Landscape of the Maritime Provinces: A Reconnaissance." *Acadiensis* 10.

Ensminger, Robert F. 1980. "A Search for the Origin of the Pennsylvania Barn." *Pennsylvania Folklife* 30, no. 2.

Epp, Frank. 1974. *Mennonites in Canada, 1786–1920.* Toronto: Macmillan of Canada.

Erixon, Sigurd. 1938. "Hur Sverige och Finland Mötas." *Rig* 21.

Erpestad, David, and David Wood. n.d. "The Architectural History of South Dakota." Vermillion, S.D.: State Historical Preservation Center. Draft manuscript.

Espinosa, J. Manuel. 1939. "The Recapture of Santa Fe, New Mexico, by the Spaniards—December 29–30, 1693." *Hispanic American Historical Review* 19.

———. 1944. "Our Debt to the Franciscan Missionaries of New Mexico." *The Americas* 1.

Evans, E. Estyn. 1974. "Folk Housing in the British Isles in Materials Other than Timber." In *Man and Cultural Heritage: Papers in Honor of Fred B. Kniffen,* H. J. Walker and W. G. Haag, eds. Baton Rouge: School of Geoscience, Louisiana State University.

Evans, William R. 1896. *History of the Welsh Settlements in Jackson and Gallia Counties of Ohio.* Philip G. Davies, trans. Utica, N.Y.: Thomas Griffiths.

Fapso, Richard J. 1977. *Norwegians in Wisconsin.* Madison: State Historical Society of Wisconsin.

Fapso, Richard J., and Mark H. Knipping. 1975. "The Knud Crispinusen Fossebrekke House: A Norwegian Settler's Cabin in the Woods, circa 1845." Old World Wisconsin Research Report.

Farion, Anna. 1978. "Homestead Girlhood." In *Land of Pain—Land of Promise,* Harry Piniuta, trans. and ed. Saskatoon: Western Producer Prairie Books.

Faust, Albert G. 1909. *The German Element in the United States.* Vol. 1. New York: Houghton Mifflin.

Federal and State Indian Reservations and Indian Trust Areas. 1974. Washington: U.S. Department of Commerce.

References

Fitchen, John. 1968. *The New World Dutch Barn*. Syracuse, N.Y.: Syracuse University Press.

Fontenot, Mary Alice. 1976. "The Pieux Fence: A Standard Fixture on Early Acadian Farms." *Attakapas Gazette* 11.

Ford, Thomas R., ed. 1967. *The Southern Appalachian Region*. Lexington: University of Kentucky Press.

Forman, Henry Chandlee. 1967. *The Architecture of the Old South: The Medieval Style 1585–1850*. New York: Russell and Russell; originally published in 1948.

Foster, George M. 1953. "Cofradia and Compadrazgo in Spain and Spanish America." *Southwestern Journal of Anthropology* 9.

Foster, James S. 1870. *Outlines of History of the Territory of Dakota and Emigrant's Guide to the Free Lands of the Northwest*. Yankton, Dakota Territory: McIntyre and Foster.

Fox, Paul. 1970. *The Poles in America*. New York: Arno Press.

Francaviglia, Richard V. 1970. "The Mormon Landscape: Definition of an Image in the American West." *Proceedings of the Association of American Geographers* 2.

———. 1979. *The Mormon Landscape: Creation and Perception of a Unique Image in the American West*. New York: AMS Press.

Franciscan Fathers. 1952. "Home Heating, Navajo Style." *The Padre's Trail* (January). St. Michael's, Ariz.

Freeze, Karen Johnson. 1980. "Czechs." In *Harvard Encyclopedia of American Ethnic Groups,* Stephan Thernstrom et al., eds. Cambridge: Harvard University Press.

Frolec, Václav. 1974. *Lidová Architektura na Moravě a ve Slezsku*. Brno, Czechoslovakia: Blok.

Funk, Harold. 1970. "Daut Darp." *Mennonite Life* 25.

Gailey, Alan. 1984. *Rural Houses of the North of Ireland*. Edinburgh: John Donald.

Gallop, Rodney. 1970. *A Book of the Basques*. Reno: University of Nevada Press.

Gastil, Raymond D. 1975. *Culture Regions of the United States*. Seattle: University of Washington Press.

Gauthier-Larouche, George. 1974. *L'évolution de la Maison rurale tradtionelle dans la région de Québec*. Quebec: Université Laval.

Gentilicore, R. Louis. 1957. "Vincennes and French Settlement in the Old North West." *Annals of the Association of American Geographers* 47.

Gilbert, Dorothy A. 1989. *Recent Portuguese Immigrants to Fall River, Massachusetts*. New York: AMS Press.

Gilkey, George R. 1968. "The United States and Italy: Migration and Repatriation." In *World Migration in Modern Times,* Franklin D. Scott, ed. Englewood Cliffs, N.J.: Prentice Hall.

Gillenwater, Mack H. 1972. "Cultural and Historical Geography of Mining Settlements in the Pocohontas Coal Field of Southern West Virginia, 1880–1930." Ph.D. dissertation, University of Tennessee.

Glassie, Henry H. 1963. "The Appalachian Log Cabin." *Mountain Life and Work* 39, no. 4.

———. 1965a. "The Old Barns of Appalachia." *Mountain Life and Work* 40.

———. 1965b. "Southern Mountain Houses: A Study in American Folk Culture." Master's thesis, Cooperstown Graduate Program, State University of New York College at Oneonta.

———. 1968. *Pattern in the Material Folk Culture of the Eastern United States*. Philadelphia: University of Pennsylvania Press.

———. 1975. *Folk Housing in Middle Virginia*. Knoxville: University of Tennessee Press.

———. 1978. "The Types of the Southern Mountain Cabin." In *The Study of American Folklore*, 2nd ed., Jan Brunvand, ed. New York: Norton.

References

428

———. 1986. "Irish." In *America's Architectural Roots,* Dell Upton, ed. Washington, D.C.: Preservation Press.

Golab, Caroline. 1977. *Immigrant Destinations.* Philadelphia: Temple University Press.

Goodman, James M. 1982. *The Navajo Atlas.* Norman: University of Oklahoma Press.

Goresky, Isidore. 1975. "Early Ukrainian Settlement in Alberta." In *Ukrainians in Alberta,* Isidore Goresky et al., eds. Edmonton: Ukrainian Pioneers Association of Alberta.

Graham, Ian Charles C. 1956. *Colonists from Scotland: Emigration to North America, 1707–1783.* Ithaca. American Historical Association by Cornell University Press.

Greissman, B. Eugene, ed. 1972. "The American Isolates," *American Anthropologist* 74.

Gritzner, Charles. 1971a. "Construction Materials in Folk Housing Tradition: Considerations Governing Their Selection in New Mexico." *Pioneer America* 6.

———. 1971b. "Log Housing in New Mexico." *Pioneer America* 3.

———. 1974a. "Construction Materials in a Folk Housing Tradition: Considerations Governing Their Selection in New Mexico." *Pioneer America* 6.

———. 1974b. "Hispano Grist Mills in New Mexico." *Annals of the Association of American Geographers* 64, no. 4.

———. 1979–1980. "Hispanic Log Construction of New Mexico." *El Palacio* 85.

———. 1983. "Cultural Landscapes." In *Borderlands Sourcebook: A Guide to the Literature on Northern Mexico and the American Southwest,* Ellwyn R. Stoddard, Richard L. Nostrand, and Jonathan P. West, eds. Norman: University of Oklahoma Press.

———. 1990. "Log Barns of Hispanic New Mexico." *Journal of Cultural Geography* 10 (Spring/Summer).

Guillet, Edwin. 1933. *Early Life in Upper Canada.* Toronto: University of Toronto Press.

———. 1963. *Pioneer Days in Upper Canada.* Toronto: University of Toronto Press.

Hackett, Charles W. 1911. "The Revolt of the Pueblo Indians of New Mexico in 1680." *Quarterly of the Texas State Historical Association* 15.

Hackett, Charles W., ed., and Charmion C. Shelby, trans. 1942. *Revolt of the Pueblo Indians of New Mexico and Otermin's Attempted Reconquest, 1680–1682.* Vols. 7–9. Albuquerque: University of New Mexico Press.

Haile, Berard. 1942. "Why the Navajo Hogan?" *Primitive Man* 15.

———. 1954. *Property Concepts of the Navajo Indians.* Anthropology Series no. 6. Washington, D.C.: Catholic University of America.

Hale, Frederick, ed. 1984. *Danes in North America.* Seattle: University of Washington Press.

Hall, Basil. 1829. *Travels in North America in the Years 1827 and 1828.* Vol. 1. Edinburgh: Cadell.

Hall, John W. 1970. "Louisiana Survey Systems: Their Antecedents, Distribution, and Characteristics." Ph.D. dissertation, Louisiana State University.

Hall, Robert. 1982. "Fort Mose: Black Fortress in Spanish Florida." Paper presented at the Southern Conference on Afro-American Studies, New Orleans.

Halvorson, Morris. [1939?] *Our Norwegian Ancestors of 1868.* Privately printed.

Hammond, George P. 1952. "Oñate's Effort to Gain Political Autonomy for New Mexico." *Hispanic American Historical Review* 32.

Hanna, Charles A. [1902] 1968. *The Scotch Irish.* Vols. 1 and 2. Baltimore: Genealogical Publishing Co.

Hardy, J. H. 1913. "The Ruthenians in Alberta." *Onward.*

Haring, Clarence H. 1947. *The Spanish Empire in America.* New York: Oxford University Press.

Harris, Richard C[ole] 1966. *The Signeurial System in Early Canada: A Geographical Study.* Madison: University of Wisconsin Press.

Harris, R[ichard] Cole, ed. 1987. *Historical Atlas of Canada.* Toronto: University of Toronto Press.

Harris, R[ichard] Cole, and John Warkentin. 1974. *Canada before Confederation.* New York: Oxford University Press.

Harris, Richard Robert. 1974. "Spatial Relationships of Anglo Culture Contact Centers and the Navajo Culture Landscape in the Chinle Valley, Arizona." Master's thesis, University of Arizona, Tucson.

Hart, John Fraser. 1984. "Resort Areas in Wisconsin." *Geographical Review* 74, no. 2.

Harte, Thomas J. 1963. "The Social Origins of the Brandywine Community." *Phylon* 24.

Hartmann, Edward G. 1967. *Americans from Wales.* Boston: Christopher Publishing House.

Haskell, J. Loring. 1987. *Southern Athapaskan Migration, A.D. 200–1750.* Tsaile, Ariz.: Navajo Community College Press.

Heck, Robert W. 1978. "Building Traditions in the Acadian Parishes." In *The Cajuns: Essays on Their History and Culture,* Glenn R. Conrad, ed. Lafayette: University of Southwestern Louisiana.

Helgeson, Thor [1915?] *Fra "Indianernes Lande."* Minneapolis. Privately printed.

Henderson, Alice C. 1937. *Brothers of Light: The Penitentes of the Southwest.* New York: Harcourt, Brace.

Henderson, David B. 1968. "Impacts of Ethnic Homogeneity and Diversity on the Cultural Landscape of Door County, Wisconsin." Master's thesis, Department of Geography, University of Wisconsin, Milwaukee.

Henderson, Erick. 1983. "Social Organization and Seasonal Migrations among the Navajos." *The Kiva* 48, no. 14.

Herman, Bernard L. 1985. "Time and Performance: Folk Houses in Delaware." In *American Material Culture and Folklife,* Simon J. Bronner, ed. Ann Arbor, Mich.: UMI Research Press.

Hester, James J. 1962. *Early Navajo Migrations and Acculturations in the Southwest.* Papers in Anthropology, no. 6, Museum of New Mexico.

Hill, G. W. 1942. "The People of Wisconsin according to Ethnic Stocks, 1940." *Wisconsin's Changing Population.* Madison: Bulletin of the University of Wisconsin.

Hoglund, A. William. 1960. *Finnish Immigrants in America 1880–1920.* Madison: University of Wisconsin Press.

Hohol, Demjan. 1985. *The Grekul House: A Land Use and Structural Inventory.* Historic Sites Service, Occasional Paper no. 14. Edmonton: Alberta Culture, Historical Resources Division.

Holand, Hjalmar R. 1928. *Coon Valley.* Minneapolis: Augsburg Publishing House.

Holmes, Fred L. 1948. *Old World Wisconsin: Around Europe in the Badger State.* Eau Claire, Wisc.: E. M. Hale.

Holmio, Armas K. E. 1967. *Michiganin Suomalaisten Historia.* Hancock, Mich.: Michiganin Suomalaisten Historia-Seura.

Hoover, J. W. 1931. "Navajo Nomadism." *Geographical Review* 21, no. 3.

Houston, Virginia H. T. 1961. "Surveying in Texas." *South-western Historical Quarterly* 65.

"How Foreigners Became Canadian." 1907. *Manitoba Free Press.* October 5.

Howison, John. 1821. *Sketches of Upper Canada.* Edinburgh: Oliver and Boyd.

Hrbkova, Sarka B. 1919. "Bohemians in Nebraska." *Publications of the Nebraska State Historical Society* 19.

Hubbard, Chester D. 1977. *Hooghan Hazaagi Bo Hoo' Aah: The Learning of That Which Pertains to the Home.* Tsaile, Ariz.: Navajo Community College Press.

Hulan, Richard. 1975. "Middle Tennessee and the Dogtrot House." *Pioneer America* 7, no. 2.

Humeniuk, Peter [1979?] *Hardships and Progress of Ukrainian Pioneers: Memoirs from Stuartburn Colony and Other Points.* Steinbach, Manitoba: Derksen Printers.

Humphreys, Barbara. 1974. *The Architectural Heritage of the Rideau Corridor.* Ottawa: Parks Canada.

Hvidt, Kristian. 1976. *Danes Go West.* Hyldgaardsminde, Rebild, Denmark: Rebild National Park Society.

Ilmonen, S. 1923. *Amerikan Suomalaisten Historia.* Jyväskylä, Finland: Tekijan Kustannuksella.

Isham, Norman Morrison, and Albert F. Brown. 1986. "Early Rhode Island Houses." In *Common Places: Readings in America Vernacular Architecture,* Dell Upton and John Michael Vlach, eds. Athens: University of Georgia Press.

Jackson, J. B. 1953–1954. "Pueblo Architecture and Our Own." *Landscape* 3.

Jackson, Richard H. 1980. "The Use of Adobe in the Mormon Culture Region." *Journal of Cultural Geography* 1.

James, Bartlett B., and J. Franklin Jameson, eds. 1913. "Journal of Jaspar Danckaerts, 1679 and 1680." *Original Narratives of Early American History.* New York: Charles Scribner's Sons.

Jeanton, C., and A. Duraffour. 1935. *L'habitation Paysanne en Bresse.* Paris: Librairie E. Droz.

Jennings, Francis. 1982. "Indians and Frontiers in Seventeenth-Century Maryland." In *Early Maryland in a Wider World,* David B. Quinn, ed. Detroit: Wayne State University.

Jett, Stephen C. 1978a. "Navajo Seasonal Migration Patterns," *The Kiva* 44, no. 1.

———. 1978b. "The Origins of Navajo Settlement Patterns." *Annals of the Association of American Geographers* 68, no. 3.

———. 1980. "The Navajo Homestead: Situation and Site." *Yearbook of the Association of Pacific Coast Geographers* 41.

———. 1987. "Cultural Fusion in Native-American Architecture: The Navajo Hogan." In *A Cultural Geography of North American Indians,* Thomas E. Ross and Tyrel G. Moore, eds. Boulder: Westview Press.

Jett, Stephen C., and Virginia E. Spencer. 1981. *Navajo Architecture: Forms, History, Distributions.* Tucson: University of Arizona Press.

Johansen, Johannes and Soren Bache. 1949. "An Immigrant Exploration." *Norwegian-American Studies and Records* 14.

Johansen, John P. 1937. *Immigrant Settlements and Social Organization in South Dakota.* Brookings: South Dakota State College.

Johnson, Hildegard Binder. 1976. *Order upon the Land.* New York: Oxford University Press.

Jones, David M. 1946. *A Celebration of the Ninety-second Anniversary of the Founding of Jefferson Furnace, September 2, 1946,* Oak Hill, Ohio.

Jones, Emrys. 1964. *Human Geography.* New York: Frederick A. Praeger.

Jones, Oakah L., Jr. 1979. *Los Paisanos: Spanish Settlers on the Northern Frontier of New Spain.* Norman: University of Oklahoma Press.

Jones, Suzi. 1976. "Regionalization: A Rhetorical Strategy." *Journal of the Folklore Institute* 13, no. 1.

Jordan, Terry G. 1966. *German Seed in Texas Soil: Immigrant Farmers in Nineteenth-Century Texas.* Austin: University of Texas Press.

———. 1974. "Antecedents of the Long-Lot in Texas." *Annals of the Association of American Geographers* 64.

———. 1978. *Texas Log Buildings: A Folk Architecture.* Austin: University of Texas Press.

———. 1985. *American Log Buildings: An Old World Heritage.* Chapel Hill: University of North Carolina Press.

Jordan, Terry G., and Matti Kaups, 1989. *The American Backwoods Frontier.* Baltimore: Johns Hopkins University Press.

Julian, George W. 1887. "Land Stealing in New Mexico." *North American Review* 145.

Kahlert, John. 1978. "Devout Belgian Settlers Built Shrines out of Faith, Gratitude." *Door County Advocate,* pt. 2. Sturgeon Bay, Wisconsin.

Kantowicz, Edward R. 1984. "Polish Chicago: Survival through Solidarity." In *Ethnic Chicago,* Melvin G. Holli and Peter d'A. Jones, eds. Grand Rapids, Mich.: Wm. B. Eerdman.

Karolevitz, M. Jill. 1987. "Lakeport Church Celebrates Restoration." *Yankton* [South Dakota] *Press and Dakotan.*

Kaups, Matti. 1971. "Speculations and Geographic Myths: Patterns of Finnish Settlement in the Lake Superior Region." *Michigan Academician* 3.

———. 1975. "The Finns in the Copper and Iron Ore Mines of the Western Great Lakes Region, 1864–1905: Some Preliminary Observations." In *The Finnish Experience in the Western Great Lakes Region: New Perspectives,* Michael G. Karni, Matti E. Kaups, and Douglas J. Ollila, eds. Vammala, Finland: Institute for Migration Studies, University of Turku.

———. 1976. "A Finnish Savusauna in Minnesota." *Minnesota History* 45.

———. 1978. "Finnish Place Names as a Form of Ethnic Expression in the Middle West, 1880–1977." *Finnish Americana* 1.

———. 1981. "Log Architecture in America: European Antecedents in a Finnish Context." *Journal of Cultural Geography* 2.

———. 1983. "Finnish Log Houses in the Upper Middle West, 1890–1920." *Journal of Cultural Geography* 3, no. 2.

———. 1985. "Economies and Buildings on Finnish Immigrant Farms in the Upper Middle West." Paper presented at the Scandinavian Immigration Conference, Luther College, Decorah, Iowa.

Kaups, Matti, and Cotton Mather. 1968. "Eben: Thirty Years Later in a Finnish Community in the Upper Peninsula of Michigan." *Economic Geography* 44.

Kavli, Guthorm. 1958. *Norwegian Architecture Past and Present.* Oslo: Dreyers Forlag.

Kawashima, Yasuhide. 1974. "Indians and Southern Colonial Statutes." *Indian Historian* 7.

Kaye, Vladimir J. 1964. *Early Ukrainian Settlements in Canada, 1895–1900.* Toronto: University of Toronto Press for the Ukrainian Canadian Research Foundation.

———. 1984. *Dictionary of Ukrainian Canadian Biography of Pioneer Settlers of Alberta, 1891–1900.* Edmonton: Ukrainian Pioneers Association of Alberta.

Keech, Roy A. 1934. "Pueblo Dwelling Architecture." *El Palacio* 36.

Kelley, Klara B. 1986. *Navajo Land Use: An Ethnoarchaeological Study.* Orlando, Fla. Academic Press.

Kemrer, Meade. 1974. "The Dynamics of Western Navajo Settlement, A.D. 1750–1900: An Archaeological-Dendrochronological Analysis." Ph.D. dissertation, University of Arizona, Tucson.

Kent, Susan. 1984. *Analyzing Activity Areas: An Ethnoarcheological Study of the Use of Space.* Albuquerque: University of New Mexico Press.

Kivisto, Peter. 1989. *The Ethnic Enigma.* Philadelphia: Balch Institute Press.

Kluckhohn, Clyde, and Dorothea Leighton. 1962. *The Navajo.* Rev. ed. Garden City, N.Y.: Doubleday Anchor Books.

Kluckhohn, Clyde, W. W. Hill, and Lucy Wales Kluckhohn. 1971. *Navaho Material Culture.* Cambridge: Belknap Press of Harvard University Press.

Kniffen, Fred B. 1936. "Louisiana House Types." *Annals of the Association of American Geographers* 26.

Kniffen, Fred B. 1965. "Folk Housing—Key to Diffusion." *Annals of the Association of American Geographers* 55.

Kniffen, Fred, and Henry Glassie. 1966. "Building in Wood in the Eastern United States." *Geographical Review* 56.

Knipmeyer, William. 1956. "Settlement Succession in Eastern French Louisiana." Ph.D. dissertation, Louisiana State University.

Knipping, Mark H., and Richard J. Fapso. 1978. "The Andres Ellingsen Kvaale Farm: Early Norwegian Commercial Architecture, circa 1865." Old World Wisconsin Research Report.

Kolehmainen, John I., and George W. Hill. 1951. *Haven in the Woods: The Story of Finns in Wisconsin.* Madison: State Historical Society of Wisconsin.

Konrad, Victor. 1982. "Against the Tide: French Barn Building Traditions in the St. John Valley of Maine." *American Review of Canadian Studies* 12, no. 2.

Kosmina, T. V. 1980. *Sil'ske zhytlo Podillia, Kinets 19–20 st.* (The Rural house of Podillia at the end of the nineteenth and in the twentieth centuries). Kiev: Naukova Dumka.

Kotecki, M. D., and R. R. Rostecki. 1984. *Ukrainian Churches of Manitoba: An Overview Study.* Winnipeg: Historic Resources Branch, Department of Culture, Heritage and Recreation. Unpublished research report.

Krissdotter, Morine. 1982. "Ingolf's Pillars: The Changing Icelandic House." *Landscape* 26, no. 2.

Krueger, Lillian. 1945. "Motherhood on the Frontier." *Wisconsin Magazine of History* 29, no. 2.

Kubler, George. 1972. *The Religious Architecture of New Mexico in the Colonial Period and since the American Occupation.* Albuquerque: University of New Mexico Press for the School of American Research.

Kurath, Hans. 1949. *A Word Geography of the Eastern United States.* Ann Arbor: University of Michigan Press.

Kusela, Zenon. 1963. "Folk Architecture." *Ukraine: A Concise Encyclopedia.* Toronto: University of Toronto Press.

Laatsch, William G., and Charles F. Calkins. 1986. "The Belgian Roadside Chapels of the Door Peninsula, Wisconsin." *Journal of Cultural Geography* 7, no. 1.

Lakeport (South Dakota) Committee. 1988. Lakeport newsletter, July 1, 1988.

Landgraf, John Leslie. 1954. *Land-Use in the Ramah Navaho Area, New Mexico.* Papers of the Peabody Museum of American Archaeology and Ethnology (Harvard University) 42, no. 1.

Lauvriere, Emile. 1924. *La Tragédie d'un peuple.* 2 vols. Paris: Editions Bossard.

Leblanc, Dudley J. 1932. *The True Story of the Acadians.* Lafayette, La.: Private printing.

———. 1966. *The Acadian Miracle.* Lafayette, La.: Evangeline.

Ledohowski, Edward M., and David K. Butterfield. 1983. *Architectural Heritage: The Eastern Interlake Planning District.* Winnipeg: Historic Resources Branch, Department of Cultural Affairs and Historic Resources, Province of Manitoba.

Lehr, John C. 1973. "Ukrainian Houses in Alberta." *Alberta Historical Review* 21, no. 4.

———. 1975. "Changing Ukrainian House Styles." *Alberta History* 23, no. 1.

———. 1976. *Ukrainian Vernacular Architecture in Alberta.* Historic Sites Service Occasional Paper no. 1. Edmonton: Alberta Culture, Historical Resources Division.

———. 1977. "The Government and the Immigrant: Perspectives on Ukrainian Block Settlement in the Canadian West." *Canadian Ethnic Studies* 9, no. 2.

———. 1980. "The Log Buildings of Ukrainian Settlers in Western Canada." *Prairie Forum* 5, no. 2.

———. 1981. "Colour Preferences and Building Decoration among Ukrainians in Western Canada." *Prairie Forum* 6, no. 2.

———. 1982. "The Landscape of Ukrainian Settlement in the Canadian West." *Great Plains Quarterly* 2, no. 2.

———. 1985. "Kinship and Society in the Ukrainian Pioneer Settlement of the Canadian West." *Canadian Geographer* 29, no. 3.

———. 1986. Personal communication with Christopher Martin, state folklorist for North Dakota.

Lewis, Nathan. 1897. "The Last of the Narragansetts." *Proceedings of the Worcester Society of Antiquity* 16.

Leyburn, James G. 1966. *The Haitian People.* New Haven: Yale University Press.

Libecap, Gary D., and George Alter. 1982. "Agricultural Productivity, Partible Inheritance, and the Demographic Response to Rural Poverty: An Examination of the Spanish Southwest." *Explorations in Economic History* 19.

Lindal, W. J. 1967. *The Icelanders in Canada.* Ottawa: Viking Printers.

Little-Stokes, Ruth. 1979. *An Inventory of Historic Architecture, Caswell County, North Carolina.* Yanceyville, N.C.: Caswell County Historical Society.

Lloyd, John. 1969. "The Norwegian Laftehus." In *Shelter and Society,* Paul Oliver, ed. New York: Frederick A. Praeger.

Long, Amos, Jr. 1972. *The Pennsylvania German Family Farm: A Regional Architecture and Folk Cultural Study of An American Agricultural Community.* Publications of the Pennsylvania German Society no. 8. Breiningsville, Pa.

Lopez, Thomas R., Jr. 1974 *Prospects for the Spanish American Culture of New Mexico.* San Francisco: R&E Research Associates.

Lossing, Benson J. 1877. "The Last of the Pequods." In *The Indian Miscellany,* W. W. Beck, ed. Albany, N.Y.: J. Munsell.

Lounsbury, John F. 1955. "Farmsteads in Puerto Rico and Their Interpretative Value." *Geographical Review* 45.

MacGregor, J. G. 1969. *Vilni Zemli—Free Lands.* Toronto: McClelland and Stewart.

Maillet, Antoine. 1971. *La Sagouine.* Montreal: Lemeac.

———. 1979. *Pélagie-la-Charette.* Paris: Grosset.

Manitoba Historic Resources Branch. 1981. *St. Michael's Ukrainian Greek Orthodox Church.* Winnipeg: Department of Cultural Affairs and Historical Resources.

Mannion, John J. 1974. *Irish Settlements in Eastern Canada: A Study of Cultural Transfer and Adaptation.* Toronto: University of Toronto Press.

Manucy, Albert. 1962. *The Houses of St. Augustine.* St. Augustine, Fla.: St. Augustine Historical Society.

Margry, Pierre. ca. 1974. *Journal of the Frigate "Le Marin."* Henri de Ville Du Sinclair, trans. Ocean Springs, Miss.: Blossman.

Marquez, Teresa. 1985. "The Condition of Hispanics in the U.S. Today." Special Libraries Association, Geography and Map Division *Bulletin* 142.

Martin, Chester. 1973. *Dominion Lands Policy.* Carlton Library, ed. by Lewis H. Thomas, no. 69. Toronto: McClelland and Stewart.

Mather, Cotton, and Matti Kaups. 1963. "The Finnish Sauna: A Cultural Index to Settlement." *Annals of the Association of American Geographers* 53.

Mather, Eugene Cotton, and John Fraser Hart. 1954. "Fences and Farms." *Economic Geography* 44.

Mauzy, Wayne. 1937. "Architecture of the Pueblos." *El Palacio* 42.

McAllester, David P., and Susan W. McAllester. 1980. *Hogans: Navajo Houses and House Songs.* Middletown, Conn.: Wesleyan University Press.

McCarty, Frankie. 1969. "Land Grant Disputes Began More than 250 Years Ago." Albuquerque: *Albuquerque Journal.*

McDonald, Forrest, and Ellen Shapiro McDonald. 1980. "The Ethnic Origins of the American People, 1790." *William and Mary Quarterly,* 3rd series, vol. 37.

McIlwaine, H. R., ed. 1928. *Executive Journals of the Council of Colonial Virginia* 3 (May 1, 1705–October 23, 1721). Richmond: Virginia State Library.

McIlwraith, Thomas F. 1981. "The Diamond Cross: An Enigmatic Sign in the Rural Ontario Landscape." *Pioneer America* 13.

McKenzie, Ruth. 1967. *Leeds and Grenville: Their First Two Hundred Years*. Toronto: McClelland and Stewart.

McMullen, Ann. 1982. "Woodsplint Basketry of the Eastern Algonkian." *Artifacts* 10.

McNickle, D'Arcy. 1962. *The Indian Tribes of the United States: Ethnic and Cultural Survival*. New York: Oxford University Press.

McNitt, Frank. 1972. *Navajo Wars: Military Campaigns, Slave Raids, and Reprisals*. Albuquerque: University of New Mexico Press.

McNutt, Thomas. 1924. "Galicians and Bukowinians." In *The Story of Saskatchewan and Its People,* John Hawkes, ed. Chicago-Regina: S. J. Clarke.

McWhiney, Grady. 1988. *Cracker Culture: Celtic Ways in the Old South*. Tuscaloosa: University of Alabama Press.

Mead, Colonel D. 1832. "The Last Indians of Virginia." *Atlantic Journal* 1.

Meinig, D. W. 1986. *The Shaping of America: A Geographical Perspective on 500 Years of History*. New Haven: Yale University Press.

Mencil, Václav. 1980. *Lidová Architektura v Ceskoslvensku*. Prague: Academia Nakadatelstvi Ceskoslovenske' Akadeniaved.

Mercer, Henry C. 1926. "The Origin of Log Houses in the United States." *Papers of the Bucks County Historical Society* 5.

Merritt, Carole. 1984. *Historic Black Resources*. Atlanta: Historic Preservation Section, Georgia Department of Natural Resources.

Metzgar, Joseph V. 1974. "The Ethnic Sensitivity of Spanish New Mexicans: A Survey and Analysis." *New Mexico Historical Review* 49.

Mills, Edward. 1971. *Early Settlement in Ontario*. Manuscript Report no. 182, Ottawa: Parks Canada.

Mindeleff, Cosmos. 1898a. "Navajo Houses." Bureau of American Ethnology, *Annual Report* 17. Washington, D.C.: Government Printing Office.

———. 1898b. "Origin of the Cliff Dwellings." *Journal of the American Geographical Society* 30.

Mitchell, Robert D. 1972. "The Shenandoah Valley Frontier." *Annals of the Association of American Geographers* 62, no. 3.

———. 1978. "The Formation of Early American Cultural Regions: An Interpretation." In *European Settlement and Development in North America: Essays on Geographic Change in Honour and Memory of Andrew Hill Clark,* James R. Gibson, ed. Toronto: University Press of Toronto.

Mochow, Marion J. 1968. "Stockbridge-Munsee Cultural Adaptations: Assimilated Indians." *Proceedings of the American Philosophical Society* 112.

Moffett, Marian, and Lawrence Wodehouse. 1984. *The Cantilever Barn in East Tennessee*. Knoxville: University of Tennessee School of Architecture.

Montell, Lynwood. 1970. *The Saga of Coe Ridge: A Study in Oral History*. Knoxville: University of Tennessee Press.

Montell, William L., and Michael Lynn Morse. 1976. *Kentucky Folk Architecture*. Lexington: University of Kentucky Press.

Moody, T. W., F. X. Martin, and F. J. Byrne. 1982. *A New History of Ireland*. Vol. 8, *A Chronology of Irish History to 1976*. Oxford: Clarendon Press.

———. 1984. *A New History of Ireland*. Vol. 9, *Maps, Genealogies, Lists*. Oxford: Clarendon Press.

Moogk, Peter. 1977. *Building a Home in New France*. Toronto: McClelland and Stewart.

Moore, Tyrel G., Jr. 1975. "The Role of Ferry Crossings in the Development of the Transportation Network in East Tennessee, 1790–1974." Master's thesis, University of Tennessee.

Morgan, John T. 1986. "The Decline of Log House Construction in Blount County, Tennessee." Ph.D. dissertation, University of Tennessee.

Morgan, John [T.], and Joy Medford. 1980. "Log Houses in Grainger County, Tennessee." *Tennessee Anthropologist* 5, no. 2.

Morrison, Hugh. 1952. *Early American Architecture*. New York: Oxford University Press.

Morrow, William W. 1923. *Spanish and Mexican Private Land Grants*. San Francisco: Bancroft-Whitney.

Morse, Jedidiah. 1822. *A Report to the Secretary of War of the United States, on Indian Affairs*. New Haven.

Mortensen, Enok. 1961. *Seventy-five Years at Danebod*. Askov, Minnesota: American Publishing.

Munch, Peter A. 1980. "Norwegians." *Harvard Encyclopedia of American Ethnic Groups*, Stephen Thernstrom, ed. Cambridge: Belknap Press of Harvard University Press.

Murphy, David. 1986. "Czechs." In *America's Architectural Roots: Ethnic Groups That Built America*, by Dell Upton. Washington, D.C.: Preservation Press.

Nabokov, Peter, and Robert Easton. 1989. *Native American Architecture*. New York: Oxford University Press.

Nahachewsky, Andriy. 1985. *Ukrainian Dugout Dwellings in East Central Alberta*. Historic Sites Occasional Paper no. 11. Edmonton: Alberta Culture.

Naismith, Robert J. 1985. *Buildings of the Scottish Countryside*. London: Victor Gollancz.

Nash, Gary G. 1978. "Notes on the History of Seventeenth-Century Missionization in Colonial America." *American Indian Culture and Research Journal* 2.

Newton, Milton B., Jr. 1967. "The Peasant Farm of St. Helena Parish, Louisiana: A Cultural Geography." Ph.D. dissertation, Louisiana State University.

———. 1971. "Louisiana House Types: A Field Guide." *Mélanges* 2.

———. 1974. "Cultural Preadaptation and the Upland South." In *Man and Cultural Heritage: Papers in Honor of Fred B. Kniffen*, H. J. Walker and W. G. Haag, eds. Baton Rouge: School of Geoscience, Louisiana State University.

———. 1985. "Louisiana Folk Houses." In *Louisiana Folklife: A Guide to the State*, Nicholas R. Spitzer, ed. Baton Rouge: Louisiana Folklife Program, Division of the Arts.

Nielsen, Marie Clawson, [196–] "Uncle Ted Talks." Tyler, Minnesota. Unpublished manuscript.

Noble, Allen G. 1984a. "Identifying Ethnic Regions in Ohio." *Ohio Geographers* 12.

———. 1984b. *Wood, Brick and Stone: The North American Settlement Landscape*. Vol. 1, *Houses*. Amherst: University of Massachusetts Press.

———. 1984c. *Wood, Brick and Stone: The North American Settlement Landscape*. Vol. 2, *Barns and Farm Structures*. Amherst: University of Massachusetts Press.

———. 1985. "Rural Ethnic Islands." In *Ethnicity in Contemporary America*, Jesse O. McKee, ed. Dubuque, Iowa: Kendall-Hunt.

"Old Catholic Church." 1980. In "Historic Resources of the Northern and Central Townships of Yankton County." Nomination by Yankton County, South Dakota, to the National Register of Historic Places.

"Old St. Wenceslaus Catholic Parish House." 1987. Nomination by Bon Homme County, South Dakota, to the National Register of Historic Places.

Oleskow, Josef. 1985. *O Emigratsii* (On Emigration). L'viv, U.S.S.R.: Michael Kachkowskyi Society.

O'Malley, James R. 1972. "The 'I' House: An Indicator of Agricultural Opulence in Upper East Tennessee." Master's thesis, University of Tennessee.

———. 1977. "The 'I' House: An Indicator of Agricultural Attainment in the Southern Appalachian Valley." In *West Virginia and Appalachia: Selected Read-*

ings, Howard G. Adkins, ed. Dubuque, Iowa: Kendall-Hunt.

O'Malley, James R., and John B. Rehder. 1978. "The Two-Story Log House in the Upland South." *Journal of Popular Culture* 11.

Olmsted, Frederick Law. 1857. *A Journey through Texas.* New York: Dix, Edwards.

Olson, James S. 1979. *The Ethnic Dimension in American History.* New York: St. Martin's Press.

Olynyk, M. D., K. M. Lausman, and E. Oram. 1980. *The Fedoryshyn Cottage at Caliento, Manitoba: An Analytical Study Report.* Winnipeg: Historic Resources Branch, Province of Manitoba.

Osa, Gretchen. 1989. "The Overland: The Last Basque Hotel." In *Essays in Basque Social Anthropology and History,* William A. Douglass, ed. Basque Studies Program Occasional Papers Series, no. 4. Reno: University of Nevada.

Oszuscik, Philippe. 1981. "A Creole Tradition: Gumbo." *Big Thicket* [Museum] *Bulletin* 70. (Saratoga, Texas.)

———. 1983. "French Creole Housing on the Gulf Coast: The Early Years." *Pioneer America Society Transactions* 6.

———. 1985. "The French Creole Cottage and Its Caribbean Connection." In *Material Culture of the French and Germans in the Mississippi Valley,* Michael Roark, ed. Cape Girardeau: University of Southeast Missouri Press.

———. 1986. "The Carolina Heritage in Mobile and Southwest Alabama." *Pioneer America Society Transactions* 9.

Ott, Sandra. 1981. *The Circle of Mountains: A Basque Sheepherding Community.* Oxford: Oxford University Press.

Page, Gordon B. 1937. "Navajo House Types." *Museum* [of Northern Arizona] *Notes* 9, no. 9.

Palanuk, Agnes. 1974. *The Ukrainians in North Dakota.* Belfield, N.D.: North Dakota Ukrainian Pioneer Days Committee.

Parfitt, Gilbert. 1941. "Ukrainian Cottages." *Architecture Canada* 18.

Parker, N. Howe. 1855. *Iowa as It Is in 1855; A Gazeteer for Citizens and a Handbook for Emmigrants* [sic]. Chicago: Keen and Lee.

Pech, Stanley Z. 1969. *The Czech Revolution of 1848.* Chapel Hill: University of North Carolina Press.

Perrin, Richard W. E. 1960–1961. "John Bergen's Log House: An Architectural Remnant of Old Muskego." *Wisconsin Magazine of History* 44, no. 1.

Petersen, Albert J. 1976. "The German-Russian House in Kansas: A Study in Persistance of Form." *Pioneer America* 8, no. 1.

Phillips, Yvonne. 1964. "The Bousillage House." *Louisiana Studies* 3.

Pierson, George W. 1968. "The M-Factor in American History." In *World Migration in Modern Times,* Franklin D. Scott, ed. Englewood Cliffs, N.J.: Prentice-Hall.

Plumbe, John, Jr. 1839. *Sketches of Iowa and Wisconsin.* St. Louis: Chambers, Harris and Knapp. Reprint. Iowa City, Iowa: The State Historical Society of Iowa, 1948.

Porter, Frank W., III. 1979a. "A Century of Accommodation: The Nanticoke in Colonial Maryland." *Maryland Historical Magazine* 74.

———. 1979b. "Strategies for Survival: The Nanticoke in a Hostile World." *Ethnohistory* 26.

———. 1982. "Backyard Ethnohistory: Understanding Indian Survivals in the Middle Atlantic Region." *Virginia Social Science Journal* 17.

———. 1984. "Indian Communities in Southern Maryland." *Almanack: Newsletter of the National Colonial Farm.*

———. 1985. "American Indian Basketry in the Middle Atlantic Region: Material Survival and Changing Function." *Material Culture* 17.

———. 1986. *Strategies for Survival: American Indians in the Eastern United States.* Westport, Conn.: Greenwood Press.

Post, Lauren C. 1940. "Acadian Animal Caste in Southwest Louisiana: Some Sociological Observations." *Rural Sociology* 5.

———. 1962. *Cajun Sketches*. Baton Rouge: Louisiana State University.

Powter, A. 1977. *Metis Log Building in Saskatchewan*. Ottawa: Engineering and Architecture Branch, Dept. of Indian and Northern Affairs, Government of Canada.

Przybycien, Frank E. n.d. *Utica: A City Worth Saving*. Utica: Dodge-Graphic Press.

Purvis, Thomas L. 1984. "The European Ancestry of the United States Population, 1790." *William and Mary Quarterly*. 3rd series, vol. 41, no. 1.

Quinn, David B. 1979. "Juan de Oñate and the Founding of New Mexico, 1595–1609." In *The Extension of Settlement in Florida, Virginia and the Spanish Southwest*, David B. Quinn, ed. New York: Arno Press.

Rafinesque, C. S. 1832. "The Last Indians of New Jersey." *Atlantic Journal* 1.

Raitz, Karl B., Richard Ulack, and Thomas R. Leinbach. 1984. *Appalachia: A Regional Geography*. Boulder, Colo: Westview Press.

Rank, Gustav. 1962. *Die Bauernhausformen im Baltischen Raum*. Würzburg: Holzner-Verlag.

Raulston, J. Leonard, and James W. Livingood. 1977. *Sequatchie: A Story of the Southern Cumberlands*. Knoxville: University of Tennessee Press.

Reaman, G. Elmore. 1957. *The Trail of the Black Walnut*. Toronto: McClelland and Stewart.

Records of private land claims adjudicated by the U.S. Court of Private Land Claims, 1891–1904. University of New Mexico Library, Albuquerque. Also at Bureau of Land Management, Santa Fe.

Records of Private Land Claims Adjudicated by the U.S. Surveyor-General, 1855–1890. University of New Mexico Library, Albuquerque. Also at Bureau of Land Management, Santa Fe.

Redekop, Calvin. 1969. *The Old Colony Mennonites*. Baltimore: Johns Hopkins University Press.

Redfield, Robert. 1947. "The Folk Society." *American Journal of Sociology* 52.

———. 1955. *The Little Community*. Chicago: University of Chicago Press.

Reed, Allen D., and Jonathon C. Horn. 1990. "Early Navajo Occupation of the American Southwest: Reexamination of the Dinetah Phase." *Kiva* 55.

Rehder, John B., John Morgan, and Joy L. Medford. 1979. "The Decline of Smokehouses in Grainger County, Tennessee." *West Georgia College Studies in the Social Sciences* 18.

Rehder, Karen. 1989. "Observations of Folk Houses as Found in the Eastern Tennessee Region." Unpublished data in Special Collections, John C. Hodges Library, University of Tennessee.

Renehan, Alois B. 1923. *The Pueblo Indians and Their Land Grants: The Pioneers and Their Families, Their Descendants and Grantees Occupying Parts of the Pueblo Indian Land Grants in New Mexico*. Albuquerque: T. Hughes.

"Report on the Stuartburn Colony." 1898. Ottawa: Public Archives of Canada. Aug. 30.

Richardson, A. J. H., Genevieve Bastien, Doris Dube, and Marthe Lacombe. 1984. *Qúebec City: Architects, Artisans and Builders*. Ottawa: National Museum of Man.

Richtik, James M. 1975. "The Policy Framework for Settling the Canadian West, 1870–1880." *Agricultural History* 49.

Riedl, Norbert F., Donald B. Ball, and Anthony P. Cavender. 1976. *A Survey of Traditional Architecture and Related Material Folk Culture Patterns in the Normandy Reservoir, Coffee County, Tennessee*. Department of Anthropology Report of Investigations, no. 17. Knoxville: University of Tennessee and Tennessee Valley Authority.

Rikkinen, Kalevi. 1977. *Suomen Asutusmaantiede*. Helsinki, Finland: Kustannusosakeyhtiö Otava.

Roark, Michael. 1984. "Imprint of the French in North America: Long-Lots in the Mid-Mississippi Valley." Paper delivered at Pioneer America Society, Cape Girardeau, Mo.

Robin, C. C. 1966. *Voyage to Louisiana, 1803–1805.* Stuart O. Landry, ed. and trans. New Orleans: Pelican.

Robinson, W. Stitt. 1959. "Tributary Indians in Colonial Virginia." *Virginia Magazine of History and Biography* 67.

Robison, R. Warren. 1975. "Louisiana Acadian Domestic Architecture." In *The Culture of Acadiana,* Steven L. Del Sesto and Jon L. Gibson, eds. Lafayette: University of Southwestern Louisiana.

Roemer, Ferdinand. 1935. *Texas.* Oswald Mueller, trans. San Antonio: Standard Printing Co.

Roessel, Robert. 1983. "Navajo History, 1850–1923." In *Handbook of North American Indians,* Alfonso Ortiz, ed. Vol. 10, *Southwest.* Washington, D.C.: Smithsonian Institution Press.

Roucek, Joseph S. 1967. *The Czechs and Slovaks in America.* Minneapolis: Lerner Publications.

Rountree, Helen C. 1972. "Powhatan's Descendants in the Modern World: Community Studies of the Two Virginia Indian Reservations, with Notes on Five Non-Reservation Enclaves." *Chesopiean* 10.

Rushton, William F. 1979. *The Cajuns.* New York: Farrar Straus Giroux.

"St. Wenceslaus Catholic Church and Parish House." 1984. Nomination by Bon Homme County, South Dakota, to the National Register of Historic Places.

Salisbury, Neal. 1974. "Red Puritans: The Praying Indians of Massachusetts Bay and John Eliot." *William and Mary Quarterly* 31.

Samojlovych, V. P. 1972. *Ukrains'ke Narodne Zhytlo* (The Ukrainian Folk Dwelling). Kiev: Nankova Dumka.

———. 1973. "Architectural and Artistic Peculiarities of Ukrainian National Dwelling." *Ethnologica Slavica* 5.

Sawyer, Claire M. 1961. *Some Aspects of the Fertility of a Tri-Racial Isolate.* Washington, D.C.: Catholic University of America.

Schell, Herbert S. 1975. *History of South Dakota.* 3rd ed. Lincoln: University of Nebraska Press.

Schmidt, Gustavus. 1851. *The Civil Law of Spain and Mexico.* New Orleans: Thomas Rea.

Scholes, France V. 1935. "Civil Government and Society in New Mexico in the Seventeenth Century." *New Mexico Historical Review* 10.

Scofield, Edna. 1936. "The Evolution and Development of Tennessee Houses." *Journal of the Tennessee Academy of Science* 11, no. 4.

Scott, Franklin D. 1968. "The Great Migration from Europe." In *World Migration in Modern Times,* Franklin D. Scott, ed. Englewood Cliffs, N.J.: Prentice-Hall.

Selkurt, Claire Elaine. 1973. "The Domestic Architecture and Cabinetry of Luther Valley, A Norwegian-American Settlement." Master's thesis, University of Minnesota.

Sheehan, Bernard W. 1973. *Seeds of Extinction: Jeffersonian Philanthropy and the American Indian.* Chapel Hill: University of North Carolina Press.

Sherman, William C. 1983. *Prairie Mosaic: An Ethnic Atlas of Rural North Dakota.* Fargo: North Dakota Institute for Regional Studies.

Shinkle, James D. 1965. *Fort Sumner and the Bosque Redondo Reservation.* Roswell, N.M.: Hall-Poorbaugh Press.

Shufeldt, R. W. 1889. "The Evolution of House-Building among the Navajo Indians." *United States National Museum Proceedings* 15.

Simmons, Marc 1980–1981. "The Pueblo Revolt: Why Did It Happen." *El Palacio* 86.

Simpson, Lesley B. 1950. *The Encomienda in New Spain: The Beginning of Spanish Mexico.* Berkeley: University of California Press.

Sklenar, Joe, ed. 1955. *Farm Atlas and Historical Review of Audubon County, Iowa.* Audubon, Iowa: Sklenar.

Sloane, Eric. 1956. *American Yesterday.* New York: Funk and Wagnalls.

———. 1967. *An Age of Barns.* New York: Funk and Wagnalls.

Smith, [H.] McKelden. 1978. "Guilford County: The Architectural Traditions in an Exclusively Vernacular Landscape." In *Carolina Dwelling: Towards Preservation of Place,* Doug Swaim, ed. Raleigh: North Carolina State University.

Smith, H. McKelden. 1979. *Architectural Resources, An Inventory of Historic Architecture.* Raleigh: North Carolina Department of Cultural Resources, Division of Archives and History.

Smith, William Carlson. 1970. *Americans in the Making.* New York: Arno Press.

Sorensen, Clara. n.d. "Glimpses from My Eighty Years" (unpublished manuscript), Tyler, Minnesota.

Speck, Frank G. 1915. "Family Hunting Band as the Basis of Algonkian Social Organization." *American Anthropologist* 17.

Speck, Frank G., and Loren Eiseley. 1939. "Significance of Hunting Territory Systems of the Algonkians in Social Theory." *American Anthropologist* 41.

Speers, C. W. 1897. Winnipeg. Letter to W. F. McCreary. R.G. 76, Bol. 144, File 34214, pt. 1 (40035), Public Archives of Canada.

Spencer, Virginia E., and Stephen C. Jett. 1971. "Navajo Dwellings of Rural Black Creek Valley, Arizona-New Mexico." *Plateau* 43:4.

Stanislawski, Dan. 1947. "Early Spanish Town Planning in the New World." *Geographical Review* 37.

Steensberg, Axel. 1949. *Danske Bondemøbler.* Kobenhavn: Alfr. G. Hassings, Forlag.

———. 1963. *Dagligliv I Danmark I Det Nittende og Tyvende Aarhundrede.* Bind I., Kobenhavn: Nyt Nordisk Forlag Arnold Busck.

Stella, Antonio. 1975. *Some Aspects of Italian Immigration to the United States.* New York: Arno Press.

Stern, Theodore. 1952. "Chickahominy: The Changing Culture of a Virginia Indian Community." *Proceedings of the American Philosophical Society* 96.

Stevens, Sylvester K., and Donald H. Kent, eds. 1943. *The Papers of Col. Henry Bouquet.* Harrisburg: Pennsylvania Historical and Museum Commission.

Stewart, Janice S. 1953. *The Folk Arts of Norway.* Madison: University of Wisconsin Press.

Stilgoe, John R. 1982. "Chimayo." *Common Landscapes of America, 1580 to 1845.* New Haven: Yale University Press.

Stortroen, A. J. 1932. "Norwegian Immigrant Letters." *Wisconsin Magazine of History* 15, no. 3.

Stout, Wilbur. 1933. "The Charcoal Iron Industry of the Hanging Rock District, Its Influence on the Early Development of the Ohio Valley." *Ohio State Archeological and Historical Society Quarterly* 1.

Struble, Michael T. 1989. "Ty Capels and the Residual Patterns of Welsh Settlement upon the Landscape of Southeastern Ohio." *Material Culture* 12.

Sullivan, Dennis R. 1962. "Ecological Distributions of the Brandywine Population in Charles County, Maryland." Master's thesis, Catholic University of America.

Suomen, Tilastollinen Päätoimisto. 1922. *Suomen Tilastollinen Vuosikirja.* Helsinki, Finland: Valtioneuvoston Kirjapaino.

Sutton, Imre. 1975. *Indian Land Tenure: Bibliographical Essays and a Guide to the Literature.* New York: Clearwater.

Swadesh, Frances L. 1974. *Los Primeros Pobladores: Hispanic Americans of the Ute Frontier.* South Bend, Ind.: Notre Dame University Press.

References

"Tabor Log Schoolhouse." 1983. Nomination by Bon Homme County, South Dakota, to the National Register of Historic Places.

Tate, Bill. 1966. *The Penitentes of the Sangre de Cristo*. Truchas, New Mexico: Tate Gallery.

Taylor, Theodore W. 1972. *The States and Their Indian Citizens*. Washington, D.C.: U.S. Department of the Interior, Bureau of Indian Affairs.

Tentchoff, Dorice. 1975. "Cajun French and French Creole: Their Speakers and the Questions of Identities." In *The Culture of Acadiana*. Steven Del Sesto and Jon Gibson, eds. Lafayette: University of Southwestern Louisiana.

Thomas, Peter, Frank Johnson, and Jonah Yazzie. 1974. "Hogan Building at Rock Point, Arizona." *Tsa 'Aszi* 1, no. 2.

Thompson, Gerald. 1976. *The Army and the Navajo: The Bosque Redondo Reservation Experiment, 1864–1868*. Tucson: University of Arizona Press.

Thompson, S. Harrison. 1943. *Czechoslovakia in European History*. Princeton: Princeton University Press.

Thrower, Norman J. G. 1966. *Original Survey and Land Subdivision*. Chicago: Rand McNally.

Tishler, William H. 1984. "Built from Tradition: Wisconsin's Rural Ethnic Folk Architecture." *Wisconsin Academy Review* 30, no. 2.

———. 1986. "Early Buildings, Farmsteads and Landscapes in the Coon Valley Norwegian Settlement of Wisconsin." Madison: University of Wisconsin, Department of Landscape Architecture.

———. 1987. "Namur Belgian-American District." Nomination by State Historical Society of Wisconsin to the National Register of Historic Places.

Tishler, William H., and Michael Koop. 1984. "Norwegian Settlement and Folk Architecture in Coon Valley Wisconsin." Madison: University of Wisconsin, Department of Landscape Architecture.

Toivonen, Anna-Lena. 1963. *Etelä-Pohjanmaan Valtamerentakainen Siirtolaisus 1867–1930*. Helsinki, Finland: Suomen Historiallinen Seura, Historiallisia Tutkimuksia: 66.

Toledano, Roulhac, Mary Louise Christovich, Samuel Wilson, Jr., and Sally K. Evans. 1974. *New Orleans Architecture*. Vol. 4, *The Creole Faubourgs*. Gretna, La.: Pelican.

Torrez, Robert J. 1979. "The Jacal in the Tierra Amarilla." *El Palacio* 85.

Tremblay, Marc-Adelard, John Collier, Jr., and Tom T. Sasaki. 1954. "Navajo Housing in Transition." *America Indigena* 14, no. 3.

Tremblay, Marc-Adelard, and Marc Laplante. 1977. *Famille et parente en Acadie*. Publications in Ethnology, no. 3. Ottawa: National Museum of Man.

Trewartha, Glenn T. 1948. "Some Regional Characteristics of American Farmsteads." *Annals of the Association of American Geographers* 38.

Tuan, Yi-Fu, Cyril E. Everard, and Jerold G. Widdison. 1969. *The Climate of New Mexico*. Santa Fe: New Mexico State Planning Office.

Twitchell, Ralph E. 1919. *Spanish Colonization in New Mexico in the Oñate and De Vargas Periods*. Santa Fe: Historical Society of New Mexico.

Tyler [Minnesota] *Herald,* July 11, 1907.

Underhill, Ruth M. 1956. *The Navajos*. Norman: University of Oklahoma Press.

U.S. Bureau of Land Management. 1905. "Fernando de Taos." *Records of Private Land Claims Adjudicated by the U.S. Court of Private Land Claims, 1891–1904*. Washington, D.C.: Government Printing Office.

U.S. Bureau of Statistics. 1893. *Arrivals of Alien Passengers and Immigrants in the United States from 1820 to 1892*. Washington, D.C.: Government Printing Office.

U.S. Department of Agriculture, Human Resources Branch, Economic Development Division, Economic Research Service. n.d. Washington, D.C. Unpublished data.

U.S. Department of Commerce and Labor. 1904. *Statistical Abstract of the United States: 1903*. Washington, D.C.: Government Printing Office.

U.S. Department of Commerce, Bureau of the Census. 1922. *Fourteenth Census of the United States, Population, 1920*. Vol. 3. Washington, D.C.: Government Printing Office.

U.S. Department of Commerce, Bureau of the Census. 1936. *United States Census of Agriculture, 1935*. Vol. 2, part 3, "The Western States." Washington, D.C.: Government Printing Office.

U.S. Department of Commerce, Bureau of the Census. 1946. *1945 Census of Agriculture*. Vol. 1, part 30, "New Mexico and Arizona." Washington, D.C.: Government Printing Office.

U.S. Department of Commerce, Bureau of the Census. 1956. *1954 Census of Agriculture*. Vol. 1, part 30, "New Mexico and Arizona." Washington, D.C.: Government Printing Office.

U.S. Department of Commerce, Bureau of the Census, 1975. *1970 Census of Population*. PC (S1)-105.

U.S. Department of Commerce, Bureau of the Census. 1981. *1978 Census of Agriculture*. Vol. 1, part 31, "New Mexico." Washington, D.C.: Government Printing Office.

U.S. Department of Commerce, Bureau of the Census. 1982. *1980 Census of Population*. Vol. 1, part 33, "New Mexico." Washington, D.C.: Government Printing Office.

U.S. Department of Commerce, Bureau of the Census. 1983. *1980 Census of Population*. Vol. 1, part 33, "New Mexico." Washington, D.C.: Government Printing Office.

U.S. Department of Commerce, Bureau of the Census. 1983. *1982 Census of Agriculture*. Vol. 1, part 31, "New Mexico." Washington, D.C.: Government Printing Office.

U.S. Department of Commerce, Bureau of the Census. n.d. "The 182 Lowest-Ranking Counties in the U.S., Ordered by Per Capita Income in 1959." Washington, D.C. Unpublished data.

U.S. Department of Labor, Commissioner General of Immigration. 1921. *Annual Reports for 1920*. Washington, D.C.: Government Printing Office.

U.S. Immigration Commission. 1911. *Abstracts of Reports of the Immigration Commission*. Vol. 1. Washington, D.C.: Government Printing Office.

University of Texas, Institute of Texan Cultures. 1970. *The German Texans*. San Antonio: University of Texas.

Valonen, Niilo. 1975. "Zu den ältesten Schichten der finnischen Hauskultur." *Ethnologia Europaea* 8, no. 2.

Vassburg, David E. 1974. "The Tierras Baldias: Community Property and Public Lands in Sixteenth Century Castile." *Agricultural History* 48.

Vavrousek, Bohemul. 1925. *Dedina: 516 Fotografii Lidovych staveb v Repubice Céskoslovenské*. Prague: Vesmiru.

Veyrin, Phillippe. 1955. *Les Basques*. Paris: B. Arthaud.

Vlach, John. 1975. "Sources of the Shotgun House: African and Caribbean Antecedents for Afro-American Architecture." Ph.D. dissertation, Indiana University.

———. 1976. "The Shotgun House: An African Architectural Legacy," parts 1 and 2. *Pioneer America* 8, nos. 1 and 2.

———. 1987. *The Afro-American Tradition in Decorative Arts*. Cleveland: Cleveland Museum of Art.

Vondracek, Paul P. 1963. "History of the Early Czech Settlements in South Dakota." Master's thesis, University of South Dakota.

Vrooman, Nicholas Curchin, and Patrice Avon Marvin, eds. 1982. *Iron Spirits.* Fargo: North Dakota Folk Council on the Arts.

Vuorela, Toivo. 1975. *Suomalainen Kansankulttuuri.* Porvoo and Helsinki, Finland: Werner Soderstrom Osakeyhtiö.

Walker, Mack. 1968. "The German Background of Emigration." In *World Migration in Modern Times,* Franklin D. Scott, ed. Englewood Cliffs, N.J.: Prentice-Hall.

Warburton, Maranda. 1985. *Culture Change and the Navajo Hogan.* Ann Arbor: University Microfilms International (8610389).

Ward, Albert A. 1968. "Investigation of Two Hogans at Toonerville." *Plateau* 40, no. 4.

Ward, David. 1971. *Cities and Immigrants: A Geography of Change in Nineteenth-Century America.* New York: Oxford University Press.

Warkentin, John. 1959. "Mennonite Agricultural Settlements of Southern Manitoba." *Geographical Review* 49, no. 3.

Wasastjerna, Hans R. 1957. *Minnesotan Suomalaisten Historia.* Duluth, Minn.: Minnesotan Suomalais-Amerikkalainen Historiallinen Seura.

Weeks, David. 1947. "The Agrarian System of the Spanish American Colonies." *Journal of Land and Public Utility Economics* 23.

Weigle, Marta. 1976. *Brothers of Light, Brothers of Blood.* Albuquerque: University of New Mexico Press.

Wertenbaker, Thomas J. 1938. *The Founding of American Civilization: The Middle Colonies.* New York: Charles Scribner's Sons.

Weslager, C. A. 1969. *The Log Cabin in America.* New Brunswick, N.J.: Rutgers University Press.

West, Robert C. 1986. *An Atlas of Louisiana Surnames of French and Spanish Origin.* Baton Rouge: Geoscience Publications, Louisiana State University.

Westphall, Victor. 1983. *Mercedes Reales, Hispanic Land Grants of the Upper Río Grande Region.* Albuquerque: University of New Mexico Press.

Weynes, Josef. 1963. *Bakhuis en broadbakken in Vlaanderen,* Sint Martens-Latem, Belgique.

White, Richard. 1983. *The Roots of Dependency: Subsistence, Environment, and Social Change among the Choctaws, Pawnees, and Navajos.* Norman: University of Oklahoma Press.

White, Koch, Kelley, and McCarthy. 1971. *Land Title Study.* Santa Fe: New Mexico State Planning Office.

Wilhelm, Hubert G. H. 1981. "A Lower Saxon Settlement Region in Western Ohio." *Pioneer America Society Transactions* 4.

———. 1982. *The Origin and Distribution of Settlement Groups: Ohio 1950.* Athens: Ohio University.

———. 1986a. "Owl Holes: A Settlement Residual in Southeastern Ohio." *Ohio Geographers* 16.

———. 1986b. "The Route West: German Immigration in Ohio before 1850, with Emphasis on the Riverine Area." In *French and German Folk Landscapes in the Mississippi Valley,* Michael Roark, ed. Cape Girardeau, Mo.: Center for Regional Heritage, Southeast Missouri State College.

Wilhelm, Hubert G. H., and Michael Miller. 1974. "Half-Timber Construction: A Relic Building Method in Ohio." *Pioneer America* 6.

Williams, Walter L., ed. 1979. *Southeastern Indians since the Removal Era.* Athens: University of Georgia Press.

Willoughby, Charles C. 1902. "Coiled Basketry." *Science* 16.

Wilmsen, Edwin N. 1960. "The House of the Navajo." *Landscape* 10, no. 1.

Wilson, Charles Reagan, and William R. Ferris, Jr., eds. 1989. *Encyclopedia of Southern Culture.* Chapel Hill: University of North Carolina Press.

Wilson, Eugene M. 1970. "The Single Pen House in the South." *Pioneer America* 2, no. 1.

———. 1971. "Some Similarities between American and European Folk Houses." *Pioneer America* 3, no. 2.

———. 1975. *Alabama Folk Houses.* Montgomery: Alabama Historical Commission.

Winberry, John J. 1974. "The Log House in Mexico." *Annals of the Association of American Geographers* 64, no. 1.

Winsor, Justin. 1895 (1972 reprint). *The Mississippi Basin: The Struggle in America between England and France, 1697–1763.* Freeport, N.Y.: Books for Libraries Press.

Winzerling, Oscar W. 1955. *Acadian Odyssey.* Baton Rouge: Louisiana State University.

Wittke, Carl. 1962. "The Germans of Cincinnati." *Bulletin of the Historical and Philosophical Society of Ohio* 20.

Wonders, William C., and Mark A. Rassmussen. 1980. "Log Buildings of West Central Alberta." *Prairie Forum* 5, no. 2.

Woodham-Smith, Cecil. 1962. *The Great Hunger.* New York: Harper and Row.

Woodsfield [Ohio] Chamber of Commerce. 1969. *History of Monroe County, 1883.* (Based on the H. H. Hardesty history, 1882.) Woodsfield, Ohio.

Wright, Martin. 1958. "The Antecedents of the Double-Pen House Type." *Annals of the Association of American Geographers* 48.

Wyatt, Barbara, ed. 1987. *Wisconsin Cultural Resource Plan.* Madison: State Historical Society of Wisconsin.

Wytrwal, Joseph A. 1961. *America's Polish Heritage.* Detroit: Endurance Press.

Yap, Angelita Q. 1961. *A Study of a Kinship System: Its Structural Principles.* Washington, D.C.: Catholic University of America.

Zavala, Silvio. 1943. *New Viewpoints on the Spanish Colonization of America.* Philadelphia: University of Pennsylvania Press.

Zelinsky, Wilbur. 1951. "Where the South Begins, the Northern Limits of the Cis-Appalachian South in Terms of Settlement Landscape." *Social Forces* 30.

———. 1973. *The Cultural Geography of the United States.* Englewood Cliffs, N.J.: Prentice-Hall.

Zvarych, Petro. 1962. "Do pytannya: postupu v materiyal'ni kulturi ukrains'kykh poselentsivu kanadi" (On the problem of development and progress of material culture of Ukrainian settlers in Canada). *Zbirnyk na poshanu Zenona Kuzeli.* Paris: Zapyskynaukovoho tovarystva im Shevchenka.

References

Contributors

Signe T. Nielsen Betsinger is professor of design, housing, and apparel at the University of Minnesota, St. Paul, and past president of the Board of Directors of the Danish Immigrant Museum. She is the author of *Danish Immigrant Houses: Glimpses from Southwestern Minnesota.*

Charles F. Calkins is professor of geography and former vice president of academic affairs at Carroll College, Waukesha, Wisconsin. He also is executive director of the Pioneer America Society and coauthor of the *Atlas of Minnesota Occupancy.*

Alvar W. Carlson is professor and chair of geography at Bowling Green State University. He is the author of *The Spanish American Homeland: Four Centuries in the Río Arriba* and also serves as editor of the *Journal of Cultural Geography.*

Brian Coffey is associate professor and head of geography at the State University of New York College at Geneseo. His articles have appeared in several journals, including *Canadian Geographer, Material Culture,* and *Ontario History.*

Malcolm L. Comeaux is professor of geography at Arizona State University. He is the author of *Arizona: A Geography* and *Atchafalaya Swamp Life: Settlement and Folk Occupations.*

William A. Douglass is professor and coordinator of Basque studies at the University of Nevada, Reno. He is coauthor of *Basque Sheepherders of the American West* and author of *Emigration in a South Italian Town: An Anthropological History,* among other books.

Peter Ennals is professor and head of geography at Mount Allison University, New Brunswick, Canada, and adjunct professor in the School of Graduate Studies at Saint Mary's University, Nova Scotia. His articles have appeared in *Acadiensis, American Review of Canadian Studies, Canadian Geographical Journal,* and other journals.

Stephen C. Jett is professor of geography at the University of California-Davis. Among his books are *Navajo Architecture: Forms, History, Distributions* and *Navajo Wildlands: "As Long as the Rivers Shall Run."*

Matti Enn Kaups is professor of geography and ethnohistory at the University of Minnesota, Duluth, and professor of Scandinavian studies at the University of Minnesota, Minneapolis. He is coauthor of *The American Backwoods Frontier: An Ethnic and Ecological Interpretation* and author of *Finnish Folk Architecture in the Lake Superior Region,* among other books. In 1991 he was awarded the Order of the White Rose of Finland.

William G. Laatsch is professor of regional analysis and geography at the University of Wisconsin, Green Bay, and vice chair of the Wisconsin Historic Preservation Review Board. His articles have appeared in *Cultural Ecology, Pioneer America,* and other journals.

John C. Lehr is professor of geography at the University of Winnipeg, Manitoba. He is the author of *Ukrainian Vernacular Architecture in Alberta.* He is past president of the Society for the Study of Architecture and also served as chairman of the Manitoba Heritage Council.

Gerlinde Leiding is professor of architecture and planning at the University of Texas, Austin. She is the author of *Texas Border Architecture: Eagle Pass, Texas, and Guerrero, Coahuila, Mexico.*

Allen G. Noble is professor and head of geography at the University of Akron. Among his many books is the two-volume work *Wood, Brick and Stone: The North American Settlement Landscape.*

Philippe Oszuscik is associate professor of architectural history at the University of South Alabama. He is the author of *Louisiana's Gothic Revival.*

Frank W. Porter III is director of the Chelsea House Foundation for American Indian Studies in New York City. He is also general editor of *Indians of North America,* a fifty-three–volume collection in preparation. Among his many books are *Indians in Maryland and Delaware* and *Strategies for Survival: American Indians in the Eastern United States.*

John E. Rau is national register coordinator for the South Dakota Historical Preservation Center. His articles have appeared in *Old House Journal, South Dakota History,* and other journals.

John B. Rehder is associate professor of geography at the University of Tennessee. His articles have appeared in the *Journal of Geography, Journal of Popular Culture,* and other journals.

Michael T. Struble works for the State of Ohio. A political scientist-geographer interested in Welsh settlement groups, he has published in *PAST.*

William H. Tishler is professor of landscape architecture at the University of Wisconsin, Madison. He is the editor of *American Landscape Architecture: Designers and Places* and coauthor of *Frederick Law Olmsted, Sr., Founder of Landscape Architecture in America.* He was also the designer of the master plan for Old World Wisconsin, an outdoor museum of ethnic culture.

Hubert G. H. Wilhelm is professor of geography at Ohio University. He is producer of *The Barn Builders,* a video documentary, and his articles have appeared in *Pioneer America, Geoscience and Man* and other journals.

Contributors

_____

446

Index

Brainerd, Rev. David, 124
Brethren. *See* Czech, Brethren
brick houses: Belgian, 198–99; Danish, 222; English, in Ontario, 51; German (Ohio), 67; Scots, in Ontario, 53
British, the, 14, 31
bryggerset, 218
buccaneers, 137
buda, 313
Bukovyna, 309, 314, 315, 325
"bull's-eye" window, 199
bungalows, 42

C

caballerías, 347
cabinets, 152
caille, 162
Cajun: barn, 183; farmsteads, 181, 191; house, 182
Cajuns, 17, 142–44, 177–92
caliche, 358
California, 110, 380
camelback houses, 163, 164
Canada, 9, 44–59, 177, 309–30, 331; avoidance of, by Scandinavians, 11; migration from, to American Midwest, 212; Maritime Provinces, 29–43
Canadian Icelandic house, 12
casa-corral houses, 355
catalpa trees, 190
cedar, 250, 258, 261
cemeteries: Appalachian, 116; Czech, 303; Finnish, 266; Ukrainian, 330; Welsh, 83, 92
center-hall plan, 41
chalkrock, 290, 295
chambre, 35
chapels, 83–88; Belgian, 204–9
chapel style house, 69
charcoal furnaces, 89
Charleston, 97, 98, 174
Charleston single house, 174
chicken coops: Cajun, 184; Czech, 293; Norwegian, 236
chimney: Acadian, 37, 38; Appalachian, 105, 107, 108, 109, 111; Cajun house, 182; clay, 34, 46; Czech, 293, 296; Finnish, 259; French Creole, center, 148; German gable, 69; Norwegian, 233, 235; Ukrainian, 314
chinaberry tree, 190
chinking: Czech, 291; Finnish, 251; German (Texas), 368, 374; Navajo, 336;

Norwegian, 233–34; Spanish-American, 356
churches: American Indian, 130; Czech, 302–3; French Creole, 144; German (Ohio), 66, 69, 71; Ukrainian, 314, 327–28
Cincinnati, 64
cisterns, 144
coiled baskets, 158
colombage bousillé, 33. *See also* nogging, brick
colombage pierrotté, 33
color preferences: Acadian houses, 42; Czech interiors, 297; Ukrainian houses, 323, 327
Coon Valley, Wis., 232, 233–38
coquina, 170
corbeled-log hogan, 336
cordwood walls, 249
Corn Laws, 80
cottonwood, 301
Creoles, 17, 136–56; cottages of, 159
cribbed-log hogan, 338
cross gable, 41
cross passage, 37
cruck structures, 104, 106
cuisine (kitchen), 35
cultural: adjustment, 405; assimilation, 24; borrowing, 4, 39, 279; broadening, 3; change, 127; devolution, 4, 31; inertia, 404; pluralism, 400; rebound, 377
Cumberland house, 107
Cutover Area, 246, 248, 249, 250, 254, 260
cypress, 180, 187
Czech: barns, 298; Brethren, 287; fraternal societies, 287; immigration, 287; material culture, 289
Czechs, 10, 285–306

D

Dakota Territory, 288
Danes, 13, 211–25; migration of, 212–14
Delaware, 79, 96
Dinétah, 331, 332, 335
dogtrot house, 107; adoption by Blacks, 173; description, 109; possible origin in Appalachia, 118; use by Germans in Texas, 369
Dominion Lands Act, 268, 309, 312
Dominion Land Survey (Canada), 311–13
Door Peninsula, Wis., 10, 195–96
dormers, 258, 279

Index

Books in the Series

Designed by Edward D. King.

Composed by Brushwood Graphics, Inc.
in New Baskerville text and display.

Printed on 60-lb., Glatfelter Offset, A-50 shade,
and bound in Holliston Roxite
by The Maple Press Company.